ISBN 978-0-260-18044-5
PIBN 10932815

# FOURTH ANNUAL REPORT

OF THE

# PRINCIPAL

OF THE

# RHODE ISLAND SCHOOL FOR THE DEAF,

## PROVIDENCE, R. I.,

FOR THE

## YEAR ENDING DECEMBER 31,

## 1881.

PROVIDENCE:
E. L. FREEMAN & CO., PRINTERS TO THE STATE.
1882.

# FOURTH ANNUAL REPORT

OF THE

# PRINCIPAL

OF THE

# RHODE ISLAND SCHOOL FOR THE DEAF,

## PROVIDENCE, R. I.,

FOR THE

## YEAR ENDING DECEMBER 31,

## 1881.

PROVIDENCE:

E. L. FREEMAN & CO., PRINTERS TO THE STATE.

1882.

# RHODE ISLAND SCHOOL FOR THE DEAF,

## CORNER OF BENEFIT AND HALSEY STREETS,

## PROVIDENCE, R. I.

UNDER THE SUPERVISION OF THE.

# STATE BOARD OF EDUCATION.

# REPORT.

*To the Honorable the State Board of Education:*

GENTLEMEN: — I beg leave to submit herewith my report for the year ending December 31, 1881.

Respectfully,

JOSEPH W. HOMER,

*Principal.*

DECEMBER 31, 1881.

| NAMES OF PUPILS. | RESIDENCE. | AGE. (Approx ) | DATE OF ADMISSION. |
|---|---|---|---|
| Kinyon, Ada J......... | Providence............. | 21 | April 2, 1877.. |
| Cole, Frank L........... | Valley Falls............. | 20 | " 2, " .. |
| Bauer, Emily M........ | Wanskuck, Providence.. | 15 | " 2, " .. |
| Morlock, William T..... | Providence............. | 14 | " 2, " .. |
| Hackman, Harry, Jr..... | " ...... ...... | 13 | " 2, " .. |
| Sprague, Lily R......... | ... .......... ... | 17 | " 8, 1878.. |
| Wallace, M. Amey. ..... | Woodville, N. Providence | 10 | " 15, " .. |
| Catlow, Mary A......... | Providence............. | 10 | " 22, " .. |
| Jencks, Lyman H........ | " ...... .......... | .......... | Sept. 29, 1879.. |
| Mowry, Grace G........ | .. ............. | 8 | Nov. 19, " .. |
| Slavin, Joseph.......... | Pawtucket............. | 9 | Jan. 28, 1880.. |
| Goodspead, Bertha...... | Providence............. | 7 | Mar. 9, " .. |
| Slavin, Margaret........ | " ............. | 9 | April 5, " .. |
| Riley, Thomas.......... | East Providence......... | 8 | " 5, " .. |
| Wood, Francis J....... | Pawtucket............. | 8 | " 5, " .. |
| Degnan, Bartley........ | Providence............. | 26 | May 3, " .. |
| Sheldon, Mary E ....... | Arnold's Mills, Cumberland. | 13 | Sept. 6, " .. |
| Lynch, James E....... ... | Wanskuck, Providence.. | 6 | " 6, " .. |
| Hall, Annie I.......... | Providence............. | 16 | " 9, " .. |
| Dorgan, Michael J....... | Slatersville, N. Smithfield, | 10 | Oct. 4, " .. |
| Leighton, Charles....... | Olneyville, Johnston..... | 20 | " 4, " .. |
| Swift, Mary E. ........ | Providence............. | 9 | Nov. 2, " .. |
| Bellows, Herbert G...... | Walpole, N. H.......... | 17 | " 12, " .. |
| Mallon, Mary A.......... | East Providence......... | 12 | " 29, " .. |
| White, Sarah........... | Providence............. | 10 | Sept. 5, 1881.. |
| Commin, Rock.......... | Albion, Lincoln.......... | 10 | Oct. 3, " .. |
| Provençal, Joseph....... | " " ........... | 10 | " 3, " .. |
| Potvin, William......... | River Point, Warwick .. | 12 | " 24, " .. |
| McDonnell, Thomas..... | Providence............. | 11 | Nov. 28, " .. |

| CAUSE OF DEAFNESS. (As far as known.) | AGE WHEN MADE DEAF. (Approx.) | REMARKS. |
|---|---|---|
| Severe illness........ | 8 months..... | |
| Scarlet fever........ | 2½ years...... | Left Feb. 15, 1881. At work with Hood & Chamberlain, Valley Falls. |
| Brain fever (?).. ... | 6½ years...... | Left June 30, 1881. At work in the Wanskuck Mill. |
| Congenital, or lung fever at 9 months. | ............. | |
| Congenital.... .... | ............. | |
| Disease of the ears.. | 12 y'rs. 8 mos. | |
| Congenital........... | ...... ... | |
| Scarlet fever.... ... | 3 years....... | Absent most of the year. |
| Congenital........ .... | ............ | Killed Nov. 22, 1881, aged 6 years 7 mos. |
| Congenital..... .... | ............ | |
| —— (?) fever...... | 2 years....... | |
| Scarlet fever........ | 5 y'rs. 8 mos.. | |
| Congenital........ .... | ............ | At R. I. R. C. Orphan Asylum. |
| Congenital........ ..... | ............ | At R. I. R. C. Orphan Asylum, until June 30. Absent since June 30. |
| Disease of the ears.. | 2 years...... | |
| —— —— (?)........ | 5 (?) years.... | Left March 1, 1881. At work with William H. Perry. |
| Scarlet fever... .... | 5 years.. .... | Supported by the State at Children's Home, Tobey Street. |
| Brain fever........ | 2 y'rs. 2 mos.. | Left Sept. 27, 1880. Re-entered Dec. 27, 1881. |
| Severe cold.... .... | 10 y'rs.,...... | Absent since Oct. 13. |
| Brain fever......... | 3 y'rs ....... | Supported by the State at R. I. R. C. Orphan Asylum. |
| Catarrh........... | 5 y'rs ....... | Semi-deaf. |
| Scarlet fever........ | 6 y'rs. 10 mos. | Absent most of the year. |
| Cerebro-spinal meningitis. | 2 years....... | Not a State beneficiary. Left June 30, 1881. |
| Scarlet fever........ | 6 years...... | |
| Lung fever.......... | 2 y'rs. 6 mos.. | Absent since Nov. 2. |
| Lung fever........ | 3 years...... | Board at R. I. R. C. Orphan Asylum, paid one-half by the State. Absent since Nov. 10. |
| Lung fever...... ... | 4 years...... | Board at R. I. R. C. Orphan Asylum, paid one-half by the State. Absent since Dec. 1. |
| Congenital...... .... | .... .. ...... | |
| Congenital, or tumor in ears at 10 mos. | ............. | |

## SUMMARY.

Number of pupils, from date of opening the school, April 2, 1877,
    to Dec. 31, 1880. ...................................... ...............  28
Number of pupils who have entered since Dec. 31, 1880. .......   5

    Whole number of pupils who have attended the school...  33
    Number who have left the school....................   9

Number of pupils Dec. 31, 1881............................  24

Number of males..................................... ............  16
  "   " females............................... ....................  13

Whole number of pupils who have attended during the year 1881.  29

Number of semi-mutes (including one semi-deaf)..............   8
Number of deaf-mutes (including those congenitally deaf, and
    those made deaf in infancy before receiving any idea of
    language through the ear)............................. .........  21

    Total..................... .................................  29

*Residences of all who have attended during the year 1881.*

Providence ..............................................  ...........  16
Woodville, North Providence...............................   1
East Providence....................................... ..............   2
Albion, Lincoln........ ................................ .... ...........   2
Arnold's Mills, Cumberland............................. ......  1
Valley Falls,    "  .............. .......... ... ... .......  1
                                                                             2
Johnston, Olneyville..................................,...........   1
Pawtucket........................................................   2
River Point, Warwick........................................   1
Slatersville, North Smithfield............. ......... ..............   1

    Total from Rhode Island...... ......................  28
Walpole, N. H........... .... ..........................   1

    Total..................................................  29

A sad vacancy has been caused by the death of our youngest and most promising pupil, Lyman H. Jencks. He was killed by a furniture wagon while playing near his home during the November vacation. He had crept under the wagon which was heavily loaded, and while clinging to a large plank suspended under it, he was thrown off and killed almost instantly. The exact nature of the accident is not known, but enough is known to show that he would probably have met with the same fate even if he had not been deaf.

From the foregoing summary it will be seen that the number of pupils has been increased by only one this year, although, considering the number of deaf and dumb children in the State, the increase should have been much larger. Moreover, the average attendance of those who are nominally pupils has been very unsatisfactory. In fact, the success of the school is so seriously impaired by the irregularity of attendance, that I would call your attention especially to the subject, and respectfully recommend that decided measures be taken to remedy the evil.

The year has added, of course, to the experience and skill of the teachers, and decided improvements have been made in methods of instruction employed, and in quality of work accomplished.

But in order to produce really satisfactory results, radical changes need to be made in the organization of the school. For, although it is serving a good purpose, in arousing an interest in the work of educating the deaf and dumb children of the State, and in showing what can, and what ought to, be done for them, it is not adapted to their present needs. It ought to be situated in a central locality; a Home should be established in connection with it for the benefit of children from the country, a dozen of whom are at hand; and the School and Home together should be under one management, and constitute what, in time, should become an institution for deaf-mutes, worthy of the State.

Since this School was opened, the State has been gradually realizing that its deaf and dumb children have been unfortunately, although unwittingly, neglected. Accordingly, it has from year to year made additional provision for their welfare; and at its last session the Legislature passed an amendment to the General Statutes, placing it within the power of His Excellency, the Governor, to furnish aid at his discretion to persons in the country wishing to send children to the School. A small proportion of the appropriation has been drawn, and seven petitioners have been aided; but the needs of the recipients have been only partially supplied, and consequently the object has been only partially accomplished.

The State has acknowledged its obligation to educate these children, to a certain extent. But, if its object and intention is to give them such an education as they really need, it must be still more liberal in its patronage, and as fast as occasion seems to require, take definite steps toward the establishment of an institution. For this alone will suffice to perform the necessary work, as I have attempted to show by the following statements:

I. The deaf-mutes of the State, as a class, have never yet been properly educated, and many of them have received no instruction whatever.

In 1817 the American Asylum was founded at Hartford, Conn., and until 1876 the only educated deaf-mutes of this State, were those who, with rare exceptions, had been sent to that institution.

Between 1817 and 1876, only fifty-nine deaf children of this State, or an average of one annually, received any instruction. Since 1876, forty-three have received instruction, or an average of at least eight annually.

In 1876, ten children were at Hartford; this year thirty-six have been under instruction (twenty-nine at this school, and seven at Hartford and elsewhere), while at least thirty others have not been under instruction.

II. It is not only impracticable, but unjust, to attempt to educate them, without bringing them together under one roof and one management.

In the fifty-third report of the American Asylum, printed in 1869, the principal says:

"Deaf-mutes must have a special education. As they constitute so small a portion of the community, but one individual being found within the limits of a township, it is impracticable to collect them in districts, as in the case of hearing children. It is better for the sake of economy, as well as efficiency generally, to gather the deaf-mutes of a State into one school."

To show how truly these statements are borne out by facts, I have prepared the following

## LIST:

*Showing the residences of sixty-five deaf children in this State.*

Bristol................................................... 2

Cumberland.....!......................................... 1

"     Valley Falls................................. 2

                       —   3

Coventry................................................. 1

Cranston, Pawtuxet...................................... 1

East Providence......................................... 3

Glocester................................................ 1

Johnston, Olneyville .................................... 1

Lincoln.................................................. 1

"     Albion ..................................... 2

"     Central Falls............................... 1

                       4

Little Compton........................................... 1

Newport................................................. 1

North Providence, Woodville.... ........................ 1

North Smithfield, Slatersville............................ 1

Providence.............................................. 26

"       Wanskuck................................ 3

                     —   29

Pawtucket............................................... 4

Scituate, Hope.......................................... 2

"     South................................... 1

                     —   3

Smithfield............................................... 2

Warwick................................................. 1

"     River Point.............................. 1

                     —   2

Warren.................................................. 1

Westerly................................................ 2

Woonsocket............................................. 2

                      ——
                      65

It will be generally acknowledged that these children are all equally deserving of an education at the hands of the State; yet, while some of them are receiving aid, varying in amount from $16 to $175 each per annum, others are receiving no aid whatever.

III. It is even more an act of economy than of charity, for States to educate their deaf mutes *liberally*.

In the report of the American Asylum referred to above, occur the following statements:

"The institutions for the deaf and dumb of this country are distinctively educational. * * * They receive only pupils who are capable of being instructed, and retain them only so long as may suffice to effect that object."

This is true; and although a spirit of charity must necessarily enter into the work of such institutions, yet those who watch the rapid intellectual development of their inmates, their power of language increasing, and their faces brightening from year to year, are impressed with the fact that it "pays" to educate them.

For loss of hearing, although a great deprivation and, when occurring in childhood, often followed by loss of speech, need by no means prevent the unfortunate ones from being educated into a condition of independence. Deaf-mutes can only be considered as intelligent beings, capable of becoming workers for good or evil, constructive or destructive, producers or consumers, self-supporting or paupers, according as they are educated or neglected.

Such institutions possess a certain economical value also, in tending to attract laborers, and in binding them to the

State.   Especially in a manufacturing community like ours,
is it essential to take measures to turn this floating population into a permanent one.   To illustrate, I will state that
this year there have come into the school three deaf-mute
boys, children of French operatives.   Another one I know
to be at a French institution in Canada; and three others,
living in the State last year, have since moved away.   The
restlessness of the French, and of this class especially, is pro-
verbial.   Many of them leave mortgaged farms in Canada
and come here with a determination, often carried out, to
save enough of their earnings to pay off the mortgages, and
return to Canada.   But they are usually well-behaved, industrious and desirable members of the community, and
would it not be a gain to the State if they could be induced
to stay here ?

And in the case of the seven families above mentioned,
numbering, perhaps, seventy or eighty members—for these
families are usually large—can it be doubted that the education of their deaf-mute boys would have a decided influence in keeping them in the State ?

In spite, however, of the migratory nature of mill operatives, the population of Rhode Island increased twenty-
seven per cent. between 1870 and 1880 — a much larger
increase than that of most other states — and owing to its
situation, its wealth, its manufacturing enterprise, and its
railroad facilities, it will increase, perhaps, even more
rapidly during the next decade.   And is not such an increase
of population another reason why such an institution is
needed now, even if never before?

In considering such a question as this we naturally look for precedent, and find that every other state in the Union supports an Institution for Deaf-Mutes, excepting Maine, New Hampshire, Vermont, Delaware, New Jersey and Florida; and in Maine the nucleus of an institution has been formed by a growing day-school in Portland.

The State of New York has adopted a wise and liberal policy in this matter. Its statutes allow every deaf-mute in the State, between the ages of six and twenty-five, to receive twelve, or, if desirable, fourteen years of instruction, at an annual expense "not to exceed three hundred dollars." It has now six institutions, whose inmates number twelve hundred pupils, (exclusive of those from other states,) each of whom costs the public about two hundred and sixty dollars annually, or altogether about $312,000.

Five years have elapsed, since this subject was first brought before the Legislature of Rhode Island, and steps taken toward the opening of this school. Slowly it has developed into its present condition. But is it not time now for a more rapid growth? Is Rhode Island justified in disregarding longer the claims of so many of its deaf-mute children, or in delaying longer to furnish proper means of educating them?

I submit these questions to you, into whose hands the education of the public has been entrusted, for your serious consideration.

JOSEPH W. HOMER.

## TO PARENTS OF DEAF CHILDREN.

This school is for the benefit of children incapacitated through deafness or dumbness, total or partial, from receiving proper instruction in common schools.

The aim of the school is to teach deaf children to use the English language with the spontaneity, correctness, and enjoyment of hearing children, as far as this is practicable.

The more advanced and intelligent pupils are taught the higher branches of education, but the *actual use of the English language* is considered of first importance.

It is very desirable that deaf children be sent to school at as early an age as possible — especially if they are also dumb. A parent will be amply repaid by sending a child as young as five or six years, even at some inconvenience.

If a child who has learned to talk is made deaf by disease, he should immediately upon his recovery be sent to a school where his speech will be retained, and where he will be taught to understand from the lips.

In such cases it is common to delay so long that serious loss of speech results.

Every effort should be made to encourage the child to retain the use of his voice. He should be taught to pronounce common words, but no attempt should be made to teach him *the names* of the letters of the alphabet.

Writing lessons should also be given him at home. It will

save much time if, when he enters school, he is able to write the names of common objects with which he is familiar.

The school hours are from 9 A. M. to 1 P. M. on every week day except Saturday. Open to visitors on Fridays from 10 to 12.

The next summer vacation will begin Friday, June 30, 1882. The school will re-open Monday, September 4, 1882.

Terms of admission may be obtained on application to the principal of the school, corner of Benefit and Halsey streets, or at 55 Waterman street, or at the office of the Commissioner of Public Schools, 104 North Main street, Providence. R. I.

# FIFTH ANNUAL REPORT

OF THE

# PRINCIPAL

OF THE

# IODE ISLAND SCHOOL FOR THE DEAF,

PROVIDENCE, R. I.,

FOR THE

## YEAR ENDING DECEMBER 31,

## 1882.

PROVIDENCE:

E. L. FREEMAN & CO., PRINTERS TO THE STATE.

1883.

# FIFTH ANNUAL REPORT

OF THE

# PRINCIPAL

OF THE

# RHODE ISLAND SCHOOL FOR THE DEAF,

PROVIDENCE, R. I.,

FOR THE

## YEAR ENDING DECEMBER 31,

## 1882.

PROVIDENCE:

E. L. FREEMAN & CO., PRINTERS TO THE STATE.

1883.

# RHODE ISLAND SCHOOL FOR THE DEAF,

CORNER OF FOUNTAIN AND BEVERLY STREETS,

## PROVIDENCE, R. I.

UNDER THE SUPERVISION OF THE

# STATE BOARD OF EDUCATION.

HIS EXCELLENCY ALFRED H. LITTLEFIELD, Governor, *ex-officio*, PRESIDENT.

HIS HONOR HENRY H. FAY, Lieutenant-Governor, *ex-officio*.

| | |
|---|---|
| REV. DANIEL LEACH, . . . . . . | Providence. |
| DWIGHT R. ADAMS, . . . . . . . | Centreville. |
| REV. CHARLES J. WHITE, . . . . . | Woonsocket. |
| REV. GEORGE L. LOCKE, . . . . . . | Bristol. |
| DAVID S. BAKER, JR., . . . . . . | Wickford. |
| LUCIUS D. DAVIS, . . . . . . . | Newport. |

SECRETARY:

THOMAS B. STOCKWELL, Commissioner of Public Schools, *ex-officio*.

PRINCIPAL:

KATHARINE H. AUSTIN,
Successor to Joseph W. Homer, who resigned in March, 1882.

ASSISTANT TEACHERS:

ARDELIA C. DEWING, ELLEN J. KERR.

# REPORT.

*To the Honorable the State Board of Education:*

GENTLEMEN:—I herewith submit my report for the year ending December 31, 1882.

Respectfully,

KATHARINE H. AUSTIN,

*Principal.*

DECEMBER 31, 1882.

## TABULAR REPORT OF THE PUPILS OF THE RHODE ISLAND

| Names of Pupils. | Residence. | Age. (Approx.) | Date of Admission. |
|---|---|---|---|
| Kinyon, Ada J. | Providence. | 22 | April 2, 1877 |
| Morlock, William T. | " | 15 | " 2, " |
| Hackman, Harry, Jr. | " | 14 | " 2, " |
| Sprague, Lily R. | " | 18 | " 8, 1878. |
| Wallace, M. Amey | Woodville, North Providence. | 11 | " 15, " |
| Catlow, Mary A. | Providence. | 11 | " 22, " |
| Mowry, Grace G. | " | 9 | Nov. 19, 1879. |
| Slavin, Joseph | Pawtucket. | 10 | Jan. 28, 1880. |
| Goodspead, Bertha | Providence. | 8 | Mar. 9, " |
| Slavin, Margaret | " | 10 | April 5, " |
| Riley, Thomas | " | 9 | " 5, " |
| Wood, Francis J. | Central Falls, Lincoln. | 9 | " 5, " |
| Tucker, Arthur | Providence. | 9 | " 19, " |
| Sheldon, Mary E. | Arnold's Mills, Cumberland. | 14 | Sept. 6, " |
| Lynch, James E. | Wanskuck, Providence. | 7 | " 6, " |
| Hall, Annie I. | Providence. | 17 | " 9, " |
| Dorgan, Michael J. | Central Falls, Lincoln. | 11 | Oct. 4, " |
| Leighton, Charles | Olneyville, Johnston. | 21 | " 4, " |
| Swift, Mary E. | Providence. | 10 | Nov. 2, " |
| Mallon, Mary A. | East Providence. | 13 | " 29, " |
| White, Sarah | Providence. | 11 | Sept. 5, 1881. |
| Commin Rock. | Albion, Lincoln. | 11 | Oct. 3, " |
| Provençal, Joseph | " " | 11 | " 3, " |
| Potvin, William | River Point, Warwick. | 13 | " 24, " |
| McDonnell, Thomas | Providence. | 12 | Nov. 28, " |
| Sprague, Florence M. | " | 13 | May 1, 1882. |
| Langevin, Ambroise | Valley Falls, Lincoln. | 23 | June 14, " |
| Brownell, Lester R. | Little Compton. | 7 | " 15, " |
| Ingham, Sarah A. | Wanskuck, Providence. | 13 | " 21, " |
| Fournier, Jean B. | Oakland, Burrillville. | 17 | Sept. 4, " |
| Radcliffe, Eliza | Lonsdale, Lincoln. | 10 | " 13, " |
| Dolan, Katharine | Providence. | 6 | Nov. 6, " |
| Moon, Ina G. | Washington, Coventry. | 10 | " 24, " |

## SCHOOL FOR THE DEAF FOR THE YEAR ENDING DEC. 31, 1882.

| CAUSE OF DEAFNESS, AS FAR AS KNOWN. | AGE WHEN MADE DEAF. (Approx.) | REMARKS. |
|---|---|---|
| Severe illness | 8 months | Scarcely any previous instruction. |
| Congenital, or lung fever at 9 months. | | No previous instruction. |
| Unknown | 2 years | No previous instruction. |
| Disease of the ears | 12 years, 8 months. | Left school Feb. 2, 1882. At work in C. W. Jencks & Bros. box manufactory. |
| Congenital | | No previous instruction. |
| Scarlet fever | 3 years | Re-entered April 17, 1882. Absent since June 21, 1882. Expects to return as soon as possible. |
| Congenital | | |
| ——? fever | 2 years | No previous instruction. |
| Scarlet fever | 5 years, 8 months. | |
| Congenital | | No previous instruction. Inmate of R. C. Orphan Asylum, Prairie Avenue. |
| Congenital | | Re-entered April 10, 1882. Absent May 11, to Oct. 10, 1882. Hears very loud sounds. |
| Disease of the ears | 2 years | No previous instruction. |
| Whooping cough. Semi-deaf | 3 years | Re-entered June 6, 1882. |
| Scarlet fever | 5 years | Supported by the State at Children's Home, Tobey street. |
| Brain fever | 2 years, 2 months. | No previous instruction. |
| Severe cold | 10 years | Left school Oct. 2, 1882. Employed in a family. |
| Brain fever | 3 years | No previous instruction. Supported by State at R. C. Orphan Asylum, Prairie Avenue. |
| Catarrh. Semi-deaf | 5 years | Removed to Lowell, Mass. Left School Oct. 20, 1882. |
| Scarlet fever | 6 years, 10 months. | |
| Scarlet fever | 6 years | |
| Lung fever | 2 years, 6 months. | No previous instruction. Re-entered April 10, 1882. |
| Lung fever | 3 years | No previous instruction. Re-entered April 11, 1882. |
| Lung fever | 4 years | No previous instruction. Re-entered April 11, 1882. |
| Congenital | | No previous instruction. Hears very loud sounds. |
| Congenital, or tumor in ears at 10 months. | | No previous instruction. Hears very loud sounds. |
| Scrofulous tendency ; also scarlet fever at 5. Semi-deaf. | 11 years | Only two months previous instruction. Left school June 28, 1882. At work in a mill. Hopes to return. |
| ——? fever. | 2 years | No previous instruction. Widowed mother removed to Providence to educate the child. |
| Congenital | | Permitted to attend temporarily for improvement of speech. Left school Nov. 14, 1882. |
| Hears perfectly | | Had attended a French school in Province of Quebec for a year and a half. |
| Scarlet fever | 3 years | Four months' instruction previous to her illness. |
| Scarlet fever | 6 years | No previous instruction. |
| Congenital, or illness at 2 years | | Very little previous instruction. Hears shrill voices. |
| Congenital, or illness at 3 months | | |

## SUMMARY.

Number of pupils, from date of opening the school, April 2, 1877,
to Dec. 31, 1881...................................... 33

Number of pupils who have entered since Dec. 31, 1881........ 8

Whole number of pupils who have attended the school... 41

Number who have left the school .................... 14

Number of pupils, Dec. 31, 1882......................... 27

Number of girls............... .............. ............ 17

"    " boys... ........................................ 16

Whole number of pupils who have attended the school during
the year ..................................... 33

Number of semi-mutes (including three semi-deaf)........... 14

Number of deaf-mutes (including those congenitally deaf, and
those made deaf in infancy, before receiving any idea of language through the ear)........ .................... 18

Number of children with perfect hearing, but imperfect speech,
allowed to attend temporarily.... .................... 1

Total................................................ 33

*Residences of all who have attended during the year* 1882.

Providence.......... .......... ...................... 19

Pawtucket 2, (1 of whom has removed to Central Falls)........ 1

Central Falls 2, (1 boarding in Providence)............... .... 1

Wanskuck.......... .......................... 2

Albion..:.......... ...................... 2

Woodville ....... .... ................... 1

Valley Falls........... .................. 1

East Providence 2, (1 removed to Providence)............... 1

Olneyville.......... .................................. 1

Lonsdale .................................................... 1
Arnold's Mills, Cumberland, (boarding in Providence) 1.
Nasonville (and more recently Oakland) 1.
Oakland, (previously Nasonville)........................... 1
River Point............................................... 1
Washington Village ....................................... 1
Slatersville, (removed to Central Falls) 1.
Little Compton, (at present in Providence) 1.

　　　　　　　　　　　　　　　　　　　　　　　　　　　—

　17 localities.... .. ..................................... 33

In connection with the foregoing tabular report and summary, it may be interesting to examine the growth of the
school from year to year. This will be seen to have been
by no means uniform, for

The number of pupils present at the opening of the school, April
　　2, 1877, was........................................... 5
The number who attended the school between April 2, 1877, and
　　Dec. 31, 1878, was....................................... 10
The number during the year ending Dec. 31, 1879, was........ 13
　　"　　　"　　　"　　"　　"　　"　　"　31, 1880, "　........ 28
　　"　　　"　　　"　　"　　"　　"　　"　31, 1881, "　........ 29
　　"　　　"　　　"　　"　　"　　"　　"　31, 1882, "　........ 33

The large increase apparent in 1880, is mainly due to the
fact that in the course of that year, the census-returns became available, furnishing the names of deaf children who
were sought out and induced to attend the school. Notwithstanding the care used by the former and the present
principal, in following up slight clues, there are indications
that there may be a considerable number of deaf children in
the State, as yet quite unknown to the teachers of this
2

school. For example, since November 1st, two little girls have been admitted, of whose existence we had never heard before October 27th. One of them was promptly reported by the mother of a promising lad who has been in attendance for a year. This parent regrets as lost time, the four preceding years, during which she was ignorant that there was a school for the deaf in Providence. The relatives of the child last admitted, living fourteen miles out of town, had not known of the school until their attention was at- . tracted by a recent article in a Providence paper.

It is gratifying to detect an increased regularity of attendance since the removal of the school in September, from Benefit street to the present more central location. We expect to see the difference more strongly marked in the inclement season which is approaching.

The gain of a third room is a great advantage to the school, as the most casual visitor can easily understand.

Moreover, through the courtesy of the teachers of the Free Kindergarten, our pupils have enjoyed the use of a spacious room on the first floor, for marching and simple calisthenics. These exercises were at first shared with the children of the Kindergarten, but of late, they have oc-curred immediately after the dispersion of the latter, at 12 o'clock. They prove valuable, not only in supplying physi-cal training and wholesome amusement, but as aids toward developing the sense of rhythm, necessarily defective in congenitally deaf persons.

The methods of instruction pursued in the school, are sub-stantially those of last year. The appliances, devised or adapted by the former principal, at the expense of much careful thought, continue to be of very great service to the present teachers. The problem of the exact apportionment of attention to the various claims of the pupil's mind, is one which besets all educators, but especially, perhaps, the teachers of the deaf. Since the education of deaf students *must* progress slowly, how shall it be made to progress the least slowly? Since written language, lip-reading and articulation are each important, how shall we adjust the right proportion of time for each? How shall a term of school-years produce the best results for the pupil's life-time?

These and other delicate questions demand for their solution, all the sound judgment, ingenuity, enthusiasm and sense of responsibility which can be brought to bear upon them. In other words, absolute success is well-nigh unattainable. Yet the results secured by faithful teachers under a good general system, are such as constantly to stimulate them toward a nicer adaptation of means to ends, and toward a juster balancing of the ends themselves.

To speak in more detail would be to repeat what previous reports have said. One of the principal aims of the school is to give the pupils a command of written language. An individual possessing this, necessarily has the power of thinking with some clearness, of communicating with his fellow-men and of gaining access to the best literature. For persons *congenitally* deaf, the process is a very long one. Therefore it can hardly be commenced too early.

The ability to understand speech by watching the movements of the lips, is obviously of great value; hence all the pupils have daily practice in this art.

The power of articulation can be developed in varying degrees. Every child who has attended the school for a few weeks, can utter some words which in his mind are asso- ciated with ideas and with written forms. We cherish even the minimum attainment in this direction, while aiming at the maximum, and daily training is given to all, with some very satisfactory results of conversation, in the case of chil- dren congenitally deaf, as well as of those who retain more or less recollection of sounds.

It is a pleasant duty here to pay tribute to the marked fidelity and success of the assistant-teachers, as witnessed day by day, in the varied experiences of the schoolroom.

At the suggestion of the School Commissioner, in Septem- ber, an afternoon-session was established for the benefit of certain pupils living out of the city. It is held from half- past one to half-past three o'clock, on Mondays, Wednesdays and Fridays, the three teachers taking alternate charge. The arrangement has two advantages.

I. It tends to equalize the benefits of the school, other- wise unevenly shared in consequence of the inconvenient times at which the Albion trains and the Wanskuck omnibus start. For instance, two lads of eleven, who had heretofore returned to their homes in Albion by the 11.30 train, now remain on three days in each week, until the 4.05 train, there being no intermediate one.

II. It provides a safe place of waiting for several children who go home in the River Point cars at 2.45, the Wanskuck omnibus at 3, and the Providence and Springfield cars at 4.30. For the oversight of this class, the principal remains at the school-house on Tuesdays and Thursdays until 2.

Thus the only pupil, who on those two days has much time remaining, is a trustworthy youth of seventeen, who is encouraged to spend it at the Public Library.. The librarian and his assistants have always co-operated most cordially with the teachers of this school, in trying to meet the needs of the pupils. The same is true of the lady in attendance upon the Library of the Union for Christian Work.

Thanks are due to our former co worker, Miss Ellen Shaw, now of the Horace Mann School for the Deaf in Boston, for the gift of various useful articles of school apparatus; to Miss Adeline Brown for five large, delicately-tinted lithographs, suitably framed, which increase the attractiveness of our schoolrooms; to several ladies, who, from time to time, have given clothing needed by the poorer pupils; and to the " Children's Mission " connected with the First Congregational Church, for five pairs of new shoes and rubbers.

The chairman of the 9th ward visiting committee of the Women's City Missionary Society, in September, offered to the school some of the tickets contributed by citizens for "poor women's and children's excursions." These were given to the pupils whose parents could not afford to buy them. Others paid their own fare, and thus about a score of happy boys and girls under the care of their teachers, passed several hours at Rocky Point on a pleasant day after the close of the excursion season. As there was scarcely another visitor on the grounds, the time was spent in greater freedom than would have been possible in summer, and the children's enjoyment seemed complete.

Acknowledgment is hereby made of the receipt during the past year, of the Nebraska Mute Journal, a semi-monthly sheet, printed and published at the Nebraska Institute for the Deaf and Dumb.

There are frequent proofs that the existence of the Rhode Island School is becoming more and more generally known in the State, and that its very nature appeals to the sympathy and curiosity of the citizens. It is earnestly to be hoped that persons into whose hands this report may come, will not fail to apprise the principal of the school, or the Commissioner of Public Schools, of any cases of total or partial deafness among young people, which, they may have reason to believe, are unknown to those officers. Such cases will be promptly investigated, to the probable advantage of the body politic.

The conduct of the pupils who have left their studies to enter active life, justifies the Rhode Island School for the Deaf in claiming a full share of the State's inspiring motto: " Hope."

KATHARINE H. AUSTIN.

## TO PARENTS OF DEAF CHILDREN.

This school is for the benefit of children incapacitated through deafness or dumbness, total or partial, from receiving proper instruction in common schools.

The aim of the school is to teach deaf children to use the English language with the spontaneity, correctness, and enjoyment of hearing children, as far as this is practicable.

The more advanced and intelligent pupils are taught the higher branches of education, but the *actual use of the English language* is considered of first importance.

It is very desirable that deaf children be sent to school at as early an age as possible — especially if they are also dumb. A parent will be amply repaid for sending a child as young as five or six years, even at some inconvenience.

If a child who has learned to talk is made deaf by disease, he should immediately upon his recovery be sent to a school where his speech will be retained, and where he will be taught to understand from the lips.

In such cases it is common to delay so long that serious loss of speech results.

Every effort should be made to encourage the child to retain the use of his voice. He should be taught to pronounce common words, but no attempt should be made to teach him *the names* of the letters of the alphabet.

Writing lessons should also be given him at home. It will

save much time if, when he enters school, he is able to write the names of common objects with which he is familiar.

The school hours are from 9 A. M. to 1 P. M. on every week day except Saturday. Open to visitors on Fridays from 10 to 12.

The next summer vacation will begin Friday, June 29, 1883. The school will re-open Monday, September 3, 1883. Tuition is free to residents of this State. Application for admission may be made to the principal of the school, or to the Commissioner of Public Schools, 104 North Main street, Providence, R. I.

.Б.. В

# SIXTH ANNUAL REPORT

OF THE

# PRINCIPAL

OF THI

# IODE ISLAND SCHOOL FOR THE DEAF,

## PROVIDENCE. R. I.

FOR THE

### YEAR ENDING DECEMBER 31,

## 1883.

PROVIDENCE:
E. L. FREEMAN & CO., PRINTERS TO THE STATE,
1884.

# SIXTH ANNUAL REPORT

OF THE

# PRINCIPAL

OF THE

# RHODE ISLAND SCHOOL FOR THE DEAF,

## PROVIDENCE, R. I.

FOR THE

### YEAR ENDING DECEMBER 31,

## 1883.

---

PROVIDENCE:

E. L. FREEMAN & CO., PRINTERS TO THE STATE.

1884.

# RHODE ISLAND SCHOOL FOR THE DEAF.

### CORNER OF FOUNTAIN AND BEVERLY STREETS.

## PROVIDENCE, R. I.

UNDER THE SUPERVISION OF THE

# STATE BOARD OF EDUCATION.

HIS EXCELLENCY AUGUSTUS O. BOURN, Governor, *ex-officio*,
PRESIDENT.

HIS HONOR OSCAR J. RATHBUN, Lieutenant-Governor, *ex-officio*.

| | |
|---|---|
| REV. DANIEL LEACH, . . . . . . | Providence. |
| DWIGHT R. ADAMS, . . . . . . . | Centreville. |
| REV. CHARLES J. WHITE, . . . . | Woonsocket. |
| REV. GEORGE L. LOCKE, . . . . . | Bristol. |
| DAVID S. BAKER, JR., . . . . . | Wickford. |
| LUCIUS D. DAVIS, . . . . . . | Newport. |

SECRETARY:

THOMAS B. STOCKWELL, Commissioner of Public Schools, *ex-officio*.

PRINCIPAL:

KATHARINE H. AUSTIN.

ASSISTANT TEACHERS:
ARDELIA C. DEWING,     ELLEN J. KERR.

# REPORT.

*To the Honorable the State Board of Education:*

GENTLEMEN :—I herewith submit my report for the year ending December 31, 1883.

Respectfully,

KATHARINE H. AUSTIN,

*Principal.*

DECEMBER 31, 1883.

## TABULAR REPORT OF THE PUPILS OF THE RHODE ISLAND

| NAMES OF PUPILS. | RESIDENCE. | AGE. (Approx.) | DATE OF ADMISSION. |
|---|---|---|---|
| Kinyon, Ada J. | Providence | 23 | April 2, 1877 |
| Morlock, William T. | " | 16 | " 2, " |
| Hackman, Harry Jr. | " | 15 | " 2, " |
| Sprague, Lily R. | " | 19 | " 8, 1878 |
| Wallace, M. Amey | Woodville, North Providence | 12 | " 15, " |
| Catlow, Mary A. | Providence | 12 | " 22, " |
| Mowry, Grace G. | " | 10 | Nov. 19, 1879 |
| Slavin, Joseph H. | Pawtucket | 11 | Jan. 28, 1880 |
| Goodspeed, Bertha | Providence | 9 | Mar. 9, " |
| Slavin, Margaret | " | 11 | Apr. 5, " |
| Riley, Thomas | " | 10 | " 5, " |
| Wood, Francis J. | Central Falls, Lincoln | 10 | " 5, " |
| Tucker, Arthur | Providence | 10 | " 19, " |
| Sheldon, Mary E. | Arnold's Mills, Cumberland | 15 | Sept. 6, " |
| Lynch, James E. | Wanskuck, Providence | 8 | " 6, " |
| Dorgan, Michael J | Valley Falls, Lincoln | 12 | Oct. 4, " |
| Swift, Mary E. | Providence | 11 | Nov. 2, " |
| Mallon, Mary A | East Providence | 14 | " 29, " |
| White, Sarah | Providence | 12 | Sept. 5, 1881 |
| Commin, Rock | Albion, Lincoln | 12 | Oct. 3, " |
| Provençal, Joseph | " " | 12 | " 3, " |
| Potvin, William | River Point, Warwick | 14 | " 24, " |
| McDonnell, Thomas | Providence | 13 | Nov. 28, " |
| Sprague, Florence M | " | 14 | May 1, 1882 |
| Brownell, Lester R | Little Compton | 8 | June 15, " |
| Fournier, Jean B. | Woonsocket | 18 | Sept. 4, " |
| Radcliffe, Eliza | Lonsdale, Lincoln | 11 | " 13, " |
| Dolan, Katharine | Providence | 7 | Nov. 6, " |
| Moon, Ina G | Washington, Coventry | 11 | " 24, " |
| Lorimer, John F. | Providence | 11 | April 18, 1883 |
| Woodley, Abby M | " | 6 | May 7, " |
| Nolan, Rosanna | Rumford, East Providence | 9 | Sept. 3, " |
| Avery, Edward S. | Providence | 8 | " 21, " |

## SCHOOL FOR THE DEAF FOR THE YEAR ENDING DEC. 31, 1883.

| CAUSE OF DEAFNESS, AS FAR AS KNOWN. | AGE WHEN MADE DEAF. (Approx.) | REMARKS. |
|---|---|---|
| Severe illness .................. | 8 months.. ....... | ............................................................. |
| { Congenital, or lung fever at 9 } months. | .................. | ............................................................. |
| Unknown.................... | 2 years, 6 months.. | { Left school September 10, 1883. Now at the } American Asylum, Hartford. |
| Disease of the ears............. | 12 years, 8 months. | { In attendance four months. Left School } Oct. 29, 1883, to learn a trade. |
| Congenital...................... | .................. | ..................................................... |
| Scarlet fever.................... | 3 years........... | { Re-entered March 5, 1883. Has considerable } hearing. |
| Congenital...................... | ... ............ | .................................................. |
| ——? fever................... | 1 year, 9 months... | ............................................................. |
| Scarlet fever.................... | 5 years, 8 months.. | ............................................................. |
| Congenital...................... | .................. | { Inmate of R. C. Orphan Asylum. Left school } Oct. 15. Now at school in Montreal. |
| Congenital .................. | .................. | Can hear shrill tones................ |
| Disease of the ears............. | 2 years........... | Left school June 29, 1883. Removed to Chicago. |
| Whooping cough............ ... | 3 years,.......... | Can hear voices somewhat raised. |
| Scarlet fever.................. | 5 years.......... | ..................................................... |
| Brain fever.................... | 2 years, 2 months.. | ............................................................. |
| Brain fever.................... | 3 years.......... | ............................................................. |
| Scarlet fever.................... | 6 years, 10 months. | ............................................................. |
| Scarlet fever.................... | 6 years .......... | ..................................................... |
| Lung fever............. ....... | 2 years, 6 months.. | Can imperfectly hear shrill tones. |
| Lung fever ................... | 3 years........... | { Struck by a locomotive, July 18th; died July } 20th, 1883. |
| Lung fever.................... | 4 years........... | Left school June 29. Removed to Canada. |
| Congenital .................. | .................. | Can hear shrill tones. |
| { Congenital, or tumor in ears } at 10 months. | .................. | Can hear shrill tones. |
| { Scrofulous tendency, also scar- } let fever at 5. | 11 years.......... | { In school only three days during 1883. Left } school Oct. 18. Has considerable hearing. |
| Congenital.................. ..... | ........ ..... | ..................................................... |
| Scarlet fever.................... | 3 years........... | { Left school October 5, 1883. Removed to } Glasgo, Conn. |
| Scarlet fever . ............... | 6 years........... | ..................................................... |
| Congenital, or illness at 2 years. | .................. | .......................................... |
| Congenital, or illness at 3 months | .................. | Can hear shrill tones. |
| Scarlet fever ................. | { Probably before } the age of two. | Can hear loud tones. |
| Chronic inflammation of throat.. | { Discovered in } her third year. | Can hear very loud tones. |
| Scarlet fever ................. | 9 weeks. ........ | ............................................................. |
| Canker ...................... | 3 weeks........... | Can imperfectly hear shrill tones. |

## SUMMARY.

| | |
|---|---|
| Number of pupils, from date of opening the school, April 2, 1877, to Dec. 31, 1882.............................................. | 41 |
| Number of pupils who have entered the school since Dec. 31, 1882, | 4 |
| Whole number of pupils who have attended the school.... | 45 |
| Number who have left the school ..................... | 20 |
| Number of pupils, Dec. 31, 1883.......................... | 25 |
| Number of girls who have attended school during the year ..... | 17 |
| "    boys    "    "    "    "    "    ..... | 16 |
| Whole number of pupils during the year..................... | 33 |
| Number congenitally deaf, or made deaf before the age of two... | 15 |
| Number who lost hearing between the ages of two and four..... | 10 |
| Number who lost hearing after the age of four ............... | 8 |
| | 33 |
| Number who can hear any tones of the human voice........... | 11 |

*Residences of all who have attended during the year 1883.*

| | |
|---|---|
| Providence................................................. | 18 |
| Albion..................................................... | 2 |
| Watchemoket.............................................. | 1 |
| Rumford .................................................. | 1 |
| Wanskuck................................................. | 1 |
| Woodville................................................. | 1 |
| Pawtucket ................................................ | 1 |
| Central Falls ............................................. | 1 |
| Valley Falls............................................... | 1 |
| Lonsdale.................................................. | 1 |
| Arnold's Mills, Cumberland, (boarding in Providence).......... | 1 |

Oakland, Burrillville, (and more recently Woonsocket)......... 1
River Point............................ .... .............. 1
Washington Village................................... 1
Little Compton, (family living in Providence for the sake of edu-
  cating the child)....... ............................ 1
                                                        ___
  16 localities.................. .................... 33

The number of pupils in the school during the whole or
a part of the year 1883 is the same as for 1882. The average daily attendance, however, has been larger than in any
preceding year.

For 1883 it has been. ........................21.9 pupils.
 " 1882 it was....................................18.    "
 " 1881   "    ....................................14.
 " 1880   "    ....................................14.4
 " 1879   "    .................................... 9.3
 " 1878   "    ....:.................................. 7.7

Since the last report was presented, a shadow has been
cast upon the school by the death of a pupil. During the
summer vacation Rock Commin of Albion, a lad about
twelve years old, while standing on the railroad track within
a few rods of his home, was struck by a locomotive, and so
injured that he died, after two days' unconsciousness. He
had been a member of this school for more than a year, and
had manifested winning traits of character.

The peril of being off one's guard in streets and in the
vicinity of railroads, is a lesson which the teachers take
much pains to impress, and which the pupils are, for the
most part, apt to learn, usually developing very satisfactory

2

habits of caution and self-reliance. Care is taken to provide trustworthy companions for the younger children on their way to and from school.

The tri-weekly afternoon-session of two hours, established in September, 1882, besides continuing to serve its original purpose, has been used as a valuable opportunity for bringing certain pupils up to the level of their classes, and in a few cases, for the well-being of children whose parents liked that they should be occupied among books instead of being at home in the afternoon. It will be remembered that this session was arranged for the benefit of two or three pupils living out of town, whom the cars or omnibus did not accommodate in regard to returning home. Such are allowed to go at about 11 o'clock on Tuesdays and Thursdays, and on the other three days they remain until half-past three. The school house, moreover, is open every day until two o'clock, under the care of a teacher, that a few children who leave town shortly after that hour, may have a suitable place of waiting.

In preparing the summary on page 26, there has been the usual difficulty in accurately classifying the pupils in respect to deafness and muteness. If possible, a line should be drawn between children who retain any recollection of sounds and those who do not. In the present report, the age of two has been chosen as approximating the true line of division. Yet there are two pupils by no means deficient in ability who have always seemed to their instructors like congenital deaf mutes, although they are said to have retained their hearing until about the ages of five and six. In these cases, no instruction was given from that time until they were admitted to this school at the ages of twelve and ten respectively. It is to be noted that they are reported by their friends to have talked well before losing their hearing. The term "semi-mute," often applied to persons who become deaf after infancy, would be highly inappropriate to these and some other pupils who have lost hearing power since the age of two.

The term "semi-deaf," if used in the Rhode Island School at the present time, must cover a very wide range,—from a boy who hears a voice slightly raised, to one who can catch but indistinctly vowel-sounds uttered with the teacher's utmost force. Even this faint power of hearing is of value to the child, but he is not semi-deaf, in the ordinary acceptation of the prefix "semi."

As it is obviously very important to guard the eyesight of deaf persons, several pupils whose eyes did not appear to be in a normal condition, were, last summer, taken to the R. I. Hospital for examination. After careful inspection, Dr. Capron prescribed glasses in most instances, and Mr. Putney, the well-known optician, kindly furnished them at less than half price, upon learning that the children needing them, were in straitened circumstances.

The course of instruction pursued in the school, is the same as heretofore, in its general aims and methods. The teachers cannot but feel that they are gradually adjusting the methods to the aims with greater accuracy, thus economizing time which is invaluable, in an education necessarily slow. Most instructors of the deaf, whether by the oral,

the manual, or the combined system, would probably agree
with the experienced Principal of a certain Institution conducted on the combined plan, that it is of the first importance to give pupils a free use of *written* language.
This is not easily accomplished. As, in the case of hearing
persons who study a foreign language, the preponderance of
judgment appears to be in favor of a system uniting the
advantages of the "natural" with those of the "scientific"
method, so to the teachers in this school for the deaf, it
seems most reasonable to encourage idiomatic and colloquial
forms of speech, at the same time that they try to avail
themselves of whatever regularity can be discovered in the
English language, and to give the learner the benefit of all
practicable classification of forms.

In assigning the first place to the teaching of written language, there is no disloyalty to other standards upheld in
the R. I. School for the Deaf from its beginning. Articulation and the power of understanding speech by watching
the lips of a speaker, continue to seem priceless possessions,
only to be relinquished in rare cases. Even the little attainment in these directions that can be secured by a dull child
whose sight is imperfect, may be of some moral and intellectual value to the child himself and of some service as a
means of communication. Relatives would be unnatural
indeed, who should take no pleasure in hearing articulate
utterance, however imperfect; while the satisfaction must
be inexpressible, of those parents whose careful training,
anticipating and supplementing that of teachers, is rewarded
by the intelligible and fluent speech of a congenitally deaf
child.

Such a member of this school was recently invited to read aloud in the Chinese Sunday School maintained by the Beneficent Congregational Church, as was also a well educated blind boy, for the sake of giving to Chinamen some idea of what is done for the deaf and the blind in Christian countries. On this occasion, it was not merely the partial judgment of teachers which regarded the little girl's reading of the Lord's Prayer as distinct and agreeable.

The school is indebted to numerous friends for gifts serviceable in illustrating lessons, and for clothing needed by a few of the poorer children. Among these benefactors are the "Children's Mission" connected with the First Congregational Church, Miss Lily R. Sprague and Mr. Thomas F. Burns, formerly members of the school, and Mr. Denis Provençal, father of a pupil.

The library, now numbering 310 volumes, has been increased by welcome gifts from the School Commissioner. The children are fond of taking these books to their homes, and it is considered highly desirable to foster the love of books, even where, as among the younger scholars, it chiefly consists in a liking for the illustrations and for finding here and there a familiar word.

The receipt of the Nebraska Mute Journal, issued at the Nebraska Institution for the Deaf and Dumb, and of recent numbers of the Mute's Companion, published at the Minnesota School, is hereby acknowledged with thanks.

In response to the request for information contained in the last annual report, and mailed to the Postmasters of the State, names of two deaf children in different localities, were received. One proved to be that of an eligible pupil, and at the age of nine and a half years, her school education has commenced. Her parents would have been glad to send her to a day school for the deaf, three or four years earlier, had they known that such existed within their reach.

The request is earnestly renewed, that persons who may chance to see this report, will send to the Principal or to the School Commissioner, the addresses of children too deaf to attend ordinary schools with profit.

KATHARINE H. AUSTIN.

## TO PARENTS OF DEAF CHILDREN.

This school is for the benefit of children incapacitated through deafness or dumbness, total or partial, for receiving proper instruction in common schools.

The aim of the school is to teach deaf children to use the English language with the spontaneity, correctness, and enjoyment of hearing children, as far as this is practicable.

The more advanced and intelligent pupils are taught the higher branches of education, but the *actual use of the English language* is considered of first importance.

It is very desirable that deaf children be sent to school at as early an age as possible—especially if they are also dumb. A parent will be amply repaid for sending a child as young as five or six years, even at some inconvenience.

If a child who has learned to talk is made deaf by disease, he should immediately upon his recovery be sent to a school where his speech will be retained, and where he will be taught to understand from the lips.

In such cases it is common to delay so long that serious loss of speech results.

Every effort should be made to encourage the child to retain the use of his voice. He should be taught to pronounce common words, but no attempt should be made to teach him *the names* of the letters of the alphabet.

Writing lessons should also be given him at home. It will save much time if, when he enters school, he is able to write the names of common objects with which he is familiar.

The school hours are from 9 A. M. to 1 P. M. on every week day except Saturday. Open to vistors on Fridays from 10 to 12.

The next summer vacation will begin Friday, June 27, 1884. The school will re-open Monday, September 1, 1884. Tuition is free to residents of this State. Provision is made for defraying the traveling expenses of indigent pupils. Application for admission may be made to the principal of the school, or to the Commissioner of Public Schools, 104 North Main street, Providence, R. I.

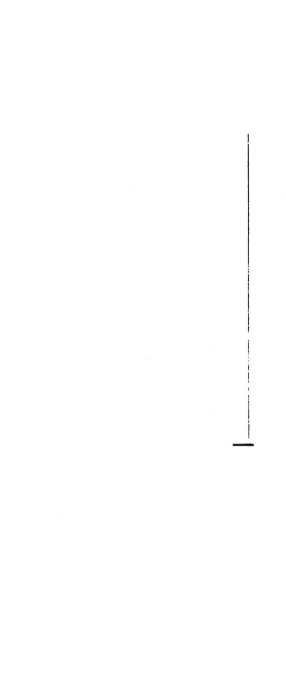

# SEVENTH ANNUAL REPORT

OF THE

# PRINCIPAL

OF THE

# RHODE ISLAND SCHOOL FOR THE DEAF,

PROVIDENCE, R. I.

FOR THE

YEAR ENDING DECEMBER 31,

1884.

PROVIDENCE:
E. L. FREEMAN & CO., PRINTERS TO THE STATE.
1885.

# RHODE ISLAND SCHOOL FOR THE DEAF.

## CORNER OF FOUNTAIN AND BEVERLY STREETS.

## PROVIDENCE, R. I.

UNDER THE SUPERVISION OF THE

# STATE BOARD OF EDUCATION.

HIS EXCELLENCY AUGUSTUS O. BOURN, Governor, *ex-officio*.

PRESIDENT.

HIS HONOR OSCAR J. RATHBUN, Lieutenant-Governor, *ex-officio*,

| | |
|---|---|
| REV. DANIEL LEACH, | Providence. |
| DWIGHT R. ADAMS, | Centreville. |
| REV. CHARLES J. WHITE, | Woonsocket. |
| REV. GEORGE L. LOCKE, | Bristol. |
| DAVID S. BAKER, JR., | Wickford. |
| LUCIUS D. DAVIS, | Newport. |

SECRETARY:

THOMAS B. STOCKWELL, Commissioner of Public Schools, *ex-officio*.

PRINCIPAL:

KATHARINE H. AUSTIN.

ASSISTANT TEACHERS:

ARDELIA C. DEWING,    ELLEN J. KERR.

# REPORT.

*To the Honorable the State Board of Education:*

GENTLEMEN:—I herewith submit my report for the year ending December 31, 1884.

Respectfully,

KATHARINE H. AUSTIN,

*Principal.*

DECEMBER 31, 1884.

## TABULAR REPORT OF THE PUPILS OF THE RHODE ISLAND

| NAMES OF PUPILS. | RESIDENCE. | AGE. (Approx.) | DATE OF ADMISSION. |
|---|---|---|---|
| Kinyon, Ada J | Providence | 24 | April 2, 1877 |
| Morlock, William T | " | 17 | " 2, " |
| Wallace, M. Amey | Woodville, North Providence .. | 13 | " 15, 1878 |
| Catlow, Mary A | Providence | 13 | " 22, " |
| Mowry, Grace G | " | 11 | Nov. 19, 1879 |
| Flavin, Joseph H | Pawtucket | 12 | Jan. 28, 1880 |
| Goodspeed, Bertha | Providence | 10 | Mar. 9, " |
| Riley, Thomas | " | 11 | April 5, " |
| Tucker, Arthur | " | 11 | " 19, " |
| Sheldon, Mary E | Arnold's Mills, Cumberland.... | 16 | Sept. 6, " |
| Lynch, James E | Wanskuck, Providence, | 9 | " 6, " |
| Dorgan, Michael J | Valley Falls, Lincoln | 13 | Oct. 4, " |
| Swift, Mary E | Providence | 12 | Nov. 2, " |
| Mallon, Mary A | East Providence | 15 | " 29, " |
| White, Sarah | " " | 13 | Sept. 5, 1881 |
| Potvin, William | River Point, Warwick | 15 | Oct. 24, " |
| McDonnell, Thomas | Providence | 14 | Nov. 28, " |
| Brownell, Lester R | Little Compton | 9 | June 15, 1882 |
| Radcliffe, Eliza | Lonsdale, Lincoln | 12 | Sept. 13, " |
| Dolan, Katharine | Providence | 8 | Nov. 6, " |
| Moon, Ina G | Washington, Coventry | 12 | " 24, " |
| Lorimer, John F. | Providence | 12 | Apr. 18, 1883 |
| Woodley, Abby M | " | 7 | May 7, " |
| Nolan, Rosanna | Rumford, East Providence | 10 | Sept. 3, " |
| Avery, Edward S | Providence | 9 | " 21, " |
| Baker, Mary Louisa | East Providence | 26 | May 13, 1884 |
| Addison, Eleanor J | Pawtucket | 14 | " 19, " |
| Addison, Susan B | " | 12 | " 19, " |
| Goodwin, James H | Providence | 9 | Oct. 7, " |
| Holloway, Mary Ellen | Centreville, Warwick | 8 | " 20, " |

## SCHOOL FOR THE DEAF FOR THE YEAR ENDING DEC. 31, 1884.

| Cause of Deafness, as far as Known. | Age when made Deaf. (Approx.) | Remarks. |
|---|---|---|
| Severe illness, | 8 months | |
| Congenital, or lung fever at 9 months. | | |
| Congenital | | |
| Scarlet fever | 3 years | Has considerable hearing. |
| Congenital | | Absent from city during summer and autumn. |
| —? fever | 1 year, 9 months | |
| Scarlet fever | 5 years, 8 months | |
| Congenital | | Can hear very loud tones. |
| Whooping cough | 3 years | Can hear voices somewhat raised. |
| Scarlet fever | 5 years | |
| Brain fever | 2 years, 2 months | Can hear very shrill tones. |
| Brain fever | 3 years | |
| Scarlet fever | 6 years, 10 months | |
| Scarlet fever | 6 years | |
| Lung fever | 2 years, 6 months | Can hear very shrill tones. |
| Congenital | | Can hear shrill tones. |
| Congenital, or tumor in ears at 10 months. | | Can hear shrill tones. |
| Congenital | | |
| Scarlet fever | | |
| Congenital, or illness at 2 years | | Can hear very shrill tones. |
| Congenital, or illness at 3 months | | Can hear shrill tones. |
| Scarlet fever | Probably before the age of 2. | Can hear loud tones. |
| Chronic inflammation of throat | Discovered in her third year. | Can hear very loud tones. |
| Scarlet fever | 9 weeks | |
| Canker | 3 weeks | Can hear very shrill tones. |
| Scrofula | 13 years | Absent since Sept. 24. |
| Hears perfectly | | Attends this school in order to take charge of deaf sister in going and returning. |
| Lung fever | 5 months | Can hear very shrill tones. |
| Scarlet fever | 4 years | Can hear loud tones. |
| Scarlet fever | Discovered at the age of 5. | |

## SUMMARY.

| | |
|---|---|
| Number of pupils, from date of opening the school, April 2, 1877, to Dec. 31, 1883.............................................. | 45 |
| Number of pupils who have entered the school since Dec. 31, 1883....................................................... | 5 |
| | — |
| Whole number who have attended the school........... | 50 |
| Number who have left the school..................... | 22 |
| | — |
| Number of pupils, Dec. 31, 1884......................... | 28 |
| Number of girls who have attended school during the year..... | 18 |
| "    boys    "      "      "      "      "    .... . | 12 |
| | — |
| Whole number of pupils during the year......... ........... | 30 |
| Average attendance..................................21.57 | |
| | — |
| Number congenitally deaf, or made deaf before the age of two.. | 15 |
| Number who lost hearing between the ages of two and four.... | 6 |
| Number who lost hearing after the age of four............... | 8 |
| Number having perfect hearing....................... ......... | 1 |
| | — |
| | 30 |
| Number who can hear any tones of the human voice........... | 15 |

*Residences of all who have attended during the year 1884.*

| | |
|---|---|
| Providence, including Wanskuck............................ | 15 |
| Watchemoket, East Providence............................ | 1 |
| Rumford, East Providence................................. | 1 |
| East Providence.... ..................................... | 2 |
| Woodville, North Providence.............................. | 1 |
| Pawtucket................................................ | 3 |

The number of changes in the school during the year 1884 has been small. Except in one or two instances, the attendance has been as regular as could be expected, in view of the fact that some of the pupils retain a delicacy of constitution, from which their deafness originally resulted. A number have been taken to the Rhode Island Hospital for treatment of diseases of the ear and the eye, and several still go there on Saturday mornings, to their decided benefit.

It will be seen from the tabular report that at least one-third of the pupils became either wholly or partially deaf from scarlet fever. These sad consequences emphasize the wisdom of the rigid rule enforced by the Superintendent of Health, forbidding the attendance at the public schools of children living in districts where cases of scarlet fever are in progress.

In a few instances serious affections of the sight result from the same causes which produced deafness. These appeal with especial force to the watchfulness of teachers and physicians, and every effort is made to retard the advance of blindness, and to furnish the mind with as varied resources as possible, in order to soften the fate which may await such children.

As in former years, the regular attendance of certain pupils, whose means are very limited, has been facilitated by the gift of shoes from the "Children's Mission" connected with the First and Westminster Congregational Churches. Representatives of the Women's City Missionary Society and various individuals have also promptly responded to the pupils' needs, as made known by the teachers.

Instructors of the deaf are increasingly awake to the possibility of developing hearing, where even the least exists. Many children who have been considered "deaf and dumb" are found, upon careful trial, to possess more or less "*vowel hearing.*" This power, if utilized, becomes a considerable factor in teaching articulation, and after a time the child's hearing seems to have improved, because, having become familiar with the dim sound of certain words, he can recognize them, as he could not have done without special training. His case then somewhat resembles that of an adult whose hearing power has grown very dull. Such a person catches the meaning of many sentences which he but partially hears, while if he were addressed in a foreign language he could not repeat a single word, because they would all be unfamiliar. A flexible ear-tube is very serviceable in the exercises here indicated, and has been much used during the past year.

The work of the three school-rooms has proceeded very much as heretofore. Each of the teachers has devised some new methods and prepared new appliances for pursuing them. They all attended the Convention of Articulation Teachers, held in New York, from June 25th to 28th, and found its essays and discussions highly profitable. As guests of the New York Institution for the Improved Instruction of Deaf Mutes, they, with more than one hundred other teachers, representing thirty-eight schools, were most hospitably entertained. Some parents of deaf children and students of social science were also present. One of the Vice-Presidents was the Rev. William Stainer, of London, England, who has the superintendence of eight schools in that city, conducted upon the oral plan. Professor A. Graham Bell, the President of the Convention, is devoting much attention to experiments in the education of the deaf, and to the collection of statistics in regard to the danger of forming a "deaf variety of the human race." He has established a small private school in Washington, D. C., where, under his own supervision, his theories may be tested.

Although teachers of the deaf are far from being unanimous in their views, it would be conceded by the most conservative instructor or observer that the movement has been toward a larger proportion of articulation-teaching and a smaller proportion of sign-teaching. In 1867 the first oral schools in America were established, one being the New York Institution for the Improved Instruction of Deaf Mutes; the other being Miss Rogers' little group of pupils in Billerica, Mass., a nucleus which has since become the well-known Clarke Institution at Northampton.

The twenty-five institutions for the deaf previously existing in the United States were sign schools. At present there are fifty-five schools, only nine of which are conducted on the old plan. Twelve are oral schools, and thirty-four combine the two methods. The same tendencies are very noticeable in England, Italy and France. Germany has long been the chief home of the oral system.

It is an established fact that fewer pupils can be instructed by one teacher under the oral than under the manual system. And a pressing need of the Rhode Island school is that of an additional teacher in the lowest division, where there is now the unusually large number of twelve children, at different stages of advancement. When it is remembered that, according to the plan always pursued in this school, each teacher trains her own pupils in articulation—a work requiring much time—it will be seen that even efforts as diligent and efficient as Miss Kerr's cannot secure the best results, unless supplemented by more assistance than her present co-laborers can furnish.

Feeling confidence that this lack will soon be supplied, we anticipate in the coming year the satisfaction of seeing the foundations of education laid with greater rapidity and security than can now be done. The whole up-building of the speech, the intellect and the character of deaf children, is a peculiarly slow and delicate work. Its great importance may well spur teachers to enthusiastic and persistent labors, and should also make every member of the community prompt to report to the proper authorities the names of any young persons who are too deaf to attend ordinary schools.

KATHARINE H. AUSTIN.

## GIFTS RECEIVED DURING THE YEAR 1884.

*Rubbers and other Shoes.*—From the "Children's Mission" connected with the First and Westminster Congregational Churches.

*Shoes and Clothing.*—From Mrs. John Binning, Chairman of 9th Ward Committee, Women's City Missionary Society; Mrs. Wm. Porter, Chairman of 3d Ward Committee, Women's City Missionary Society.

*Clothing.*—From Mrs. A. G. Lorimer, Mrs. Wm. Sayles, Pawtucket, Mrs. Edw. G. Billings, Master Pearl Iron, Mrs. J. O. Austin.

*Cards and Ornaments.*—From Miss Josephine Pitman.

*Candy and Fruit.*—From Mrs. Horace Jenks.

*Specimens for Cabinet.*—From Miss Adeline Brown, Miss Lily R. Sprague.

*Framed Portrait of Gen. Grant.*—From Mr. and Mrs. Chas. S. Cleveland.

*Twelve Copies Jacobs' Primary Lessons, Part I.*—From Mrs. George F. Woodley.

*Nebraska Mute Journal.*—From Nebraska Institution for the Deaf.

*Mute's Companion.*—From Minnesota Institution.

*Deaf Mute Optic.*—From Arkansas Institution.

*"Our Children's School Journal."*—From Western New York Institution.

## STUDIES PURSUED DURING THE YEAR 1884.

### LOWEST DIVISION.

Drill in Articulation.
Lessons in reading from Monroe's Chart.
Exercises in Lip-reading.
Names of miscellaneous objects.
    "  " persons in the school-room.
    "  " parts of the body.
    "  " articles of clothing.
Numerals.
Colors.
Description of pictures.
Verbs.
Phrases and simple sentences.
Peet's Language Lessons.
Questions of practical value.
Simple addition.
Drawing: Kindergarten books; Tile-patterns with colored pencils.
Miscellaneous work.

### SECOND DIVISION.

Articulation and Lip-reading.
Latham's Reader.

Parker & Marvel's Supplementary Reading for Primary Schools.

Hutton's Question Book.

Exercises in asking and answering questions.

  "  " defining words.

  "  " forming sentences.

  "  " writing descriptions of pictures.

Addition, Subtraction, Simple Multiplication.

Geography commenced.

Drawing: Forbriger's Tablets; Tile-patterns with colored pencils.

Miscellaneous work.

### FIRST DIVISION.

Articulation exercises.

Lip-reading exercises.

Language lessons, prepared by teacher and memorized by pupils.

Stickney's Language Lessons.

Journals and letters.

Monteith's 1st Lessons in Geography, and other exercises in Geography.

MS. lessons on History of the United States.

Arithmetic: through Long Division and simple examples in analysis.

Drawing: Forbriger's Tablets; Tile-patterns; Painting on silk.

Miscellaneous work.

## TO PARENTS OF DEAF CHILDREN.

This school is for the benefit of children incapacitated through deafness or dumbness, total or partial, for receiving proper instruction in common schools.

The aim of the school is to teach deaf children to use the English language with the spontaneity, correctness and enjoyment of hearing children, as far as this is practicable.

The more advanced and intelligent pupils are taught the higher branches of education, but the *actual use of the English language* is considered of first importance.

It is very desirable that deaf children be sent to school at as early an age as possible—especially if they are also dumb. A parent will be amply repaid for sending a child as young as five or six years, even at some inconvenience.

If a child who has learned to talk is made deaf by disease, he should immediately upon his recovery be sent to a school where his speech will be retained, and where he will be taught to understand from the lips.   In such cases it is common to delay so long that serious loss of speech results.

Every effort should be made to encourage the child to retain the use of his voice.   He should be taught to pronounce common words, but no attempt should be made to teach him *the names* of the letters of the alphabet.

Writing lessons should also be given him at home.   It will save much time if, when he enters school, he is able to write the names of common objects with which he is familiar.

The school hours are from 9 A. M. to 1 P. M. on every week day, except Saturday.   Open to visitors on Fridays, from 10 to 12.

The next summer vacation will begin Friday, June 26, 1885.   The school will re-open Monday, September 7, 1885. Tuition is free to residents of this State.   Provision is made for defraying the travelling expenses of indigent pupils. Application for admission may be made to the Principal of the school, or to the Commissioner of Public Schools, 104 North Main street, Providence, R. I.

# EIGHTH ANNUAL REPORT

OF THE

# PRINCIPAL

OF THE

# ODE ISLAND SCHOOL FOR THE DEAF,

PROVIDENCE, R. I.

FOR THE

# YEAR ENDING DECEMBER 31,

# 1885.

PROVIDENCE:

E. L. FREEMAN & SON, PRINTERS TO THE STATE.

1886.

# EIGHTH ANNUAL REPORT

OF THE

# PRINCIPAL

OF THE

# RHODE ISLAND SCHOOL FOR THE DEAF,

## PROVIDENCE, R. I.

FOR THE

## YEAR ENDING DECEMBER 31,

## 1885.

---

PROVIDENCE:

E. L. FREEMAN & SON, PRINTERS TO THE STATE.

1886.

# RHODE ISLAND SCHOOL FOR THE DEAF.

### CORNER OF FOUNTAIN AND BEVERLY STREETS.

## PROVIDENCE, R. I.

UNDER THE SUPERVISION OF THE

# STATE BOARD OF EDUCATION.

His Excellency George Peabody Wetmore, Governor, *ex-officio,*

PRESIDENT.

His Honor Lucius B. Darling, Lieutenant-Governor, *ex-officio.*

| | |
|---|---|
| Samuel H. Cross, . . . . . . | Westerly. |
| George A. Littlefield, . . . . . . | Newport. |
| Rev. Daniel Leach, . . . . . . | Providence. |
| Dwight R. Adams, . . . . . . | Centreville. |
| Rev. Charles J. White, . . . . . . | Woonsocket. |
| Rev. George L. Locke, . . . . . | Bristol. |

SECRETARY :

Thomas B. Stockwell, Commissioner of Public Schools, *ex-officio.*

PRINCIPAL :

Anna M. Black.

ASSISTANT TEACHERS :

Ardelia C. Dewing,    Ellen J. Kerr,    Emma F. Dunlop.

# REPORT.

To the Honorable the State Board of Educatio1

GENTLEMEN:—I herewith submit my repor
ending December 31, 1885.

Respectfully,

ANNA M. BI

DECEMBER 31, 1885.

## TABULAR REPORT OF THE PUPILS OF THE RHODE ISLAND

| NAMES OF PUPILS. | RESIDENCE. | AGE. (Approx.) | DATE OF ADMISSION. |
|---|---|---|---|
| Kinyon, Ada J.................. | Providence..................... | 24 | April 2, 1877........ |
| Morlock, William T........ .... | " ..................... | 17 | " 2, " ........ |
| Wallace, M. Amey.............. | Woodville, North Providence... | 13 | " 15, 1878........ |
| Catlow, Mary A................ | Providence..... ............. | 13 | " 22, " ........ |
| Slavin, Joseph H.............. | Pawtucket......... ........... | 12 | Jan. 28, 1880........ |
| Goodspeed, Bertha..... ........ | Providence.. ................. | 10 | Mar. 9, " ........ |
| Riley, Thomas................. | " ..................... | 11 | April 5, " ........ |
| Tucker, Arthur................ | " ..................... | 11 | " 19, " ........ |
| Sheldon, Mary E.............. | Arnold's Mills, Cumberland.... | 16 | Sept. 6, " ........ |
| Lynch, James E.............. | Wanskuck, Providence......... | 9 | " 6, " ........ |
| Dorgan, Michael J............. | Valley Falls, Lincoln.......... | 13 | Oct. 4, " ........ |
| Swift, Mary E........ ......... | Providence..................... | 12 | Nov. 2, " ........ |
| Mallon, Mary A................ | East Providence............... | 15 | " 2, " ........ |
| White, Sarah.................. | " " ............. | 13 | Sept. 5, 1881........ |
| Potvin, William............... | River Point, Warwick......... | 15 | Oct. 24, " ........ |
| McDonnell, Thomas.... ........ | Providence..................... | 14 | Nov. 28, " ........ |
| Brownell, Lester R............ | Little Compton............... | 9 | June 15, 1882........ |
| Radcliffe, Eliza............... | Lonsdale, Lincoln.............. | 12 | Sept. 13, " ........ |
| Dolan, Katharine.............. | Providence.... ............... | 8 | Nov. 6, " ........ |
| Moon, Ina G.................. | Washington, Coventry......... | 12 | " 24, " ........ |
| Lorimer, John F.............. | Providence..................... | 12 | April 18, 1883........ |
| Woodley, Abby M.............. | " ..................... | 7 | May 7, " ........ |
| Nolan, Rosanna................ | Rumford, East Providence..... | 10 | Sept. 3, " ........ |
| Avery, Edward S.............. | Providence..................... | 9 | " 21, " ........ |
| Baker, Mary Louisa........... | East Providence............... | 26 | May 13, 1884........ |
| Addison, Susan B.............. | Pawtucket......... ...... .... | 12 | " 19, " ........ |
| Goodwin, James H............. | Providence..................... | 9 | Oct. 7, " ........ |
| Holloway, Mary Ellen.......... | Centreville, Warwick.......... | 8 | " 20, " ........ |
| Harris, William H............ | Providence..................... | 14 | Feb. 21, 1885........ |
| Cole, Egbert T................ | South Scituate..... ........... | 16 | Mar. 10, " ........ |
| Herzog, Ernest J. H.......... | Olneyville..................... | 12 | " 10, " ........ |
| Provingal, Joseph..... ........ | Albion.............. .......... | 13 | Sept. 23, " ........ |

## SCHOOL FOR THE DEAF FOR THE YEAR ENDING DEC. 31, 1885.

| Cause of Deafness, as far as Known. | Age when made Deaf. (Approx.) | Remarks. |
|---|---|---|
| Severe illness...................... | 8 months.......... .... | ................................................... |
| { Congenital, or lung fever at 9 { months................... | ...... .. ........... | { Did not re-enter in Sept., 1885. Learning { cabinet trade. |
| Congenital...................... | | ................................................... |
| Scarlet fever....... ............. | 3 years............. | Has considerable hearing. |
| ——? fever...................... | 1 year, 9 months.... | ................................................... |
| Scarlet fever......... .......... | 5 years, 8 months... | ................................................... |
| Congenital.... ............... | | Can hear very loud tones. |
| Whooping cough............... | 3 years............. | Can hear voices somewhat raised. |
| Scarlet fever.................... | 5 years............. | ................................................... |
| Brain fever.................... | 2 years, 2 months... | Can hear very shrill tones. |
| Brain fever.................... | 3 years............. | ................................................... |
| Scarlet fever......... .......... | 6 years, 10 months.. | ................................................... |
| Scarlet fever.... ......... | 6 years.... ........ | Left Feb. 27 to work in Jencks' box shop. |
| Lung fever....................... | 2 years, 6 months... | Can hear very shrill tones. |
| Congenital..................... | | Can hear shrill tones. |
| { Congenital, or tumor in ears { at 10 months............... | | Can hear shrill tones. |
| Congenital........ ........... | | .... ............................................. |
| Scarlet fever.................. | | ................................................... |
| Congenital, or illness at 2 years. | | { Can hear very shrill tones. Did not re-enter { in September, 1885. |
| Congenital, or illness at 3 months | | Can hear shrill tones. |
| Scarlet fever.................... | { Probably before { the age of 2. | Can hear loud tones. |
| Chronic inflammation of throat.. | { Discovered in her { third year. | Can hear very loud tones. |
| Scarlet fever.................... | 9 weeks..... ...... | ................................................... |
| Canker.... ... ..... .......... | 3 weeks.......... .. | { Can hear very shrill tones. Removed from { the State, March 2, 1885. |
| Scrofula....................... | 13 years ............ | { Absent since Sept. 24. Left on account of { loss of sight. |
| Lung fever..................... | 5 months.. .... .... | Can hear very shrill tones. |
| Scarlet fever.................... | 4 years............. | Can hear loud tones. |
| Scarlet fever.................... | { Discovered at the { age of 5. | ................................................... |
| Catarrh.... ... ............... | | Can hear voices somewhat raised. |
| Congenital........ ............ | | ................................................... |
| Congenital........ ........... | | Previously taught in a German school. |
| Lung fever..................... | 4 years............. | { Removed from Providence. Afterward re- { turned to Albion to live. |

## SUMMARY.

Number of pupils, from date of opening the school, April 2, 1877,
  to Dec. 31, 1884 .........................................  50
Number of pupils who have entered the school since Dec. 31,
  1884 ......................................................   4
                                                            ——
  Whole number who have attended the school ...........  54
  Number who have left the school .....................  27
                                                            ——
Number of pupils, Dec. 31, 1885 ..........................  27

Number of girls who have attended school during the year ......  16
  "   boys   "      "      "      "      "      ......  16
                                                            ——
Whole number of pupils during the year ......................  ·32
Average attendance ........................................21.03

Number congenitally deaf, or made deaf before the age of two..  15
Number who lost hearing between the ages of two and four ....   7
Number who lost hearing after the age of four ...............  10
                                                            ——
                                                              32
Number who can hear any tones of the human voice ..........  15

*Residences of all who have attended during the year 1885.*

Providence, including Wanskuck .........................  15
Rumford, East Providence ...............................   1
East Providence ........................................   3
Woodville, North Providence ............................   1
Pawtucket ..............................................   2
Albion .................................................   1
Olneyville .............................................   1
South Scituate .........................................   1

Valley Falls............................................... 1

Lonsdale.................................................. 1

Arnold's Mills, Cumberland (boarding in Providence).......... 1

River Point, Warwick...................................... 1

Centreville, Warwick...................................... 1

Washington Village, Coventry.............................. 1

Little Compton, (family living in Providence for the sake of educating the child.......................................... 1

15 localities............................................. 32

Except in one or two instances, the attendance during the last year has been very regular. There have been two changes in the corps of teachers. Miss Katharine H. Austin, the Principal since March, 1882, ceased to have charge of the school at the close of the last term. There are many indications in the school, that during that time she labored faithfully and earnestly in the discharge of the absorbing and onerous duties of her position, both for the present and future prosperity of the school. There was some delay in the appointment of her successor, and during the interval, the efficient body of assistant teachers carried forward, not only their especial class work, but the additional duties of the Principal. The selection was made in October, but the new Principal did not arrive until the latter part of November following.

The school also made a great step forward, and a pressing need, which had long been felt, was supplied by securing the services of an additional teacher. Although this school is young and small as compared with most other State institutions, there are very nearly as many grades of advancement as in schools of a larger growth, or in schools in general.

It should be well understood—but I am afraid it is not, hence the necessity of reiteration—that the system of instruction employed in this school is that which was long ago taught in Germany, the chief home of the oral system, and is known as the German or Oral method. It is generally admitted that fewer pupils can be taught by one teacher in this than by the manual method. It has been only within the last twenty years that this system was adopted in America, and in that time it has been subjected to changes—our national pride would lead us to say improvements—and adaptation of appliances to suit our American ideas and genius. I may add that since its introduction, eighteen years ago, it has been constantly and steadily growing in favor and proportions.

In this method, instruction is given by word of mouth, and the recitations of the pupils are oral. Written work should always be supplementary. The manual alphabet and signs are never taught. The meaning and adaptation of the spoken words in the acquirement of general knowledge, especially with beginners, are taught and illustrated with objects, pictures, and description of size, shape, distance, position, action, etc.; to the full and complete understanding: as in the generality of schools, not alone for the deaf, but for the hearing also. This, I suppose, accounts for the so often reiterated assertion, that "The language of signs or gestures is the natural language of mankind." Every influence should be brought to bear in encouraging the pupil to make spoken language the medium of thought and the ordinary means of communication with the world of hearing people. It seems to be expected by many who are so hard to convince, and when convinced are of the same opinion still, that the utility and advantage of this method should be estimated by the number of " natural " voices that are developed. They seem to forget that many hearing people have peculiarities of utterance, occasioned by imperfect vocal organization, or, more often, by careless habits of speech. The function or practice of such a voice is never doubted, or its right to be heard questioned. Did any one ever know of a hearing person resorting to the use of a tablet or the manual alphabet because of a peculiarity or even unpleasantness in the sound of his voice ?

" Natural "! Is not anything natural that belongs to us individually,—given by birth or acquired through native ability ? Is it not natural for a person afflicted with catarrh to have a nasal quality of voice, or head-tone, as it is often called ; or one with a bronchial trouble to experience difficulties in tone or quality called by musicians and elocutionists, timbre ? Is it more of a misfortune for us to listen to them than for them to realize their defect ? If, through the want of hearing, the voice cannot acquire, or loses some powers of inflection, modulation and intonation, should the deaf be restricted ? We believe that even imperfect speech and speech-reading are better means of communicating with a world of hearing and speaking people than the language of signs, which, however " natural " to the deaf, is more unfamiliar than the dead languages to the world at large. If we were destined to remove and abide in a foreign country, we would think it advisable to acquire a knowledge of the language of that country; and not by any manner of means would we be satisfied with the ability simply to read and write it, but we would think it positively necessary to learn to *speak* it for purposes of utility as well as pleasure.

The importance of educating the deaf cannot be estimated. Committees have, from time to time, made it their business and taken much pains to trace the lives of graduates of various institutions for the deaf, and have found in some instances 90 per cent. of them self-supporting—working at different trades and professions. I have been told that a number of the Government clerks at Washington are deaf. A former pupil of this school, a young man totally deaf, of pleasant, intelligent face and manly bearing, dropped in upon us the other day. He has a fluent, pleasing voice, and converses with ease and grace. I asked him if he generally talked or made use of the tablet in conversing with persons in his business connections. He replied, "I *always* talk, and have very little difficulty in understanding others. I never tell or remind any one that I am deaf. If, as sometimes happens, a person is hard to understand," [laughing] "I manage to keep out of his way rather than tell him that I am deaf or ask him to write." This young man is at work in one of the machine shops of the city and earns a support not only for himself, but for a sister and younger brother, and has made some gifts of clothing to some in the school that need such assistance. Is it any wonder that his teachers look upon him with respect and pride?

Teachers of the deaf are sometimes called fanatics, and why not? The whole up-building of the speech, intellect and character of deaf children is a peculiarly slow and delicate work: not to be accomplished in a half-hearted, methodical manner, but demanding the utmost indomitable energy and patience; and, in its results, calculated to inspire its teachers to the loftiest heights of enthusiasm.

We would that every member of this community and all others were awakened to that degree of interest, that would prompt them to seek out and report to the proper authorities, the names of those children,—and we feel there are many such,—too deaf to be benefitted by attendance at an ordinary school, and who are too often neglected, or whose parents think they are too poor to make the exertion to send them to a school designed especially for such. There are many possible ways of pushing forward, by effort and liberality, the education of the deaf in this city and State, and raising this good and important work to a higher standard.

ANNA M. BLACK.

## GIFTS RECEIVED DURING THE YEAR 1885.

*Rubbers and other Shoes.*—From the " Children's Mission" connected with the First and Westminster Congregational Churches.

*Clothing.*—From "The Irrepressible Society," Mrs. Edward G. Billings, Mrs. J. O. Austin, Mrs. Alvin Johnson, Mrs. G. F. Woodley, Miss Olney, Thomas Burns.

*Cards and Ornaments.*

*Candy and Fruit.*

*Specimens for Cabinet.*—From Mary E. Swift, Bertha Goodspeed, Amey Wallace, William Morlock, Mrs. George M. Woodley.

*Publications.*—"Nebraska Mute Journal," from Nebraska Institution for the Deaf; "Mute Companion," from Minnesota Institution; "Deaf Mute Optic," from Arkansas Institution; "Our Children's School Journal," from Western New York Institution; "Kentucky Deaf Mute," from Kentucky Institution; "Students' Workshop," Healdsburg, Cal.; "Readings in Line Writing," from Dr. A. Graham Bell, Washington, D. C.; "Maryland Bulletin," from the Maryland School for the Deaf and Dumb; "Kansas Star," from the Kansas Institution for the Education of the Deaf and Dumb; "Deaf Mute Progress," Indianapolis, Ind.; "Howard Times," from Sockanosset School, Howard, R. I.

## STUDIES PURSUED DURING THE YEAR 1885.

### LOWEST DIVISION.

Drill in Articulation.

Lessons in reading from Monroe's Chart.

Exercises in Lip-reading.

Names of miscellaneous objects.

" " persons in the school-room.

" " parts of the body.

" " articles of clothing.

Numerals.

Colors.

Description of pictures.

Verbs.

Phrases and simple sentences.

Peet's Language Lessons.

Questions of practical value.

Simple addition.

Drawing: Kindergarten books; Tile-patterns with colored pencils.

Miscellaneous work.

### SECOND DIVISION.

Articulation and Lip-reading.

Latham's Reader.

Parker & Marvel's Supplementary Reading for Primary Schools.

Hutton's Question Book.

Exercises in asking and answering questions.

      "     " defining words.

      "     " forming sentences.

      "     " writing descriptions of pictures.

Addition, Subtraction, Simple Multiplication.

Geography commenced.

Drawing: Forbriger's Tablets; Tile-patterns with colored pencils.

Miscellaneous work.

### FIRST DIVISION.

Articulation exercises.

Lip-reading exercises.

Language lessons, prepared by teacher and memorized by pupils.

Stickney's Language Lessons.

Journals and letters.

Cornell's First Steps in Geography, and other exercises in Geography.

MS. lessons on History of the United States.

Arithmetic: through Long Division and simple examples in analysis.

Drawing: Forbriger's Tablets; Tile-patterns; Painting on silk.

Miscellaneous work.

## TO PARENTS OF DEAF CHILDREN.

This school is for the benefit of children incapacitated through deafness or dumbness, total or partial, for receiving proper instruction in common schools.

The aim of the school is to teach deaf children to use the English language with the spontaneity, correctness and enjoyment of *hearing* children, as far as this is practicable.

The more advanced and intelligent pupils are taught the higher branches of education, but the *actual use of the English language* is considered of first importance.

It is very desirable that deaf children be sent to school at as early an age as possible—especially if they are also dumb. A parent will be amply repaid for sending a child as young as five or six years, even at some inconvenience.

If a child who has learned to talk is made deaf by disease, he should immediately upon his recovery be sent to a school where his speech will be retained, and where he will be taught to understand from the lips. In such cases it is common to delay so long that serious loss of speech results.

Every effort should be made to encourage the child to retain the use of his voice. He should be taught to pronounce common words, but no attempt should be made to teach him *the names* of the letters of the alphabet.

Writing lessons should be given him at home. It will save much time if, when he enters school, he is able to write the names of common objects with which he is familiar.

The school hours are from 9 A. M. to 1 P. M. on every week day, except Saturday. Open to visitors on Fridays, from 10 to 12.

The next summer vacation will begin Friday, June 25, 1886. The school will re-open Monday, September 6, 1886. Tuition is free to residents of this State. Provision is made for defraying the travelling expenses of indigent pupils. Application for admission may be made to the Principal of the school, or to the Commissioner of Public Schools, 104 North Main street, Providence, R. I.

# NINTH ANNUAL REPORT

OF THE

# PRINCIPAL

OF THE

# RHODE ISLAND SCHOOL FOR THE DEAF,

## PROVIDENCE, R. I.

FOR THE

## YEAR ENDING DECEMBER 31,

## 1886.

---

PROVIDENCE:

E. L. FREEMAN & SON, PRINTERS TO THE STATE.

1887.

# RHODE ISLAND SCHOOL FOR THE DEAF.

CORNER OF FOUNTAIN AND BEVERLY STREETS.

PROVIDENCE, R. I.

UNDER THE SUPERVISION OF THE

# STATE BOARD OF EDUCATION.

HIS EXCELLENCY GEORGE PEABODY WETMORE, Governor, *ex-officio*, PRESIDENT.

HIS HONOR LUCIUS B. DARLING, Lieutenant-Governor, *ex-officio*.

| | |
|---|---|
| REV. DANIEL LEACH, | Providence. |
| DWIGHT R. ADAMS, | Centreville. |
| SAMUEL H. CROSS, | Westerly. |
| GEORGE A. LITTLEFIELD, | Newport. |
| REV. CHARLES J. WHITE, | Woonsocket. |
| REV. WILLIAM N. ACKLEY, | Warren. |

SECRETARY :

THOMAS B. STOCKWELL, Commissioner of Public Schools, *ex-officio*.

PRINCIPAL :

ANNA M. BLACK.

ASSISTANT TEACHERS :

ABDELIA C. DEWING,   ELLEN J. KERR,   EMMA F. DUNLOP.

MRS. E. T. SMITH, Teacher of Drawing.

# REPORT.

*To the Honorable the State Board of Education:*

GENTLEMEN:—I herewith submit my report for the year ending December 31, 1886.

Respectfully,

ANNA M. BLACK,

*Principal.*

DECEMBER 31, 1886.

## TABULAR REPORT OF THE PUPILS OF THE RHODE ISLAND

| Names of Pupils. | Residence. | Age. (Approx.) | Date of Admission. |
|---|---|---|---|
| Kinyon, Ada J............ ....... | Providence..................... | 26 | April 2, 1877......... |
| Wallace, M. Amey.............. | Woodville, North Providence... | 15 | " 15, 1878......... |
| Slavin, Joseph H............... | Pawtucket...................... | 14 | Jan. 28, 1880......... |
| Goodspeed, Bertha............. | Providence..................... | 12 | Mar. 9, " ......... |
| Riley, Thomas.................. | " .................. ........... | 13 | April 5, " ......... |
| Tucker, Arthur........... .... | " .................. ........... | 13 | " 19, " ......... |
| Sheldon, Mary E... ........... | Arnold's Mills, Cumberland.... | 18 | Sept. 6, " ......... |
| Lynch, James E................. | Wanskuck, Providence......... | 11 | " 6, " ......... |
| Dorgan, Michael J............. | Valley Falls, Lincoln.. ........ | 15 | Oct. 4, " ......... |
| Swift, Mary E.................. | Providence..................... | 14 | Nov. 2, " ......... |
| White, Sarah................... | East Providence............... | 13 | Sept. 5, 1881. |
| Potvin, William............... | River Point, Warwick.......... | 17 | Oct. 24, " ......... |
| McDonnell, Thomas............ | Providence..................... | 16 | Nov. 28, " ......... |
| Brownell, Lester R............. | Little Compton................ | 10 | June 15, 1882. ....... |
| Radcliffe, Eliza............. ... | Lonsdale, Lincoln............. | 14 | Sept. 13, " ......... |
| Moon, Ina G................... | Washington, Coventry......... | 12 | Nov. 24, " .... .... |
| Lorimer, John F....... ........ | Providence..................... | 14 | April 18, 1883......... |
| Woodley, Abby M.............. | " .................. ........... | 8 | May 7, " ......... |
| Nolan, Rosanna................ | Rumford, East Providence...... | 12 | Sept. 3, " ......... |
| Addison, Susan B.............. | Pawtucket...................... | 14 | May 19, 1884....... |
| Goodwin, James H............. | Providence..................... | 11 | Oct. 7, " ......... |
| Holloway, Mary Ellen.... ...... | Centreville, Warwick........... | 10 | " 20, " ......... |
| Harris, William H............. | Providence..................... | 16 | Feb. 21, 1885......... |
| Cole, Egbert T.......... ...... | South Scituate................. | 17 | Mar. 10, " ......... |
| Herzog, Ernest J. H............. | Geneva, Providence ....... ... | 13 | " 10, " ......... |
| Provingal, Joseph.............. | Albion.................. | 15 | Sept. 23, " ......... |
| Walker, Mabel................. | Providence. | 14 | Jan. 6, 1886.... .... |
| Terrace, Nettie................ | " .................. ........... | 7 | April 19, " ......... |
| Beauchesne, Alphonse........... | Central Falls. ................. | 9 | Oct. 25, " ......... |
| Schultz, Frederick. ......... .... | Providence..................... | 9 | Nov. 1, " ......... |
| Sullivan, Nellie................ | Newport....... .............. | 6 | " 12, " ......... |
| Grant, Edith....... .... ........ | Providence..................... | 4 | Dec. 13, " ......... |

## SCHOOL FOR THE DEAF FOR THE YEAR ENDING DEC. 31, 1886.

| Cause of Deafness, as far as Known. | Age when made Deaf. (Approx.) | Remarks. |
|---|---|---|
| Severe illness...... .... ....... | 8 months.......... | ........................................................ |
| Congenital..... ... ............. | 1 year ...... | ........................................................ |
| ——? fever................... | 1 year, 9 months.... | ..................................... .................. |
| Scarlet fever................... | 5 years, 8 months... | ........................................................ |
| Congenital..... ............... | | Can hear very loud tones. |
| Whooping cough.... .......... | 3 years.............. | Can hear voices somewhat raised. |
| Scarlet fever.................... | 5 years......... .... | ........................................................ |
| Brain fever... ..... ........... | 2 years, 2 months... | Can hear very shrill tones. |
| Brain fever................... | 3 years........ ... | |
| Scarlet fever................... | 6 years, 10 months.. | ........................................................ |
| Lung fever.................... | 2 years, 6 months... | Can hear very shrill tones. |
| Congenital..... ...... ...... | | Can hear shrill tones. |
| { Congenital, or tumor in ears at 10 months.. .............. | | Can hear shrill tones. |
| Congenital.. ................ | | ........................................................ |
| Scarlet fever................ | | ........................................................ |
| Congenital, or illness at 3 months | | Can hear shrill tones. |
| Scarlet fever.. ....... ......... | { Probably before the age of 2. | Can hear loud tones. |
| Chronic inflammation of throat.. | { Discovered in her third year. | Can hear very loud tones. |
| Scarlet fever.................... | 9 weeks.......... | ............................. .................. |
| Lung fever.................... | 5 months.......... | Can hear very shrill tones. |
| Scarlet fever.................... | 4 years.... ........ | Can hear loud tones. |
| Scarlet fever................... | { Discovered at the age of 5. | ........................................ |
| Catarrh......... ...... ..... | | Can hear voices somewhat raised. |
| Congenital................ ...... ... | | { Unable to attend school much of the time on account of difficulty of obtaining board. |
| Congenital........ ... ......... | | Previously taught in a German school. |
| Lung fever.................... | 4 years............ | ........................................................ |
| Scarlet fever................... | 3 years............. | ................... .............................. |
| ............................... | ......... ..... ... | { Reported mute; afterward sent to the School for Feeble-minded. |
| Scarlet fever.................... | 4 years............ | ...... ............................. |
| ............................... | ...... ... | Admitted on trial; not deaf. |
| Scarlet fever.................... | 2 years............ | ......... .. .............. ......... |
| Tumor in ears................. | 6 months.......... | ........................................................ |

## SUMMARY.

Number of pupils, from date of opening the school, April 2, 1877,
to Dec. 31, 1885........................................ 54

Number of pupils who have entered the school since Dec. 31,
1885............................. ............................ 6

                                           ——

     Whole number who have attended the school........... 60

     Number who have left the school.................... 32

                                           ——

Number of pupils Dec. 31, 1886........................... 28

                                           ——

Number of girls who have attended school during the year...... 16

    "     " boys "    "    "    "    "    "    " ... .. 16

                                           ——

     Whole number of pupils during the year...... ........ 32

     Average attendance...................... ...........24.05

Number congenitally deaf, or made deaf before the age of two.. 13

Number who lost hearing between the ages of two and four..... 8

Number who lost hearing after the age of four............... 9

                                           ——

                                           30

Two dismissed because they were not deaf, but feeble minded... 2

                                           ——

                                           32

Number who can hear any tones of the human voice.......... 13

NOTE.—Two pupils have taken lessons in drawing in the R. I. School of Design; and two others have attended an Industrial School on Saturdays.

NOTE.—Three persons hard of hearing have had private instruction in speech-reading.

*Residences of all who have attended during the year 1886.*

Providence, including Wanskuck and Geneva...... ......... 16

Rumford, East Providence........ ........................ 1

East Providence...................................................  1
Woodville, North Providence.....................................  1
Pawtucket........................................................  2
Albion...........................................................  1
Central Falls....................................................  1
South Scituate...................................................  1
Valley Falls.....................................................  1
Lonsdale.........................................................  1
Arnold's Mills, Cumberland (boarding in Providence)..........  1
River Point, Warwick.............................................  1
Centreville, Warwick.............................................  1
Washington Village, Coventry....................................  1
Little Compton (family living in Providence for the sake of edu-
    cating the child)............................................  1
Newport..........................................................  1

16 localities.......................................  32

There have been no changes during the year in the corps
of teachers. Two pupils have left; one removed from the
State, and circumstances made it advisable for the other to
remain at home. Two were admitted to the school on trial,
and when it was ascertained that they were not deaf, but
backward on account of being feeble minded, their friends
were recommended to send them to the institution designed
especially for such. Two others have been very irregular
on account of vagrant habits acquired through neglect in
their home training. They had been allowed to live in the
streets until they were unwilling to brook the slightest restraint for their improvement in behavior or instruction.
One other was kept at home on account of our inability to
procure a suitable boarding place for him in the city, and

2

he lived too far away for it to be practicable for him to return to his home every day. We hope now that a permanent place has been secured for him, through the kindly aid of the Y. M. C. A. Two girls, boarded at the "Children's Home," have been detained from school on account of contagious diseases prevailing at the "Home," although they themselves were not affected. All of these could, I think, have been retained in the school and their regular attendance secured, if we had had a suitable boarding department connected with the school. We have had six additions during the year, and one pupil, named above, returned after a long absence.

The prospects of the school have brightened in many respects. I think its work is much better known and appreciated than one year ago; and there have been many substantial proofs thereof in the interest shown and gifts made to the school. The prizes offered by Mrs. Henry Lippitt were a great incentive to improvement in articulation and speech-reading. Others, whose names do not appear among our list of donors, have visited our school and expressed their appreciation, wonder and delight at the immense amount of patience, skill and energy expended, and the results accomplished, thus giving great encouragement and positive help to the earnest, devoted teachers and pupils.

A public examination and exhibition was held last June, near the close of the school year. The attendance was good and the company much interested. I think all the members of the State Board of Education were present. Many spoke in terms of high commendation and pleasure of the attainments of the pupils, in which they did themselves and teachers great credit.

Our great and pressing need now is a boarding department in connection with the school, especially for those who come from a distance, and for others who would come if such accommodations were provided; also for those too poor to avail themselves of these privileges of education without other provision, a home where proper care, restraint and security can be thrown around those who have, or might acquire, idle and vicious habits, or might be injured in other ways by being exposed to the daily temptations and dangers of city streets and other thoroughfares. Such a home would be a great benefit, indeed, to any deaf child attending school, particularly to those taught by the oral method, for, as I sought to show in my remarks at our exhibition last June, it is of the utmost importance that these children who have never heard, or have lost their hearing at an early age, should become in some measure accustomed to speech-reading at the age that the majority of children learn to talk through the medium of hearing,—just as though that were the usual manner of learning to talk and understand speech. Thus they are kept from forgetting the words learned before they became deaf, and taught new words, and by this means have a more nearly equal start in their education with the generality of children. Again, the deaf need, like all children, careful moral training, which cannot begin at too early an age. This early training, or a large part of it at least, can be much better given at home by the parents, or some anxious, loving

one who understands what is needed, and is able and willing
to give the time and patience required, and to make every
effort to accomplish the desired end.   This we find exceedingly rare; therefore in the large majority of cases a home
school is the only place where these children can get this
early training, and the teacher and attendant the only ones
who can be relied upon to give it.

Then again, in behalf of the pupils of any age and degree
of progress, when deaf children are taught to talk and educated by means of speech, they need the most persistent and
painstaking watchfulness, in school and out of school, in
order that speech and speech-reading may become a strong
and fixed habit with them, and used as the constant medium
of communication, or they will attain to a very imperfect
degree of proficiency in speech-reading, and form careless,
loose habits of articulation,—a sort of mongrel dialect, half
talk, half gesticulation.   Nearly all of the best speech-readers
are those who have had this early and persistent and exclusive training.   Usually it has been when parents, friends and
teachers have all combined to work for one precious attainment—blessed speech.   The lost sense is replaced by speech-
reading, the doorway to the benighted mind thrown open
and the light enters.   These ends, for a large majority of
our deaf, can best be attained in a home or boarding school.

There are many discouraging difficulties to be overcome
and hard contests to be fought, in this work of teaching the
deaf, but many of these can be much more easily and successfully met, and victory won, in a temporary home for the
pupils, than in a school where the influence and results of

the daily recitations and training are counteracted, and all but lost at times, by the hindrances, absences, and careless and sometimes even wrong influences to which the little ones are subjected out of school hours. In an especial and trying manner is this found true in regard to oral training.

I give all due honor to those parents who take a deep and vital interest in this matter of educating their deaf children, and aid the good work in every way they can. They could do so much, so much for these unfortunate ones, if only they would learn how, and persevere. The Report of the Clarke Institution at Northampton, Mass., contains the copy of a letter written by a mother to the principal of the school. I have taken the liberty to give some extracts from it. I am tempted to copy it entire, it is so right to the point. I wish that the parents of every one of our deaf pupils might take it to heart. The deaf daughter of this mother, after several years' training at the Clarke Institution, at home, and under Prof. Bell, was sent to a boarding school entirely among the hearing. It was her ambition to become as thoroughly educated as any hearing girl. The same requirements were made of her as of her classmates, and her marks represented her standing by the scale of measurement applied to them. Her recitations were to be made in class, orally, and she was questioned in her turn as the others, depending solely on her lip-reading ability. The mother writes:

"She has, since her school days ended, continued reading aloud, and, in her turn, being *read to*, while she repeats sentence by sentence aloud as she reads it from my lips. I think she may never be willing to dispense with this exercise as a training for her voice and practice

in lip-reading.  Any mother can help her deaf child immeasurably
taking a half hour out of her day and dividing it between these t
exercises with the child.

*        *        *        *        *        *        *        *

"One thing I cannot say too earnestly or with too grateful recog
tion: Miss Rogers * insisted that I should *always correct E—
faulty English*, not letting it pass because her meaning could nev
theless be understood; and that I should use in talking with her t
*variety of words* in which we clothe our thoughts for the heari
people about us, *not* translating them into the expressions *alrea
familiar* to her, which would tend to restrict her use of languaᵩ
Miss Rogers has been—is still—a very thorn in my conscience, p:
testing in every way against maternal indolence.  She would ne
let me, peacefully, save myself trouble which were better taken 1
my child.  I can never forget my breathless suspense while awaiti
her verdict, after E——'s first home vacation, as to whether, on 1
return to Northampton, she found the child had kept the grou
gained before leaving school, or whether, to my dire disgrace, she h
retrograded.  Ah, me!  those little exercise books, brought home 1
daily vacation practice, make daily exactions of us, 'in season a
out of season,' but in the retrospect those same intrusive books beco1
the recording volumes of our little victories, our conflicts with so1
obstinate consonant or elusive vowel sound, our perseverance und
discouragements, or perhaps that conquest of self which wins patier
to control impatience and subdues the natural, quick irritability i1
the gentle firmness which must be the never-failing reliance and su
port of the dear deaf child entrusted to us.  It is an unspeakal
precious thought that the tender, loving Father of us all should tr1
one of His little ones, requiring carefullest care, to us!

"May I say one word more, O mothers of the deaf?  This child
mine naturally takes her place in society, naturally presides as t
care-taking elder sister, because we have never held her to be exce

---

* Former Principal at Northampton.

tional, have never let her feel that she was different from any other, where the feeling could be warded off; have never let the other children of the family form the thought, 'It is different with E—— because she is deaf.' We began at the beginning with the determination that she should hold her natural place everywhere, that we would try to fit her for it, and then try to maintain her in it by making her feel that her deafness need not disqualify her. A maimed *character* would be a vital loss, but a maimed *ear* need not impair her usefulness, or her delightsomeness to those around her. Let us make our children whole as nearly as we may, with God's continual help. With Him, working together, let us shape in them symmetrical souls; then, how slight an impairment to the child's well-being will seem an unhearing ear!"

I would reiterate in closing: there are many possible ways of pushing forward, by effort and liberality, the education of the Deaf in this City and State, and raising this good and important work to a higher standard. Let our great anxiety about this matter amount to a hand-to-hand, and shoulder-to-shoulder movement to obtain that which is right and best in this work, and let us not rest until we do obtain it.

ANNA M. BLACK.

## GIFTS RECEIVED DURING THE YEAR 1886.

*Rubbers, Shoes and Clothing.*—From the "Children's Mission" connected with the First and Westminster Congregational Churches, "The Irrepressible Society," Mrs. Abner Sackett, Mrs. Ferdinand Read, Mrs. Henry Lippitt, Mr. N. L. Berry, Miss Mabel Walker, Mr. Thomas Burns, Mr. James Cook.

*Cards, Ornaments and Books.*—From Mrs. S. S. Keene, Miss Julia Halsey, Mrs. R. B. Hubbard, Grace C. Berry, "a Friend," and a teacher.

*Candy and Fruit.*—From Miss Edna R. Gardiner, and a teacher.

*Specimens for Cabinet.*—From the Teachers and Pupils, Colorado, Nevada, Utah, California and Yellowstone specimens.

*Periodicals for Pupils' Reading.*—From Mrs. R. B. Hubbard, Mrs. G. R. Holden, Miss S. A. Waterman.

*Publications.*—"Nebraska Mute Journal," from Nebraska Institution for the Deaf; "Mute Companion," from Minnesota Institution; "Our Children's School Journal," from Western New York Institution; "Kentucky Deaf Mute," from Kentucky Institution; "Maryland Bulletin," from the Maryland School for the Deaf and Dumb; "Kansas Star," from the Kansas Institution for the Education of the Deaf and Dumb; "Deaf Mute Index," from Colorado Institution; "New Method for the Deaf," from the Voice and Hearing School, Englewood, Ill.; "The Silent Observer," from the Tennessee Institution.

*Reports.*—From most of the Schools for the Deaf.

*Periodicals provided for the School.*—For the Teachers: "The Annals for the Deaf," and "The Voice." For the Pupils: "The Youth's

Companion," "Wide Awake," "Harper's Young People," "Our Little Men and Women," "Our Little Ones," "Baby Days." These tend to encourage and cultivate a taste for general and instructive reading.

### PRIZES OFFERED.

*Lippitt Fund.*—For best progress and improvement in Articulation, Speech-reading, General Reading and Deportment. Ernest Herzog took the prize for Speech-reading; Thomas McDonnell, for Articulation; Mary Swift, for General Reading; Susie Addison, for Deportment.

# COURSE OF STUDY.

## BEGINNING CLASS.

### FIRST YEAR.

*First Term.*—Extending from the 1st Monday in September to the Christmas holidays.

I. Language.
    1. Articulation and speech-reading.
        *a.* Elements; all, if possible.
        *b.* As soon as child has learned to utter the combinations that form words, such as the most familiar nouns and pronouns, explain or show what they signify. Such words as *papa, mamma,* I [eye], you, me, toe, shoe, thumb, mouth, tooth, fan, one, two, three, four, five, home, etc.,—whatever comes easiest.

II. Writing—Always to supplement speech, except in very rare cases. Letters representing the elements and words when uttered, figures and tracing tablets.

III. Drawing—Kindergarten tablets.

IV. Calisthenics.

*Second Term.*—Extending from 1st Monday after New Years to the latter part of March.

I. Language.
    1. Articulation and speech-reading.
        *a.* Complete elements, with combinations. See charts.
        *b.* Words: nouns, pronouns and adjectives; names of familiar objects, persons, parts of body, articles of food, clothing, etc.
        *c.* Verbs in the present tense.

II. Arithmetic.

    1. Numerals and counting to 10.

III. Writing.

    1. As above.

    2. Tracing Book, No. I.

IV. Drawing.

    1. Kindergarten tablets.

V. Calisthenics.

*Third Term.*—Extending from early April to first of July.

I. Language.

    1. Articulation and speech-reading.

        *a.* Review elements. Thorough drill in combinations; be able to pronounce words at sight.

        *b.* As above.

        *c.* " "

        *d.* Simple sentences, as "I eat the apple, I eat bread, etc.; I hold the book; Bring me the cup, etc."

II. Arithmetic.

    1. Numerals and counting to 20.

    2. Addition and Subtraction to 10.

III. Writing.

    1. Teacher give verbs and blanks to fill out into sentences.

    2. Copy Book, No. I.

IV. Drawing.

    1. As above.

V. Calisthenics.

### SECOND YEAR.

*First Term.*

I. Language.

    1. Articulation and speech-reading.

        *a.* Drill on elements.

        *b, c, d.* As above.

*e.* Description of actions.

*f.* Colloquial phrases.

II. Arithmetic.

    1. Numerals and counting.

    2. Addition and Subtraction.

III. Writing.

    1. Everything pupil can speak he is taught to write.

    2. Copy Book, No. I.

IV. Drawing.

    1. Inventive; combinations of straight lines.

V. Calisthenics.

*Second Term.*

I. Language.

    1. Articulation and speech-reading.

        *a, b, c, d, e, f.* As above.

        *g.* Prepositions, verbs in progressive form, commands, qu

        tions and answers.

II. Arithmetic.

    1. Numerals and counting.

    2. Addition and Subtraction.

III. Writing.

    1. As above.

    2. Copy Book, No. I.

IV. Drawing.

    1. As above.

V. Calisthenics.

*Third Term.*

I. Language.

    1. Articulation and speech-reading.

    As above.

    2. Reading chart.

    3. Jacobs' Reader, No. I., to page 54.

II. Arithmetic.

    1. Numerals and counting to 100.

    2. Addition and Subtraction to 50.

III. Writing.

    1. As above.

    2. Copy Book, No. I.

IV. Drawing.

    1. As above.

V. Calisthenics.

## SECOND GRADE.

### FIRST YEAR.

*First Term.*

I. Language.

    1. Articulation and speech-reading.

    2. Reading chart.

    3. Jacobs' Reader, No. I., from page 54.

    4. Conversation, colloquial phrases, questions and answers; Hutton, to page 10.

    5. Verbs; progressive form, past and perfect.

        *a.* Description of pictures, actions, etc.

        *b.* Latham's First Lessons in Language, to page 46.

II. Arithmetic.

    1. Barton's Language Lessons in Arithmetic, to lesson 6.

    2. Tables; Addition and Subtraction to 100.

III. Geography.

    1. Place lessons; Map of Table-Top.

IV. Writing.

    1. Copy Book, No. II.

    2. Lessons in Note Books.

V. Drawing.

    1. Names of lines, straight and curved; invented figures and combinations.

VI. Calisthenics.

*Second Term.*

I. Language.
    1. Articulation and speech-reading.
    2. Reading chart.
    3. Jacobs' Reader, No. I.
    4. As above. Hutton, to page 18.
    5. Verbs, etc., as above. Latham, to page 70.

II. Arithmetic.
    1. Barton, to lesson 12.
    2. Tables; Addition and Subtraction.

III. Geography.
    1. Map of School-room.

IV. Writing.
    1. Copy Book, No. II.
    2. Lessons in Note Books.

V. Drawing.
    1. As above.

VI. Calisthenics.

*Third Term.*

I. Language.
    1. Articulation and speech-reading.
    2. Jacobs' Reader, No. I.; finish.
    3. As above. Hutton, to page 21.
    4. As above. Finish Latham.

II. Arithmetic.
    1. Barton, to lesson 15.
    2. Tables; Addition and Subtraction

III. Geography.
    1. Map of School-room; boundaries.

IV. Writing.
    1. Copy Book, No. III.
    2. Lessons in Note Books.

V. Drawing.

    As above.

VI. Calisthenics.

SECOND YEAR.

*First Term.*

I. Language.

    1. Articulation and speech-reading.

    2. As above.   Hutton, to page 26.

    3. Miss Sweet's Language Lessons;  No. I., to page 29.

II. Arithmetic.

    1. Barton, to lesson 18.

    2. Practical;  Addition, Subtraction and Multiplication.

III. Geography.

    1. Map of floor [second] of School building, with boundaries.

IV. Writing.

    1. Copy Book, No. III.

    2. Lessons in Note Books.

V. Drawing.

    1. Book No. I.;  Prang.

VI. Calisthenics.

*Second Term.*

I. Language.

    1. Articulation and speech-reading.

    2. As above.   Hutton, to page 31.

    3. As above.   Sweet, No. I., to page 60.

    4. Reading Book;  Parker & Marvel, No. I., to page 83.

II. Arithmetic.

    1. Barton, to lesson 23.

    2. Practical;  Addition, Subtraction, Multiplication and Division.

III. Geography.

    1. Map of School building;  boundaries.

IV. Writing.
    1. Copy Book, No. IV.
    2. Lessons in Note Books.

V. Drawing.
    1. Book No. I.; Prang.

VI. Calisthenics.

*Third Term.*

I. Language.
    1. Articulation and speech-reading.
    2. Hutton, to page 35.
    3. Sweet, No. I.; finish.
    4. Parker & Marvel, No. I.; finish.

II. Arithmetic.
    1. Barton, to page 26.
    2. Practical; Four fundamental principles.

III. Geography.
    1. Map of School-yard; boundaries.

IV. Writing.
    1. Copy Book, No. IV.
    2. Lessons in Note Books.

V. Drawing.
    1. Book No. II.

VI. Calisthenics.

## THIRD GRADE.

### FIRST YEAR.

*First Term.*

I. Language.
    1. Jacobs' Reader, No. II.
    2. Hutton's Colloquial Phrases, to page 45.
    3. Sweet's Lessons, No. II., to page 35.
    4. Reader; Parker & Marvel, No. II., to page 40.
    5. Descriptions of pictures.
    6. Letter writing.

II. Arithmetic.
    1. Barton, to page 50.
    2. Practical.

III. Geography.
    1. Map of City.

IV. Writing.
    1. Copy Book, No. IV.
    2. Copying in Note Books, letters, etc.

V. Drawing.
    1. Book No. II.

VI. Calisthenics.

*Second Term.*

I. Language.
    1. Jacobs, No. II.
    2. Hutton, to page 55.
    3. Sweet, No. II., to page 70.
    4. Parker & Marvel, No. II., to page 80.
    5. As above.
    6. As above.

II. Arithmetic.
    1. Barton, to page 75.
    2. Practical.

III. Geography.
    1. Map of County and State.

IV. Writing.
    1. Copy Book, No. IV.
    2. As above.

V. Drawing.
    1. Book No. III.

VI. Calisthenics.

*Third Term.*

I. Language.

    1. Jacobs, No. II.; finish.
    2. Hutton, to page 65.
    3. Sweet, No. II.; finish.
    4. Parker & Marvel, No. II.
    5. As above.
    6. As above.

II. Arithmetic.
    1. Barton, to page 100.
    2. Practical.

III. Geography.
    1. Cornell's First Steps.
    Map of New England States.

IV. Writing.
    1. Copy Book, No. V.
    2. As above.

V. Drawing.
    1. Book No. III.

VI. Calisthenics.

SECOND YEAR.

*First Term.*

I. Language.
    1. Hutton; finish.
    2. Parker & Marvel; finish.
    3. Readings: Newspapers and magazines, and reproduction
       pupils' own language.
    4. Powell's Language Series; Part I., to page 60.
    5. As above.　Journals.

II. Arithmetic.
    1. Barton, to page 125.
    2. Practical.

III. Geography.
    1. Cornell; United States.

IV. Writing.
1. Copy Book, No. V.
2. As above.

V. Drawing.
1. Book No. IV.

VI. Calisthenics.

*Second Term.*

I. Language.
1. Powell; Part I., to page 125.
2. Readings: Newspapers and magazines, and reproduction.
3. Journals, etc.
4. Conversation and dialogues.

II. Arithmetic.
1. Barton, to page 150.
2. Practical.

III. Geography.
1. Cornell; from page 3 to 23.

IV. Writing.
1. Copy Book, No. V.
2. As above.

V. Drawing.
1. Book No. IV.

VI. Calisthenics.

*Third Term.*

I. Language.
1. Powell, Part I.; finish.
2. Reading; as above.
3. Journals; as above.
4. Conversation and dialogues.

II. Arithmetic.
1. Barton; review.
2. Practical.

III. Geography.
    1. Cornell, to page 41 and review.

IV. Writing.
    1. Copy Book, No. V.
    2. As above.

V. Drawing.
    1. Book No. IV.

VI. Calisthenics.

## FOURTH GRADE.

### FIRST YEAR.

*First Term.*

I. Language.
    1. Powell; Part II.
    2. Readings, and talks of what is read.
    3. Journals, composition.
    4. Review of difficult words and phrases in sentence-making.
    5. Conversation, dialogues, etc.

II. Arithmetic.
    1. Barton, from page 150.
    2. Practical.

III. Geography; Harper.

IV. History; local.

V. Writing.

VI. Drawing.

VII. Calisthenics.

[To be filled out.]

## TO PARENTS OF DEAF CHILDREN.

This school is for the benefit of children incapacitated through deafness, total or partial, for receiving proper instruction in common schools.

The aim of the school is to teach deaf children to use the English language with the spontaneity, correctness and enjoyment of *hearing* children, as far as this is practicable.

"Without language there can be no thought, no reason;" and as the highest aim of all instruction is the culture of the mental and moral nature in man, our first effort should be to furnish the deaf with a medium through which knowledge can be imparted and obtained. This can be done by signs, by the finger alphabet, and by speech. Our method is the latter, or oral method, by which the deaf can be educated and, at the same time, furnished with the usual and most convenient way of communication in society and in the world at large.

It is very desirable that deaf children be sent to school at as early an age as possible. A parent will be amply repaid for sending a child as young as five or six years, even at some inconvenience.

If a child who has learned to talk is made deaf by disease, he should immediately upon his recovery be sent to a school where his speech will be retained, and where he will be taught to understand from the lips. In such cases it is common to delay so long that serious loss of speech results.

Speech-reading is an invaluable acquisition for those who are semi-deaf or even hard of hearing, as well as for those congenitally or totally deaf.

Every effort should be made to encourage the child to retain the use of his voice. He should be taught to pronounce common words, but no attempt should be made to teach him *the names* of the letters of the alphabet.

The school hours are from 9 A. M. to 1 P. M. on every week day, except Saturday. Open to visitors on Fridays, from 10 to 12.

The next summer vacation will begin Friday, July 1, 1887. The school will re-open Monday, September 5, 1887. Tuition is free to residents of this State. Provision is made for defraying the travelling expenses of indigent pupils. Application for admission may be made to the Principal of the school, or to the Commissioner of Public Schools, 104 North Main street, Providence, R. I.

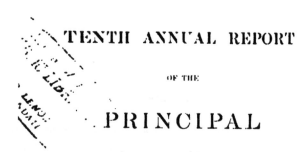

# TENTH ANNUAL REPORT

OF THE

# PRINCIPAL

OF THE

# )DE ISLAND SCHOOL FOR THE DEAF,

## PROVIDENCE, R. I.

FOR THE

## ˉEAR ENDING DECEMBER 31,

# 1887.

PROVIDENCE:

ˉ. L. FREEMAN & SON, PRINTERS TO THE STATE.

1888.

# TENTH ANNUAL REPORT

OF THE

# PRINCIPAL

OF THE

# RHODE ISLAND SCHOOL FOR THE DEAF,

PROVIDENCE, R. I.

FOR THE

# YEAR ENDING DECEMBER 31,

# 1887.

PROVIDENCE:

E. L. FREEMAN & SON, PRINTERS TO THE STATE.

1888.

# RHODE ISLAND SCHOOL FOR THE DEAF.

CORNER OF FOUNTAIN AND BEVERLY STREETS,

PROVIDENCE, R. I.

UNDER THE SUPERVISION OF THE

# STATE BOARD OF EDUCATION.

HIS EXCELLENCY JOHN W. DAVIS, Governor, *ex-officio*,

PRESIDENT.

HIS HONOR SAMUEL R. HONEY, Lieutenant-Governor, *ex-officio.*

| | |
|---|---|
| REV. WILLIAM N. ACKLEY, | Warren. |
| FRANK E. McFEE, | Woonsocket. |
| REV. DANIEL LEACH, | Providence. |
| DWIGHT R. ADAMS, | Centreville. |
| SAMUEL H. CROSS, | Westerly. |
| GEORGE A. LITTLEFIELD, | Newport. |

SECRETARY:

THOMAS B. STOCKWELL, Commissioner of Public Schools, *ex-officio.*

PRINCIPAL:

ANNA M. BLACK.

ASSISTANT TEACHERS:

ARDELIA C. DEWING,    ELLEN J. KERR,    EMMA F. DUNLOP.
MRS. E. T. SMITH, Teacher of Drawing.

SCHOOL FOR THE DEAF FOR THE YEAR ENDIN(

| Cause of Deafness, as far as Known. | Age when made Deaf. (Approx.) | Rem |
|---|---|---|
| Severe illness............ ......... | 8 months ............ | ................. |
| ——? fever................... | 1 year, 9 months.... | ............... ..... |
| Scarlet fever................. | 5 years, 8 months... | ................. ..... |
| Congenital........ .. | .......... ...... | Could not be kept } vagrant habits. |
| Whooping cough............. | 3 years.............. | Can hear loud tones. |
| Scarlet fever............... | 5 years.............. | ..... ....... ........ |
| Brain fever................. | 2 years, 2 months.. | ................ . ... |
| Scarlet fever................... | 6 years, 10 months.. | .............. ....... |
| Lung fever.................... | 2 years, 6 months... | ................... |
| Congenital................... | ... ........... .. | Left on account of sick |
| Congenital, or tumor in ears at 10 months .... ......... | .......... .... .... | ................. |
| Congenital................. | ............. .. .... | |
| Scarlet fever................. | ................ | ................. |
| Congenital, or illness at 3 months | .............. ...... | Slight degree of hearir |
| Scarlet fever........... | Probably before the age of 2. | Can hear loud tones. |
| Chronic inflammation of throat. | Discovered in her third year. | Slight degree of hearir |
| Scarlet fever................ | 9 weeks............. | ................... ... |
| Lung fever.................... | 5 months.......... | ................. .. |
| Scarlet fever................. | 4 years............. | Left on account of trou |
| Scarlet fever................ | Discovered at the age of 5. | ................. |
| Congenital............... .... | ............. ...... .. | Left school to work on |
| Congenital................. | .... ............. | Previously taught in a |
| Lung fever................. | 4 years............. | Left school to work lu |
| Scarlet fever............... | 3 years............. | ................... .... |
| Scarlet fever................. | 4 years..... ... | ................. ...... |
| Scarlet fever............... | 2 years | ................. ... |
| Tumor in ears................ | 6 months........... | ................. |
| Congenital................. | .... ......... .... | ........ . ........ |
| Brain fever.... ............. | 6 months . ......... | Has slight degree of h }(0) |
| Meningitis................ . . | 2 years, 6 months.. | ............. ....... |
| Fever....... ............ | 2 years............. | ........ ............. |
| Scarlet fever............ .... | 2 years............. | ......... .......... |
| ........ ............ ... | ............ | Attending for instructi |
| Typhoid fever.......... ....... | 3 years, 6 months.. | ............. |
| Scarlet fever............. | 6 years... .......... | } Hard of hearing. reading only, |
| Congenital .............. | ............... | Hard of hearing. |
| Scarlet fever ............... | 9 years............. | Hard of hearing. |

## TABULAR REPORT OF THE PUPILS OF THE RHODE ISLA[ND]

| Names of Pupils. | Residence. | Age. (Approx.) | Date o Admissi[on] |
|---|---|---|---|
| Kinyon, Ada J....... ........ | Providence.................... | 27 | April 2, 187[ ] |
| Slavin, Joseph H............... | Pawtucket.... .............. | 15 | Jan. 28, 188[ ] |
| Goodspeed, Bertha............. | Providence....... ....... ... | 13 | Mar. 9, " |
| Riley, Thomas................. | " ................... | 14 | April 5, " |
| Tucker, Arthur.. ........... | " ................... | 14 | " 19, " |
| Sheldon, Mary E.............. | " ................... | 19 | Sept. 6, " |
| Lynch, James E................ | Wanskuck, Providence........ | 12 | " 6, " |
| Swift, Mary E......... ...... | Providence.... ............. | 15 | Nov. 2, " |
| White Sarah.................... | East Providence............... | 15 | Sept. 5, 188[ ] |
| Potvin, William.............. | River Point, Warwick.......... | 18 | Oct. 24, " |
| McDonnell, Thomas...... ..... | Providence.................... | 17 | Nov. 28, " |
| Brownell, Lester R............. | " | 12 | June 15, 188[ ] |
| Radcliffe, Eliza ........ ........ | Lonsdale, Lincoln............. | 15 | Sept. 13, " |
| Moon, Ina G.................... | Washington, Coventry.......... | 14 | Nov 24. " |
| Lorimer, John F............... | Providence................... | 15 | April 18, 188[ ] |
| Woodley Abby M.... ......... | " ................... | 9 | May 7, " |
| Nolan, Rosanna............... | Rumford, East Providence. ... | 13 | Sept. 3, " |
| Addison Susan B.............. | Pawtucket........... ........ | 15 | May 19, 188[ ] |
| Goodwin, James H............. | Providence................. | 12 | Oct. 7, " |
| Holloway, Mary Ellen.. ....... | Pawtucket.................... | 12 | " 20, " |
| Cole, Egbert T............. | South Scituate................ | 19 | Mar. 10, 188[ ] |
| Herzog, Ernest J H............ | Geneva, Providence........... | 14 | " 10, " |
| Provincal, Joseph..... ........ | Albion.... ................... | 16 | Sept. 23, " |
| Walker, Mabel. ... ....... | Providence.... ............. | 15 | Jan. 6, 188[ ] |
| Beauchesne, Alphonse.......... | Central Falls.... .............. | 10 | Oct. 25, " |
| Sullivan, Nellie ................ | Newport.................... ... | 7 | Nov. 12, " |
| Grant, Edith....,............ | Providence.... ............. | 4 | Dec. 13, " |
| Cole, Luella...... ............ | South Scituate................ | 7 | Mar. 28, 188[ ] |
| Chevers, C. Herbert............ | East Providence.... ........... | 8 | April 26, " |
| Jacques, George A.............. | Pawtucket.................... | 8 | May 11, " |
| Cove, Margaret................ | Woonsocket..... ............. | 8 | Sept. 5, " |
| Green, Sarah...... ...... | Hope ............. .. .... | 12 | " 12, " |
| Andrews, Wilhelmina...... ... | Providence...... ......... ... | 15 | " 20, " |
| Francis, Manuel................ | Bristol..................... ... | 8 | " 26, " |
| Balch, Grace A................ | East Providence Centre........ | 10 | Oct. 10, " |
| Staunton, Annie................ | Providence........ ........... | 6 | Nov. 14, " |
| Reynolds, Ella E............... | Merino, Johnston.... ........... | 16 | Dec. 4. " |

## SCHOOL FOR THE DEAF FOR THE YEAR ENDING DEC. 31, 1887.

| CAUSE OF DEAFNESS, AS FAR AS KNOWN. | AGE WHEN MADE DEAF. (Approx.) | REMARKS. |
|---|---|---|
| Severe illness | 8 months | |
| —— ? fever | 1 year, 9 months | |
| Scarlet fever | 5 years, 8 months | |
| Congenital | | { Could not be kept in school on account of vagrant habits. |
| Whooping cough | 3 years | Can hear loud tones. |
| Scarlet fever | 5 years | |
| Brain fever | 2 years, 2 months | |
| Scarlet fever | 6 years, 10 months | |
| Lung fever | 2 years, 6 months | |
| Congenital | | Left on account of sickness. |
| { Congenital, or tumor in ears at 10 months | | |
| Congenital | | |
| Scarlet fever | | |
| Congenital, or illness at 3 months | | Slight degree of hearing. |
| Scarlet fever | { Probably before the age of 2. | Can hear loud tones. |
| Chronic inflammation of throat. | { Discovered in her third year. | Slight degree of hearing |
| Scarlet fever | 9 weeks | |
| Lung fever | 5 months | |
| Scarlet fever | 4 years | Left on account of trouble with ears. |
| Scarlet fever | { Discovered at the age of 5. | |
| Congenital | | Left school to work on a farm. |
| Congenital | | Previously taught in a German school. |
| Lung fever | 4 years | Left school to work in a mill. |
| Scarlet fever | 3 years | |
| Scarlet fever | 4 years | |
| Scarlet fever | 2 years | |
| Tumor in ears | 6 months | |
| Congenital | | |
| Brain fever | 6 months | Has slight degree of hearing. |
| Meningitis | 2 years, 6 months | |
| Fever | 2 years | |
| Scarlet fever | 2 years | |
| | | Attending for instruction in articulation only. |
| Typhoid fever | 3 years, 6 months | |
| Scarlet fever | 6 years | { Hard of hearing. Attending for speech reading only. |
| Congenital | | Hard of hearing. |
| Scarlet fever | 9 years | Hard of hearing. |

## SUMMARY.

Number of pupils, from date of opening the school, April 2, 1877,
to Dec. 31, 1886........................................ 60

Number of pupils who have entered the school since Dec. 31,
1886................................................ 10
_____
Whole number who have attended the school........... 70

Number who have left the school.................... 42
_____
Number of pupils Dec. 31, 1887........................ 28
_____
Number of girls who have attended school during the year...... 21

    "   " boys "  "   "    "    "    "   " ... . 16
_____
Whole number of pupils during the year................ 37

Average attendance................................24.85
_____
Number congenitally deaf, or made deaf before the age of two... 16

Number who lost hearing between the ages of two and four..... 8

Number who lost hearing after the age of four...... .......... 12
_____
    36

One not deaf, taking lessons in articulation only.............. 1
_____
    37

Number who have any degree of hearing..................... 12

*Residences of all who have attended during the year 1887.*

| | |
|---|---:|
| Providence, including Wanskuck and Geneva | 17 |
| Rumford, East Providence | 1 |
| East Providence | 3 |
| Pawtucket | 4 |
| Albion | 1 |
| Central Falls | 1 |
| South Scituate | 2 |
| Lonsdale | 1 |
| River Point, Warwick | 1 |
| Washington Village, Coventry | 1 |
| Newport | 1 |
| Woonsocket | 1 |
| Hope | 1 |
| Bristol | 1 |
| Merino, Johnston | 1 |
| 15 localities | 37 |

There have been no changes during the year in the corps of teachers. Five pupils have left. One could not be retained on account of vagrant habits, acquired through neglect of home training, and too much street training. Two were obliged to leave on account of sickness. Two have left school to engage in work. Four girls are now boarded by the State at the "Children's Home." Five of our girls have been admitted to the Cooking School for one lesson a week. One boy attends the R. I. School of Design. All of our children except the very smallest ones of the beginning class, have been under the tuition of Mrs. E. T. Smith in drawing; and most of them have made progress creditable to themselves and to their teacher. Mrs. Smith has the happy faculty of training their hearts as well as their hands to follow her lead. She will start a class in clay modeling next term. There have been ten additions to the school during the year—more than ever before in any one year. A number of improvements have been made in the furnishing and arrangement of the school-rooms. Some books have been added to the library.

At our public examination and exhibition last June, many spoke in terms of commendation and pleasure of the attainments of the pupils, and the advancement made since the previous examination. Year by year the work of the school is becoming much better known, and consequently more thoroughly appreciated. One substantial evidence thereof is the increased interest shown in the school. The prizes offered by Mrs. Henry Lippitt have been made a regular and permanent feature. The "Children's Home" and "Children's Mission" have been ever ready to extend a helping hand. Other friends have been generous and hearty in expressions of interest; accompanied by something more substantial when needed. All these things go very far toward keeping some children in school, who could not otherwise attend, and encourage and cheer the teachers and pupils. Yea, more, such appreciation as this, accompanied by a more liberal appropriation from the State, or individual endowment, would establish beyond question that the founding of this school was a good and beneficent thought, and destine it to grow to be one of the, not only necessary, but honored and permanent institutions of the

State: as such schools have become in nearly every State in the Union. The United States is doing more and greater things than any other country in the world toward educating and making self-supporting, useful, gifted and honored citizens of our children of the fettered ear. Once we went to other nations to learn how to teach our deaf; now they come to us.

With all these anxious longings and high hopes I cannot but think that it is passing strange, that notwithstanding the issuing of circulars and reports, and various other advertisements, so many whom our school is designed to benefit, are in total ignorance or neglect of the privilege offered them. It is estimated and frequently quoted that there is one fit subject for a school for the deaf in every 1500 people. In Martha's Vineyard and some other communities the proportion is much greater. On studying the census reports, the reports of the Hartford and other schools where some of our deaf have been educated, our own reports and other statistics, it cannot be proven in any way that there is that proportion in Rhode Island.

The population of Rhode Island being 304,284, the above estimate would give about 200 deaf in this State. The last census records 91 deaf and *dumb*. This probably does not include all who have been taught a longer or shorter time at the Rhode Island School for the Deaf within the last ten years; for some of those had never lost their voices and all have been or are being taught to talk; some leaving, however, before they had made much proficiency. It may include most of the deaf of Rhode Island, who in past years have been taught at other schools. This would leave less than 50 who have not been educated. Besides this, however, the census records 500 deaf (not dumb). I suppose this includes persons of all ages and all stages and degrees of deafness. It may be that out of this number there are 30 or 40 more who either have been, or ought to be educated at our school. At a rough estimate and lowest count, there are 50 persons in our State who ought to be, but are not members of the Rhode Island School for the Deaf. I would be more than glad if some fertile brain would devise some plan of ascertaining to a nearer certainty just how many there are, and how to get them into school. I confess that it is a subject that has caused me no little thought, anxiety and effort. I expect to keep on trying; but if there are 50 who ought to be in the School for the Deaf, it is high time that every resident of the State made it his interest to assist us to reach and educate all who need this special instruction. Our system is for, not only the deaf-mutes, but for those who are hard of hearing. Speech-reading is our specialty. Articulation is taught through the process of noting the muscular action and expression of the vocal organs, which we term speech-reading. I will say here that a course of speech-reading would be a great assistance to any one of almost any age who has become hard of hearing.

Our State is not singular in respect to the neglect of the privileges offered for the education of its deaf. It is claimed that in many of the States there are twice as many deaf children growing up in absolute ignorance, as there are of those under instruction ; and this, not because ample provision has not been made for them, but advantage is not taken of it. It is calculated that there are over 7,000 deaf children in the United States, who are growing up in ignorance through the more deplorable ignorance, careless selfishness or at best, thoughtlessness, of their parents and guardians. There is an urgent call in this direction for a compulsory education law.

Rhode Island provides this school for the free education of all the deaf in the State ; and any outside of the State who will pay tuition. By this I mean, not only all of the so-called deaf-mutes, but the semi-deaf; all that are too deaf to be benefited by the ordinary instruction in the public schools. There is no limit in our State as to age and length of time allowed for attendance. The little one is *so little* in knowledge and mental development that the teacher ought to begin where the mother usually begins with a hearing child; that is, as young as possible, or as soon as possible after the child loses his hearing ; while habits are easily formed and the vocal organs mobile and flexible ; or, if the child has once talked, in order to preserve his voice or his remembrance of the language once acquired. Children so soon forget how to talk if they lose their hearing, or when it becomes impaired. Right here, I would say, that it is surprising how many children who have once talked, and have lost their hearing by disease, are allowed to forget how to talk on account of the neglect of home training or school privileges.

It is asserted by some of our educators, who advocate the

use of signs for teaching the deaf, that persons of intelligence and education acquire the art of speech-reading with comparative ease, and that those taught by the "eclectic" system become better speech-readers and more fluent articulators than those taught exclusively by the oral system. For this reason the mind of the deaf child just beginning to learn, should first and all along, be disciplined and informed by means of the manual signs. This is said to prepare the way and render easier the teaching of speech and speech-reading. This is not my experience, or the experience of those who have been a much longer time in this work than have I. First, in regard to laying the foundation, I prefer to start with the speech movement of the vocal organs—call them facial *signs* if you will, I have no special objection to that word in its general sense. For, while it is true, that context is one of the keys to speech-reading; still it is mainly built on a cultivated habit of perception and accurate observation. The eyes are trained to detect the slightest and most delicate shades and variations in the muscular action and expression of the vocal and facial organs which mean words, and words mean ideas. No time is better to begin to train into this habit of nice observation than very early childhood. What does all our system of kindergarten, and object and illustrative teaching mean, if it does not mean just this? Teach a child two ways of gaining a thing—manual signs and lip signs, and he will not select and adopt that which will be of the most benefit to him, speech; but he will choose the easier, at the loss of all the facility he would obtain by the persistent, constant and exclusive practice of the other. Just as wise, I think, are those parents, who do not take their children to any particular church, or teach them the moral right or wrong of any course of action; leaving them to choose as the conscience or intuition dictates as they grow older. The trouble is, that when it comes to selecting for themselves, the conscience itself, by which they could be guided, seems to be lacking, and the intuition left to run riot, will do so still. The ability to choose wisely belongs to "those, who by reason of use have their senses exercised to discern both good and evil."

I have given lessons in speech-reading to a number of adults, intelligent and well-informed people, who had become very hard of hearing. The few who persevered against all obstacles and difficulties and acquired a facility in the art, have told me time and again, that it was the most difficult thing that they had ever tried to learn, and their great regret has always been, that they had the habits of years to contend against, always exclaiming, "If I were only younger, I know, I could learn this so much easier!" More give it up in disgust or despair, than persevere. Is it strange, when so few adults undertake any new acquisition or accomplishment which requires indomitable and long continued practice? Of those who have been taught by the, so-called, "combined method" or allowed and encouraged to use signs; some that I have known, who settled down to life in an institution, where far the larger part of their associates are the sign taught deaf who do not talk at all, give up almost entirely trying to practice speech-

reading, and seem to forget what knowledge they had obtained of it; even in some cases, neglecting to talk themselves; or they accompany speech with the gesture language,
so little do they go into general society.    Others, who are
obliged to mingle with the world at large, and seldom meet
one of their kind, either deprive themselves of social intercourse or resort to the tablet, as a means of communication.

In a city, working side by side in the same shop, are two
totally deaf men.   Both became deaf at about the same age,
eight or nine years, I think.   One was educated at a school
where the pupils were once taught exclusively by means of
manual signs.   The other man has been taught in an exclusively oral school.   As far as can be ascertained, they are
equally intelligent.   I have questioned both parties and
other workmen in the shop, carefully.   The former is a
very poor speech-reader, and seldom trusts himself to depend upon it in his every day intercourse, but uses a tablet
most of the time.   The other one mingles freely with all,
talks fluently and reads speech with ease.   He appears in
every respect as though he heard, and has no marked peculiarities.   I inquired particularly of one who knew both
men intimately, which he thought had the advantage of the
other, both from a business and a social point of view.   He
replied, "The one taught by the oral method most decid-
edly.   It does not admit of a question among any of their
associates."

Herein is another very astonishing thing.   The great out-
cry all over the land, from almost every institution for the
deaf in this country, is against irregularity of attendance,

and against the children leaving school when they have hardly had a fair start in their education. When once started in school, these children should be kept regularly and steadily there for a longer time, if possible, than hearing children. The teacher is the best judge as to their capacities, difficulties and the length of time that should be given to educate the deaf. They labor under many disadvantages all through life. For the uneducated deaf, life must indeed be hard and hopeless, to say the least, with little possibility of enjoyment. It should be our aim, and their parents aim, to lessen these disadvantages as effectually as possible, by giving them, at least, as liberal an education as the State provides, to render them self-supporting and capable of performing the duties and enjoying the privileges of life. The parents of the deaf do not consider sufficiently, that the loss of education is a serious hindrance to their advancement in life, socially, in business, in every respect; and more than that, renders them more liable to fall into idle and vicious habits.

Deaf children differ from hearing children only in their lack of one sense. Let us endeavor to make up this deficiency as much as possible by inducing them to attend a school adapted to their needs. There is the same difference in mental capacity, disposition, emotions, in short, they are very much like children in general; and should have the same intellectual and moral training. It is high time that every one realized that fact. Sometimes when people admit the truth of all this, there seems a fatality about their drifting into the same opinion still,—that there is something

"queer" or "strange" about the deaf. People will call
our schools for the deaf "Asylums," and look upon their
pupils or students as "inmates." In the past ages there
was some excuse for this. Aristotle discouraged all effort
to instruct the deaf-born, and Lucretius wrote: "To instruct
the deaf, no art could reach, no care improve them and no
wisdom teach." We read that Martin Luther was the first
one to strenuously advocate the education of the deaf, but
until the middle of the last century little effort had been
made to instruct them or improve their condition. Braid-
wood, a Scotchman, and Heinecke, a German, did more at the
start than any other two men to perfect the art of teaching
the deaf-born to talk. Many of our educated deaf in this
day and age fill places of high trust and responsibility in
the civil service. There are clerks, farmers, artists, mechanics, business men and women of intelligence, industry
and success. Some have risen to positions of credit and
honor in the fine arts and literature. This success is due
largely to the industrial training given in most of the institutions. We have no reason to be ashamed of some of the
pupils that have gone out from our own school and are
now in business; not alone as to business capacity and
steadiness of habits, but also as to their ability to make a
practical, everyday use of their attainments in speech-reading and articulation.

At the convention of the New York State Association of
Deaf-Mutes, held in Syracuse, N. Y., in August last, the following was reported: "Those in attendance at this convention are principally graduates of the institutions of the

State and now engaged in the common battle of life. They can set a true value upon the education they have secured, and their suffrages would doubtless be unanimous in recommending that all now in school stay there as long as possible. The State is generous in the time allowed each pupil in the institutions, and faithful adherence to the course of instruction is necessary to a ripened graduation. But it is a lamentable fact that altogether too many pupils are withdrawn before they have completed a good half of the course, thus destroying their chances for a completed education. The usual excuse given is that parents wish to realize upon the immature labor of the pupils, but they forget that the power to command remunerative employment would be greatly enhanced by that part of the education they foolishly throw away. It is against such a pernicious practice that this association can and should take its strongest stand."

The convention unanimously passed the following resolution :

*Resolved*, that the practice of parents withdrawing pupils from schools for the deaf before the completion of their education is one that is so obviously unjust to the pupil that it calls for the severest censure of this Association.

Some of the Teachers have enjoyed the privilege during the year of visiting other schools. One spent two weeks at the Clarke Institution, Northampton, studying their ways and means. Another visited the Boston School. The Principal had the rare privilege over a year ago of attending the Eleventh National Convention of American Instructors of the Deaf held at the California Institution for the Deaf, Berkeley, Cal. In many respects this convention was the most remarkable gathering ever held. Over 250 members took part in its deliberations and discussions, and a valuable printed report of its proceedings has been issued for reference. The benefits derived from such a meeting of the many master minds in this special branch of education, the talks and comparisons of methods of teaching, to see how other teachers instruct; what new and original ways to get the pupils to learn, not to speak of the grand opportunity for travel and the royal welcome and lavish entertainment extended to us by the Sunset State, were worth years of monotonous plodding. It brightens and enthuses, makes the work seem more worth the doing, the results good for the aiming, and the success worthy of the strongest, most subtile intellect and lofty enthusiasm. No kind of teaching requires more whole souled devotion and self-absorption, than this work of teaching the deaf.

I cannot close without urging the importance of doing all in our power as a State, in our appropriations, appointments and equipments to render our school a success, and one of the most beneficial and honored of its kind. Let not the lack of any needed additional outlay of means of any kind hinder or hamper its special purpose or render the work any the less efficient. Let it be said of our State through our school, with all due reverence. "He hath done all things well: he maketh both the deaf to hear, and the dumb to speak."

## GIFTS RECEIVED DURING THE YEAR 1887.

*Rubbers, Shoes and Clothing.*—From the "Children's Mission" connected with the First and Westminster Congregational Churches, "The Union Congregational Benevolent Society," Mrs. Adnah Sackett, Mrs. George Holden, Mrs. Henry. Billings, Miss Mabel Walker, Mrs. Taft, Mrs. P. H. Rose, Mrs. C. Le Gierse, Miss Mabel Richmond, Abby Woodley.

*Cards, Ornaments and Books.*—From Miss Aborn, Mrs. R. B. Hubbard and other Friends and Teachers.

*Cake, Ice Cream, Candy and Fruit.*—From Mrs. Albert Walker, Mrs. Geo. F. Woodley and Teachers.

*Specimens for Cabinet.*—From the Teachers and Pupils.

*Publications.*—"Nebraska Mute Journal," from Nebraska Institution for the Deaf; "The Companion," from Minnesota Institution; "Our Children's School Journal," from Western New York Institution; "Kentucky Deaf Mute," from Kentucky Institution; "Maryland Bulletin," from the Maryland School for the Deaf and Dumb; "Kansas Star," from the Kansas Institution for the Education of the Deaf and Dumb; "Deaf Mute Index," from Colorado Institution; "New Method for the Deaf," from the Voice and Hearing School, Englewood, Ill.; "The Silent Observer," from the Tennessee Institution; "Texas and Juvenile Ranger," from Texas Deaf and Dumb Asylum; "The Voice," from the Mississippi Institution for the Deaf; "The Register," from Central New York Institution, Rome, N. Y.

*Reports.*—From most of the Schools for the Deaf.

*Periodicals provided for the School.*—For the Teachers: "The Annals for the Deaf," and "The Voice." For the Pupils: "The Youth's Companion," "Wide Awake," "Harper's Young People," "Our Little Men and Women," "Our Little Ones," "Baby Days." These tend to encourage and cultivate a taste for general and instructive reading. They are bound at the end of the year and make quite an addition to the School Library.

### PRIZES OFFERED.

*Lippitt Fund.*—For best progress and improvement in Articulation, Speech-reading, Construction of Sentences, General Reading, Penmanship, Attendance and Deportment. Mary Holloway took the prize for Speech-reading; Alphonse Beauchesne, for Articulation; Joseph Provençal, for Construction of Sentences; Arthur Tucker, for General Reading; Joseph Slavin, for Penmanship; Lester Brownell, for Regular Attendance; Ernest Herzog, for Deportment.

# COURSE OF STUDY.

## BEGINNING CLASS.

### [FIRST YEAR.]

*First Term.*—Extending from the 1st Monday in September to the Christmas holidays.

I. Language.
  1. Articulation and speech reading.
      *a.* Elements; all, if possible.
      *b.* As soon as child has learned to utter the combinations that form words, such as the most familiar nouns and pronouns, explain or show what they signify. Such words as *papa, mamma, I* [*eye*], *you, me, toe, shoe, thumb, mouth, tooth, fan, one, two, three, four, five, home, etc.,*—whatever comes easiest.

II. Writing—Always to supplement speech, except in very rare cases. Letters representing the elements and words when uttered, and figures on slates.

III. Calisthenics—Breathing, vocal and physical.

*Second Term.*—Extending from 1st Monday after New Year's to the latter part of March.

I. Language.

    1. Articulation and speech-reading.

        *a.* Complete elements, with combinations.　See charts.

        *b.* Words: nouns and pronouns ; names of familiar objects, persons, parts of body, articles of food, clothing, etc.

II. Arithmetic.

    1. Numerals and counting to 5.

III. Writing.

    1. As above.

IV. Drawing.

    1. Kindergarten tablets.

V. Calisthenics; as above.

*Third Term.*—Extending from early April to first of July.

I. Language.

    1. Articulation and speech-reading.

        *a.* Review elements.　Thorough drill in combinations ; be able to pronounce words at sight.

        *b.* As above.

        *c.* Commands—Such as, *come, go, look, watch. sit, stand, turn, pass, etc.*

        *d.* Simple sentences and phrases, as "*I eat the apple, I eat bread, etc.; I hold the book; Bring me the cup; Good morning; Good bye, etc.*"

II. Arithmetic.

    1. Numerals and counting to 10.

III. Writing.

    1. Tracing Book, No. I.

IV. Drawing.

    1. As above.

V. Calisthenics; as above.

## SECOND GRADE.

[SECOND YEAR.]

*First Term.*

I. Language.

    1. Articulation and speech-reading.
        *a.* Drill on elements.
        *b, c, d.* As above, with adjectives.
        *e.* Colloquial phrases.

II. Arithmetic.

    1. Numerals and counting to 20.
    2. Addition and Subtraction to 10.

III. Writing.

    1. Everything pupil can speak he is taught to write.
    2. Copy Book, No. I.

IV. Drawing.

    1. Inventive; combinations of straight lines.

V. Calisthenics; as above.

*Second Term.*

I. Language.

    1. Articulation and speech-reading.
        *a, b, c, d, e.* As above.
        *f.* Prepositions and verbs describing actions, commands, questions and answers.

II. Arithmetic.

    1. Numerals and counting.
    2. Addition and Subtraction.

III. Writing.

    1. As above.

    2. Copy Book, No. I.

IV. Drawing.

    1. As above.

V. Calisthenics; as above.

*Third Term.*

I. Language.

    1. Articulation and speech-reading, as above.

    2. Reading chart.

II. Arithmetic.

    1. Numerals and counting.

    2. Addition and Subtraction.

III. Writing.

    1. As above.

    2. Copy Book, No. I.

IV. Drawing.

    1. As above.

V. Calisthenics; as above.

## THIRD GRADE.

### [THIRD YEAR.]

*First Term.*

I. Language.

    1. Articulation and speech-reading.

    2. Reading chart.

    3. Conversation, colloquial phrases, questions and answers; F
ton, to page 10.

    4. Verbs; present, past and future.

II. Arithmetic.

    1. Barton's Language Lessons in Arithmetic, to lesson 6. (Text-books are used when we approve of their general plan. We do not confine ourselves closely to any one here named.)

    2. Tables; Addition and Subtraction.

III. Geography.

    1. Place lessons; Map of Table-top.

IV. Writing.

    1. Copy Book, No. II.

    2. Lessons in Note Books.

V. Drawing.

    1. Invented figures and combinations, formed from straight and curved lines.

VI. Calisthenics; as above.

*Second Term.*

I. Language.

    1. Articulation and speech-reading.

    2. Reading chart.

    3. As above. Hutton, to page 18.

    4. Verbs, etc., as above.

II. Arithmetic.

    1. Barton, to lesson 12.

    2. Tables; Addition and Subtraction.

III. Geography.

    1. Map of School-room.

IV. Writing.

    1. Copy Book, No. II.

    2. Lessons in Note Books.

V. Drawing.

    1. As above.

VI. Calisthenics.

*Third Term.*

I. Language.

    1. Articulation and speech-reading.

    2. Reading chart.

    3. As above. Hutton, to page 21.

    4. As above.

II. Arithmetic.

    1. Barton, to lesson 15.

    2. Tables; Addition and Subtraction.

III. Geography.

    1. Map of School-room; boundaries.

1V. Writing.

    1. Copy Book, No. III.

    2. Lessons in Note Books.

V. Drawing.

    1. As above.

VI. Calisthenics.

## FOURTH GRADE.

### [FOURTH YEAR.]

*First Term.*

I. Language.

    1. Articulation and speech-reading.

    2. As above. Hutton, to page 26.

    3. Miss Sweet's Language Lessons No. I., to page 29 with changes of tenses.

II. Arithmetic.

    1. Barton, to lesson 18.

    2. Practical; Addition, Subtraction and Multiplication.

III. Geography.

    1. Map of floor of school building, with boundaries.

IV. Writing.

    1. Copy Book, No. III.

    2. Lessons in Note Books.

V. Drawing.

    1. Prang, Book No. I.

VI. Calisthenics.

*Second Term.*

I. Language.

    1. Articulation and speech-reading.

    2. Hutton, to page 31.

    3. Sweet, No. I., as above, to page 60.

    4. Reading Book; Parker & Marvel, No. I.

II. Arithmetic.

    1. Barton, to lesson 23.

    2. Practical; Addition, Subtraction, Multiplication and Division.

III. Geography.

    1. Map of school building; boundaries.

IV. Writing.

    1. Copy Book, No. IV.

    2. Lessons in Note Books.

V. Drawing.

    1. Prang, Book No. I.

VI. Calisthenics.

*Third Term.*

I. Language.

    1. Articulation and speech-reading.

    2. Hutton, to page 35.

    3. Sweet, No. I., finish.

    4. Parker & Marvel, No. I.

5

II. Arithmetic.

    1. Barton, to page 21.

    2. Practical; Four fundamental principles.

III. Geography.

    1. Map of school-yard; boundaries.

IV. Writing.

    1. Copy Book, No. IV.

    2. Lessons in Note Books.

V. Drawing.

    1. Book No. I.

V. Calisthenics.

## FIFTH GRADE.

### [FIFTH YEAR.]

*First Term.*

I. Language.

    1. Hutton's Colloquial Phrases, to page 45.

    2. Sweet's Lessons, No. II., to page 30.

    3. Reader; Parker & Marvel, No. I., finish.

    4. Descriptions of pictures.

    5. Letter writing.

II. Arithmetic.

    1. Barton, to page 36.

    2. Practical.

III. Geography.

    1. Map of city.

IV. Writing.

    1. Copy Book, No. IV.

    2. Copying in Note Books, letters, etc.

V. Drawing.

    1. Book No. II.

VI. Calisthenics.

*Second Term.*

I. Language.
  1. Hutton, to page 55.
  2. Sweet, No. II., to page 60.
  3. Parker & Marvel, No. II.
  4. As above.
  5. As above.

II. Arithmetic.
  1. Barton, to page 50.
  2. Practical.

III. Geography.
  1. Map of county and State.

IV. Writing.
  1. Copy Book, No. IV.
  2. As above.

V. Drawing.
  1. Book No. II.

V. Calisthenics.

*Third Term.*

I. Language.
  1. Hutton, to page 65.
  2. Sweet, No. II., to page 80.
  3. Parker & Marvel, No. II.
  4. As above.
  5. As above.

II. Arithmetic.
  1. Barton, to page 60.
  2. Practical.

III. Geography.
  1. Cornell's First Steps.
  2. Map of New England States.

IV. Writing.
    1. Copy Book, No. V.
    2. As above.

V. Drawing.
    1. Book No. II.

VI. Calisthenics.

## SIXTH GRADE.

### [SIXTH YEAR.]

*First Term.*

I. Language.
    1. Hutton.
    2. Sweet, No. II., finish.
    3. Parker & Marvel, No. II.
    4. Powell's Language Series, Part I., to page 37.
    5. As above.   Journals.

II. Arithmetic.
    1. Barton, to page 80.
    2. Practical.

III. Geography.
    1. Cornell; United States.

IV. Writing.
    1. Copy Book, No. V.
    2. As above.

V. Drawing.
    1. Book No. III.

VI. Calisthenics.

*Second Term.*

I. Language.
    1. Hutton.
    2. Powell, Part I., to page 63.
    3. Parker & Marvel, No. II., finish.

VII. Drawing.

VIII. Calisthenics.

*Third Term.*

I. Language.

    1. Powell, Part I., finish.

    2, 3, 4, 5, 6. As above.

II. Arithmetic.

    1, 2. As above.

III. Geography.

IV. History.

V. Physiology, Blaisdell.

VI. Writing.

VII. Drawing.

VIII. Calisthenics.

        [Eighth Grade work to be filled

## SEVENTH GRADE.

### [SEVENTH YEAR.]

*First Term.*

I. Language.
    1. Powell, Part I., to 105.
    2. Readings, and talks of what is read.
    3. Journals, composition.
    4. Review of difficult words and phrases in sentence-making.
    5. Conversation, dialogues, etc.

II. Arithmetic.
    1. Barton, to page 150.
    2. Practical.

III. Geography; Harper.

IV. History; local.

V. Physiology; Child's Book of Health, Blaisdell.

VI. Writing.

VII. Drawing.

VIII. Calisthenics.

*Second Term.*

I. Language.
    1. Powell; Part I., to page 138.
    2, 3, 4, 5. As above.
    6. Powell; Part II.

II. Arithmetic.
    1. Barton.
    2. Practical.

III. Geography; Harper.

IV. History; Goodrich, United States.

V. Physiology, Blaisdell.

VI. Writing.

VII. Drawing.

VIII. Calisthenics.

*Third Term.*

I. Language.
　　1. Powell, Part I., finish.
　　2, 3, 4, 5, 6. As above.

II. Arithmetic.
　　1, 2. As above.

III. Geography.

IV. History.

V. Physiology, Blaisdell.

VI. Writing.

VII. Drawing.

VIII. Calisthenics.

[Eighth Grade work to be filled out.]

# TO PARENTS OF DEAF CHILDREN.

This school is for the benefit of children incapacitated through deafness, total or partial, for receiving proper instruction in common schools.

The aim of the school is to teach deaf children to use the English language with the spontaneity, correctness and enjoyment of *hearing* children, as far as this is practicable.

"Without language there can be no thought, no reason;" and as the highest aim of all instruction is the culture of the mental and moral nature in man, our first effort should be to furnish the deaf with a medium through which knowledge can be imparted and obtained. This can be done by signs, by the finger alphabet, and by speech. Our method is the latter, or oral method, by which the deaf can be educated and, at the same time, furnished with the usual and most convenient way of communication in society and in the world at large.

It is very desirable that deaf children be sent to school at as early an age as possible. A parent will be amply repaid for sending a child as young as five or six years, even at some inconvenience.

# ELEVENTH ANNUAL REP

OF THE

# PRINCIPAL

OF THE

# IODE ISLAND SCHOOL FOR T

## PROVIDENCE, R I

FOR THE

## YEAR ENDING DECEMBE

# 1888.

PROVIDENCE:
E. L. FREEMAN & SON, PRINTERS TO THE S
1889.

# ELEVENTH ANNUAL REPORT

OF THE

## PRINCIPAL

OF THE

# ODE ISLAND SCHOOL FOR THE DEAF,

PROVIDENCE, R. I.

FOR THE

YEAR ENDING DECEMBER 31,

# 1888.

PROVIDENCE:

E. L. FREEMAN & SON, PRINTERS TO THE STATE.

1889.

# ELEVENTH ANNUAL REPORT

OF THE

# PRINCIPAL

OF THE

# RHODE ISLAND SCHOOL FOR THE DEAF,

## PROVIDENCE, R. I.

FOR THE

## YEAR ENDING DECEMBER 31,

# 1888.

PROVIDENCE:

E. L. FREEMAN & SON, PRINTERS TO THE STATE.

1889.

# RHODE ISLAND SCHOOL FOR THE DEAF,

### CORNER OF FOUNTAIN AND BEVERLY STREETS,

### PROVIDENCE, R. I.

---

#### UNDER THE SUPERVISION OF THE

# STATE BOARD OF EDUCATION.

---

HIS EXCELLENCY ROYAL C. TAFT, Governor, *ex-officio*,

#### PRESIDENT.

HIS HONOR ENOS LAPHAM, Lieutenant-Governor, *ex-officio*.

| | |
|---|---|
| REV. WILLIAM N. ACKLEY, | Warren. |
| FRANK E. McFEE, | Woonsocket. |
| REV. DANIEL LEACH, | Providence. |
| DWIGHT R. ADAMS, | Centreville. |
| SAMUEL H. CROSS, | Westerly. |
| GEORGE A. LITTLEFIELD, | Newport. |

---

#### SECRETARY :

THOMAS B. STOCKWELL, Commissioner of Public Schools, *ex-officio*.

---

#### PRINCIPAL :

#### ANNA M. BLACK.

---

#### ASSISTANT TEACHERS :

ARDELIA C. DEWING,     ELLEN J. KERR,     EMMA F. DUNLOP,
MRS. E. T. SMITH, Teacher of Drawing.

# REPORT.

---

*To the Honorable, the State Board of Education:*

GENTLEMEN:—I herewith submit my report for the year ending December 31, 1888.

Respectfully,

ANNA M. BLACK,

*Principal.*

DECEMBER 31, 1888.

## TABULAR REPORT OF THE PUPILS OF THE RHODE ISLAND

| NAMES OF PUPILS. | RESIDENCE. | AGE. (Approx.) | DATE OF ADMISSION. |
|---|---|---|---|
| Slavin, Joseph H............. | Pawtucket........ ........... | 16 | Jan. 28, 1880........ |
| Goodspeed, Bertha........... | Providence......... .......... | 14 | March 9, " ........ |
| Tucker, Arthur ............... | " .................... | 15 | April 19, " ........ |
| Sheldon, Mary E............. | " .................... | 20 | Sept. 6, " ........ |
| Lynch, James E.............. | Wanskuck, Providence......... | 13 | " 6, " ........ |
| Swift, Mary E.............. | Providence ............ .... | 16 | Nov. 2, " ........ |
| McDonnell, Thomas........... | " .................... | 18 | " 28, 1881........ |
| Brownell, Lester R........... | " ....,......... | 13 | June 15, 1882........ |
| Radcliffe, Eliza............... | Lonsdale, Lincoln............. | 16 | Sept. 13, " ......,. |
| Moon, Ina G................. | Washington, Coventry .... .... | 15 | Nov. 24, " ........ |
| Lorimer, John F............. | Providence.... ......... ....... | 16 | April 18, 1883........ |
| Woodley, Abby M............. | " . .... | 10 | May 7, " ........ |
| Nolan, Rosanna............... | Rumford, East Providence...... | 14 | Sept. 3, " ......... |
| Holloway, Mary Ellen......... | Pawtucket.................. .. | 13 | Oct. 20, 1884........ |
| Herzog, Ernest J. H........... | Providence................ | 15 | March 10, 1885...... .. |
| Walker, Mabel............... | Providence.... ............ | 16 | Jan. 6, 1886........ |
| Beauchesne, Alphonse .... ... | Central Falls............... | 11 | Oct. 25, " ....... |
| Sullivan, Nellie............... | Newport ................. | 8 | Nov. 12, " ........ |
| Grant, Edith.................. | Providence ....... .. ........ | 5 | Dec. 13, " ........ |
| Cole, Luella.................. | South Scituate............. | 8 | March 28, 1887........ |
| Chevers, C. Herbert........... | Providence................ | 9 | April 26, " ........ |
| Jacques, George A..... ...... | Pawtucket................... | 9 | May 11, " .... ... |
| Cove, Margaret.... ......... | Woonsocket................ | 9 | Sept. 5, " ........ |
| Green, Sarah.................. | Hope.......... ......... | 13 | " 12, " ........ |
| Andrews, Wilhelmina......... | Providence................ | 16 | " 20, " ........ |
| Francis, Manuel............... | Bristol.................. | 9 | " 26, " ........ |
| Balch, Grace A ............... | East Providence Centre........ | 11 | Oct. 10, " ...... |
| Reynolds, Ella E... ......... | Providence................... | 17 | Dec. 4, " ...... |
| Whipple, Ethel G............. | Diamond Hill ............. | 16 | May 21, 1888 ...... |
| Barnes, Joseph S..... ........ | Pawtucket...... ......... | 6 | " 23, " ........ |
| Canning, Thomas F........... | Woonsocket ............... | 7 | Sept. 3, " ........ |
| Hackett, Clara L ............. | Providence.... ........... | 5 | " 20, " ........ |
| Trudell, Albertina ............. | Warren.......... ... | 9 | Nov. 14, " ........ |
| Gill, Eva G .................. | Providence................ | 6 | Dec. 10, " ........ |

SCHOOL FOR THE DEAF FOR THE YEAR ENDING DEC. 31, 1888.

| CAUSE OF DEAFNESS, AS FAR AS KNOWN. | AGE WHEN MADE DEAF, (Approx.) | REMARKS. |
|---|---|---|
| ——? fever | 1 year, 9 months | Left school to work in a cigar shop. |
| Scarlet fever | 5 years, 8 months | |
| Whooping cough | 3 years | Can hear loud tones. |
| Scarlet fever | 5 years | |
| Brain fever | 2 years, 2 months | |
| Scarlet fever | 6 years, 10 months | |
| Congenital, or tumor in ears at 10 months. | | |
| Congenital | | |
| Scarlet fever | About 5 years | Nearly blind. |
| Congenital, or illness at 3 months | | Slight degree of hearing. |
| Scarlet fever | Probably before the age of 2. | Can hear loud tones. |
| Chronic inflammation of throat. | Discovered in her third year. | Slight degree of hearing. |
| Scarlet fever | 9 weeks | |
| Scarlet fever | Discovered at the age of 5. | |
| Congenital | | Previously taught in a German school. |
| Scarlet fever | 3 years | |
| Scarlet fever | 4 years | |
| Scarlet fever | 2 years | |
| Tumor in ears | 6 months | |
| Congenital | | |
| Brain fever | 6 months | Has slight degree of hearing. |
| Meningitis | 2 years, 6 months | |
| Fever | 2 years | |
| Scarlet fever | 2 years | |
| | | Attending for instruction in articulation only. |
| Typhoid fever | 3 years, 6 months | |
| Scarlet fever | 6 years | Hard of hearing. Attending for speech reading only. |
| Scarlet fever | 9 years | Hard of hearing. |
| | | Not deaf but feeble-minded. Left school in October, 1888. |
| Congenital | | Has slight degree of hearing. |
| Congenital | | |
| Congenital | | Hard of hearing. |
| Paralysis | 3 years | |
| Scarlet fever | 5 years | |

## SUMMARY.

Number of pupils, from date of opening the school, April 2, 1877,
to Dec. 31, 1887......................................    70

Number of pupils who have entered the school since Dec. 31,
1887.....  .......  ...  ................................    6
                                                      ————
Whole number who have attended the school ..........    76
Number who have left the school ......................    45
                                                      ————
Number of pupils Dec. 31, 1888 ..........................    31
                                                      ————
Number of girls who have attended school during the year......    21
  "      boys    "        "         "         "     ......    13
                                                      ————
Whole number of pupils during the year........  .......    34
Average attendance...............................25.05
                                                      ————
Number congenitally deaf, or made deaf before the age of two...    16
Number who lost hearing between the ages of two and four.....    9
Number who lost hearing after the age of four and doubtful cases.    9
                                                      ————
                                                           34
Number who have any degree of hearing....................    10

*Residences of all who have attended during the year 1888.*

Providence, including Wanskuck and Geneva .................  ....    17
Rumford, East Providence.....  ..  .........................    1
East Providence.................... ...  ..................    1
Pawtucket ,......................................    2
Central Falls...................................    1
South Scituate......... .........  ...................  .......    1
Lonsdale.......................................    1

It is much the same with institutions as with individuals
and nations, the happiest and the most prosperous have the
least variety in their history.    Another mile-post has been
reached in the records of our school.    As usual we are
expected to take a retrospect and report progress, short-
comings, etc.    As I look back over the year of strong,
faithful, earnest work on the part of teachers and pupils, I
feel sure that it has made its impress on the present, and
will tell in the future prosperity and success of the school.
In the report, it will appear in the form of bare statistics
and course of study, which, though dry as summer dust,
are necessarily of interest and importance in public records,
and interwoven in the very nature of development and
culture.    If the majority of our friends and patrons find
little or nothing that is striking or novel in our reports,
they need not thereby conclude that year by year the R. I.
State School for the Deaf is not becoming better known
and appreciated, and its usefulness and necessity being made
more and more apparent.

Most of the new pupils that have entered during the past
two years have been a younger class of children.    This is

2

as it should be. They are the ones that can be best and most benefitted by instruction, especially when they are taught to speak and speech is used as a medium of intelligence and instruction. It does not, however, follow that they should be removed early from school. Deaf children should begin at an earlier age, and be kept at school a longer time than hearing children. Hearing children are already provided with language, the conveyer of instruction; and are far advanced on the road of intelligence when they begin school; and in the very nature of the case, they, having fewer obstacles and difficulties in their way, learn much more easily and rapidly. Strange, that this needs reiterating so often, when it is such a self-evident fact; and stranger still,—passing strange,—that many parents and guardians of the deaf cannot or will not realize this necessity. We have been much troubled by irregularity of attendance in some cases, and we are losing from our numbers, ever and anon, pupils from 14 to 20 years of age. Some of them, starting late, have not yet made a living, every-day habit of speech and speech-reading, and have but just entered the portal of intellectual training; others only beginning to taste the stronger meats of a feast of reason. These learners, being well grown and strong in body, have been taken from school, in spite of the earnest protestations of the teachers, and put to work for those at home, or to earn a few dollars a week. What a price to pay for the loss of an education; yea, more, intelligence and ability to communicate with their fellow men! These, children in mind and judgment, if not in years and size, are not capable of choosing for themselves, and their guardians fail to insist on the much needed application to school advantages. The excuse generally made by these guardians is, that their children want to and will leave school to work, because they want to earn money; or that they, the parents, cannot afford to keep their children at school when they can earn something for their own support. Afford it! They cannot afford *not* to do it! They are placing a few dollars in the way of the deaf child's best good, and perchance their own as well. It sometimes happens that uneducated deaf mutes do succeed to a limited degree in business; but where competition is great, as it frequently is, they are at a tremendous disadvantage, and become more or less a burden on their friends and the community. Even taking a selfish view of the matter, the educated deaf person, nine times out of ten, will be better fitted for all the interests and enjoyments of life and home; yea, I might say, Heaven as well.

We held our public exhibition and examination in June. The Governor and other officials, and members of the State Board of Education, patrons and friends, showed their appreciation by crowding the rooms to their utmost capacity.

The "Children's Home," where five of our girls are boarded, the "Children's Mission" and other friends, have been generous and hearty in expressions of interest and other kindnesses. May the time soon come when our school shall be more liberally provided for, especially as to a provision for more and better home, industrial and mechanical training, giving to our deaf the practical and much needed preparation for earning their living, and a

more nearly equal start in life as young men and women
with their hearing brothers and sisters.  In this as well as
in other respects, may our school take its stand among the
strongest and best of the ample and efficient institutions of
this kind in which our country abounds.

England has shown her appreciation of America's front
rank in this branch of education, by sending for one, then
another of our most eminent and honored specialists in this
line, to present before the British Royal Commission our
methods of teaching the deaf.  America once sought to
learn of other nations, now they come to her.

There is a mistake which people often make in regard to
small schools.  They do not appreciate, in the first place,
why they should not be as large as others.  They seldom
take into consideration the comparative size of the States,
or the numbers these schools are intended to serve.  We
have as large a proportion of deaf in our school as have
other States; larger than some, admitting that we have the
same proportion of deaf needing an education, which is by
no means certain.  Then, in respect to the work accomplished, a false estimate is often made.  In our little school
of about thirty pupils, we have as many grades as are
usually found in a school of from 100 to 400; and a teacher
is expected to do as well by a class of from one to four
grades, and mayhap other duties besides, as another teacher
will do with a class of one grade in a large school.  It is
not among human possibilities for such to be the case, and
absurd and unjust to expect it.

Six of our girls have attended the Industrial Training

School, and have had one lesson a week in cooking, &c., and have made good progress. One boy has attended the "R. I. School of Design," and is doing excellent and creditable work in drawing, modeling and wood carving.

Mrs. E. T. Smith, our drawing teacher, finding it necessary to discontinue her classes in our school, the committee have secured the services of Miss A. M. White, the Supervisor of the Industrial Art Department in the city public schools, to take charge of that department in our school.

With the hope that the new year will open with bright prospects of renewed and greater appreciation on the part of the State, patrons and friends in general, and that with increased means and facilities, the affairs of the school may be conducted with greater vigor and efficiency on the part of the officers and teachers, I close.

ANNA M. BLACK.

# TO PARENTS OF DEAF CHILDREN.

This school is for the benefit of children incapacitated through deafness, total or partial, for receiving proper instruction in common schools.

The aim of the school is to teach deaf children to use the English language with the spontaneity, correctness and enjoyment of *hearing* children, as far as this is practicable.

"Without language there can be no thought, no reason;" and as the highest aim of all instruction is the culture of the mental and moral nature in man, our first effort should be to furnish the deaf with a medium through which knowledge can be imparted and obtained. This can be done by signs, by the finger alphabet, and by speech. Our method is the latter, or oral method, by which the deaf can be educated and, at the same time, furnished with the usual and most convenient way of communication in society and in the world at large.

It is very desirable that deaf children be sent to school at as early an age as possible. A parent will be amply repaid for sending a child as young as five or six years, even at some inconvenience.

If a child who has learned to talk is made deaf by disease he should immediately upon his recovery be sent to a school where his speech will be retained, and where he will be taught to understand from the lips. In such cases it is common to delay so long that serious loss of speech results.

Speech-reading is an invaluable acquisition for those who are semi-deaf or even hard of hearing, as well as for those congenitally or totally deaf.

Every effort should be made to encourage the child to retain the use of his voice. He should be taught to pronounce common words by watching the lip motion and facial expression, or by feeling the muscular action or the breath; but no attempt should be made to teach him *the names* of the letters of the alphabet.

The school hours are from 9 A. M. to 1 P. M. on every week day, except Saturday. Open to visitors on Fridays, from 10 to 12.

The next summer vacation will begin Friday, June 28, 1889. The school will re-open Monday, September 2, 1889. Tuition is free to residents of this State. Provision is made for defraying the travelling expenses of indigent pupils. Application for admission may be made to the Principal of the school, or to the Commissioner of Public Schools, 104 North Main Street, Providence, R. I.

# TWELFTH ANNUAL REPORT

OF THE

# PRINCIPAL

OF THE

# TATE SCHOOL FOR THE DEAF,

PROVIDENCE. R. I.

FOR THE

## YEAR ENDING DECEMBER 31,

# 1889.

PROVIDENCE:

E. L. FREEMAN & SON, PRINTERS TO THE STATE.

1890.

OF THE

# PRINCIPAL

OF THE

# TATE SCHOOL FOR TH

PROVIDENCE, R. I

FOR THE

## YEAR ENDING DECEMBER

# 1889.

PROVIDENCE:

E. L. FREEMAN & SON, PRINTERS TO THE

1890.

# TWELFTH ANNUAL REPORT

OF THE

# PRINCIPAL

OF THE

# STATE SCHOOL FOR THE DEAF,

PROVIDENCE, R. I.

FOR THE

YEAR ENDING DECEMBER 31,

# 1889.

# STATE SCHOOL FOR THE DEAF,

CORNER OF FOUNTAIN AND BEVERLY STREETS,

PROVIDENCE, R. I.

•

UNDER THE SUPERVISION OF THE

# STATE BOARD OF EDUCATION.

HIS EXCELLENCY HERBERT W. LADD, Governor, *ex-officio*,

PRESIDENT.

HIS HONOR DANIEL G. LITTLEFIELD, Lieutenant-Governor, *ex-officio*.

| | |
|---|---|
| REV. WM. N. ACKLEY, | Narragansett Pier. |
| FRANK E. McFEE, | Woonsocket. |
| LUCIUS B. DARLING, | Pawtucket. |
| DWIGHT R. ADAMS, | Centreville. |
| SAMUEL H. CROSS, | Westerly. |
| | Newport. |

SECRETARY :

THOMAS B. STOCKWELL, Commissioner of Public Schools, *ex-officio*.

PRINCIPAL :

LAURA DE L. RICHARDS.

ASSISTANT TEACHERS :

| | |
|---|---|
| ARDELIA C. DEWING, | EMMA F. DUNLOP, |
| LAURA A. WHEATON, | A. EVELYN BUTLER. |

ABBIE M. WHITE, Teacher of Drawing.

# ˙ REPORT.

---

*To the Honorable, the State Board of Education:*

GENTLEMEN:—I herewith submit my report for the year ending December 31, 1889.

Respectfully,

LAURA DE L. RICHARDS,

*Principal.*

DECEMBER 31, 1889.

## TABULAR REPORT OF THE PUPILS OF THE STATE SCHOOL

| Names of Pupils. | Residence. | Age. (Approx.) | Date of Admission. |
|---|---|---|---|
| Goodspeed, Bertha.............. | Providence..................... | 16 | March 9, 1880........ |
| Sheldon, Mary E................ | " ................ ...... | 21 | Sept. 6, " ........ |
| Lynch, James E.......... ... | Wanskuck, Providence.......... | 14 | " 6, " ... ... .. |
| Swift, Mary E................... | Providence..................... | 17 | Nov. 2, " ........ |
| Brownell, Lester R.............. | " ................ | 14 | June 15, 1882........ |
| Radcliffe, Eliza.... ........... | Lonsdale, Lincoln.............. | 17 | Sept. 13, " ........ |
| Moon, Ina G........... . .... ... | Washington, Coventry.......... | 16 | Nov. 24, " ... ... |
| Woodley, Abby M.......... .... | Providence..................... | 11 | May 7, " ........ |
| Nolan, Rosanna................ | Rumford, East Providence..... | 15 | Sept. 3, " ........ |
| Holloway, Mary Ellen.......... | Central Falls.................... | 14 | Oct. 20, 1884........ |
| Herzog, Ernest J. H........... | Providence..................... | 16 | March 10, 1885........ |
| Walker, Mabel......... ...... | " .... ...... ......... | 17 | Jan. 6, 1886........ |
| Beauchesne, Alphonse..... ... | Central Falls.................... | 12 | Oct. 25, " ........ |
| Sullivan, Nellie.... ............ | Newport....................... | 9 | Nov. 12, " ........ |
| Grant, Edith................... | Providence.......... .... ...... | 6 | Dec. 13, " ........ |
| Cole, Luella .. . .............. | South Scituate................... | 9 | March 28, 1887........ |
| Chevers, C. Herbert... ....... | Providence............ .... .... | 10 | April 26, " ........ |
| Jacques, George A ............ | Pawtucket.... .... .......... | 10 | May 11, " ........ |
| Cove, Margaret................ | Woonsocket... .............. | 10 | Sept. 5, " ........ |
| Green, Sarah.................. | Hope....................... ...... | 14 | " 12, " ........ |
| Francis, Manuel............... | Bristol........................ . | 10 | " 26, " ........ |
| Balch, Grace A.......... ...... | East Providence Centre.... .... | 12 | Oct. 10, " ........ |
| Reynolds, Ella E........... .. | Providence................... | 18 | Dec. 4, " ........ |
| Canning, Thomas F....... ... | Woonsocket.................... | 8 | Sept. 3, 1888........ |
| Hackett, Clara L.... ...... .... | Providence............ .... ...... | 6 | " 20, " ........ |
| Trudell, Albertina.... ........ | Warren....................... | 10 | Nov. 14, " ........ |
| Gill, Eva G.... ............... | Providence..................... | 7 | Dec. 10, " ........ |
| Goldenofsky, Moses. .......... | Woonsocket.................... | 6 | April 29, 1889........ |
| Dolan, Peter........ . ........ | Providence..................... | 8 | June 1, " ........ |
| Hackett, Laura... ............. | " ........ ........... | 4 | Nov. 11, " ........ |

## FOR THE DEAF FOR THE YEAR ENDING DECEMBER 81, 1889.

| Cause of Deafness, as far as Known. | Age when made Deaf. (Approx.) | Remarks. |
|---|---|---|
| Scarlet fever | 5 years, 8 months | |
| Scarlet fever | 5 years | |
| Brain fever | 2 years, 2 months | |
| Scarlet fever | 6 years, 10 months | |
| Congenital | | |
| Scarlet fever | About 5 years | Nearly blind. |
| Congenital, or illness at 8 months | | Slight degree of hearing. |
| Chronic Inflammation of throat. | Discovered in her third year. | Slight degree of hearing. |
| Scarlet fever | 9 weeks | |
| Scarlet fever | Discovered at the age of 5. | |
| Congenital | | Previously taught in a German school. |
| Scarlet fever | 8 years | |
| Scarlet fever | 4 years | |
| Scarlet fever | 2 years | |
| Tumor in ears | 6 months | |
| Congenital | | |
| Brain fever | 6 months | Slight degree of hearing. |
| Meningitis | 2 years, 6 months | |
| Fever | 2 years | |
| Scarlet fever | 2 years | |
| Typhoid fever | 3 years, 6 months | |
| Scarlet fever | 6 years | Hard of hearing.    Attending for speech reading only. |
| Scarlet fever | 9 years | Hard of hearing. |
| Congenital | | |
| Congenital | | Hard of hearing. |
| Paralysis | 3 years | |
| Scarlet fever | 5 years | |
| Scarlet fever | 8 years | |
| Humor | 8 years | Hard of hearing. |
| Congenital | | |

## SUMMARY.

Number of pupils from date of opening the school, April 2, 1877,
    to Dec. 31, 1888.........................................

Number of pupils who have entered the school since Dec. 31,
    1888.....................................................
                                                                    —

    Whole number who have attended the school...........
    Number who have left the school.....................
                                                                    —

Number of pupils Dec. 31, 1889..................... ........

Number of girls who have attended school during the year......
    "   boys   "      "      "      "  ......

    Whole number of pupils during the year...............
    Average attendance.................... ......... ...    2
Number congenitally deaf, or made deaf before the age of two..
Number who lost hearing between the ages of two and four....
Number who lost hearing after the age of four, and doubtful cases.
                                                                    —

Number who have any degree of hearing......... ...........

*Residences of all who have attended during the year 1889.*

Providence, including Wanskuck and Geneva.................
Rumford, East Providence...................... ..........
East Providence.......................... ......
Pawtucket ................................. ......
Central Falls................... ....... .................
South Scituate......................... ..................
Lonsdale............. ............. .................
Washington Village, Coventry......: ....................

Having assumed charge of the school at the beginning of
ie fall term, upon the resignation of Miss Anna M. Black,
ie former efficient principal, my knowledge of the school
ork the past year is necessarily quite limited.  So far as
can learn, the history of the school since the last report
is been one of quiet progress, while the teachers have per-
rmed their onerous duties with zealous faithfulness and
ccess.  The attendance generally has been very regular.
ie number of pupils present last session was thirty-one.
ie number this session, to date, is thirty—twenty-three
ni-mutes and seven congenital mutes.  The early instruc-
n of semi-mutes, who have been taught nothing before
ning to school, is often more difficult than that of con-
nital mutes.  But after a time the benefit of the language
ey retain is seen, and they are then generally able to
vance more rapidly than the congenital mutes who en-
ed with them.  There are, however, exceptions, some
ngenital mutes excelling in everything they undertake.
Three of the boys left at the close of the school year to
ter into active life.  These have been taken from school,
spite of the earnest entreaties of their teachers, and put
the way of earning a few dollars.  When will the parents
id guardians learn and appreciate the inestimable value of

a thorough education to these children, and that it requires a much longer time for them to gain an education than for hearing children? Yet as a rule the number of school years allowed them is much less. One reason for this is that many of our children are found in the homes of the poor, whose every effort is put forth to gain a livelihood. Some through misguided affection, some through carelessness, and some through ignorance keep their children at home when they should be in school. In April the school sustained a loss in the resignation of Miss Ellen J. Kerr, who for eight years was a valuable teacher here. On the resignation of Miss Kerr, Miss Laura A. Wheaton and Miss A. Evelyn Butler were appointed teachers, and thus a long felt need of the addition of a fourth teacher to our corps was supplied.

We have deemed it advisable to re-grade the classes, which we find very advantageous to both teachers and pupils, and in so doing have formed a new department,—a kindergarten for the children too young to grasp ideas rapidly,—and we look forward to good results if it is properly conducted.

Our blind and deaf and dumb pupil, Eliza Radcliffe, under Miss Dewing's instruction, is making good progress. She is now provided with books printed in raised type, which make the instruction more easy. Yet it must be borne in mind that she requires individual attention, and that she takes a large part of her teacher's time.

We have recently formed a sewing class, where we hope to see some practical work done. Several of the pupils have been taken to the Rhode Island Hospital for treatment, greatly to their relief. One of the boys is attending the Rhode Island School of Design, and also, through the liberality of a lady, a class in Wood Carving at the Friends' School with very gratifying results.

We beg leave to call your attention to our great need of a Home for those of our pupils who live at too great a distance from the city to be able to attend school. Three are now boarded at the Children's Home on Tobey Street, one at the Home of the S. P. C. C. on Doyle Avenue, and two in private families, while others are waiting to come, and would be with us if we could care for them. By providing us a home you will increase our influence, and enable us to carry on our work to greater advantage and with much greater success.

Notwithstanding the fact that the school has been in existence so long, and is so well known, constant effort is necessary to find deaf children, and to bring to the knowledge of their parents and friends what can be done for them, and what the State so liberally provides. And the request is earnestly renewed that those who may chance to see this report will send to the School Commissioner or Principal the addresses of children too deaf to attend ordinary schools with profit.

Our thanks are gratefully tendered to Miss Helen M. Lathrop for books for the pupils' library; to Mrs. Phillips, Mrs. Walker, Mrs. Sacket, and Miss Richmond for clothing; to the Children's Mission, for shoes and rubbers; to the Rhode Island Society for Encouragement of Domestic In-

2

dustry for admission to the State Fair; to the Rhode Island
Island Horticultural Society for admission to the Floral
Exhibition; and to the parents and teachers for refresh-
ments on different occasions.

### LIPPITT FUND PRIZES.

For greatest progress and improvement in Articulation,
Alphonse Beauchesne, Herbert Chevers.   For Speech Read-
ing, Grace Balch, Maggie Cove.   For Construction of Sen-
tences, Mary Holloway, Abby Woodley.   For General
Reading, Mary Swift.   For Penmanship, Ella Reynolds,
Bertie Trudell, Joseph Barnes.   For Attendance, Nellie
Sullivan.   For Deportment, Luella Cole.

# COURSE OF STUDY.

## KINDERGARTEN.

### FIRST YEAR.

a. KINDERGARTEN EXERCISES.

b. ARTICULATION.

c. LANGUAGE.

d. ARITHMETIC.

e. PENMANSHIP.

a. Paper cutting and folding; drawing and modeling in clay; designing in shoe pegs; stick laying; embroidery designs sewed on pricked sewing cards; lessons in form and color in all exercises.

b. Elements, combinations, simple words and sentences, with reading them from the lips.

c. Nouns; objects in class-room, articles of dress, articles of food, different parts of the body, with a limited number of verbs. Adjectives; good, bad, large, small, &c.

d. Counting and writing numbers, with addition and subtraction to 10.

e. Writing on slate and with lead pencil.

## PRIMARY COURSE.

SECOND, THIRD, AND FOURTH YEARS.

> *a.* ARTICULATION.
> *b.* LANGUAGE.
> *c.* ARITHMETIC.
> *d.* GEOGRAPHY.
> *e.* PENMANSHIP.
> *f.* DRAWING.

*a.* Drill in elements, combinations and words, and reading them from the lips.

*b.* Thorough review of first year work. Nouns and verbs continued. Adjectives continued; their comparison. Pronouns as in first year, adding myself, himself, herself with the plurals, and the relatives who and which. Adverbs; not, often, never, &c. Elliptical sentences; action and picture writing; journal and letter writing, and simple stories.

*c.* Practical exercises in addition, subtraction, multiplication, and division; United States currency; simple fractions.

*d.* School-room, building and yard, city, and a limited knowledge of the State.

*e.* Copy-book writing.

## INTERMEDIATE COURSE.

FIFTH, SIXTH, AND SEVENTH YEARS.

> *a.* ARTICULATION.
> *b.* LANGUAGE.
> *c.* ARITHMETIC.
> *d.* GEOGRAPHY.
> *e.* HISTORY.
> *f.* PENMANSHIP.
> *g.* DRAWING.
> *h.* CALISTHENICS.

*a.* Drill in elements, combinations, syllables; words and sentences continued as in Primary Course.

*b.* Nouns, pronouns, adjectives, adverbs, prepositions and conjunctions continued as in Primary Course. Drill in active and passive voices; action and picture writing; stories from Natural History; journal and letter writing.

*c.* Mental and written addition, subtraction, multiplication, and division, with practical examples; United States currency and simple fractions continued.

*d.* City, State, and New England States.

*e.* Simple historical stories in connection with geography.

*f.* Copy-book writing twice a week.

*g.* Object drawing.

### HIGHER COURSE.

#### EIGHTH, NINTH, AND TENTH YEARS.

*a.* ARTICULATION.

*b.* LANGUAGE.

*c.* ARITHMETIC.

*d.* GEOGRAPHY.

*e.* HISTORY.

*f.* PHYSIOLOGY.

*g.* PENMANSHIP.

*h.* DRAWING.

*i.* CALISTHENICS.

*a.* Drill in difficult combinations and words.

*b.* Composition; journal and letter writing; miscellaneous reading; newspapers and magazines; lessons on general subjects.

*c.* Mental, written and practical.

*d.* Geographical Reader; Manual of Commerce.

*e.* History of the United States; Outline of General History.

*g.* Copy book.

*h.* Free-hand and object drawing and designing.

# TO PARENTS OF DEAF CHILDREN.

This school is for the benefit of children incapacitated through deafness, total or partial, for receiving proper instruction in common schools.

The aim of the school is to teach deaf children to use the English language with the spontaneity, correctness, and enjoyment of *hearing* children as far as this is practicable.

"Without language there can be no thought, no reason;" and as the highest aim of all instruction is the culture of the mental and moral nature in man, our first effort should be to furnish the deaf with a medium through which knowledge can be imparted and obtained. This can be done by signs, by the finger alphabet, and by speech. Our method is the latter, or oral method, by which the deaf can be educated and, at the same time, furnished with the usual and most convenient way of communication in society and in the world at large.

It is very desirable that deaf children be sent to school at as early an age as possible. A parent will be amply repaid for sending a child as young as five or six years, even at some inconvenience.

If a child who has learned to talk is made deaf by disease he should immediately upon his recovery be sent to a school where his speech will be retained, and where he will be taught to understand from the lips. In such cases it is common to delay so long that serious loss of speech results.

Speech reading is an invaluable acquisition for those who are semi-deaf or even hard of hearing, as well as for those congenitally or totally deaf.

Every effort should be made to encourage the child to retain the use of his voice. He should be taught to pronounce common words by watching the lip motion and facial expression, or by feeling the muscular action or the breath; but no attempt should be made to teach him *the names* of the letters of the alphabet.

The school hours are from 9 A. M. to 1 P. M. on every week day, except Saturday. Open to visitors on Fridays, from 10 to 12.

The next summer vacation will begin Friday, June 27, 1890. The school will re-open Monday, September 1, 1890. Tuition is free to residents of this State. Provision is made for defraying the travelling expenses of indigent pupils. Application for admission may be made to the Principal at the school, corner Fountain and Beverly streets, or to the Commissioner of Public Schools, 104 North Main Street, Providence, R. I.

# THIRTEENTH ANNUAL REPORT

OF THE

# PRINCIPAL

OF THE

# TATE SCHOOL FOR THE DEAF,

## PROVIDENCE, R. I.,

FOR THE

## YEAR ENDING DECEMBER 31.

# 1890.

PROVIDENCE, R. I.
E. L. FREEMAN & SON, PRINTERS TO THE STATE.

# THIRTEENTH ANNUAL REPORT

OF THE

# PRINCIPAL

OF THE

# STATE SCHOOL FOR THE DEAF,

PROVIDENCE, R. I.,

FOR THE

YEAR ENDING DECEMBER 31,

# 1890.

---

PROVIDENCE:

E. L. FREEMAN & SON, STATE PRINTERS.

1891.

# STATE SCHOOL FOR THE DEAF,

CORNER OF FOUNTAIN AND BEVERLY STREETS,

PROVIDENCE, R. I.

UNDER THE SUPERVISION OF THE

# STATE BOARD OF EDUCATION.

HIS EXCELLENCY JOHN W. DAVIS, Governor, *ex-officio*,

PRESIDENT.

HIS HONOR WM. T. C. WARDWELL, Lieutenant-Governor, *ex-officio*.

| | |
|---|---|
| PERCY D. SMITH, . . . . . | Chepachet. |
| J. HOWARD MANCHESTER, . . . | Bristol. |
| LUCIUS B. DARLING, . . . . | Pawtucket. |
| DWIGHT R. ADAMS, . . . . | Centreville. |
| SAMUEL H. CROSS, . . . . | Westerly. |
| FRANK E. THOMPSON, . . . | Newport. |

SECRETARY:

THOMAS B. STOCKWELL, Commissioner of Public Schools, *ex-officio*.

PRINCIPAL:

LAURA DE L. RICHARDS.

ASSISTANT TEACHERS:

| | |
|---|---|
| ARDELIA C. DEWING, | EMMA F. DUNLOP, |
| A. EVELYN BUTLER, | FANNIE D. GLADDING. |

CLARA F. ROBINSON, Teacher of Drawing.

# REPORT.

To the Honorable, the State Board of Education:

GENTLEMEN:—I herewith submit my report for the year ending December 31, 1890.

Respectfully,

LAURA DE L. RICHARDS,

*Principal.*

DECEMBER 31, 1890.

### TABULAR REPORT OF THE PUPILS OF THE STATE SCHOOL

| Names of Pupils. | Residence. | Age. (Approx.) | Date of Admission. |
|---|---|---|---|
| Goodspeed, Bertha...... | Providence............... | 16 | March 9, 1880. |
| Sheldon, Mary E....... | Providence...... ..... ..... | 22 | Sept. 6, " . |
| Lynch, James E ....... | Wanskuck, Providence...... | 15 | " 6, " . |
| Swift, Mary E.......... | Providence...... ...... .... | 18 | Nov. 2, " . |
| Brownell, Lester R..... | " ............... | 15 | June 15, 1882. |
| Radcliffe, Eliza ........ | Lonsdale, Lincoln .......... | 18 | Sept. 18, " . |
| Moon, Ina G............ | Washington, Coventry....... | 17 | Nov. 24, " . |
| Woodley, Abby M...... | Providence............... | 12 | May 7, " . |
| Nolan, Rosanna......... | Rumford, East Providence... | 16 | Sept. 3, " . |
| Holloway, Mary Ellen.... | Central Falls............ .... | 15 | Oct. 20, 1884. |
| Herzog, Ernest J. H.. ... | Providence ............ | 17 | March 10, 1885. |
| Walker, Mabel...... ... | " ............... | 18 | Jan. 6, 1886. |
| Beauchesne, Alphonse... | Central Falls............ | 13 | Oct. 25, " |
| Sullivan, Nellie......... | Newport .................. | 10 | Nov. 12, " . |
| Grant, Edith............ | Providence .............. | 7 | Dec. 13, " . |
| Cole, Luella.......... | South Scituate............ | 10 | March 28, 1887. |
| Chevers, C. Herbert..... | Providence............... | 11 | April 26, " . |
| Jacques, George A...... | Pawtucket................ | 11 | May 11, " . |
| Cove, Margaret. ....... | Woonsocket.... ........... | 11 | Sept. 5, " |
| Green, Sarah........ .. | Hope .................... | 15 | " 12, " . |
| Francis, Manuel......... | Bristol.................... | 11 | " 26, " . |
| Balch, Grace A........ | East Providence Centre...... | 13 | Oct. 10, " . |
| Reynolds, Ella E ...... | Providence.... ............ | 19 | Dec. 4, " |
| Canning, Thomas F..... | Woonsocket........... .. | 9 | Sept. 3, 1888. |
| Hackett, Clara L....... | Providence............... | 7 | " 20, " . |
| Trudell, Albertina....... | Warren ................ .. | 11 | Nov. 14, " . |
| Gill, Eva G............ | Providence.......... ...... | 8 | Dec. 10, " . |
| Goldenofsky, Moses...... | Woonsocket............. | 7 | April 29, 1889. |
| Dolan, Peter......... ... | Providence............ .. | 9 | June 1, " . |
| Hackett, Laura.......... | " ............... | 5 | Nov. 11, " . |
| Dumais, Leander.... ... | Central Falls ............. | 10 | May 7, 1890. |
| Maker, Dora C......... | Providence............ .. | 7 | " 19, " . |
| Egan, Frederick........ | | 8 | Sept. 1, " . |
| Fletcher, Henrietta M.... | Harris, Coventry........... | 7 | " 1. " |
| Poulin, R. Delima....... | Woonsocket.... ........... | 17 | " 15, " |
| Hudson, Alice.......... | Providence .............. | 27 | " 24, " . |
| Duhamel, M. Alma.. ... | Woonsocket ...... ... ... | 11 | Oct. 8, " . |
| Baillergeron, Joseph..... | " ............... | 8 | " 8, " . |
| Dyson, Ethel........... | Providence............... | 6 | " 23, " . |
| Trudeau, Leonel,....... | Woonsocket............ | 9 | Nov. 19, " . |
| O'Brien, William T..... | Providence .. ............ | 9 | Dec. 1, " . |

## FOR THE DEAF FOR THE YEAR ENDING DECEMBER 31, 1890.

| CAUSE OF DEAFNESS, AS FAR AS KNOWN. | AGE WHEN MADE DEAF. (Approx.) | REMARKS. |
|---|---|---|
| Scarlet fever.................... | 5 years, 8 months . | .................... |
| Scarlet fever.................... | 5 years........... | .................... |
| Brain fever..................... | 2 years, 2 months. | .................... |
| Scarlet fever.................... | 6 years, 10 months | .................... |
| Congenital...................... | | |
| Scarlet fever.................... | About 5 years .... | Nearly blind. |
| Congenital, or illness at 3 months | .................... | Slight degree of hearing. |
| Chronic Inflammation of throat . | { Discovered in her third year. | { Slight degree of hearing. |
| Scarlet fever.................... | 9 weeks........... | |
| Scarlet fever.................... | { Discovered at the age of 5. | { .................... |
| Congenital...................... | .................... | Previously taught in a German School. |
| Scarlet fever.................... | 3 years........... | .................... |
| Scarlet fever.................... | 4 years........... | .................... |
| Scarlet fever.................... | 2 years........... | .................... |
| Tumor in ears................... | 6 months.......... | .................... |
| Congenital...................... | | |
| Brain fever..................... | 6 months.......... | Slight degree of hearing. |
| Meningitis...................... | 2 years, 6 months. | .................... |
| Fever........................... | 2 years........... | .................... |
| Scarlet fever.................... | 2 years........... | |
| Typhoid fever................... | 3 years, 6 months. | |
| Scarlet fever.................... | 6 years........... | { Hard of hearing. Attending for speech reading only. |
| Scarlet fever.................... | 9 years........... | Hard of hearing. |
| Congenital...................... | | |
| Congenital...................... | .................... | Hard of hearing |
| Paralysis....................... | 3 years........... | .................... |
| Scarlet fever................... | 5 years........... | .................... |
| Scarlet fever................... | 3 years........... | .................... |
| Humor.......................... | 3 years........... | Hard of hearing |
| Congenital...................... | | |
| Typhoid fever................... | 4 years........... | .................... |
| Scarlet fever................... | 3 years........... | Hard of hearing. |
| Meningitis...................... | 7 years........... | .................... |
| Congenital...................... | | |
| Inflammation of brain.......... | 1 year........... | |
| Measles........................ | 4 years........... | |
| Scarlet fever................... | | |
| Congenital...................... | | |
| Congenital...................... | | Hard of hearing. |
| Congenital...................... | | |
| Run over....................... | | Hard of hearing. |

## SUMMARY.

Number of pupils from date of opening the school, April 2, 1877,
  to Dec. 31, 1889.................................................

Number of pupils who have entered the school since Dec. 31,
  1889 ........................................................

Whole number who have attended the school............
Number who have left the school.......................

Number of pupils Dec. 31, 1890.............................

Number of girls who have attended school during the year......
  "    boys    "      "      "      "      "    .......

Whole number of pupils during the year...............
Average attendance ................................. 27
Number congenitally deaf, or made deaf before the age of two...
Number who lost hearing between the ages of two and four.....
Number who lost hearing after the age of four, and doubtful cases.

—

Number who have any degree of hearing....................

*Residences of all who have attended during the year 1890.*

Providence, including Wanskuck..ι.............  ............
Rumford, East Providence ...............................
East Providence.........  .........  ...........................  ...
Pawtucket.......  ........................................
Central Falls ........................................
Valley Falls.........  ............  ...........  ........
South Scituate..............  ..........  ..............
Lonsdale................................................

The year just closed has been in many respects successful. The number of pupils at the time of the last report
was thirty; eleven have since been admitted, a much larger
number than in any previous year. In the spring two of
the older girls left school. One removed from town, and
the other, whom we had boarded in a private family for
some months, went home and was taken out of school.
She is now at the Clarke Institution in Northampton, having been sent there by a friend of our school because it
seemed advisable for her to be in a boarding school. The
blind, deaf and dumb girl and one other have not returned
because they had become tired of the long rides in the cars.
You will please bear in mind the strain upon these children,
especially the smaller ones, from these long journeys in the
cars, and we have six who come *regularly* from Woonsocket.

The number now present in school is thirty-six, and two
more are expected to return after the holidays. Notwithstanding the care taken in following up slight clues, there
are indications that there are a number of deaf children in the State unknown to us. The attendance has been
very regular and the progress made by the pupils very

2

gratifying. Conscientious and careful labor on the part of the teachers has met with good results.

We feel that the classes are in better condition for work than last year, as they have again been re-graded. Our aim is to have but one grade in a class. We have not been able to secure it in all the classes, but we are working toward that end. We teach all our pupils to speak and to read the speech of others from their lips, but we must first teach those who come to us as deaf mutes the use of ordinary language. In March, Miss Laura A. Wheaton resigned her position, and Miss Fannie D. Gladding was appointed to fill the vacancy; and Miss Clara F. Robinson has charge of the drawing, which was for two years under the charge of Miss Abbie M. White, teacher of drawing in the public schools of Providence.

Two pupils go regularly to the Rhode Island Hospital for treatment. One of the boys continues his lessons at the R. I. School of Design, and in wood carving at the Friends' School, and we hope by the sale of the articles he makes there that he will be able to pay his tuition, which has formerly been paid by a friend. As time passes we see more and more the need of a home, or boarding school, where the boys can receive manual training, and the girls be instructed in house-work and sewing. The sewing class, started a year ago, has been, as far as could be expected, a success. But we must consider how little can be done in sewing in less than two hours a week. These pupils need systematic instruction in an industrial as well as educational department, and had we them constantly with us they could

receive such instruction daily. Another loud call for a
boarding school is that we may care for our own at home,
and not be obliged to call upon private generosity to send
pupils to other institutions. At present four pupils are
boarded at the Children's Home on Tobey street, and
another is expected at the beginning of the year. If we
could but have the constant oversight of these children we
might serve them much better than we are now doing and
extend our influence greatly.

Our thanks are gratefully tendered the Children's Mission
for shoes; the Mt. Pleasant King's Daughters for clothing;
Mrs. Wm. Gammell for a box of oranges; His Excellency,
Gov. Davis, for bananas; Mr. Balch for ice cream, and to
our many friends for the kind interest they have taken in
the school.

### PERIODICALS.

The receipt of the following periodicals is thankfully acknowledged, and their continuance respectfully requested.

Mute's Companion, Faribault, Minn.; Daily Paper for
Our Little People, Rochester, N. Y.; "Our Children's
School Journal", The Deaf Mute Journal, New York;
Maryland Bulletin, Frederick, Md.; The Deaf Mute Voice,
Jackson, Miss.; Kentucky Deaf Mute, Danville, Ky.; The
Goodson Gazette, Staunton, Va.; Kansas Star, Olathe, Kan-
sas; Deaf Mute Optic, Little Rock, Ark.; Deaf Mute In-
dex, Colorado Springs, Col.; Juvenile Ranger, Austin,
Texas; The Register, Rome, N. Y.; Nebraska Mute Jour-
nal, Omaha, Neb.; New Method for the Deaf, Englewood,

Ill.; Weekly News, Berkeley, Cal. We also thank Miss Jeanie Lippitt for furnishing us Harper's Weekly, Mrs. H. B. Gardner for one year of St. Nicholas, The Century Co. for back numbers of the Century magazine.

Periodicals provided for the School:

For the teachers; The Annals for the Deaf, The Silent Educator. For the pupils; Harper's Young People, Our Little Men and Women, The Pansy, Wide Awake, Our Little Ones.

### LIPPITT FUND PRIZES.

#### *Articulation.*

| | |
|---|---|
| Mary Swift, | Ernest Herzog, |
| Alphonse Beauchesne, | Herbert Chevers, |
| Ina Moon, | Eva Gill. |

#### *Lip Reading.*

| | |
|---|---|
| Mary Swift, | Luella Cole, |
| Abbie Woodley, | Clara Hackett, |
| Ina Moon, | Nellie Sullivan. |

#### *Language.*

| | |
|---|---|
| Grace Balch, | Ernest Herzog, |
| Mary Swift, | Luella Cole, |
| Mary Holloway, | Maggie Cove, |
| Mary Sheldon, | Moses Goldenofsky. |

#### *Penmanship.*

| | |
|---|---|
| Grace Balch, | James Lynch, |
| Mary Sheldon, | Manuel Francis, |
| Lester Brownell, | Edith Grant. |

*Neatness.*

| | |
|---|---|
| Ina Moon, | Lester Brownell, |
| James Lynch, | Mabel Walker, |

Peter Dolan.

*Regular Attendance.*

Sarah Green.

# COURSE OF STUDY.

## KINDERGARTEN

### FIRST YEAR.

    *a.* KINDERGARTEN EXERCISES.

    *b.* ARTICULATION.

    *c.* LANGUAGE.

    *d.* ARITHMETIC.

    *e.* PENMANSHIP.

*a.* Paper cutting and folding; drawing and modeling in clay; designing in shoe pegs; stick laying; embroidery designs sewed on pricked sewing cards; lessons in form and color in all exercises.

*b.* Elements, combinations, simple words and sentences, with reading them from the lips.

*c.* Nouns; objects in class-room, articles of dress, articles of food, different parts of the body, with a limited number of verbs. Adjectives; good, bad, large, small, &c. Personal pronouns.

*d.* Counting and writing numbers, with addition and subtraction to 10.

*e.* Writing on slate and with lead pencil.

## PRIMARY COURSE.

### SECOND, THIRD, AND FOURTH YEARS.

    *a.* ARTICULATION.
    *b.* LANGUAGE.
    *c.* ARITHMETIC.
    *d.* GEOGRAPHY.
    *e.* PENMANSHIP.
    *f.* DRAWING.

*a.* Drill in elements, combinations and words, and reading them from the lips.

*b.* Thorough review of first year work. Nouns and verbs continued. Adjectives continued ; their comparison. Pronouns as in first year, adding myself, himself, herself with the plurals, and the relatives who and which. Adverbs ; not, often, never, &c. Elliptical sentences ; action and picture writing ; journal and letter writing, and simple stories.

*c.* Practical exercises in addition, subtraction, multiplication, and division ; United States currency ; simple fractions.

*d.* School-room, building and yard, city, and a limited knowledge of the State.

*e.* Copy-book writing.

## INTERMEDIATE COURSE.

### FIFTH, SIXTH, AND SEVENTH YEARS.

    *a.* ARTICULATION.
    *b.* LANGUAGE.
    *c.* ARITHMETIC.
    *d.* GEOGRAPHY.
    *e.* HISTORY.
    *f.* PENMANSHIP.
    *g.* DRAWING.
    *h.* CALISTHENICS.

*a.* Drill in elements, combinations, syllables; words and sentences
  continued as in Primary Course.

*b.* Nouns, pronouns, adjectives, adverbs, prepositions and conjunctions continued as in Primary Course. Drill in active and passive voices; action and picture writing; stories from Natural
  History; journal and letter writing.

*c.* Mental and written addition, subtraction, multiplication, and divi-
  ion, with practical examples; United States currency and simple fractions continued.

*d.* City, State, and New England States.

*e.* Simple historical stories in connection with geography.

*f.* Copy-book writing twice a week.

*g.* Object drawing.

### HIGHER COURSE.

EIGHTH, NINTH, AND TENTH YEARS.

  *a.* ARTICULATION.
  *b.* LANGUAGE.
  *c.* ARITHMETIC.
  *d.* GEOGRAPHY.
  *e.* HISTORY.
  *f.* PHYSIOLOGY.
  *g.* PENMANSHIP.
  *h.* DRAWING.
  *i.* CALISTHENICS.

*a.* Drill in difficult combinations and words.

*b.* Composition; journal and letter writing; miscellaneous reading;
  newspapers and magazines; lessons on general subjects.

*c.* Mental, written, and practical.

*d.* Geographical Reader; Manual of Commerce.

*e.* History of the United States; Outline of General History.

*g.* Copy book.

*h.* Free-hand and object drawing and designing.

# TO PARENTS OF DEAF CHILDREN.

This school is for the benefit of children incapacitated through deafness, total or partial, for receiving proper instruction in common schools.

The aim of the school is to teach deaf children to use the English language with the spontaneity, correctness, and enjoyment of *hearing* children as far as this is practicable.

"Without language there can be no thought, no reason;" and as the highest aim of all instruction is the culture of the mental and moral nature in man, our first effort should be to furnish the deaf with a medium through which knowledge can be imparted and obtained. This can be done by signs, by the finger alphabet, and by speech. Our method is the latter, or oral method, by which the deaf can be educated and, at the same time, furnished with the usual and most convenient way of communication in society and in the world at large.

It is very desirable that deaf children be sent to school at as early an age as possible. A parent will be amply repaid for sending a child as young as five or six years, even at some inconvenience.

If a child who has learned to talk is made deaf by disease he should immediately upon his recovery be sent to a school where his speech will be retained, and where he will be taught to understand from the lips.  In such cases it is common to delay so long that serious loss of speech results.

Speech reading is an invaluable acquisition for those who are semi-deaf or even hard of hearing, as well as for those congenitally or totally deaf.

Every effort should be made to encourage the child to retain the use of his voice.  He should be taught to pronounce common words by watching the lip motion and facial expression, or by feeling the muscular action or the breath; but no attempt should be made to teach him *the names* of the letters of the alphabet.

The school hours are from 9 A. M. to 1½ P. M. on every week day, except Saturday.  Open to visitors on Fridays, from 10 to 12.

The next summer vacation will begin Friday, June 26, 1891.  The school will re-open Monday, September 7, 1891.  Tuition is free to residents of this State.  Provision is made for defraying the travelling expenses of indigent pupils.  Application for admission may be made to the Principal at the school, corner Fountain and Beverly streets, or to the Commissioner of Public Schools, 104 North Main Street, Providence, R. I.

# FOURTEENTH ANNUAL REPORT

OF THE

# PRINCIPAL

OF THE

# STATE SCHOOL FOR THE DEAF,

PROVIDENCE, R. I.,

FOR THE

YEAR ENDING DECEMBER 31,

# 1891.

PROVIDENCE:
E. L. FREEMAN & SON, STATE PRINTERS,
1892.

# STATE SCHOOL FOR THE DEAF,

CORNER OF FOUNTAIN AND BEVERLY STREETS,

PROVIDENCE, R. I.

.

UNDER THE SUPERVISION OF THE

# STATE BOARD OF EDUCATION.

His Excellency HERBERT W. LADD, GOVERNOR, *ex-officio,*
PRESIDENT.

His Honor HENRY A. STEARNS, Lieutenant-Governor, *ex-officio.*

| | |
|---|---|
| PERCY D. SMITH, | Chepachet. |
| J. HOWARD MANCHESTER, | Bristol. |
| JOHN E. KENDRICK, | Providence. |
| DWIGHT R. ADAMS, | Centreville. |
| SAMUEL H. CROSS, | Westerly. |
| FRANK E. THOMPSON, | Newport. |

SECRETARY :

THOMAS B. STOCKWELL, Commissioner of Public Schools, *ex-officio.*

PRINCIPAL :

LAURA DE L. RICHARDS.

ASSISTANT TEACHERS :

ARDELIA C. DEWING,   SUSAN E. LITTLEFIELD,
A. EVELYN BUTLER,    FANNIE D. GLADDING.
CLARA F. ROBINSON, Teacher of Drawing.

# REPORT.

*To the Honorable, the State Board of Education:*

GENTLEMEN :—I herewith submit my report for the year ending December 31, 1891.

Respectfully,

LAURA DE L. RICHARDS,

*Principal.*

DECEMBER 31, 1891.

## TABULAR REPORT OF THE PUPILS OF THE STATE SCHOOL

| Name of Pupil. | Residence. | Age. (Approx) | Date of Admission. |
|---|---|---|---|
| Sheldon, Mary E........ .... | Providence................. | 23 | Sept.    6, 1880.. |
| Lynch, James E......... | Wanskuck, Providence...... | 16 | Sept.    6, "  .. |
| Swift, Mary E........... | Providence·.............. | 19 | Nov.    2, "  .. |
| White, Sarah .......... | East Providence............ | 21 | Sept.    5, 1881.. |
| Brownell, Lester R...... | Providence. .............. | 16 | June   15, 1882.. |
| Woodley, Abby M...... | "    ................. | 18 | May    7, "  .. |
| Nolan, Rosanna. ..... ... | Rumford, East Providence... | 17 | Sept.    8, "  .. |
| Holloway, Mary Ellen.... | Pawtucket.. .............. | 16 | Oct.   20, 1884.. |
| Herzog, Ernest J. H. .... | Providence................. | 18 | March 10, 1885.. |
| Walker, Mabel........ | "    ................ | 19 | Jan.    6, 1886.. |
| Beauchesne, Alphonse ... | Central Falls............ ... | 14 | Oct.   25,  "  .. |
| Sullivan, Nellie.......... | Newport.................. | 11 | Nov.   12, "  .. |
| Grant, Edith............ | Providence ............... | 8 | Dec.   13, "  .. |
| Cole, Luella............ · | South Scituate. ............ | 11 | March 28, 1887.. |
| Chevers, C. Herbert...... | Providence................ | 12 | April  26, "  .. |
| Jacques, George A...... | Pawtucket ................. | 12 | May   11, "  .. |
| Cove, Margaret.... ... | Woonsocket............... | 12 | Sept.    5, "  .. |
| Green, Sarah... ......... | Hope ..................... | 16 | Sept.   12, "  .. |
| Francis, Manuel.... ... | Bristol.................... | 12 | Sept.   26, "  .. |
| Balch, Grace A ......... | East Providence Centre...... | 14 | Oct.   10,  "  .. |
| Canning, Thomas F.. ... | Woonsocket................ | 10 | Sept.    3, 1888.. |
| Hackett, Clara L......... | Providence............. ... | 8 | Sept.   20.  "  .. |
| Trudell, Albertina...... | Warren.................... | 12 | Nov.   14,  "  .. |
| Gill, Eva G............ | Providence................ | 9 | Dec.   10, "  .. |
| Goldenofsky, Moses...... | Woonsocket............... | 8 | April  29, 1889.. |
| Dolan, Peter. ......... ... | Providence.. .............. | 10 | June    1, "  .. |
| Hackett, Laura.......... | Providence................ | 6 | Nov.   11, "  .. |
| Dumais, Leander ....... | Central Falls............... | 11 | May    7, 1890.. |
| Maker, Dora C......... | Providence................ | 8 | May   19, "  .. |
| Egan, Frederick....... | " | 9 | Sept.    1, "  .. |
| Fletcher, Henrietta M.... | Harris, Coventry.... .... | 8 | Sept.    1, "  .. |
| Duhamel, M. Alma. ..... | Woonsocket ............ | 12 | Oct.    8, "  .. |
| Baillargeron, Joseph..... | "    ................ | 9 | Oct.    8, "  .. |
| Dyson, Ethel............ | Providence................ | 7 | Oct.   23, "  .. |
| Trudeau, Leonel.... ..... | Woonsocket............... | 10 | Nov.   19, "  .. |
| O'Brien, William T....... | Providence................ | 10 | Dec.   11, "  .. |
| Lese, Edwin G..... .... | "    ................ | 9 | Feb,    2, 1891.. |
| Beatty, John ............ | "    ................ | 10 | April  27, "  .. |
| Courtemanche, Henry.... | Woonsocket............... | 10 | June   10, "  .. |
| Staunton, Annie L........ | Providence........... ... | 10 | Sept.    8, "  .. |
| Staunton, Bertha ..... | "    ................ | 6 | Oct.    5, "  .. |
| Marsh, James. ..... ... | "    ................ | 14 | Oct.   19, "  .. |
| Gay, Frederick .........| | "    ................ | 6 | Nov.    9, "  .. |

FOR THE DEAF FOR THE YEAR ENDING DECEMBER 31, 1891.

| Cause of Deafness as far as Known. | Age when made Deaf. (Approx.) | Remarks. |
|---|---|---|
| Scarlet fever................... | 5 years........... | ............................ |
| Brain fever...... ............. | 2 years, 2 months.. | ............................ |
| Scarlet fever...... .......... | 6 years, 10 months. | ............................ |
| Lung fever.... ............... | 2 years, 6 months.. | ............................ |
| Congenital........ ...... ..... | ............. | ............................ |
| Chronic inflammation of throat. | Discovered in her third year. | Slight degree of hearing. |
| Scarlet fever................ | 9 weeks........... | ............................ |
| Scarlet fever................ | Discovered at the age of 5. | ............................ |
| Congenital................ | ................... | Previously taught in a German School. |
| Scarlet fever... ......... ..... | 3 years........... | ............................ |
| Scarlet fever......... .. ... | 4 years........... | ............................ |
| Scarlet fever................ | 2 years........... | ............................ |
| Tumor in ears..... ... ....... | 6 months....... ... | ............................ |
| Congenital................. | ................... | |
| Brain fever................ | 6 months. ....... | Slight degree of hearing. |
| Meningitis........ .... ......... | 2 years, 6 months. | ............................ |
| Fever...... .... ...... ........ | 2 years........... | ............................ |
| Scarlet fever................ | 2 years... ...... | ............................ |
| Typhoid fever........ ........ | 3 years, 6 months | |
| Scarlet fever................... | 6 years........... | Hard of hearing. Attending for speech reading only. |
| Congenital................. | .. ........... | ............................ |
| Congenital............. ... | ................... | Hard of hearing. |
| Paralysis.... .. ......... | 3 years.. ....... | ............................ |
| Scarlet fever................. | 5 years..... ...... | .. ..... ................. |
| Scarlet fever................. | 3 years........... | ............................ |
| Humor................... | 3 years........... | Hard of hearing. |
| Congenital................ | ................... | ............................ |
| Typhoid fever... ........ | 4 years.. ... | ............................ |
| Scarlet fever................ | 3 years.. ......... | Hard of hearing. |
| Meningitis................ | 7 years........... | ............................ |
| Congenital................ | .............. | ............................ |
| Scarlet fever................ | .............. | ............................ |
| Congenital............. | .............. | ............................ |
| Congenital............ ... | .............. | Hard of hearing. |
| Congenital............ | .............. | ............................ |
| Run over.... ............... | .............. | Hard of hearing. |
| Unknown ................ | 4 years........... | Hard of hearing. |
| Congenital................ | ... | ............................ |
| Congenital................ | | ............................ |
| Brain fever................... | 1 year........... | Hard of hearing. |
| Brain fever................... | 3 years. ... | ............................ |
| A fall................ | 6 years........... | Hard of hearing. |
| Scarlet fever .. ............. | 3 years............ | ............................ |

# SUMMARY.

Number of pupils from date of opening the school, April 2, 1877,
  to Dec. 31, 1890........................................  90
Number of pupils who have entered the school since Dec. 31,
  1890....................................................   8
                                                           ———
       Whole number who have attended the school..........  98
       Number who have left the school....................  58
                                                           ———
Number of pupils Dec. 31, 1891...........................  40
                                                           ———
Number of girls who have attended school during the year.....  23
  "        boys    "         "       "       "       "     ....  20
                                                           ———
       Whole number of pupils during the year............  43
       Average attendance................................  26
Number congenitally deaf, or made deaf before the age of two..  16
Number who lost hearing between the ages of two and four.....  15
Number who lost hearing after the age of four, and doubtful cases.  12
                                                           ———
                                                           43
Number who have any degree of hearing ...................  11

*Residences of all who have attended during the year 1891.*

Providence, including Wanskuck......  ....................  23
Rumford, East Providence.................................   1
East Providence..........................................   2
Pawtucket ...............................................   2
Central Falls............................................   2
South Scituate...........................................   1
Newport..................................................   ▲

We have had but few changes during the past year. We move on quietly, but our growth is steady. School opened Sept. 8th with thirty-four pupils, and four others returned later, one a girl from East Providence who had remained at home more than three years. Five new pupils have entered. Three pupils have left since the opening of school, so that our number at present is forty in regular attendance—twenty-two girls and eighteen boys. With few exceptions the attendance has been very regular, and the general health good.

During the past two years we have regraded the classes and are enabled thereby to do much better work. The progress made throughout the school the past year has been greater than ever before, and each year will enable us to classify more closely and work more systematically.

In this school, as in schools for hearing children, it is desirable that there should be uniformity of instruction throughout the school. During the first year much time is given to voice culture. In singing the placing of the voice is considered very essential, but how much more essential that the speaking voice be so placed as to render it pleasant and agreeable! What can be more disagreeable than a harsh, high pitched voice?

Voice culture continues during the entire course, but unless a child is taught properly the first three or four years it will be utterly impossible to form correct speech as he advances. While developing the voice much time is given to language writing. Great care should be taken in preparing language lessons for beginning children. We should teach language that will be of practical value to the children in their daily life. The first few years are devoted to this work, as language is by far the most important study for our pupils. If properly taught, when fairly started they will be capable of advancing like hearing children.

But one change has occurred in our corps of instructors. Miss Emma F. Dunlop, who had been connected with the school as teacher about six years, resigned her position last June to be married, and Miss Susan E. Littlefield, a teacher of long experience, was appointed to fill the vacancy. This is as it should be, because when teachers come to us from other schools new ideas are advanced and new methods introduced.

An association was formed last year, called the American Association to Promote the Teaching of Speech to the Deaf, with Dr. A. Graham Bell, who presented the association with $25,000 as a fund, as president. It purposes to hold meetings every summer and discuss methods of instruction, and have classes taught articulation. The first meeting was held at Lake George, from July 1st until the 10th, which was very successful. Many interesting papers were read, great interest shown and benefit derived. I am very glad to say one of our number, Miss Littlefield, was present.

After the appropriation for buildings was passed, we hoped they would be ready for occupancy by this time, as we have always felt that much better work could be done with the children under our immediate care, but at present we are unable to say when they will be completed.

We have one pupil at the Rhode Island Hospital under treatment. One of the boys still continues his lessons at the Rhode Island School of Design and in wood carving at the Friends' School. By the sale of articles made there last year, he received enough to pay his tuition and took a nice sum home to his father. Three pupils are at present boarded at the Children's Home, Tobey street.

Our thanks are gratefully tendered Mrs. Adnah Sackett, the Mt. Pleasant King's Daughters, and Mrs. H. F. Lippitt, for clothing; and Mrs. Wm. Gammell for a box of oranges.

### PERIODICALS.

The receipt of the following periodicals is thankfully acknowledged, and their continuance respectfully requested:

Mute's Companion, Faribault, Minn.; Daily Paper for Our Little People, Rochester, N. Y.; Our Children's School Journal, The Deaf Mute Journal, New York; Maryland Bulletin, Frederick, Md.; The Deaf Mute Voice, Jackson, Miss.; Kentucky Deaf Mute, Danville, Ky.; The Goodson Gazette, Staunton, Va.; Kansas Star, Olathe, Kansas; Deaf Mute Optic, Little Rock, Ark.; Deaf Mute Index, Colorado Springs, Col.; Juvenile Ranger, Austin, Texas; The Register, Rome, N. Y.; Nebraska Mute Journal, Omaha, Neb.; New Method for the Deaf, Englewood,

2

Ill.; Weekly News, Berkeley, Cal. We also thank Miss Jeanie Lippitt for furnishing us Harper's Weekly.

Periodicals provided for the school:

For the teachers; The Annals for the Deaf, The Silent Educator. For the pupils; Harper's Young People, Our Little Men and Women, The Pansy, Wide Awake, Our Little Ones.

### LIPPITT FUND PRIZES.

*Articulation.*

| | |
|---|---|
| Mary Swift, | Herbert Chevers, |
| Abbie Woodley, | Eva Gill, |
| Ernest Herzog, | Moses Goldenofsky. |

*Lip Reading.*

| | |
|---|---|
| Mary Swift, | Maggie Cove, |
| Sarah Green, | Alma Duhamel. |

*Language.*

| | |
|---|---|
| Grace Balch, | Leon Dumais, |
| Albertina Trudell, | Luella Cole. |

*Penmanship.*

| | |
|---|---|
| Mary Sheldon, | Edith Grant, |
| Sarah Green, | Alma Duhamel, |
| Moses Goldenofsky. | |

*Regular Attendance.*

| | |
|---|---|
| Sarah Green, | Lester Brownell, |
| James Lynch, | Alphonse Beauchesne. |

# COURSE OF STUDY.

## KINDERGARTEN.

### FIRST YEAR.

*a.* KINDERGARTEN EXERCISES.

*b.* ARTICULATION.

*c.* LANGUAGE.

*d.* ARITHMETIC.

*e.* PENMANSHIP.

*a.* Paper cutting and folding; drawing and modeling in clay; designing in shoe pegs; stick laying; embroidery designs sewed on pricked sewing cards; lessons in form and color in all exercises.

*b.* Elements, combinations, simple words and sentences, with reading them from the lips.

*c.* Nouns; objects in class-room, articles of dress, articles of food, different parts of the body, with a limited number of verbs. Adjectives; good, bad, large, small, &c. Personal pronouns.

*d.* Counting and writing numbers, with addition and subtraction to 10.

*e.* Writing on slate and with lead pencil.

## PRIMARY COURSE.

### SECOND, THIRD, AND FOURTH YEARS.

    *a.* ARTICULATION.
    *b.* LANGUAGE.
    *c.* ARITHMETIC.
    *d.* GEOGRAPHY.
    *e.* PENMANSHIP.
    *f.* DRAWING.

*a.* Drill in elements, combinations and words, and reading them from the lips.

*b.* Thorough review of first year work. Nouns and verbs continued. Adjectives continued; their comparison. Pronouns as in first year, adding myself, himself, herself with the plurals, and the relatives who and which. Adverbs; not, often, never, &c. Elliptical sentences; action and picture writing; journal and letter writing, and simple stories.

*c.* Practical exercises in addition, subtraction, multiplication, and division; United States currency; simple fractions.

*d.* Schoolroom, building and yard, city, and a limited knowledge of the State.

*e.* Copy-book writing.

## INTERMEDIATE COURSE.

### FIFTH, SIXTH, AND SEVENTH YEARS.

    *a.* ARTICULATION.
    *b.* LANGUAGE.
    *c.* ARITHMETIC.
    *d.* GEOGRAPHY.
    *e.* HISTORY.
    *f.* PENMANSHIP.
    *g.* DRAWING.
    *h.* CALISTHENICS.

*a.* Drill in elements, combinations, syllables; words and sentences continued as in Primary Course.

*b.* Nouns, pronouns, adjectives, adverbs, prepositions and conjunctions continued as in Primary Course. Drill in active and passive voices; action and picture writing; stories from Natural History; journal and letter writing.

*c.* Mental and written addition, subtraction, multiplication, and division, with practical examples; United States currency and simple fractions continued.

*d.* City, State, and New England States.

*e.* Simple historical stories in connection with geography.

*f.* Copy-book writing twice a week.

*g.* Object drawing.

## HIGHER COURSE.

### EIGHTH, NINTH, AND TENTH YEARS.

*a.* ARTICULATION.
*b.* LANGUAGE.
*c.* ARITHMETIC.
*d.* GEOGRAPHY.
*e.* HISTORY.
*f.* PHYSIOLOGY.
*g.* PENMANSHIP.
*h.* DRAWING.
*i.* CALISTHENICS.

*a.* Drill in difficult combinations and words.

*b.* Composition; journal and letter writing; miscellaneous reading; newspapers and magazines; lessons on general subjects.

*c.* Mental, written, and practical.

*d.* Geographical Reader; Manual of Commerce.

*e.* History of the United States; Outline of General History.

*g.* Copy-book.

*h.* Free-hand and object drawing and designing.

# TO PARENTS OF DEAF CHILDREN.

This school is for the benefit of children incapacitated through deafness, total or partial, for receiving proper instruction in common schools.

The aim of the school is to teach deaf children to use the English language with the spontaneity, correctness, and enjoyment of *hearing* children as far as this is practicable.

"Without language there can be no thought, no reason;" and as the highest aim of all instruction is the culture of the mental and moral nature in man, our first effort should be to furnish the deaf with a medium through which knowledge can be imparted and obtained. This can be done by signs, by the finger alphabet, and by speech. Our method is the latter, or oral method, by which the deaf can be educated and, at the same time, furnished with the usual and most convenient way of communication in society and in the world at large.

It is very desirable that deaf children be sent to school at as early an age as possible. A parent will be amply repaid for sending a child as young as five or six years, even at some inconvenience.

:hild who has learned to talk is made d(
should immediately upon his recovery b
where his speech will be retained, and wh
;ht tô understand from the lips.   In sucl
n to delay so long that serious loss of spee
ech reading is an invaluable acquisition for
mi-deaf or even hard of hearing, as well a
nitally or totally deaf.

ery effort should be made to encourage tl
i the use of his voice.   He should be taug
ce common words by watching the lip u
l expression, or by feeling the muscular act
th; but no attempt should be made to teac
les of the letters of the alphabet.

:he school hours are from 9 A. M. to 1½ P. M
ik-day, except Saturday.   Open to visitors o
n 10 to 12.

The next Summer vacation will begin Friday
½. The school will re-open Monday, Sep
½. Tuition is free to residents of this State.
ude for defraying the travelling expenses o
ila.   Application for admission may be me
cipal at the school, corner Fountain and Bever
the Commissioner of Public Schools, 104 ı
t, Providence, R. I.

# FIFTEENTH ANNUAL REPORT

OF THE

# PRINCIPAL

OF THE

# ATE SCHOOL FOR THE DEAF,

PROVIDENCE. R. I.

FOR THE

## YEAR ENDING DECEMBER 31,

## 1892.

PROVIDENCE:

E. L. FREEMAN & SON, PRINTERS TO THE STATE.

1893.

# FIFTEENTH ANNUAL REPORT

OF THE

# PRINCIPAL

OF THE

# STATE SCHOOL FOR THE DEAF,

PROVIDENCE. R. I.

FOR THE

YEAR ENDING DECEMBER 31,

# 1892.

PROVIDENCE:

E. L. FREEMAN & SON, PRINTERS TO THE STATE.

1893.

# STATE SCHOOL FOR TI

## CORNER OF FOUNTAIN AND BEVERLY

### PROVIDENCE, R. I.

#### UNDER THE SUPERVISION OF TI

# STATE BOARD OF ED

---

His Excellency D. Russell Brown, Governor

PRESIDENT.

His Honor Melville Bull, Lieutenant-Governo

Percy D. Smith, . . . . .
J. Howard Manchester, . . .
John E. Kendrick, . . .
Dwight R. Adams, . . . .
Samuel H. Cross, . . .
Frank E. Thompson, . . . .

---

SECRETARY :

Thomas B. Stockwell, Commissioner of Public

---

PRINCIPAL :

Laura De L. Richards.

---

ASSISTANT TEACHERS :

Annie C. Allen,
Fannie D. Gladding,

Bessie L. Nixon.

# REPORT.

—  ·  —

*To the Honorable, the State Board of Education:*

GENTLEMEN:—I herewith submit my report for the year
ending December 31, 1892.

Respectfully,

LAURA De L. RICHARDS,

*Principal.*

DECEMBER 31, 1892.

## TABULAR REPORT OF THE PUPILS OF THE STATE SCHOOL

| Name of Pupil. | Residence. | Age. (Approx.) | Date of Admission. |
|---|---|---|---|
| Lynch, James E. . . . . . | Wanskuck, Providence...... | 17 | Sept. 6, 1880.. |
| Swift, Mary E........... | Providence ................ | 20 | Nov. 2, " .. |
| White, Sarah........ ... | East Providence............ | 22 | Sept. 5, 1881.. |
| Brownell, Lester R...... | Providence... . ......... | 17 | June 15, 1882.. |
| Woodley, Abby M...... | " ................ | 14 | May 7, " .. |
| Nolan, Rosanna........ | Rumford, East Providence... | 18 | Sept. 8, " .. |
| Holloway, Mary Ellen... | Pawtucket........ ........ | 17 | Oct. 20, 1884.. |
| Herzog, Ernest J. H.... | Providence ................ | 19 | March 10, 1885.. |
| Walker, Mabel ........ | " .... ....... | 20 | Jan. 6, 1886.. |
| Beauchesne, Alphonse... | Central Falls............. | 15 | Oct. 25, " .. |
| Sullivan, Nellie ........ | Newport............. ...... | 12 | Nov. 12, " .. |
| Grant, Edith............ | Providence ............... | 9 | Dec. 13, " .. |
| Cole, Luella..... ..... | South Scituate..... ...... | 12 | March 28, 1887.. |
| Chevers, C. Herbert..... | Providence ...... ...... | 13 | April 26, " .. |
| Jacques, George A....... | Pawtucket ............. | 13 | May 11, " .. |
| Cove, Margaret ........ | Woonsocket ............. | 13 | Sept. 5, " .. |
| Green, Sarah.......... .. | Hope..... ............... | 17 | Sept. 12, " .. |
| Francis, Manuel....... | Bristol ... ............... | 13 | Sept. 26, " .. |
| Balch, Grace A........ | East Providence Centre...... | 15 | Oct. 10, " .. |
| Canning, Thomas F. .. | Woonsocket ........ .... | 11 | Sept. 3, 1888.. |
| Hackett, Clara L... .. | Providence.......... | 9 | Sept. 20, " .. |
| Trudell, Albertina...... | Warren..... ............ | 13 | Nov. 14, " .. |
| Gill, Eva G ... ...... | Providence..... ........ | 10 | Dec. 10, " .. |
| Goldenofsky, Moses. ... | Woonsocket ............. | 9 | April 29, 1889.. |
| Hackett, Laura........ | Providence ......... ... | 7 | Nov. 11, " .. |
| Dumais, Leander........ | Central Falls............ | 12 | May 7, 1890.. |
| Maker, Dora C ....... | Providence ............ .... | 9 | May 19, " .. |
| Egan, Frederick... ..... | " ................ | 10 | Sept. 1, " .. |
| Fletcher, Henrietta M.... | Harris, Coventry............ | 9 | Sept. 1, " .. |
| Duhamel, M. Alma...... | Woonsocket .. ......... | 13 | Oct. 8, " .. |
| Baillargeron, Joseph..... | " ............ | 10 | Oct. 8, " .. |
| Dyson, Ethel.... ...... | Providence. ......... ..| 8 | Oct. 23, " .. |
| Trudeau, Leonel. ...... | Woonsocket ... ...... | 11 | Nov. 19, " .. |
| O'Brien, William T.. ... | Providence............. | 11 | Dec. 1, " .. |
| Lese, Edwin G......... | " .... ......... | 10 | Feb. 2, 1891.. |
| Beatty, John ......... | " ............ | 11 | April 27, " .. |
| Courtemanche, Henry... | Woonsocket ............. | 11 | June 10, " .. |
| Staunton, Annie L....... | Providence ............ | 11 | Sept. 8, " .. |
| Staunton, Bertha ...... | " ............ | 7 | Oct. 5, " .. |
| Gay, Frederick. .. | " ............ | 7 | Nov. 9, " .. |
| Jermyn, William........ | Newport............ ...... | 9 | May 5, 1892.. |
| Goodspeed, Bertha...... | Providence ................ | 19 | { Readmitted } { Oct. 1, 1892 } |
| Reynolds, Ella E........ | Cranston.... ... ........ | 20 | Dec. 5. " .. |

## FOR THE DEAF FOR THE YEAR ENDING DECEMBER 31, 1892.

| CAUSE OF DEAFNESS AS FAR AS KNOWN. | AGE WHEN MADE DEAF. (Approx.) | REMARKS. |
|---|---|---|
| Brain fever | 2 years, 2 months | |
| Scarlet fever | 6 years, 10 months | |
| Lung fever | 2 years, 6 months | |
| Congenital | | |
| Chronic inflammation of throat. | { Discovered in her third year. | } Slight degree of hearing. |
| Scarlet fever | 9 weeks | |
| Scarlet fever | { Discovered at the age of 5. | } |
| Congenital | | } Previously taught in a German School. |
| Scarlet fever | 3 years | |
| Scarlet fever | 4 years | |
| Scarlet fever | 2 years | |
| Tumor in ear | 6 months | |
| Congenital | | |
| Brain fever | 6 months | Slight degree of hearing. |
| Meningitis | 2 years, 6 months | |
| Fever | 2 years | |
| Scarlet fever | 2 years | |
| Typhoid fever | 3 years, 6 months | |
| Scarlet fever | 6 years | { Hard of hearing. Attending for speech reading only. |
| Congenital | | |
| Congenital | | Hard of hearing. |
| Paralysis | 3 years | |
| Scarlet fever | 5 years | |
| Scarlet fever | 3 years | |
| Congenital | | |
| Typhoid fever | 4 years | |
| Scarlet fever | 3 years | Hard of hearing. |
| Meningitis | 7 years | |
| Congenital | | |
| Scarlet fever | | |
| Congenital | | |
| Congenital | | Hard of hearing. |
| Congenital | | |
| Run over | | Hard of hearing. |
| Unknown | 4 years | Hard of hearing. |
| Congenital | | |
| Congenital | | |
| Brain fever | 1 year | Hard of hearing. |
| Brain fever | 3 years | |
| Scarlet fever | 3 years | |
| Congenital | | |
| Scarlet fever | | |
| Scarlet fever | | Hard of hearing. |

## SUMMARY.

Number of pupils from date of opening the school, April 2, 1877, to Dec. 31, 1892... ...................... .........    98

Number of pupils who have entered the school since Dec. 31, 1891................................................    1

         Whole number who have attended the school........ ...    99

         Number who have left the school............ .......    61

Number of pupils Dec. 31, 1892 .........................    38

Number of girls who have attended school during the year.....    24

     "      boys    "      "      "    "    "    - ...    19

         Whole number of pupils during the year..... .......    43

         Average attendance...... .............. ..........29.4

Number congenitally deaf, or made deaf before the age of two.    17

Number who lost hearing between the ages of two and four....    13

Number who lost hearing after the age of four, and doubtful cases...................... ...................... .....    13

                                                        43

Number who have any degree of hearing................,........    10

*Residences of all who have attended during the year 1892.*

Providence, including Wanskuck............................    21

Rumford, East Providence............. ..............    1

East Providence........... ... ................. .......    2

Pawtucket.... ................................. ........    1

Central Falls................................ ...............    2

South Scituate...................... ....................    1

Newport........................ .................. .......    2

Centreville.......... ......... .... ...................    1

During the year just closed forty-three pupils have received instruction. There has been a marked improvement in attendance this year, the average attendance being 29.4. School opened late in September, therefore the pupils were slow in returning. There are at present forty in regular attendance, twenty-one boys and nineteen girls. The older pupils have all returned, and take greater interest in the school than ever before. The classes are very satisfactorily graded and we hope to show much better results at the close of this school year.

The same system of instruction has been pursued as in former years and the progress made is gratifying.

As new pupils came in it became evident that another teacher was needed, and Miss Harriet C. Hall was appointed teacher the first of last January. We note two changes in the corps of instructors. Miss Littlefield, who was not strong, failed in health, and resigned her position. Miss Bessie L. Nixon was appointed to fill the vacancy. In the spring Miss Dewing, who had been connected with the school for many years, resigned and Miss Annie C. Allen, a teacher of experience from the Milwaukee Day School for the Deaf, was appointed in her place.

> the appointment of inexperienced teachers, I
dvisable to give a course of instruction in Bell's
ech and the method employed in this school of
the deaf. I, therefore, gave two lessons a week,
1 Thursday afternoons, from the first of October
st of May, to all the teachers employed in the

erican Association for Promoting the Teaching
o the Deaf held its second meeting, of ten days,
orge the last few days of June and the first of
I was very successful. The attendance was large
terest great. There were lectures on the vocal
Dr. Allen, and on the ear by Dr. Hewson, both
ysicians of Philadelphia. The lectures were very
and instructive. Another attractive feature of
rs was the very interesting instruction given by
iam Bell, of Washington, D. C., in the mechanism
very afternoon. There was also a practice class,
are shown pupils from different schools, and the
instruction employed. Great benefit was de-
these meetings, and I am glad to report that all
s in this school were in attendance.
ils are at present boarded, at the expense of the
c Children's Home, Tobey street.
y tender thanks to Miss Jeanie Lippitt, Mrs. H.
and Mrs. Wm. Gammell, Jr. for kindly remem-
children with presents, candies, and oranges, last
also, to Mrs. H. F. Lippitt, Mrs. A. L. Mason,
iends for clothing.

## PERIODICALS.

The receipt of the following periodicals is t
knowledged, and their continuance respectful
Mute's Companion, Faribault, Minn.; Dai
Our Little People, Rochester, N. Y.; O
School Journal, The Deaf Mute Journal,
Maryland Bulletin, Frederick, Md.; The Deaf
Jackson, Miss.; Kentucky Deaf Mute, Danvill
Goodson Gazette, Staunton, Va.; Kansas .
Kansas; Deaf Mute Optic, Little Rock, Ark.
Index, Colorado Springs, Col.; Juvenile Ra
Texas; The Register, Rome, N. Y.; Nebrask;
nal, Omaha, Neb.; New Method for the Deaf
Ill.; Weekly News, Berkeley, Cal. We als(
Jeanie Lippitt for furnishing us Harper's Wee

Periodicals provided for the school :

For the teachers; The Annals for the Dea
Educator. For the pupils; Harper's Young
Little Men and Women, The Pansy, Wide
Little Ones.

## LIPPITT FUND PRIZES.

### *Articulation.*

| | |
|---|---|
| Ernest Herzog, | Alma Duha |
| James Lynch, | Leonel Trud |
| Fred Egan, | John Beatty, |

Henry Courtemanche.

Owing to the appointment of inexperienced teachers, I deemed it advisable to give a course of instruction in Bell's Visible Speech and the method employed in this school of instructing the deaf. I, therefore, gave two lessons a week, Monday and Thursday afternoons, from the first of October until the first of May, to all the teachers employed in the school.

The American Association for Promoting the Teaching of Speech to the Deaf held its second meeting, of ten days, at Lake George the last few days of June and the first of July, which was very successful. The attendance was large and the interest great. There were lectures on the vocal organs by Dr. Allen, and on the ear by Dr. Hewson, both eminent physicians of Philadelphia. The lectures were very interesting and instructive. Another attractive feature of the meetings was the very interesting instruction given by Dr. A. Graham Bell, of Washington, D. C., in the mechanism of speech, every afternoon. There was also a practice class, in which were shown pupils from different schools, and the methods of instruction employed. Great benefit was derived from these meetings, and I am glad to report that all the teachers in this school were in attendance.

Four pupils are at present boarded, at the expense of the State, at the Children's Home, Tobey street.

We gladly tender thanks to Miss Jeanie Lippitt, Mrs. H. F. Lippitt, and Mrs. Wm. Gammell, Jr. for kindly remembering the children with presents, candies, and oranges, last Christmas; also, to Mrs. H. F. Lippitt, Mrs. A. L. Mason, and other friends for clothing.

## PERIODICALS.

The receipt of the following periodicals is thankfully acknowledged, and their continuance respectfully requested: Mute's Companion, Faribault, Minn.; Daily Paper for Our Little People, Rochester, N. Y.; Our Children's School Journal, The Deaf Mute Journal, New York; Maryland Bulletin, Frederick, Md.; The Deaf Mute Voice, Jackson, Miss.; Kentucky Deaf Mute, Danville, Ky.; The Goodson Gazette, Staunton, Va.; Kansas Star, Olathe, Kansas; Deaf Mute Optic, Little Rock, Ark.; Deaf Mute Index, Colorado Springs, Col.; Juvenile Ranger, Austin, Texas; The Register, Rome, N. Y.; Nebraska Mute Journal, Omaha, Neb.; New Method for the Deaf, Englewood, Ill.; Weekly News, Berkeley, Cal. We also thank Miss Jeanie Lippitt for furnishing us Harper's Weekly.

Periodicals provided for the school:

For the teachers; The Annals for the Deaf, The Silent Educator. For the pupils; Harper's Young People, Our Little Men and Women, The Pansy, Wide Awake, Our Little Ones.

### LIPPITT FUND PRIZES.

#### *Articulation.*

| | |
|---|---|
| Ernest Herzog, | Alma Duhamel, |
| James Lynch, | Leonel Trudeau, |
| Fred Egan, | John Beatty, |

Henry Courtemanche.

## *Lip Reading.*

| | |
|---|---|
| Grace Balch, | Luella Cole, |
| Abbie Woodley, | Dora Maker, |
| Bertie Trudell, | Ethel Dyson, |
| Willie O'Brien, | Henry Courtemanche, |

John Beatty.

## *Language and Penmanship.*

| | |
|---|---|
| Mary Swift, | Rosa Nolan, |
| Maggie Cove, | Willie O'Brien, |
| ·Ethel Dyson, | George Jacques. |

## *Attendance.*

| | |
|---|---|
| Alphonse Beauchesne, | Sarah Green, |
| Lester Brownell, | James Lynch. |

State of Rhode Island and Providence Pl

'REPORT

OF THE

BOARD OF TRUSTE

OF THE

RHODE ISLAND

STITUTE FOR THE

PRESENTED TO THE

GENERAL ASSEMB

AT ITS

JANUARY SESSION, 1894.

---

PROVIDENCE:

E. L. FREEMAN & SON, STATE PRINT

1894.

be taught to understand from the lips. In such cases it is common to delay so long that serious loss of speech results.

Speech reading is an invaluable acquisition for those who are semi-deaf or even hard of hearing, as well as for those congenitally or totally deaf.

Every effort should be made to encourage the child to retain the use of his voice. He should be taught to pronounce common words by watching the lip motion and facial expression, or by feeling the muscular action or the breath; but no attempt should be made to teach him *the names* of the letters of the alphabet.

This school no longer exists as a day school, but has been merged into the Rhode Island Institute for the Deaf, and will be conducted as a boarding home and school. Application for admission should be made to the Principal at the Institute, corner of East Avenue and Cypress Street, Providence.

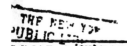

**State of Rhode Island and Providence Plantations.**

# REPORT

OF THE

# BOARD OF TRUSTEES

OF THE

# RHODE ISLAND

# STITUTE FOR THE DEAF,

PRESENTED TO THE

# GENERAL ASSEMBLY.

## JANUARY SESSION, 1891

State of Rhode Island and Providence Plantations.

# REPORT

OF THE

## BOARD OF TRUSTEES

OF THE

## RHODE ISLAND

# INSTITUTE FOR THE DEAF,

PRESENTED TO THE

## GENERAL ASSEMBLY,

AT ITS

## JANUARY SESSION, 1894.

- - -

PROVIDENCE:

E. L. FREEMAN & SON, STATE PRINTERS.

1894.

# REPORT.

*To the Honorable the General Assembly at its January Session, A. D. 1894:*

The undersigned Board of Trustees of the Rhode Island Institute for the Deaf, beg leave to make the following report, in accordance with the provisions of Chapter 922 of the Public Laws.

The original appropriation of the sum of fifty thousand dollars ($50,000) for construction was increased last year by the additional sum of four thousand dollars ($4,000).

The objects for which said appropriation was made have been substantially accomplished. In addition to minor improvements, two new and much needed servants' rooms have been finished in the attic of the main building; suitable fire escapes have been erected; hose has been supplied to connect with the stand pipes in the building; electric fire alarms have been placed in the main building and connected with an alarm box of the city fire alarm system attached to the front of the building; additional plumbing has been put in, and all has been adapted to meet the most modern requirements of scientific sanitary knowledge relating thereto. Additional furniture and books, to a limited extent, have been purchased. It might be proper to add here that valuable books and pictures have also been donated by friends of the Institute, for which proper acknowledgment has been made by vote of the Board.

Lockers and clothes closets have also been built to meet needed requirements. A new steam and hot water heater has been placed in the School building; slate blackboards have also been put up in the several school-rooms. The grounds have been graded and seeded down, and the whole surrounded by a comely and substantial picket fence painted to harmonize with the general surroundings.

There are no other imperative demands in the line of construction which may not be met from the regular appropriation for the maintenance account, and the Board, therefore, for the present, at least, think it best to close the construction account.

The Institute was formally dedicated by appropriate exercises, on the 21st of February last, the School having been opened some weeks prior thereto. Since that time the School has met the reasonable expectation of its friends, and may now be said to be in successful operation.

The School opened with 38 pupils, but the number enrolled increased to 51 before the close of the year. It is probable that the number of pupils may be still further increased during the ensuing year.

The School is in charge of a very efficient and experienced Principal in the person of Miss Laura De L. Richards, assisted by a competent body of teachers, supervisors and subordinates.

The following is a list of the present force employed at the Institute, and their respective salaries:

| | | |
|---|---|---:|
| Miss L. De L. Richards, principal............. ........ | Per annum, $1,200 00 |
| Miss F. D. Gladding, teacher.......................... | " | 450 00 |
| Miss A. E. Butler, teacher ........................... | | 450 00 |
| Miss H. C. Hall, teacher ............................. | | 350 00 |
| Miss B. L. Nixon, teacher............................ | | 350 00 |
| Miss A. W. Ely, teacher ............................. | | 250 00 |
| Miss M. A. L. Smith, teacher ........................ | | 250 00 |
| Miss F. G. Smith, supervisor......................... | " | 100 00 |
| One attendant and chamber girl......................Per month, | | 16 00 |
| One housekeeper..................................... | " | 25 00 |
| One assistant.........................................Per week, | | 2 50 |
| One cook............................................. | " | 5 00 |
| One laundress .............. .................Per month, | | 16 00 |
| One seamstress.............. ................... | " | 12 00 |
| One chamber girl..................................... | | 15 00 |
| One table girl ........... ........................ | | 15 00 |
| One scrubber................................ .......... | | 13 00 |
| One janitor............... ......................... | | 30 00 |

The sum of fifteen thousand dollars ($15,000) was appropriated last year for maintenance. By a careful attention to details, and by certain economies introduced in the purchase of supplies, the Board have been able to carry the School through the fiscal year just passed for the sum of $12,320.28, according to the Auditor's statement, thus covering into the Treasury the sum of $2,679.72. This balance, however, is apparent rather than real, for certain bills amounting to the sum of $985.66 properly chargeable to last year's account the Board were unable to get rendered in season to be audited, and which are therefore charged to the appropriation for the ensuing year, and will make the new appropriation available to the School this year less by just that amount.

It will be seen by reference to the foregoing tabulated statement, that the salary list, reckoning 40 weeks per school year, for some of the subordinates, amounts to the sum of five thousand two hundred and thirty dollars ($5,230.00), which shows that the other current expenses for maintenance amounted to the sum of eight thousand eighty-five dollars and ninety-four cents ($8,085.94).

The salary list as before stated cannot be reduced for the current year, but will rather be increased, particularly if additional teachers or subordinates are needed, and the other current expenses for maintenance, assuming an increased number of pupils, will necessarily be somewhat larger. The Board therefore respectfully ask that fifteen thousand dollars ($15,000.00) be appropriated for the maintenance of the School for the ensuing year.

The Board have received applications from pupils residing out of the State. One such pupil has been admitted to the Institute, the charge being fixed at the rate of two hundred and seventy-five dollars ($275.00) per year.

The Board have held regular meetings once each month during the year, and special meetings as occasion required.

The work of the Board has been conscientious and harmonious, and they have the satisfaction of feeling that the School is now well established and is doing an excellent service for the pupils and with ultimate beneficial results to the State.

After due consideration the Board believe that some simple and inexpensive forms of manual training can be introduced into the School with benefit to the older pupils—thus tending to enable them to be self supporting after they have finished their studies.

For further details as to the organization, conduct and status of the School, reference may be made to the report of the Principal which is hereto appended and made a part of this report.

Respectfully submitted,

D. RUSSELL BROWN, *Governor*,
MELVILLE BULL, *Lieutenant-Governor*,
*Members ex-officio.*
DANIEL B. POND, *President*,
HENRY F. LIPPITT, *Secretary*,
MRS. JEANIE L. WEEDEN,
DR. ROWLAND R. ROBINSON.
MRS. ELLEN T. McGUINNESS,
WILLIAM K. POTTER,
HOWARD SMITH,
MRS. LILLIE B. CHACE WYMAN,
MARSDEN J. PERRY,
*Board of Trustees.*

PROVIDENCE, R. I., January, 1894.

# FIRST ANNUAL REPORT

OF THE

# PRINCIPAL

OF THE

# RHODE ISLAND INSTITUTE FOR THE DEAF,

PROVIDENCE, R. I.

FOR THE

## YEAR ENDING DECEMBER 31,

## 1893.

# REPORT.

*To the Honorable the Board of Trustees of the Rhode Island Institute for the Deaf:*

GENTLEMEN :—I respectfully submit the following report for the year ending December 31, 1893 :

At the beginning of the year, January 1, 1893, we entered our new and commodious buildings and became a Boarding school with thirty-eight pupils in attendance, twenty boys and eighteen girls. Soon, before we were settled and ready to admit them, new pupils began to apply for admission, and before the close of the June term eleven were added to our number. Since the opening of the September term ten more have been admitted, making twenty-one during our first year here. The number enrolled during the year was fifty-eight ; seven have left, which leaves fifty-one in regular attendance. The average daily attendance was forty.

February twenty-first the buildings were dedicated and formally opened, when Governor Brown, with a large number of the members of the General Assembly and many other distinguished personages, were present.

The exercises were very appropriate and interesting. We listened to addresses made by Governor Brown, Mayor D. B. Pond of Woonsocket, President of the Board of Trustees, President Andrews of Brown University, and others, after which a collation was served ; then the guests inspected the buildings and visited the classes, and expressed themselves as much pleased with our new buildings, and with the work done here.

While changing from a Day to a Boarding school, work went on with but little interruption, and in this short time we can see the advantage of the change, the pupils are learning *how* to study and are becoming studious and more orderly. Language is acquired from the effort of the child to put his thoughts into words, and our great aim is to cultivate the habit of speech and the habit of reading. As this is purely an oral school, we teach speech and by speech only.

The school is delightfully situated in the most healthful part of the city, with spacious play grounds; the class-rooms are light and airy, and everything possible is done to add to the happiness and well-being of the pupils.

Shortly after the opening of the school in the new buildings, a case of scarlet fever appeared, which under the watchful care of the attending physician was confined to the one case, and shortly after there was one case of measles. Death has taken one of our number. A new pupil—a bright little fellow—had whooping cough when he was brought to us; he was taken back home and died of diphtheria before fully recovering from the first disease. Several cases of whooping cough appeared which have entirely recovered. Aside from these cases the health of the pupils has been good.

The household affairs have required considerable attention, which must always be the case when opening a new building.

The selection of assistants in all the different departments requires great care, and I can say that in this we have been very fortunate; all strive to do their best and work for the good of others.

The girls are taught sewing and they are able to do what sewing is required for the Institute. I hope that soon some industrial training will be given the boys, too. If they could be taught the Sloyd system even the smallest of the children might learn the use of tools. A shoe shop where all the mending of the children's shoes could be done, and where some might be taught the trade; and a carpenter shop and glass setting would be of use to them. It is of great importance that pupils of proper age be taught some line of daily employment, so that they may acquire habits of industry and be able to do some kind of work well, that they may gain an honest living.

As our school increased in numbers it became necessary to increase our teaching staff and Miss Alice W. Ely, a supervisor, was added to the number. At the close of school Miss Anna C. Allen left us and Miss Marie A. L. Smith was appointed teacher.

At the close of school, for the Christmas holidays, the children were made bright and happy by a beautiful Christmas tree and a visit from Santa Claus, when each pupil received both useful presents, toys and candy, by contributions from Mrs. E. D. McGuinness, Mr. Marsden J. Perry, Mr. and Mrs. W. B. Weeden, Mr. Geo. Woodley and Mrs. W. Gammell, Jr. Mr. Joseph Balch very kindly and ably personated Santa Claus, much to the amusement of the little ones who have great faith in their yearly visitor.

Our thanks are very gratefully tendered Miss Adeline Brown for some fine photographs framed; Mrs. W. B. Weeden for a set American Cyclopedia; Mrs. E. D. McGuinness and Mrs. J. C. Wyman for books for the children's library; the Misses Weeden for toys, and Mrs. W. Gammell for a box of fine oranges.

Respectfully,

LAURA DE L. RICHARDS,
*Principal.*

PROVIDENCE, January, 1894.

## TABULAR REPORT OF THE PUPILS OF THE SCHOOL

| NAME OF PUPIL. | RESIDENCE. | AGE. (Approx.) | DATE OF ADMISSION. |
|---|---|---|---|
| Lynch, James E......  .. | Wanskuck, Providence...... | 18 | Sept.   6, 1880.. |
| Swift, Mary E......  .. | Providence.....  ......  ... | 21 | Nov.   2,  "  .. |
| Brownell, Lester R.. .. | " | 18 | June  15, 1882.. |
| Nolan, Rosanna. ....... | Rumford, East Providence.. | 19 | Sept.   3,  "  .. |
| Holloway, Mary Ellen .. | Pawtucket......  ........ | 18 | Oct.  20, 1884.. |
| Herzog, Ernest J. H.  . | Providence.....  ...  .. | 20 | March 10, 1885.. |
| Beauchesne, Alphonse... | Central Falls......... .. | 16 | Oct.  25, 1886.. |
| Sullivan, Nellie.. .. .... | Newport ....  ......  ... | 13 | Nov.  12,  "  .. |
| Grant, Edith .......... | Providence.......... | 10 | Dec.  13,  "  .. |
| Cole, Luella. .. .. ...... | South Scituate.. .  ........ | 12 | March 28, 1887.. |
| Chevers, C. Herbert..... | Providence.....  ... .. | 14 | April  26,  "  .. |
| Jacques, George A..... | Pawtucket............... | 14 | May  11,  "  .. |
| Cove, Margaret.. ...... | Providence.  .......... | 13 | Sept.   5,  "  .. |
| Green, Sarah ......... | Hope. .............. | 18 | Sept.  12,  "  .. |
| Francis, Manuel........ | Bristol.. ............... | 14 | Sept.  26,  "  .. |
| Canning, Thomas F..... | Woonsocket ...  ....... | 12 | Sept.   3, 1888.. |
| Hackett, Clara L ...... | Providence............ .. | 10 | Sept.  20,  "  .. |
| Trudell, Albertina....... | Warren ...  .  ... .. | 14 | Nov.  14,  "  .. |
| Gill, Eva G............ | Providence............ | 10 | Dec.  10,  "  .. |
| Goldenofsky, Moses. | Woonsocket ..  ... .. .. | 10 | April  29, 1889.. |
| Hackett, Laura.......... | Providence.......... .. | 8 | Nov.  11,  "  .. |
| Dumais, Leander.. ..... | Central Falls.. .  ..... | 13 | May   7, 1890.. |
| Maker, Dora C ....... | Providence............ | 10 | May  19,  "  .. |
| Egan, Frederick........ | " | 11 | Sept.   1,  "  .. |
| Fletcher, Henrietta M.... | Harris, Coventry .  ....... | 10 | Sept.   1,  "  .. |
| Baillargeron, Joseph .. | Woonsocket........... | 11 | Oct.   8,  "  .. |
| Dyson, Ethel........ .. | Providence.... ...  ... | 9 | Oct.  23,  "  .. |
| Trudeau, Leonel ..... | Woonsocket........... | 12 | Nov.  19,  "  .. |
| O'Brien, William T..... | Providence............ | 12 | Dec.   1,  "  .. |
| Lese, Edwin G ........ | " | 11 | Feb.   2, 1891.. |
| Beatty, John.......... | " | 12 | April  27,  "  .. |
| Courtemanche, Henry... | Woonsocket........... | 12 | June  10,  "  .. |
| Staunton, Annie L .... | Providence.....  ...  ... | 12 | Sept.   8,  "  .. |
| Staunton, Bertha....... | " | 8 | Oct.   5,  "  .. |
| Gay, Frederick......... | " | 8 | Nov.   9,  "  .. |
| Jermyn, William ...... | Newport....  ...  ..... | 10 | May   5, 1892.. |
| Goodspeed, Bertha...... | Providence............ | 20 | { Readmitted } { Oct.   1, 1892 } |
| Mills, Annetta ........ | " | 6 | April  3, 1893.. |
| Rankin, George C... . | " | 18 | Jan.   3,  "  .. |
| Carr, David.... ...... | Pawtucket.. .......... | 6 | Jan.  27,  "  .. |
| Collins, Chester A...... | Providence............ | 4 | Jan.  30,  "  .. |
| Kleber, Fannie ..... .. | Lymansville ........... | 6 | Feb.   7,  "  .. |
| Mercier, Addie C........ | Shannock ..  .  ........ | 10 | Feb.   7,  "  .. |
| Goldstein, Clara J...... | Providence............ | 9 | March  1,  "  .. |
| Edwards, Guy C .. ..... | Plainfield, Conn........ ... | 5 | March  6,  "  .. |

## FOR THE YEAR ENDING DECEMBER 31, 1893.

| Cause of Deafness as far as Known. | Age when made Deaf. (Approx.) | Remarks. |
|---|---|---|
| Brain fever.. ... ............ | 2 years, 2 months | ....... .. .. ............ |
| Scarlet fever ... .. .......... | 6 years, 10 months | .... .. ............... |
| Congenital ... .. ........... | ..................... | ........... . ........... |
| Scarlet fever .. ....... ...... | 9 weeks.... ..... | ...... ... ... ... ... ... |
| Scarlet fever.... ...... ..... | { Discovered at the age of 5. | } ...................... |
| Congenital......... .. ..... | ..................... | } Previously taught in a German School. |
| Scarlet fever ... ..... ...... | 4 years ... ....... | ...... ................... |
| Scarlet fever ... .......... | 2 years ....... .. | ................ .. ... ... |
| Tumor in ear..... .. ..... .. | 6 months.... .. | ...................... |
| Congenital..................... | ..................... | ...................... |
| Brain fever............. .. .... | 6 months .. ... | Slight degree of hearing. |
| Meningitis ... .. ........... ... | 2 years, 6 months. | ...................... .. |
| Fever..... ............... ... | 2 years ........... | ...................... |
| Scarlet fever .. ........... .... | 2 years ........... | ...................... |
| Typhoid fever.... ... ...... | 3 years, 6 months. | ....... .. ....... |
| Congenital..................... | ..................... | ........................ . |
| Congenital..................... | ... ............. .. | Hard of hearing. |
| Paralysis. ..................... | 3 years......... | ...................... |
| Scarlet fever.................... | 5 years....... ... | ...................... |
| Scarlet fever... ..... .. ... | 3 years......... | ...................... |
| Congenital ..................... | ..................... | ...... .. ........... .. |
| Typhoid fever..... ........... | 4 years ......... | ...................... |
| Scarlet fever..... ........... | 3 years ... ....... | Hard of hearing. |
| Meningitis.................. .. | 7 years ......... | ...................... |
| Congenital..................... | ..................... | ...................... |
| Congenital..................... | ..................... | ...................... |
| Congenital..................... | ............ ... ... | Hard of hearing. |
| Congenital..................... | .... ...... ... | ...... ............ |
| Run over....................... | ...... ........ | Hard of hearing. |
| Unknown........ ......... ... | 4 years ........ | Hard of hearing. |
| Congenital ......... ........ | .. .. .... ... | ...................... |
| Congenital ..... .............. | . ... ... ... | ...................... |
| Brain fever..... ... ......... | 1 year.. .. ...... | Hard of hearing. |
| Brain fever..................... | 3 years ......... | ... ....... ............ |
| Scarlet fever........ ......... | 3 years.... ...... | ................ ....... . ... |
| Congenital.......... .. ..... | ..................... | ...................... |
| Scarlet fever ..... .......... | ........ ...... . | ................. ...... |
| Measles .................... | 3 years ......... | ...... ....... ... ... |
| ........................ ......... | .... ....... .... | Not deaf. |
| A fall........ ........... ... | 2 years ...... | ...................... |
| Measles ....... .............. | 2 years.......... | ...................... |
| Congenital..................... | ...... ...... .. | Deafness partial. |
| Scarlet fever.................. | 5 years ...... .. | ...................... |
| Typhoid fever................. | 4 years .. ....... | ...... ................... |
| Congenital..... .............. | ........... ...... | .... ............ ....... |

## TABULAR REPORT OF THE PUPILS OF THE SCHOOL

| NAME OF PUPIL. | RESIDENCE. | AGE. (Approx.) | DATE OF ADMISSION. |
|---|---|---|---|
| Desonle, Maggie ... .. | Lippitt. ... ........... .... | 8 | March 23, 1893. |
| Smith, Bernard F....... | Providence. .. ..... ... .. | 8 | April 10, " . |
| O'Conner, Mary........ | Slatersville.... ..... ........ | 6 | May 27, " . |
| Hœn, Alfred........... | . ............. ..... | | Sept. 11, " . |
| Lawton, William C.. .. | Providence. .. ... .. .... | 5 | Sept. 11, " . |
| Knowles, Grace E ..... | South Kingstown........ .. | 4 | Sept. 11, " . |
| Mowary, Melton R ..... | Pawtucket .. .. ........... | 4 | Sept. 11, " . |
| Chace, Emma E.... ... | Providence. ...... ....... .. | 15 | Sept. 11, " . |
| Thompson, George...... | " | 4 | Sept. 11, " . |
| Pulsifer, M. Hellen .... | Cranston... ..... ....... | 8 | Sept. 11, " . |
| Savard, Mary C. S. S.... | Woonsocket.. . .......... | 12 | Sept. 11, " . |
| Davis, Lillian I.. .. .... | Providence. .. ..... ...... | 6 | Sept. 11, " |
| Cole, Egbert T........ | South Scituate.. ........ - | 20 | { Readmitted Jan. 2, 1893 |

FOR THE YEAR ENDING DECEMBER 31, 1893.—*Continued.*

| CAUSE OF DEAFNESS AS FAR AS KNOWN. | AGE WHEN MADE DEAF. (Approx.) | REMARKS. |
|---|---|---|
| Congenital ... .. ... ...... | ..... .......... | ...... ......... .. ...... |
| ............ .. .... ..... | .... .. ....... | Not deaf. |
| Scarlet fever ... .. .. ........... | 1 year .. ..... | ..... ......... ........ |
| A fall. ........ ......... .. | 2 years. ... ... .. | Deafness partial. |
| Congenital.................... | ..... ......... | ......... ............. |
| Grippe. ....... .. .... ... | 2 years. .. ...... | ... ......... .. .... ... |
| Measles. ........... .......... | 2 years. .. ... | ..... ......... ...... |
| .... ....... ........ | ... .. .. .. | } Not deaf.  Impediment in speech. |
| Convulsions. ......... ..... | 3 years.... .. .. | ............... .......... |
| Measles....... .. . ...... | 6 years.... .. .. | ................. ....... |
| Congenital.................. .. | ...... .......... | ......... ......... ...... |
| Measles ...... .............. | 2 years..... ..... | Partial deafness. |
| Congenital ................. | ..... .......... | .......... .... ......... |

## SUMMARY.

Number of pupils from date of opening the State school for the deaf,
    April 2, 1877, to Dec. 31, 1893. ..,....... ....... ............. 118
Number of pupils who have entered the Institute since Dec. 31, 1892.... 21
                                                                        ———

    Whole number who have attended the school.................. 118
    Number who have left the school.......................... 68
                                                                ———

Number of pupils Dec. 31, 1893 ....... ............................ 52
                                                                ———

Number of girls who have attended school during the year......... ... 29
    "       boys    "       "       "       "       "    ... ........ 29
                                                                ———

    Whole number of pupils during the year........... .. ........ 58
    Average attendance ......... .................:..... ....... ... 49.1
Number congenitally deaf, or made deaf before the age of two ..... ... 24
Number who lost hearing between the ages of two and four. ........... 20
Number who lost hearing after the age of four, and doubtful cases.... .. 14
                                                                ———
                                                                    58

Number who have any degree of hearing.......... .................... 18

*Residences of all who have attended during the year 1893.*

Providence, including Wanskuck...................... ................ 29
Rumford, East Providence............................................ 1
Pawtucket......... ................................. .. ... ... ........ 8
Central Falls... ........ ........... .. .. ... ..................... 3
South Scituate..................... ..................... ............ 3
Newport........... ......... ...... .... ... ..................... 2
Centreville.... ........ .......... ........ ...... ............... 1
Lymansville.... .......... ........ ............. ............ .... 1
Shannock ...................... .... ...................... ....... 3
Lippitt ........ ............... . ....... ............... ......... 1
Slatersville............ .......... ........ ......... ............... 1
South Kingstown ........... ... ............ ....................... 1
Cranston.. ......... ....... ... ... ... ... ..................... 1
Woonsocket... ... ........... ... ......... ....... ........ ..... 6

Hope.......... ................................................ ................................ ......  ᴀ

Harris.......... .. ........ .... ................................ .......... ι

Bristol...... ...... .... ...... ............ ...... ... .... .......... ᴀ

Warren........................... .................... ...... ....... ι

Plainfield, Conn.............. ................................ ....... ι

19 localities.............. ........................ ............... 58

### PERIODICALS.

The receipt of the following periodicals is thankfully acknowledged, and their continuance respectfully requested :

Mute's Companion, Faribault, Minn. ; Daily Paper for Our Little People, Rochester, N. Y. ; Our Children's School Journal, The Deaf Mute Journal, New York ; Maryland Bulletin, Frederick, Md. ; The Deaf Mute Voice, Jackson, Miss. ; Kentucky Deaf Mute, Danville, Ky. ; The Goodson Gazette, Staunton, Va. ; Kansas Star, Olathe, Kansas ; Deaf Mute Optic,- Little Rock, Ark. ; Deaf Mute Index, Colorado Springs, Col. ; Juvenile Ranger, Austin, Texas ; The Register, Rome, N. Y. ; Nebraska Mute Journal, Omaha, Neb. ; New Method for the Deaf, Englewood, Ill. ; Weekly News, Berkeley, Cal. We also thank Mrs. Jeanie L. Weeden for furnishing us Harper's Weekly.

Periodicals provided for the school :

For the teachers : The Annals for the Deaf, The Silent Educator. For the pupils ; Harper's Young People, Our Little Men and Women, The Pansy, Wide Awake, Our Little Ones.

### LIPPITT FUND PRIZES AWARDED FOR

*Articulation.*

| | |
|---|---|
| Mary Swift, | Bertha Goodspeed. |
| Fred Egan, | James Lynch, |
| Frank Canning, | John Beattie, |
| Laura Hackett, | Willie Jermyn, |

Fred Gudy.

*Lip Reading.*

| | |
|---|---|
| Alphonse Beauchesne, | Eva Gill, |
| Fred Egan, | Clara Hackett, |
| Lionel Trudeau, | Annie Staunton. |

*Language.*

| | |
|---|---|
| **Mary Swift,** | Eva Gill, |
| Luella Cole, | Lionel Trudeau, |

Willie Jermyn.

*Penmanship.*

| | |
|---|---|
| Bertha Goodspeed, | Sarah Green, |
| **Maggie Cove,** | Edith Grant, |

Etta Fletcher.

# COURSE OF STUDY.

---

## KINDERGARTEN.

### FIRST YEAR.

    *a.* KINDERGARTEN EXERCISES.
    *b.* ARTICULATION.
    *c.* LANGUAGE.
    *d.* ARITHMETIC.
    *e.* PENMANSHIP.

*a.* Paper cutting and folding; drawing and modeling in clay; designing in shoe pegs; stick laying; embroidery designs sewed on pricked sewing cards; lessons in form and color in all exercises.

*b.* Elements, combinations, simple words and sentences; with reading them them from the lips.

*c.* Nouns; objects in class-room, articles of dress, articles of food, different parts of the body, with a limited number of verbs. Adjectives; good, bad, large, small, &c.

*d.* Counting and writing numbers, with addition and subtraction to 10.

*e.* Writing on slate and with lead pencil.

## PRIMARY COURSE.

### SECOND, THIRD, AND FOURTH YEARS.

    *a.* ARTICULATION.
    *b.* LANGUAGE.
    *c.* ARITHMETIC.
    *d.* GEOGRAPHY.
    *e.* PENMANSHIP.
    *f.* DRAWING.

*a.* Drill in elements, combinations and words, and reading them from the lips.

*b.* Thorough review of first year work. Nouns and verbs continued. Adjectives continued; their comparison. Pronouns as in first year, adding myself, himself, herself with the plurals, and the relatives who and which. Adverbs; not, often, never, &c. Elliptical sentences; action and picture writing; journal and letter writing, and simple stories.

*c.* Practical exercises in addition, subtraction, multiplication, and division; United States currency; simple fractions.

*d* School-room, building and yard, city, and a limited knowledge of the State.

*e.* Copy-book writing.

## INTERMEDIATE COURSE.

### FIFTH, SIXTH, AND SEVENTH YEARS.

*a.* ARTICULATION.
*b* LANGUAGE.
*c.* ARITHMETIC.
*d.* GEOGRAPHY.
*e.* HISTORY.
*f.* PENMANSHIP.
*g.* DRAWING.
*h* CALISTHENICS.

*a.* Drill in elements, combinations, syllables; words and sentences continued as in Primary Course.

*b.* Nouns, pronouns, adjectives, adverbs, prepositions and conjunctions continued as in Primary Course. Drill in active and passive voices; action and picture writing; stories from Natural History; journal and letter writing.

*c.* Mental and written addition, subtraction, multiplication, and division, with practical examples; United States currency and simple fractions continued.

*d.* City, State, and New England States.

*e* Simple historical stories in connection with geography.

*f.* Copy-book writing twice a week.

*g.* Object drawing.

## HIGHER COURSE.

### EIGHTH, NINTH, AND TENTH YEARS.

*a.* ARTICULATION.
*b.* LANGUAGE.

    *c.* ARITHMETIC.

    *d.* GEOGRAPHY.

    *e.* HISTORY.

    *f.* PHYSIOLOGY.

    *g.* PENMANSHIP.

    *h.* DRAWING.

    *i.* CALISTHENICS.

*a.* Drill in difficult combinations and words.

*b.* Composition; journal and letter writing; miscellaneous reading; newspapers and magazines; lessons on general subjects.

*c.* Mental, written and practical.

*d.* Geographical Reader; Manual of Commerce.

*e.* History of the United States; Outline of General History.

*g.* Copy book.

*h.* Free-hand and object drawing and designing.

# TO PARENTS OF DEAF CHILDREN.

This school is for the benefit of children incapacitated through deafness, total or partial, for receiving proper instruction in common schools, and is free to all pupils who belong in this State.

The aim of the school is to teach deaf children to use the English language with the spontaneity, correctness, and enjoyment of *hearing* children as far as this is practicable.

"Without language there can be no thought, no reason;" and as the highest aim of all instruction is the culture of the mental and moral nature in man, our first effort should be to furnish the deaf with a medium through which knowledge can be imparted and obtained. This can be done by signs, by the finger alphabet, and by speech. Our method is the latter, or oral method, by which the deaf can be educated, and at the same time, furnished with the usual and most convenient way of communication in society and in the world at large.

It is very desirable that deaf children be sent to school at as early an age as possible. A parent will be amply repaid for sending a child as young as five or six years, even at some inconvenience. The Board of Trustees are authorized to receive pupils between the ages of three and twenty years.

If a child who has learned to talk is made deaf by disease he should immediately upon his recovery be sent to a school where his speech will be retained, and where he will be taught to understand from the lips. In such cases it is common to delay so long that serious loss of speech results.

Speech reading is an invaluable acquisition for those who are semi-deaf or even hard of hearing, as well as for those congenitally or totally deaf.

Every effort should be made to encourage the child to retain the use of his voice. He should be taught to pronounce common words by watching the lip motion and facial expression, or by feeling the muscular action or the breath; but no attempt should be made to teach him *the names* of the letters of the alphabet.

This school no longer exists as a day school, but has been merged into the Rhode Island Institute for the Deaf, and will be conducted as a boarding home and school. Application for admission should be made to the Principal at the Institute, corner of East Avenue and Cypress Street, Providence.

State of Rhode Island and Providence Plantations.

# REPORT

OF THE

## BOARD OF TRUSTEES

OF THE

## RHODE ISLAND

# INSTITUTE FOR THE DEAF,

PRESENTED TO THE

# GENERAL ASSEMBLY,

AT ITS

## JANUARY SESSION, 1895.

PROVIDENCE:
E. L. FREEMAN & SON, PRINTERS TO THE STATE.
1895.

# REPORT OF TRUSTEES.

---

*To the Honorable the General Assembly at its January Session, A. D. 1895:*

The Board of Trustees of the Rhode Island Institute for the Deaf, in compliance with the requirement of the Public Laws, (Chapter 922) herewith respectfully presents its report for the year ending Dec. 31st, 1894.

The usual appropriation of the sum of fifteen thousand dollars ($15,000) was made for the maintenance of the Institute for the current year of 1894, of which amount the sum of $13,428.40 has been expended, and the balance, viz., $1,571.60 has been covered into the Treasury at the expiration of the fiscal year. The additional sum of $265.12 received from tuition and other sources since the opening of the school, has been turned over to the Treasury of the State.

The general expenses for maintenance, exclusive of salaries, have been $7,486.03. For salaries, including all amounts paid the Principal, the teachers, subordinate officials and assistants, the sum of $5,942.37, has been expended.

In its last annual report the Board suggested the advisability of introducing some simple forms of manual training. A committee was appointed to investigate the subject, and after a thorough examination the committee reported in favor of the introduction of sloyd and printing, at an estimated expense of about one thousand dollars ($1,000). The report was adopted by the Board, and, upon request duly presented, the Legislature, at its May Session, promptly appropriated the sum of $1,000 for that purpose.

During the summer vacation suitable rooms and facilities were prepared; sloyd tools, benches, models, etc., for a class of ten pupils at one session, were procured. A bench and tools for ordinary shop carpentering were included. A printing press and general outfit were also added. Expert instructors for the sloyd and printing classes were secured for the opening of the Fall term, and the results of establishing these classes have been entirely satisfactory.

Some radical changes were made in the teaching staff at the beginning of the Fall term and subsequently. All of the teachers of last year were renominated by the Principal, and approved by the Board, but early in the summer vacation, and while the Principal was in Europe, two of the teachers made engagements elsewhere, and, subsequently, before the opening of the Fall term, two other teachers, objecting to a rule of the Board requiring not less than two teachers to be present at the Institute over Sunday, made similar engagements. One other teacher subsequently withdrew. The vacancies were promptly filled, and the Board now feel that the present corps of teachers is fully equal, if not superior, to any that have hitherto been employed.

Entirely harmonious relations now exist between the Principal, the teachers and the pupils, and the work of the Institute is progressing surely and satisfactorily.

The Board considers the Institute fortunate in having an able, experienced and painstaking Principal to take charge of its edcational and administrative affairs.

The present force employed at the Institute and the respective salaries paid is as follows:

| | | |
|---|---|---|
| Miss L. De L. Richards, Principal.............Per annum, | $1,200 | 00 |
| Mrs. Anna C. Hurd, teacher, (first assistant) .... " | 700 | 00 |
| Miss A. Louise Steadman ................... ... | 200 | 00 |
| Miss Florence G. Smith....................... | 200 | 00 |
| Miss Sarah W. Burrill........................ | 200 | 00 |
| Miss Fannie M. Cheney ...................... | 200 | 00 |
| Miss Agnes Murch............................ | 200 | 00 |
| Mr. Richard Almgren, Instructor in Sloyd...... | 300 | 00 |
| Mr. Wm. H. Goodale, Instructor in Printing.... | 300 | 00 |
| One housekeeper............................ | 300 | 00 |
| One attendant (boys)........................Per month, | 18 | 00 |
| One attendant (girls).... ...................... " | 16 | 00 |
| One cook...................................... | 18 | 00 |
| One assistant .............. .. ............... | 12 | 00 |
| One laundress................................ | 20 | 00 |
| One seamstress ... ......................... | 15 | 00 |
| One chamber girl...... ............ .... .. .... | 15 | 00 |
| One table girl........ ..................... ... | 15 | 00 |
| One scrubber................................. | 10 | 00 |
| One janitor......... .................. .... | 30 | 00 |

The Board respectfully ask for the usual annual appropriation for maintenance, viz., the sum of fifteen thousand dollars ($15,000).

There are some things needed annually in the way of furnishings, etc., to make the Institute comfortable and homelike for its inmates, and to keep its supplies good. The Board will endeavor to so adjust the expenses as to enable it to make some modest investments in needed additional furnishings.

Much valuable information is contained in the report of the Principal to the Board, and the same is hereto appended and submitted for inspection.

It will be seen that the health of the pupils, as a whole, has been reasonably good during the year.

Regular Board meetings are held once each month, and members of the Board, individually, have made frequent visits to the Institute in the intervals of the regular meetings.

Respectfully submitted,

D. RUSSELL BROWN, *Governor.*
EDWIN R. ALLEN, *Lieutenant-Governor,*
*Members ex-officio.*

DANIEL B. POND, *President,*
HENRY F. LIPPITT, *Secretary,*
MRS. JEANIE L. WEEDEN,
DR. ROWLAND R. ROBINSON,
MRS. ELLEN T. McGUINNESS,
WILLIAM K. POTTER,
HOWARD SMITH,
MRS. LILLIE B. CHACE WYMAN,
MARSDEN J. PERRY,
*Board of Trustees.*

PROVIDENCE, R. I., January, 1895.

SECOND ANNUAL REPORT

OF THE

PRINCIPAL

OF THE

RHODE ISLAND INSTITUTE FOR THE DEAF,

PROVIDENCE, R. I.,

FOR THE

YEAR ENDING DECEMBER 31,

1894.

# REPORT OF PRINCIPAL.

---

*To the Honorable the Board of Trustees of the Rhode Island Institute for the Deaf:*

GENTLEMEN :—I respectfully submit the following report for the year ending December 31, 1894:

At the beginning of the year, January 1, 1894, there were 51 pupils in attendance—25 girls and 26 boys. Two new pupils were admitted soon after we entered upon the new year. At the close of school June 22d, five pupils were honorably discharged. Three were beyond school age and two wished to engage in work. One pupil partially deaf was withdrawn and sent to a hearing school.

Since the opening of the September term five pupils have been admitted, making seven admitted this year. Average attendance was 51.

There have been two deaths during the year. Guy C. Edwards, a bright little boy of six, went home for the Christmas holidays and was taken ill the day school re-opened and died January 4th of membraneous croup at his home in Plainfield, Conn.

Joseph I. Vient entered January 3d. He was a bright, intelligent young man of nineteen, who had never attended school, but he was anxious to learn and was delighted with each new word or expression given him. His influence over the other boys was remarkably good. But we were to have him with us only a short time. On the 16th of last November he was struck by an electric car and killed while crossing the street in front of his home in Central Falls.

2

of the school has generally been good.   German m

he early spring and there were a number of cases.

f school in September there has been unusual good b

ls of instruction pursued are substantially the same

As this is an oral school, its first object is to he

the habit of speech, so that they will speak readil

speech from their teachers and associates.

is taken in teaching language during the first few

ls may be able to express themselves clearly and i

t they may acquire a desire to read, the sitting-roon

h book-cases provided with books selected especia

of the pupils.  They, are also provided with the

pers published at other institutions for the deaf, and

er Mrs. E. G. Hurd was added to the corps of instru

er of long experience and had been connected wi

School for the Deaf in Philadelphia for a numl

Steadman was for some time a successful teache

l before engaging here.  The class of beginners is

a thoroughly trained kindergartener—Miss March

ars after graduating at one of the leading kinder

city.

t yet been able to reach all the deaf children in the

ntly hearing of new ones, and we ask all friends

f the deaf to report all such cases as come within

the principal of the school.

l is for children incapacitated through deafness, t

eceiving proper instruction in common schools, b

g in some have thus far been fruitless.  Some p

nt to the well being of the deaf child in the family.

et, as some do, to send it to school ?  They are

its hearing brothers and sisters.

rial department has been extended.  In March took

d a shoe shop was fitted up in the basement of the

building. Four boys are taught shoe-making and mending. They are under instruction three afternoons each week, doing all the repairing of the pupils' shoes.

During the summer a Sloyd room was fitted up on the first floor of the school building, with ten benches furnished with tools and models. Ten boys are instructed two afternoons each week by Mr. R. Almgren, an experienced instructor in wood work.

A printing office was fully equipped with a printing press and four cases of type. Six boys are instructed by Mr. W. H. Goodale two afternoons each week. A paper is printed semi-monthly by the pupils. A carpenter shop was also fitted up in the basement of the school-house with a full set of carpenter's tools.

The girls are still taught sewing an hour and a half each day, and they are also taught habits of neatness and industry in the care of their different rooms. We hope soon to add cooking to our list.

On Christmas the children were again delighted by a visit from Santa Claus and their customary Christmas tree. They were bountifully provided with presents, both useful articles and toys, by contributions from Mr. Marsden J. Perry and Mr. and Mrs. W. B Weeden. Mr. Raymer Weeden very successfully personated Santa Claus, giving the children who were expecting him great pleasure. Mrs. E. D. McGuinness presented the school with some fine games, which will be greatly appreciated during the evenings and rainy afternoons.

We gratefully thank Mrs. W. Gammell for a box of oranges, Mrs. C. W. Lippitt for children's clothing, Miss Adeline Brown for stereoscopic pictures, Mrs. W. B. Weeden for stereoscope and pictures, and Miss Carrie Robinson for foreign photos.

Respectfully,

LAURA De. L. RICHARDS,
*Principal.*

PROVIDENCE, January, 1895.

## TABULAR REPORT OF THE PUPILS OF THE SCHOOL

| NAME OF PUPIL. | RESIDENCE. | AGE. (Approx.) | DATE OF ADMISSION. |
|---|---|---|---|
| Lynch, James E | Wanskuck, Providence | 18 | Sept. 6, 1880 |
| Swift, Mary E | Providence | 21 | Nov. 2, 1880 |
| Nolan, Rosanna | Rumford, East Providence. | 19 | Sept. 3, 1882 |
| Herzog, Ernest J. H | Providence | 20 | March 10, 1885 |
| Beauchesne, Alphonse | Central Falls | 16 | Oct. 25, 1886 |
| Sullivan, Nellie | Newport | 13 | Nov. 12, 1886 |
| Grant, Edith | Providence | 10 | Dec. 18, 1886 |
| Cole, Luella | South Scituate | 12 | March 28, 1887 |
| Chevers, C. Herbert | Providence | 14 | April 26, 1887 |
| Jacques, George A. | Pawtucket | 14 | May 11, 1887 |
| Cove, Margaret | Providence | 13 | Sept. 5, 1887 |
| Green, Sarah | Hope | 18 | Sept. 12, 1887 |
| Francis, Manuel | Bristol | 14 | Sept. 26, 1887 |
| Canning, Thomas F | Woonsocket | 12 | Sept. 3, 1888 |
| Hackett, Clara I. | Providence | 10 | Sept. 20, 1888 |
| Trudell, Albertina | Warren | 14 | Nov. 14, 1888 |
| Gill, Eva G | Providence | 10 | Dec. 10, 1888 |
| Goldenofsky, Moses | Woonsocket | 10 | April 29, 1889 |
| Hackett, Laura | Providence | 8 | Nov. 11, 1889 |
| Dumais, Leander | Central Falls | 13 | May 7, 1890 |
| Maker, Dora C. | Providence | 10 | May 19, 1890 |
| Egan, Frederick | Providence | 11 | Sept. 1, 1890 |
| Fletcher, Henrietta M | Harris, Coventry | 10 | Sept. 1, 1890 |
| Baillargeron, Joseph | Woonsocket | 11 | Oct. 8, 1890 |
| Trudeau, Leonel | Woonsocket | 12 | Nov. 19, 1890 |
| O'Brien, William T | Providence | 12 | Dec. 1, 1890 |
| Lese, Edwin G | Providence | 11 | Feb. 2, 1891 |
| Beatty, John | Providence | 12 | April 27, 1891 |
| Courtemanche, Henry | Woonsocket | 12 | June 10, 1891 |
| Staunton, Annie L | Providence | 12 | Sept. 8, 1891 |
| Staunton, Bertha | Providence | 8 | Oct. 5, 1891 |
| Gay, Frederick | Providence | 8 | Nov. 9, 1891 |
| Jermyn, William | Newport | 10 | May 5, 1892 |
| Mills, Annetta | Providence | 6 | April 3, 1893 |
| Carr, David | Pawtucket | 6 | Jan. 27, 1893 |
| Collins, Chester A | Providence | 4 | Jan. 30, 1893 |
| Kleber, Fannie | Lymansville | 6 | Feb. 7, 1893 |
| Mercier, Addie C | Shannock | 10 | Feb. 7, 1893 |
| Goldstein, Clara J | Providence | 9 | March 1, 1893 |
| Desonie, Maggie | Lippitt | 8 | March 23, 1893 |
| Smith, Bernard F | Providence | 8 | April 10, 1893 |
| O'Conner, Mary | Slatersville | 6 | May 27, 1893 |
| Hoen, Alfred | | | Sept. 11, 1893 |
| Knowles, Grace E | South Kingstown. | 4 | Sept. 11, 1893 |
| Chace, Emma E | Providence | 15 | Sept. 11, 1893 |

## FOR THE YEAR ENDING DECEMBER 31, 1894.

| CAUSE OF DEAFNESS, AS FAR AS KNOWN. | AGE WHEN MADE DEAF. (Approx.) | REMARKS. |
|---|---|---|
| Brain fever..................... | 2 years, 2 months. | ......................... |
| Scarlet fever.................. | 6 years. 10 months | .... ..................... |
| Scarlet fever............ ...... | 9 weeks.......... | |
| Congenital..... ............. | | { Previously taught in a German school. |
| Scarlet fever................. | 4 years.......... | ..................... .... |
| Scarlet fever................. | 2 years.......... | .................... ... |
| Tumor in ear ................. | 6 months.......... | ..................... |
| Congenital..................... | | ..................... |
| Brain fever.................... | 6 months.......... | Slight degree of hearing. |
| Meningitis.................... | 2 years, 6 months. | ............. ... ......... |
| Fever......................... | 2 years.......... | |
| Scarlet fever.................. | 2 years... | ..................... .... |
| Typhoid fever................. | 3 years, 6 months. | ..................... |
| Congenital..................... | | ..................... |
| Congenital..................... | | Hard of hearing. |
| Paralysis ..................... | 3 years.......... | |
| Scarlet fever.................. | 5 years.......... | ..................... |
| Scarlet fever.................. | 3 years.......... | ..................... |
| Congenital..................... | | ..................... |
| Typhoid fever................. | 4 years.......... | ..................... |
| Scarlet fever.................. | 3 years.......... | Hard of hearing. |
| Meningitis.................... | 7 years.......... | ..................... .... |
| Congenital..................... | | ..................... |
| Congenital..................... | | |
| Congenital..................... | | ..................... .... |
| Run over...................... | | Hard of hearing. |
| Unknown...................... | 4 years.......... | Hard of hearing. |
| Congenital... ................. | | ..................... |
| Congenital..................... | | ..................... |
| Brain fever.................... | 1 year.......... | Hard of hearing. |
| Brain fever.................... | 3 years.......... | ..................... |
| Scarlet fever.................. | 3 years.......... | ... ..................... |
| Congenital..................... | | ..................... |
| Measles ...................... | 3 years.......... | ..................... |
| A fall.... ..................... | 2 years.......... | . ..................... |
| Measles....................... | 2 years.......... | ..................... |
| Congenital..................... | | Deafness partial. |
| Scarlet fever.................. | 5 years.......... | ..................... |
| Typhoid fever................. | 4 years.......... | ..................... |
| Congenital..................... | | ..................... |
| ...................... ........ | | Not deaf. |
| Scarlet fever.................. | 1 year.......... | ..................... |
| A fall......................... | 2 years.......... | Deafness partial. |
| Grippe........................ | 2 years.......... | ..................... |
| ...................... ........ | | { Not deaf. Impediment in speech. |

TABULAR REPORT OF THE PUPILS OF THE SCHOOL

| NAME OF PUPIL. | RESIDENCE. | AGE. (Approx.) | DATE OF ADMISSION. |
|---|---|---|---|
| Thompson, George........ | Providence............... | 4 | Sept. 11, 1893 . |
| Pulsifer, M. Hellen....... | River Point ............. | 8 | Sept. 11, 1893 . |
| Savard, Mary C. S. S...... | Woonsocket ............. | 12 | Sept. 11, 1893.. |
| Davis, Lillian I........... | Providence............... | 6 | Sept. 11, 1893.. |
| Cole, Egbert T ........... | South Scituate............ | 20 | { Readmitted } Jan. 2, 1893 { |
| Vient, Joseph I........... | Central Falls............. | 19 | Jan. 3, 1894.. |
| Flynn, James............. | Providence............... | 6 | Feb. 3, 1894.. |
| Pease, Walter M........... | Woonsocket........... | 5 | Sept. 10, 1894.. |
| Comfort, Mae E .......... | Newport................. | 8 | Sept. 10, 1894.. |
| Bradley, William H....... | Woonsocket............. | 11 | Oct. 1, 1894 . |
| Mudrak, Willie .......... | Geneva.................. | 4 | Oct. 13, 1894.. |
| Canney, John P .......... | Drownville............... | 9 | Dec. 3, 1894.. |

FOR THE YEAR ENDING DECEMBER 31, 1894.

| CAUSE OF DEAFNESS, AS FAR AS KNOWN. | AGE WHEN MADE DEAF. (Approx.) | REMARKS. |
|---|---|---|
| Convulsions. | 3 years. | |
| Measles. | 6 years. | |
| Congenital. | | |
| Measles | 2 years. | Partial deafness. |
| Congenital. | | |
| Scarlet fever. | 2 years. | |
| Congenital. | | |
| Grippe. | 2 years. | |
| Catarrhal fever. | 1 year, 6 months. | |
| Diphtheria. | 6 years. | |
| Congenital. | | |
| Taking quinine. | 1 year. | |

# SUMMARY.

Number of pupils from date of opening the State school for the deaf,
April 2, 1877, to Dec. 31, 1894..................................... 125

Number of pupils who have entered the Institute since Dec. 31, 1893.... 7

⎯⎯

Whole number of pupils who have attended the school....... ..... 125

Number who have left the school....... ;......................... 73

⎯⎯

Number of pupils Dec. 31, 1894......................................... 51

Number of girls who have attended school during the year.............. 27

Number of boys who have attended school during the year.............. 30

⎯⎯

Whole number of pupils during the year ......................... 57

Average attendance....................................... ................... 51

Number congenitally deaf, or made deaf before the age of two.......... 25

Number who lost hearing between the ages of two and four...... ....... 20

Number who lost hearing after the age of four, and doubtful cases....... 14

⎯⎯

57

Number who have any degree of hearing............... ................ 14

⎯⎯

*Residences of all who have attended during the year 1894.*

Geneva. ......................................................... ........ 1
Providence, including Wanskuck.............................. 27
Rumford, East Providence............................................. 1
Pawtucket.......................................................... 2
Central Falls....................................................... 3
South Scituate....................................................... 2

Newport......,.... ................................................... 3
Lymansville................................ ........................ 1
Shannock ..................................................................... ᴀ
Lippitt.... ......... ...................................................... ᴀ
Slatersville.................................. ........... .. ...... . ᴀ
South Kingstown........................................................ ᴀ
River Point.................... ....................................... ᴀ
Woonsocket...... ..... ................................................ ꜰ
Kenyon ................... ....................................... ᴀ
Hope......................................................................... ᴀ
Harris........................................................................ ᴀ
Bristol ....................................................................... ᴀ
Warren ........................ ........................................ ᴀ
Drownville.................................................................. ᴀ

Twenty-one localities .......................................... 57

## PERIODICALS.

The receipt of the following periodicals is thankfully acknowledged,
and their continuance respectfully requested :

Mute's Companion, Faribault, Minn. ; Daily Paper for Our Little
People, Rochester, N. Y. ; Our Children's School Journal, The Deaf
Mute Journal, New York ; Maryland Bulletin, Frederick, Md. ; The
Deaf Mute Voice, Jackson, Miss. ; Kentucky Deaf Mute, Danville, Ky. ;
The Goodson Gazette, Staunton, Va. ; Kansas Star, Olathe, Kansas ;
Deaf Mute Optic, Little Rock, Ark. ; Deaf Mute Index, Colorado
Springs, Col. ; Juvenile Ranger, Austin, Texas ; The Register, Rome,
N. Y. ; Nebraska Mute Journal, Omaha, Neb. ; New Method for the
Deaf, Englewood, Ill. ; Weekly News, Berkeley, Cal.

Periodicals provided for the school :

For the teachers : The Annals for the Deaf, The Silent Educator.
For the pupils : Harper's Young People, Our Little Men and Women,
The Pansy, Wide Awake, Our Little Ones.

3

LIPPITT FUND PRIZES AWARDED FOR

*Articulation.*

Eva Gill,                              Nellie Sullivan,
Clara Hackett,                         Annie Staunton.

*Lip Reading.*

Stephanie Savard,                      Luella Cole,
Fred Egan,                             Willie O'Brien,
Frank Canning,                         Henry Courtemanche.

*Language.*

Alphonse Beauchesne,                   Lionel Trudeau,
Maggie Cove,                           Addie Mercier.

*General Improvement.*

Bertie Trudel,                         Joseph Vient,
Herbert Chevers,                       Egbert Cole,
Moses Goldenofsky,                     Laura Hackett,
                  Willie Jermyn.

*General Excellence.*

Mary Swift.

# MEDICAL REPORT.

*To the Board of Trustees of the Rhode Island Institute for the Deaf:*

I have the honor to report that, during the year just past, the school has been free from any serious epidemic disease. The successful isolation of a case of whooping cough last spring has again justified your wisdom, when constructing the school building, in providing a hospital practically independent of the rest of the house. In the earlier winter several cases of follicular tonsilitis were treated there. There have been a few cases of German measles. Aside from these, general good health has prevailed, broken by an occasional minor accident or isolated case of illness, always incident to an institution for children. Last spring, by your advice, the school generally was vaccinated ; and in no case was the vaccination attended by any serious undesirable results. Animal virus was used. I want to thank the Principal and her assistants for the most painstaking and efficient way in which every suggestion concerning the care of the health of the pupils has been carried out. In no private home could better nursing and care have been given than has been provided in each case of illness that has occurred in the school this year.

Respectfully submitted,

FRANK L. DAY, M. D.,
*Attendant Physician.*

PROVIDENCE, December 31, 1894.

# FINANCIAL REPORT.

### EXPENDITURES, 1893.

| | |
|---|---:|
| Coal.............................................................. | $1,1( |
| Salaries.......... .. ............................................ | 4,57 |
| Provisions...................................................... | 3,73 |
| Gas.............. .................../........................... | 13 |
| Water.........................:................................. | 18 |
| Improvements and repairs............................. ............ | 2,08 |
| Telephone....................................................... | 8 |
| Medicines and medical attendance... ...... ........ ........... | 28 |
| Advertising..................... ................................ | 3 |
| Miscellaneous................... ................................ .... | 17 |
| Printing and stationery....... .................................. | 8 |
| | $12,4( |

Average attendance 49.1 pupils.

Cost per pupil, $253.78.

### EXPENDITURES, 1894.

| | |
|---|---:|
| Coal............ ................................................ | $78 |
| Salaries........................ ................................ | 5,9; |
| Provisions.......... ...................................... | 3,22 |
| Improvements and repairs...................................... | 2,31 |
| Medicines and medical attendance. ............................. | 28 |
| Advertising................................. .......... | 3 |
| Gas ............................................................. | 31 |
| Water............................................ .. .............. | 18 |

| | | |
|---|---:|---:|
| Telephone............................................................. | 72 | 00 |
| Printing and stationery................................ ........................... | 204 | 40 |
| Fire protection.............................. ..... .......................... | 104 | 25 |
| Miscellaneous........ ....................... ........................ | 122 | 98 |
| | | |
| | $13,532 | 65 |
| Received for tuitions, etc................. ........................ | 265 | 12 |
| | | |
| | $13,267 | 53 |

Average attendance 51 pupils.

Cost per pupil, $260.15.

| | | |
|---|---:|---:|
| Manual Training (special appropriation).... .................. ..... | 986 | 92 |
| | | |
| | $14,254 | 45 |

Total expenditures per pupil, $279.49.

# COURSE OF STUDY.

### KINDERGARTEN.

#### FIRST YEAR.

a. KINDERGARTEN EXERCISES.
b. ARTICULATION.
c. LANGUAGE.
d. ARITHMETIC.
e. PENMANSHIP.

a. Paper cutting and folding; drawing and modeling in clay; designing in pegs; stick laying; embroidery designs sewed on pricked sewing c: lessons in form and color in all exercises.
b. Elements, combinations, simple words and sentences; with reading from the lips.
c. Nouns; objects in class-room, articles of dress, articles of food, diff parts of the body, with a limited number of verbs. Adjectives; j bad, large, small, &c.
d. Counting and writing numbers, with addition and subtraction to 10.
e. Writing on slate and with lead pencil.

### PRIMARY COURSE.

#### SECOND, THIRD, AND FOURTH YEARS.

a. ARTICULATION.
b. LANGUAGE.
c. ARITHMETIC.
d. GEOGRAPHY.
e. PENMANSHIP.
f. DRAWING.

*a.* Drill in elements, combinations and words, and reading them from the lips.

*b.* Thorough review of first year work. Nouns and verbs continued. Adjectives continued; their comparison. Pronouns as in first year, adding myself, himself, herself, with the plurals, and the relatives who and which. Adverbs; not, often, never, &c. Elliptical sentences; action and picture writing; journal and letter writing, and simple stories.

*c.* Practical exercises in addition, subtraction, multiplication, and division; United States currency; simple fractions.

*d.* School-room, building and yard, city, and a limited knowledge of the State.

*e.* Copy-book writing.

### INTERMEDIATE COURSE.

#### FIFTH, SIXTH, AND SEVENTH YEARS.

*a.* ARTICULATION.
*b.* LANGUAGE.
*c.* ARITHMETIC.
*d.* GEOGRAPHY.
*e.* HISTORY.
*f.* PENMANSHIP.
*g.* DRAWING.
*h.* CALISTHENICS.

*a.* Drill in elements, combinations, syllables; words and sentences continued as in Primary Course.

*b.* Nouns, pronouns, adjectives, adverbs, prepositions and conjunctions continued as in Primary Course. Drill in active and passive voices; action and picture writing; stories from Natural History; journal and letter writing.

*c.* Mental and written addition, subtraction, multiplication, and division, with practical examples; United States currency and simple fractions continued.

*d.* City, State, and New England States.

*e.* Simple historical stories in connection with geography.

*f.* Copy-book writing twice a week.

*g.* Object drawing.

## HIGHER COURSE.

EIGHTH, NINTH, AND TENTH YEARS.

     *a.* ARTICULATION.
     *b.* LANGUAGE.
     *c.* ARITHMETIC.
     *d.* GEOGRAPHY.
     *e.* HISTORY.
     *f.* PHYSIOLOGY.
     *g.* PENMANSHIP.
     *h.* DRAWING.
     *i.* CALISTHENICS.

*a.* Drill in difficult combinations and words.

*b.* Composition; journal and letter writing; miscellaneous reading; newspapers and magazines; lessons on general subjects.

*c.* Mental, written and practical.

*d.* Geographical Reader; Manual of Commerce.

*e.* History of the United States; Outline of General History.

*g.* Copy book.

*h.* Free-hand and object drawing and designing.

# TO PARENTS OF DEAF CHILDREN.

---

This school is for the benefit of children incapacitated through deafness, total or partial, for receiving proper instruction in common schools, and is free to all pupils who belong in this State.

The aim of the school is to teach deaf children to use the English language with the spontaneity, correctness, and enjoyment of *hearing* children as far as this is practicable.

"Without language there can be no thought, no reason;" and as the highest aim of all instruction is the culture of the mental and moral nature in man, our first effort should be to furnish the deaf with a medium through which knowledge can be imparted and obtained. This can be done by signs, by the finger alphabet, and by speech. Our method is the latter, or oral method, by which the deaf can be educated, and at the same time, furnished with the usual and most convenient way of communication in society and in the world at large.

It is very desirable that deaf children be sent to school at as early an age as possible. A parent will be amply repaid for sending a child as young as five or six years, even at some inconvenience. The Board of Trustees are authorized to receive pupils between the ages of three and twenty years.

If a child who has learned to talk is made deaf by disease he should immediately upon his recovery be sent to a school where his speech will be retained, and where he will be taught to understand from the lips. In such cases it is common to delay so long that serious loss of speech results.

4

Speech reading is an invaluable acquisition for those who        semi-deaf or even hard of hearing, as well as for those congenitally or totally deaf.

Every effort should be made to encourage the child to retain the use of his voice. He should be taught to pronounce common        by watching the lip motion and facial expression, or by feeling the muscular action or the breath; but no attempt should be made to        him *the names* of the letters of the alphabet

This school no longer exists as a day school, but has been merged into the Rhode Island Institute for the Deaf, and will be conducted as a boarding home and school. Application for admission should be made to the Principal at the Institute, corner of East Avenue and Cypress Street, Providence.

State of Rhode Island and Providence Plantations.

# Report of the Board of Trustees

OF THE

# RHODE ISLAND

# NSTITUTE FOR THE DEAF,

PRESENTED TO THE

# GENERAL ASSEMBLY

AT ITS

# JANUARY SESSION, 1896.

---

PROVIDENCE:

E. L. FREEMAN & SON, PRINTERS TO THE STATE.

1896.

# REPORT OF TRUSTEES.

*To the Honorable the General Assembly at its January Session,*
*A. D.* 1896.

The Board of Trustees of the Rhode Island Institute for the Deaf herewith respectfully presents its Fourth Annual Report.

The school is gradually gaining in numbers, sixty-one pupils having been registered during the past year, and the efficiency of the school work, the development of the mental growth of the pupils and the general toning up of the Institute is now more apparent—owing no doubt to better system, more experience and skill on the part of the teachers, and the majority of the pupils reaching an age when their work counts for more, as they become appreciative of the advantages of an education and of the facilities accorded to them.

The growth of the school has called for an increase in the corps of teachers, as the classes in schools for the deaf must necessarily be small in numbers to secure the best results.

The teachers are earnest and painstaking in their efforts, harmonious in their relations with each other and with their classes, and, directed by the foresight and experience of the principal, give an assurance of continuing the good work already evidenced in many ways.

The classes in sloyd, printing, sewing and shoe-repairing, although not extensive in either branch, show manifest advantages since they were established, and bid fair to give better and wider results when we can avail ourselves of the new facilities now under construction.

The health of the school may be said to have been good during
the year, although colds and simple ailments are always more or
less prevalent among so many young people. Two cases of diphtheria, however, are to be reported as occurring the latter part of
the year, but happily recovering without serious results under
absolute hospital isolation, good nursing, and the skillful treatment of Dr. F. L. Day, physician to the institute.

For more specific information as to the school and the family,
and for valuable suggestions and recommendations, your attention
is called to the report of the principal herein presented.

The faculty, attendants, and servants now employed at the institute number twenty-two, viz.:

Miss Laura DeL. Richards...................Principal.
 "  R. E. Sparrow....................First Assistant.
 "  A. L. Steadman ........................Teacher.
 "  F. M. Cheney...........................    "
 "  A. March...............................
 "  A. D. Ward.............................
 "  A. M. Townsend........................
 "  J. L. Ruggles...........................    "
Mr. R. Almgren .....................Teacher of Sloyd.
 "  W. H. Goodale...............Teacher of Printing.
 "  P. Walpole. ........................Shoemaker.
Mrs. M. E. Oakes.......................Housekeeper.
Mr. James Rooney...........................Janitor.

Also nine other persons employed as cook, laundress, seamstress, table and chamber girls and attendants.

The total force is about the usual proportionate number required in similar institutions.

### FINANCIAL REPORT.

The sum of fifteen thousand dollars was appropriated for the
year 1895, for maintenance, and the same is accounted for as
follows:

Paid for salaries for the months of

| | |
|---|---|
| January.................................... | $557 33 |
| February.................................. | 559 00 |
| March..................................... | 565 00 |
| April...................................... | 566 00 |
| May....................................... | 580 00 |
| June...................................... | 565 00 |
| July...................................... | 48 00 |
| August.................................... | 48 00 |
| September................................. | 659 00 |
| October................................... | 673 00 |
| November................................. | 660 00 |
| December................................. | 658 00 |

| | |
|---|---|
| Total amount of salaries................. | $6,139 17 |
| "      "    " other expenses.......... | 8,553 79 |
| "       "    expended................... | $14,692 96 |
| Balance covered into treasury............ | 307 04 |
| Amount of appropriation................ | $15,000 00 |

### EXPENSES IN DETAIL.

| | |
|---|---|
| Paid Salaries............................... | $6,139 17 |
| "    Coal................................... | 724 44 |
| '    Gas.................................... | 220 74 |
| "    Water................................. | 162 01 |
| '    Ice.................................... | 88 40 |
| "    Meats, milk, etc........................ | 1,981 94 |
| "    Groceries.. .......................... | 1,916 83 |
| '    Sewer................................. | 364 00 |
| "    Improvements and repairs.............. | 934 70 |
| "    Concreting walks..................... | 275 60 |
| "    Medicines and medical attendance...... | 293 79 |
| "    Telephone............................. | 72 00 |

Paid Advertising. .......................... $33 30
   "   Printing................................ 55 50
   "   School supplies........................ 251 00
   "   Furnishings............................ 624 42
   "   Miscellaneous ......................... 553 99
                                          _____
      Total.............................. $14,692 96

For the purpose of comparison we append the items of expenditure for 1894:

Paid Salaries............................... $5,942 37
   "   Coal................................. 756 81
   '   Gas.................................. 313 69
   '   Water............................... 197 51
   "   Provisions........................... 3,237 73
   "   Improvements and repairs.............. 2,319 61
   "   Medicines and medical attendance...... 233 40
   "   Telephone............................ 72 00
   "   Advertising.......................... 27 90
   "   Printing and stationery ............... 204 40
   "   Fire protection ....................... 104 25
   "   Miscellaneous ......................... 122 98
                                          _____
      Total.............................. $13,532 65

Average attendance, 51 pupils, cost per pupil.. $260 15
Average attendance for 1895, 61 pupils, cost
      per pupil.............................. $240 87

This amount does not, of course, include the interest upon the cost of construction of the institute. It is also difficult to compare the cost per capita with that of other institutions supported under varied conditions. In the State of New York the counties are understood to appropriate $300 per pupil per annum, until twelve years of age, when they become state pupils, and the allowance to some of the schools is reduced to $260 per annum.

William R. Stewart, Commissioner, in his report (1895) to the State Board of Charities, N. Y., says, as follows:

"The extreme difficulty of imparting knowledge to the deaf, the necessity of small classes, individual instruction and sufficient teachers, has demonstrated that a per capita allowance of $300 is needed to insure the best results. Not only do public policy and the interest of the deaf require the advancement of the per capita allowance to $300 for all state pupils, but also the fact that generous provision for the education of this unfortunate class would be ultimately productive of economy to the state. The chances of the deaf requiring state or county support in latter life will be less when education is the highest, discipline the best and early advantages large and wise."

We refer to this subject as a matter of information—not for present action. The state has dealt liberally with our institution, and when the necessity arises for increased aid we feel quite sure it will be forthcoming. In the meantime we shall endeavor to carry on the institution with the same appropriation, for maintenance, as hitherto received, viz.: $15,000, which sum we respectfully ask for the ensuing year.

### IMPROVEMENTS.

At the January Session of the Legislature of 1895, upon the petition of the board, an appropriation of $10,000 was made to enable the board to make much needed improvements, by the erection of a laundry building and an addition to the school building, to contain sloyd, printing, and other rooms; an assembly and gymnasium hall, etc. These buildings are well under way and will shortly be completed. The work has not been crowded, as we desired to make our contracts for the least money, or rather to cover as much ground as possible with our appropriation.

Contracts were made with the lowest of the several competitive bidders, with an ample allowance of time, and a considerable sum has been saved by the procedure. The successful bid for the

# THIRD ANNUAL REPORT

OF THE

# PRINCIPAL

OF THE

# RHODE ISLAND INSTITUTE FOR THE DEAF,

PROVIDENCE, R. I.,

FOR THE

YEAR ENDING DECEMBER 31,

1895.

# REPORT OF PRINCIPAL.

To the Honorable the Board of Trustees of the Rhode Island Institute for the Deaf:

GENTLEMEN :—I respectfully submit the following report for the year ending December 31, 1895.

On January 1st, 1895 there were fifty-two pupils enrolled; twenty-nine boys and twenty-three girls.

Six new pupils were admitted during the winter and spring, one a boy of eighteen, who had never attended school. He is a bright, industrious boy, anxious to learn and will become, undoubtedly, a satisfactory student. When these children have been allowed to remain at home until the age of thirteen or fourteen they are slow at grasping ideas and school-room work is irksome. As the Institute and its work is better known throughout the State it is hoped that parents of deaf children will not neglect to avail themselves of its advantages. We are now trying to bring to the school a pupil of sixteen who has never attended school.

School re-opened September 10th with fifty-three pupils, and in course of time all returned, except one boy whose parents moved out of the State. Five new pupils were admitted in September and October, making eleven admitted during the year, so that our number was increased to sixty-one, thirty-four boys and twenty-seven girls, the largest attendance in the history of the school.

·We opened as a boarding school January 1st, 1893 with thirty-eight pupils.

## HEALTH.

The general health throughout the school has been good.

There have been colds and slight accidents occasionally, but they have been comparatively few when we consider the number under our care.

On the 24th of November one of the pupils was taken ill with diphtheria, which was epidemic at that time. In all probability it was contracted outside the Institute. The child was immediately taken to the hospital, which can be completely separated from the main building. There followed but one other case. The attendant who had charge of the patient until a nurse came, took the disease, but both she and the child recovered.

## SCHOOL WORK.

During the past year the work in the school-rooms has been very satisfactory, but especially so the past few months.

The children take more interest in reading than ever before, and they are learning to appreciate good and instructive books.

They are interested in the history of people and of different countries, and the teachers take an active interest in directing their reading. Such a desire to learn must stimulate the minds of these children so that they will advance, in all respects, faster than ever before. Carefully selected books are frequently added to the library, and they are taught, by collecting news items, to read the daily papers understandingly.

The teachers are provided with school papers and magazines and other necessary helps to teach.

Our most important work is to teach the use of the English language, speech-reading and speech. That the children may acquire the constant use of speech, they are first taught to understand spoken language by watching the mouths of others, *not the lips alone*, but the *tongue*, the *lips*, and the expression of the face, and thus they are taught to use speech as it is used by others.

There has been a marked improvement in deportment. The boys are more manly and the girls are more womanly. We try to make life in the Institute as home like as possible, but of course this can be done only to a certain extent, and only by the hearty coöperation of everybody, which, I can truly say, is given. And I would like here to thank the teachers for the cheerful assistance they so willingly give. Every evening some of them join the children in the sitting-rooms and take part in their conversation and games, and on Saturday evenings they teach the use of games that are both instructive and amusing.

### CHANGES.

A few changes have taken place in the corps of teachers. Miss R. E. Sparrow, for many years a teacher in Clarke Institution in Northampton, Mass., succeeded Mrs. Hurd as First Assistant. As the number of pupils increased it became necessary to add another teacher to our staff, and Miss A. D. Ward was appointed and has charge of a class of beginners in the Kindergarten department. Miss Townsend and Miss Ruggles were appointed in place of Miss Burrill and Miss Smith, who did not return after the summer vacation. Miss Gill, a teacher-in-training, assists in the class-room work a portion of each day, and observes the work done in the class-rooms the remaining time school is in session.

### INDUSTRIAL TRAINING.

Industrial training has received as careful attention as the intellectual development. Printing is taught to five boys, and a small school paper, the *What Cheer*, is issued twice a month.

Printing is very helpful in teaching the pupils how to use the English language correctly.

We hope to increase the number under instruction as soon as the addition to the school building is completed and we have more commodious quarters.

The class in Sloyd is still in charge of Mr. Almgren and the boys are doing very commendable work. At present the boys' play-room is used as the Sloyd room. When the new buildings are finished more boys can be added to the class, and we hope to form a class, in Sloyd, of girls, as it has been found practical to teach this branch of industry to them, as well as to boys.

We have an efficient shoe-maker and four boys receive instruction on three afternoons of each week in shoe-making.

The sewing, for the household, is done by the girls in the sitting-room, under a teacher of experience.

The pupils are taught regular habits of order and cleanliness in the care of their rooms and different parts of the building occupied by them.

The day before Christmas the children were made happy by a beautiful Christmas tree laden with presents provided by contributions from Mrs. Weeden and others.

### ACKNOWLEDGMENTS.

We acknowledge, with thanks, two pictures for the pupils' sitting-rooms, from Miss Adeline Brown; a box of fine oranges, from Mrs. Wm. Gammell; some children's clothing from Mrs. C. W. Lippitt; bric-a-brac, six water colors and an etching from Mr. M. J. Perry; a box of periodicals from Mrs. D. B. Pond, and we thank Mrs. Weeden and Mrs. Wyman for collecting the money, buying and framing a large photograph of the Madonna dé San Sisto, by Raphael.

Thanks are also due Mrs. S. S. Durfee for clothing, and Miss Mabelle C. Lippitt for books.

Respectfully submitted,

LAURA De L. RICHARDS,

*Principal.*

PROVIDENCE, January, 1896.

# APPENDIX.

## TABULAR REPORT OF THE PUPILS OF THE SCHOOL

| NAME OF PUPIL. | RESIDENCE. | AGE. (Approx.) | DATE OF ADMISSION. |
|---|---|---|---|
| Lynch, James E. | Wanskuck, Providence | 18 | Sept. 6, 1880 |
| Beauchesne, Alphonse | Central Falls | 16 | Oct. 25, 1886 |
| Sullivan, Nell | Newport | 13 | Nov. 12, 1886 |
| Grant, | | 10 | Dec. 13, 1886 |
| Cole, L | | | March 22, 1887 |
| Chevers, | | | |
| Jacques, | | | |
| Cove | | | |
| Fran | | | |
| Cann | | | |
| Hack | | | |
| Trud | | | |
| Gill, | | | |
| Gold | | | |
| Hack | | | |
| Dum | | | |
| Make | | | |
| Egan | | | |
| Fletc | | | |
| *Bail | | | |
| Trud | | | |
| O'Bri | | | |
| Lese, | | | |
| Beatt | | | |
| Court | | | |
| Staun | | | |
| Staun | | | 8 | Oct. 5, 1891 |
| Gay, Frederick | Providence | 8 | Nov. 9, 1891 |
| Jermyn, William | Newport | 10 | May 5, 1892 |
| Mills, Annetta | Providence | 6 | April 3, 1893 |
| Carr, David | Pawtucket | 6 | Jan. 27, 1893 |
| Collins, Chester A. | Providence | 4 | Jan. 30, 1893 |
| Kleber, Fannie | Lymansville | 6 | Feb. 7, 1893 |
| Mercier, Addie C. | Shannock | 10 | Feb. 7, 1893 |
| Goldstein, Clara J. | Providence | 9 | March 1, 1893 |
| Desonie, Maggie | Lippitt | 8 | March 23, 1893 |
| Smith, Bernard F. | Providence | 8 | April 10, 1893 |
| O'Conner, Mary | Woonsocket | 6 | May 27, 1893 |
| Hoen, Alfred | Kenyon | | Sept. 11, 1893 |
| Knowles, Grace E. | South Kingstown | 4 | Sept. 11, 1893 |
| Chace, Emma E. | Providence | 15 | Sept. 11, 1893 |
| Ladd, Joe D. | East Greenwich | 8 | Jan. 27, 1892 |
| Thompson, George | Providence | 4 | Sept. 11, 1893 |
| Pulsifer, M. Hellen | River Point | 8 | Sept. 11, 1893 |
| Savard, Mary C. S. S. | Woonsocket | 12 | Sept. 11, 1893 |
| Flynn, James | Providence | 6 | Feb. 3, 1894 |

* Deceased.

FOR THE YEAR ENDING DECEMBER 31, 1895.

| CAUSE OF DEAFNESS, AS FAR AS KNOWN. | AGE WHEN MADE DEAF. (Approx.) | REMARKS. |
|---|---|---|
| Brain fever.................... | 2 years, 2 months. | ......................... |
| Scarlet fever............. .... | 4 years... ...... | ......................... |
| Scarlet fever ............. | 2 years........ .... | ......................... |
| Tumor in ear................. | 6 months ........ | ......................... |
| Congenital................... | | ......................... |
| Brain fever......... .... ... | 6 months ........ | Slight degree of hearing. |
| Meningitis................ ... | 2 years, 6 months. | ......................... |
| Fever....................... ... | 2 years | ......................... |
| Typhoid fever............... | 3 years, 6 months. | ......................... |
| Congenital.................. | | ......................... |
| Congenital.. .................. | ... .. .......... | Hard of hearing. |
| Paralysis.............. ... ... | 3 years.... ... | ......................... |
| Scarlet fever... ............. | 5 years......... | ......................... |
| Scarlet fever................. | 3 years.... ... | ......................... |
| Congenital................... | .......... | ......................... |
| Typhoid fever . .. ..... ..... | 4 years......... | ......................... |
| Scarlet fever ................. | 3 years......... | Hard of hearing. |
| Meningitis................... | 7 years.... ...... | ......................... |
| Congenital................... | | ...... ............... |
| Congenital................... | | ......................... |
| Congenital................... | ...... ......... | Slight degree of hearing. |
| Run over.................. | | Hard of hearing. |
| Unknown................... | 4 years......... | Hard of hearing. |
| Congenital................... | | . ........ ........... |
| Congenital..... | | .... .... |
| Brain fever.. ......... .... | 1 year............ | Hard of hearing. |
| Brain fever.. ... ............ | 3 years......... | ......................... |
| Scarlet fever................. | 3 years... ..... | ......................... |
| Congenital...... | | . ...... .............. |
| Measles..................... | 3 years......... | ......................... |
| A fall........... ........ | 2 years......... | ......................... |
| Measles..................... | 2 years......... | ......................... |
| Congenital.. .... | | Deafness partial. |
| Scarlet fever ............. | 5 years.... ... | .................. ........ |
| Typhoid fever............... | 4 years......... | ......................... |
| Congenital................... | .... .. ......... | ......................... |
| ......... ...... ... | .......... .... | Not deaf. |
| Scarlet fever........ ....... | 1 year......... | ......................... |
| A fall...................... | 2 years ...... .. | Deafness partial. |
| Grippe..................... | 2 years .. ....... | { Not deaf.  Impediment in speech. |
| ......... ...... | .......... ...... | ......................... |
| Congenital............. .... | ..... .... | ......................... |
| Convulsions............. ...... | 3 years.......... | ......................... |
| Measles..................... | 6 years.......... | .................. .... |
| Congenital...... ..... ....... | .......... ... | ......................... |
| Congenital................... | | ......................... |

## TABULAR REPORT OF THE PUPILS OF THE SCHOOL

| NAME OF PUPIL. | RESIDENCE. | AGE. (Ap prox.) | DATE OF ADMISSION. |
|---|---|---|---|
| Lynch, James E. | Wanskuck, Providence | 18 | Sept. 6, 1880.. |
| Beauchesne, Alphonse | Central Falls. | 16 | Oct. 25, 1886.. |
| Sullivan, Nellie | Newport. | 13 | Nov. 12, 1886.. |
| Grant, Edith. | Providence. | 10 | Dec. 13, 1886.. |
| Cole, Luella. | South Scituate. | 12 | March 28, 1887.. |
| Chevers, C. Herbert. | Providence. | 14 | April 26, 1887.. |
| Jacques, George A. | Pawtucket. | 14 | May 11, 1887.. |
| Cove, Margaret. | Providence. | 13 | Sept. 5, 1887.. |
| Francis, Manuel. | Bristol. | 14 | Sept. 26, 1887.. |
| Canning, Thomas F. | Woonsocket. | 12 | Sept. 3, 1888 . |
| Hackett, Clara L. | Providence. | 10 | Sept. 20, 1888.. |
| Trudell, Albertina. | Warren. | 14 | Nov. 14, 1888.. |
| Gill, Eva G. | Providence | 10 | Dec. 10, 1888.. |
| Goldenofsky, Moses. | Woonsocket. | 10 | April 29, 1889.. |
| Hackett, Laura. | Providence. | 8 | Nov. 11, 1889.. |
| Dumais, Leander. | Central Falls. | 13 | May 7, 1890.. |
| Maker, Dora C. | Providence. | 10 | May 19, 1890.. |
| Egan, Frederick. | Providence. | 11 | Sept. 1, 1890.. |
| Fletcher, Henrietta M. | Johnston. | 10 | Sept. 1, 1890 . |
| *Baillargeron, Joseph. | Woonsocket. | 11 | Oct. 8, 1890.. |
| Trudeau, Leonel. | Woonsocket. | 12 | Nov. 19, 1890.. |
| O'Brien, William T. | Providence. | 12 | Dec. 1, 1890.. |
| Lese, Edwin G. | Providence. | 11 | Feb. 2, 1891.. |
| Beatty, John. | Johnston. | 12 | April 27, 1891.. |
| Courtemanche, Henry. | Woonsocket. | 12 | June 10, 1891.. |
| Staunton, Annie L. | Providence. | 12 | Sept. 8, 1891.. |
| Staunton, Bertha. | Providence. | 8 | Oct. 5, 1891.. |
| Gay, Frederick. | Providence. | 8 | Nov. 9, 1891.. |
| Jermyn, William. | Newport. | 10 | May 5, 1892.. |
| Mills, Annetta. | Providence. | 6 | April 3, 1893.. |
| Carr, David. | Pawtucket. | 6 | Jan. 27, 1893.. |
| Collins, Chester A. | Providence. | 4 | Jan. 30, 1893.. |
| Kleber, Fannie. | Lymansville. | 6 | Feb. 7, 1893.. |
| Mercier, Addie C. | Shannock. | 10 | Feb. 7, 1893.. |
| Goldstein, Clara J. | Providence. | 9 | March 1, 1893.. |
| Desonic, Maggie | Lippitt. | 8 | March 23, 1893.. |
| Smith, Bernard F. | Providence. | 8 | April 10, 1893.. |
| O'Conner, Mary. | Woonsocket. | 6 | May 27, 1893.. |
| Hoen, Alfred. | Kenyon. | .... | Sept. 11, 1893.. |
| Knowles, Grace E. | South Kingstown. | 4 | Sept. 11, 1893.. |
| Chace, Emma E. | Providence. | 15 | Sept. 11, 1893.. |
| Ladd, Joe D. | East Greenwich | 8 | Jan. 27, 1892.. |
| Thompson, George. | Providence. | 4 | Sept. 11, 1893.. |
| Pulsifer, M. Hellen | River Point | 8 | Sept. 11, 1893.. |
| Savard, Mary C. S. S. | Woonsocket. | 12 | Sept. 11, 1893 . |
| Flynn, James | Providence. | 6 | Feb. 3, 1894.. |

* Deceased.

# APPENDIX.

## TABULAR REPORT OF THE PUPILS OF THE SCHOOL

| Name of Pupil. | Residence. | Age. (Approx.) | Date of Admission. |
|---|---|---|---|
| Lynch, James E........... | Wanskuck, Providence... | 18 | Sept. 6, 1880.. |
| Beauchesne, Alphonse .. . | Central Falls............. | 16 | Oct. 25, 1886.. |
| Sullivan, Nellie....... ... | Newport................ | 18 | Nov. 12, 1886.. |
| Grant, Edith............. | Providence............. | 10 | Dec. 18, 1886.. |
| Cole, Luella........... .... | South Scituate...... .... | 12 | March 28, 1887.. |
| Chevers, C. Herbert....... | Providence...... ..... ... | | |
| Jacques, George A | | | |
| C | | | |
| F | | | |
| C | | | |
| H | | | |
| T | | | |
| G | | | |
| G | | | |
| H | | | |
| D | | | |
| M | | | |
| E | | | |
| F | | | |
| *F | | | |
| T | | | |
| O' | | | |
| Le | | | |
| Be | | | |
| Co | | | |
| St | | | |
| St | ...... ... : | Providence............. | 8 | Oct. 5, 1891.. |
| Gay, Frederick...... ..... | Providence............. | 8 | Nov. 9, 1891.. |
| Jermyn, William...:...... | Newport................ | 10 | May 5, 1892.. |
| Mills, Annetta............ ... | Providence.... .. .... | 6 | April 8, 1893.. |
| Carr, David............... | Pawtucket........... .. | 6 | Jan. 27, 1893.. |
| Collins, Chester A......... | Providence. ............ | 4 | Jan. 30, 1893.. |
| Kleber, Fannie............ | Lymansville,........... | 6 | Feb. 7, 1893.. |
| Mercier, Addie C.......... | Shannock.... ...... ... | 10 | Feb. 7, 1893.. |
| Goldstein, Clara J.......... | Providence............. | 9 | March 1, 1893.. |
| Desonie, Maggie ......... | Lippitt................. | 8 | March 23, 1893.. |
| Smith, Bernard F......... | Providence.......... .. | 8 | April 10, 1893.. |
| O'Conner, Mary.......... | Woonsocket............. | 6 | May 27, 1893.. |
| Hoen, Alfred.......... .. | Kenyon.............. ..... | .... | Sept. 11, 1893.. |
| Knowles, Grace E........ | South Kingstown....... | 4 | Sept. 11, 1893.. |
| Chace, Emma E........... | Providence............. | 15 | Sept. 11, 1893.. |
| Ladd, Joe D.............. | East Greenwich.......... | 8 | Jan. 27, 1892.. |
| Thompson, George........ | Providence... ...... | 4 | Sept. 11, 1893.. |
| Pulsifer, M. Hellen ..... | River Point ... ........ | 8 | Sept. 11, 1893.. |
| Savard, Mary C. S. S...... | Woonsocket............. | 12 | Sept. 11. 1893 . |
| Flynn, James ........... | Providence............. | 6 | Feb. 3, 1894.. |

* Deceased.

FOR THE YEAR ENDING DECEMBER 81, 1895.

| Cause of Deafness, as far as known. | Age when made deaf. (Approx.) | Remarks. |
|---|---|---|
| Brain fever.................... | 2 years, 2 months. | ....................... |
| Scarlet fever.............. .... | 4 years... ...... | |
| Scarlet fever ................ | 2 years....... .... | |
| Tumor in ear................. | 6 months ........ | |
| Congenital..................... | ................... | |
| Brain fever......... .... ... | 6 months .... ... | Slight degree of hearing. |
| Meningitis......... .......... | 2 years. 6 months. | ....................... |
| Fever....................... | 2 years | ...... ............ |
| Typhoid fever................ | 3 years, 6 months. | ....................... |
| Congenital..................... | | |
| Congenital.. ................... | .... .. .......... | Hard of hearing. |
| Paralysis..................... | 3 years........ | |
| Scarlet fever.... ........... | 5 years.......... | |
| Scarlet fever................. | 3 years.... ... | |
| Congenital..................... | | |
| Typhoid fever . .. ...... .... | 4 years........ .. | ....................... |
| Scarlet fever ............... | 3 years.......... | Hard of hearing. |
| Meningitis......... .. .... ...| 7 years.... . .... | |
| Congenital..................... | | |
| Congenital..................... | | |
| Congenital.......... ......... | ............ ........ | Slight degree of hearing. |
| Run over...................... | | Hard of hearing. |
| Unknown.................... | 4 years......... | Hard of hearing. |
| Congenital..................... | | ............... .......... |
| Congenital...... ........... | | |
| Brain fever.................. | 1 year............ | Hard of hearing. |
| Brain fever.. .... ............ | 3 years........... | ....................... |
| Scarlet fever................. | 3 years... ..... | |
| Congenital...... ........... | | ... .. ............... |
| Measles...................... | 3 years.......... | ....................... |
| A fall........... ........ | 2 years........ | |
| Measles...................... | 2 years......... | ........ ..... ...... |
| Congenital.. .... ........... | .................... | Deafness partial. |
| Scarlet fever ............. . | 5 years.... .... | ................ ......... |
| Typhoid fever................ | 4 years.......... | .... |
| Congenital.................... | .... .. .......... | |
| ................. .. .... | .... | Not deaf. |
| Scarlet fever....... .. .... | 1 year........... | ....................... |
| A fall........................ | 2 years ...... ... | Deafness partial. |
| Grippe....................... | 2 years ... ...... | |
| | | { Not deaf. Impediment in speech. |
| ................ ........ | ......... ....... | |
| Congenital............. ...... | ....................... | |
| Convulsions............. ........ | 8 years........ | ....................... |
| Measles....................... | 6 years.... .... | ............ .... |
| Congenital...... ........... | .............. .. | ....................... |
| Congenital.................... | .................... | ....................... |

TABULAR REPORT OF THE PUPILS OF THE SCHOOL

| Name of Pupil. | Residence. | Age. (Approx.) | Date of Admission. |
|---|---|---|---|
| Pease, Walter M ......... | Woonsocket............. | 5 | Sept. 10, 1894.. |
| Comfort, Mae E........... | Newport.............. .. | 8 | Sept. 10, 1894.. |
| Bradley, William H........ | Woonsocket............. | 11 | Oct. 1, 1894.. |
| Mudrak, Willie........... | Geneva................. | 4 | Oct. 13, 1894.. |
| Canney, John P........... | Providence............. | 9 | Dec. 3, 1894.. |
| Ulrich, J. Adolph........ | Providence............. | 7 | Jan. 21, 1895.. |
| Grimes, Mary............. | Newport.... .......... | 9 | Feb. 5, 1895.. |
| O'Riley, Willie F ....... | East Providence.......... | 7 | Feb. 11, 1895.. |
| Grace, Theresa ........... | Providence............. | 12 | April 10, 1895.. |
| Welsh, John.............. | Providence ............. | 7 | May 20, 1895.. |
| Roe, Albert C............ | Hope................... | 5 | Sept. 21, 1895.. |
| Stetson, Leroy W.. ........ | Warren................. | 10 | Sept. 30, 1895.. |
| Grebert, Herman........... | Bristol................. | 9 | Oct. 14, 1895.. |
| Boivert, Mary........... .. | Providence........ .. .. | 18 | Oct. 27, 1895.. |
| Smith, Idella.. .. ........ | Johnston................ | 9 | Oct. 28, 1895.. |
| Lefebre, Isaac............. | Natick................. | 18 | May 6, 1895.. |

FOR THE YEAR ENDING DECEMBER 31, 1895.

| CAUSE OF DEAFNESS, AS FAR AS KNOWN. | AGE WHEN MADE DEAF. (Approx.) | REMARKS. |
| --- | --- | --- |
| Grippe.......................... | 2 years.......... | ..... ...................... |
| Catarrhal fever. .............. | 1 year, 6 months.. | ................... ... .. |
| Diphtheria..... ............. | 6 years......... | ..... .................... |
| Congenital..................... | ............. ...... | .......................... |
| Taking quinine................. | 1 year.... ...... | .......................... |
| Scarlet fever................... | 8 years......... | .......................... |
| Measles......... ............. | 5 years... ...... | Slight degree of hearing. |
| Congenital..................... | .................... | ............ ............. |
| Congenital..................... | .................... | .......................... |
| Brain fever.... ............. | 8 years........ | .......................... |
| Inflammation in head   ...... | 4 months... ... | .......................... . |
| Fall and fever................. | 4 years.......... | Slight degree of hearing. |
| Congenital........ ..... .... | .................... | .. ...................... |
| Fever ....... .. ............ | 8 years.... ...... | .......................... |
| Congenital..................... | ........ ........ | Slight degree of hearing. |
| Scarlet Fever.... ............ | 8 years.......... | .... ............. .. ...... |

## SUMMARY.

Number of pupils from date of opening the State school for the deaf, April
2, 1877, to December 31, 1894......................................... 131
Number of pupils who have entered the Institute since Dec. 31, 1894....... 11
                                                                        ———
Whole number of pupils who have attended the school.......... ... 181
Number who have left the school......... ..... ................. 74
                                                                        ———
Number of pupils Dec. 31, 1895..................................... 61
Number of girls who have attended school during the year............... 29
Number of boys who have attended school during the year............... 34
                                                                        ———
Whole number of pupils during the year . ......................... 68
Average attendance................................................ 54
Number congenitally deaf, or made deaf before the age of two............ 33
Number who lost hearing between the ages of two and four ............. 18
Number who lost hearing after the age of four, and doubtful cases......... 18
                                                                        ———
                                                                        68
Number who have any degree of hearing..................... ............. 14

———

*Residences of all who have attended during the year 1894.*

Geneva........ .......... . ............. ................................. 1
Providence, including Wanskuck...................... ................. 25
East Providence................................. ................. ......... 1
Pawtucket................................................ ... .......... 2
Central Falls. ...................... ... ..... ................. 2
South Scituate......................................... 1
Johnston............................................. ...................... .. 3
Newport.... ....................... ...... ........................... ... 4
Lymansville .......... ......... .................................. 1
Shannock......... . ......... ................................... 1
Lippitt................................................. ......... ................ 1

South Kingstown........ ........ .. ...................................  ·
River Point............................ ... .. ................. .........  1
Woonsocket.......................... .............. ....... .. ... ....  9
Kenyon....... ...................................................... ...  :
Hope.............................. ........ .... ....................  1
Bristol.................... .. ....................................  2
Warren..... ......... ............................................  2
_____

Eighteen localities................... .. .................... .. ......  68

## PERIODICALS.

The receipt of the following periodicals is thankfully acknowledged, and their continuance respectfully requested:

Mute's Companion, Fairibault, Minn. ; Daily Paper for Our Little People, Rochester, N. Y.; Our Children's School Journal, The Deaf Mute Journal, New York; Maryland Bulletin, Frederick, Md.; The Deaf Mute Voice, Jackson, Miss.; Kentucky Deaf Mute, Danville, Ky.; The Goodson Gazette, Staunton, Va.; Kansas Star, Olathe, Kansas; Deaf Mute Optic, Little Rock, Ark.; Deaf Mute Index, Colorado Springs, Col.; Juvenile Ranger, Austin, Texas; The Register, Rome, N. Y.; Nebraska Mute Journal, Omaha, Neb.; New Method for the Deaf, Englewood, Ill.; Weekly News, Berkeley, Cal.

### LIPPITT FUND PRIZES AWARDED FOR

#### *Articulation.*

| | |
|---|---|
| Eva Gill, | Alphonse Beauchesne, |
| Leon Dumais, | Dora Maker, |
| Lionel Trudeau, | Annie Staunton, |
| Nellie Pulsifer, | Jennie Goldstein. |

#### *Lip Reading.*

| | |
|---|---|
| Eva Gill, | Willie O'Brien, |
| Nellie Sullivan, | Luella Cole, |

Moses Goldenofsky,          Addie Mercier,
Laura Hackett,              Nellie Pulsifer.

*Language.*

Stephanie Savard,           Fred Egan,
Maggie Cove,                Clara Hackett,
Joseph Baillargeron,        Jennie Goldstein.

# COURSE OF STUDY.

## KINDERGARTEN.

### FIRST YEAR.

*a*. KINDERGARTEN EXERCISES.
*b*. ARTICULATION.
*c*. LANGUAGE.
*d*. ARITHMETIC.
*e*. PENMANSHIP.

*a*. Paper cutting and folding; drawing and modeling in clay; designing in shoe pegs; stick laying; embroidery designs sewed on pricked sewing cards; lesson in form and color in all exercises.

*b*. Elements, combinations, simple words and sentences; with reading them from the lips.

*c*. Nouns; objects in class-room, articles of dress, articles of food, different parts of the body, with a limited number of verbs. Adjectives; good, bad, large, small, &c.

*d*. Counting and writing numbers, with addition and subtraction to 10.

*e*. Writing on slate and with lead pencil.

## PRIMARY COURSE.

### SECOND, THIRD, AND FOURTH YEARS.

*a*. ARTICULATION.
*b*. LANGUAGE.
*c*. ARITHMETIC.
*d*. GEOGRAPHY.
*e*. PENMANSHIP.
*f*. DRAWING.

*a.* Drill in elements, combinations and words, and reading them from the lips.

*b.* Thorough review of first year work. Nouns and verbs continued. Adjectives continued; their comparison. Pronouns as in first year, adding myself, herself, himself, with the plurals, and the relatives who and which. Adverbs; not, often, never, &c. Elliptical sentences; action and picture writing; journal and letter writing, and simple stories.

*c.* Practical exercises in addition, subtraction, multiplication, and division; United States currency; simple fractions.

*d.* School-room, building and yard, city, and a limited knowledge of the State.

*e.* Copy-book writing.

### INTERMEDIATE COURSE.

#### FIFTH, SIXTH, AND SEVENTH YEARS.

> *a.* ARTICULATION.
> *b.* LANGUAGE.
> *c.* ARITHMETIC.
> *d.* GEOGRAPHY.
> *e.* HISTORY.
> *f.* PENMANSHIP.
> *g.* DRAWING.
> *h.* CALISTHENICS.

*a.* Drill in elements, combinations, syllables; words and sentences continued as in Primary Course.

*b.* Nouns, pronouns, adjectives, adverbs, prepositions and conjunctions continued as in Primary Course. Drill in active and passive voices; action and picture writing; stories from Natural History; journal and letter writing.

*c.* Mental and written addition, subtraction, multiplication, and division, with practical examples; United States currency and simple fractions continued.

*d.* City, State, and New England States.

*e.* Simple historical stories in connection with geography.

*f.* Copy-book writing twice a week.

*g.* Object drawing.

## HIGHER COURSE.

EIGHTH, NINTH, AND TENTH YEARS.

  *a.* ARTICULATION.
  *b.* LANGUAGE.
  *c.* ARITHMETIC.
  *d.* GEOGRAPHY.
  *e.* HISTORY.
  *f.* PHYSIOLOGY.
  *g.* PENMANSHIP.
  *h.* DRAWING.
  *i.* CALISTHENICS.

*a.* Drill in difficult combinations and words.

*b.* Composition; journal and letter writing; miscellaneous reading; newspapers and magazines; lessons on general subjects.

*c.* Mental, written and practical.

*d.* Geographical Reader; Manual of Commerce.

*e.* History of the United States; Outline of General History.

*g.* Copy book.

*h.* Free-hand and object drawing and designing.

# TO PARENTS OF DEAF CHILDREN.

This school is for the benefit of children incapacitated through deafness, total or partial, for receiving proper instruction in common schools, and is free to all pupils who belong in this State.

The aim of the school is to teach deaf children to use the English language with the spontaneity, correctness, and enjoyment of *hearing* children as far as this is practicable.

"Without language there can be no thought, no reason;" and as the highest aim of all instruction is the culture of the mental and moral nature in man, our first effort should be to furnish the deaf with a medium through which knowledge can be imparted and obtained. This can be done by signs, by the finger alphabet, and by speech. Our method is the latter, or oral method, by which the deaf can be educated, and at the same time furnished with the usual and most convenient way of communication in society and in the world at large.

It is very desirable that deaf children be sent to school at as early an age as possible. A parent will be amply repaid for sending a child as young as five or six years, even at some inconvenience. The Board of Trustees are authorized to receive pupils between the ages of three and twenty years.

If a child who has learned to talk is made deaf by disease he should immediately upon his recovery be sent to a school where his speech will be retained, and where he will be taught to understand from the lips. In such cases it is common to delay so long that serious loss of speech results.

Speech reading is an invaluable acquisition for those who are

or even hard of hearing, as well as for those conge
deaf.

effort should be made to encourage the child to
his voice. He should be taught to pronounce co
watching the lip motion and facial expression,
e muscular action or the breath; but no attempt
to teach him *the names* of the letters of the alphab
hool no longer exists as a day school, but ha
ato the Rhode Island Institute for the Deaf, and
l as a boarding home and school. Application
hould be made to the Principal at the Institute,
venue and Cypress Street, Providence.

State of Rhode Island and Providence Plantations.

# REPORT OF THE BOARD OF TRUSTEES

OF THE

# RHODE ISLAND
# INSTITUTE FOR THE DEAF,

PRESENTED TO THE

## GENERAL ASSEMBLY

AT ITS

## JANUARY SESSION, 1897.

PROVIDENCE:

E. L. FREEMAN & SONS, PRINTERS TO THE STATE,

1897.

Daniel B. Pond.

# DANIEL B. POND.

In view of the death of the Hon. DANIEL B. POND, which occurred September 9, 1896, the Board of Directors of the Rhode Island Institute for the Deaf places this minute upon its records.

Mr. POND was an original Director and the first and only President of our organization. His large experience in public affairs, his integrity to every trust, whether public or private, and his devotion to duty gave him the full confidence of the Legislature and Executive of Rhode Island. At any and all times whenever our new and untried institution needed the expenditure and fostering care of the State, it had a trustworthy advocate in the person of our President.

Mayor POND, as he was familiarly called, had all the executive and administrative training, with the experience, which would especially fit him for the organization and management of a new institution and of a process of education necessarily not much understood in our community.

He brought to our affairs the full powers and devoted interest of an enlightened and philanthropic citizen. In the work of starting and adjusting a complicated system of education, his judgment was unfailing and his energy and interest were never lacking.

We, his associates, for ourselves and for the teachers and employés brought under his control, desire to express our sense of bereavement and of the almost irreparable loss in the death of our companion, director, and friend. We have dwelt upon his wisdom and prompt sagacity in the general conduct of our enterprise.

Personally, we remember his constant sympathy and ready tact which smoothed the way and helped to carry us through every emergency.

It is a consolation to the Board that the Principal and the Staff of the Institute were enabled to minister to the last hours of our suffering friend. Some of the best work of his life was done in behalf of this school, and under its roof his earthly labors were ended.

The Board directs the Secretary to send a copy of this minute to the bereaved family of our late associate, and to publish the same in the newspapers of Providence and Woonsocket.

# REPORT OF TRUSTEES.

_To the Honorable the General Assembly at its January Session, A. D. 1897._

The Board of Trustees of the Rhode Island Institute for the Deaf herewith respectfully presents its Fifth Annual Report.

Notwithstanding the epidemic, so skilfully controlled by our attending physician, Dr. Frank L. Day, which somewhat interfered with school work the first part of the year, the Institute has gone quietly on its way improving and enlarging in all directions. The addition of the new gymnasium to the school building made possible two new school-rooms, which were greatly needed. The increased facilities, and the re-grading of the classes thus necessitated, enabled the teachers to be much more thorough and efficient in their work. Only one change is noted for the year in our corps of competent and earnest teachers, the list of which, with the attendants and servants now employed at the Institute, numbering twenty-one, is appended.

MISS LAURA DEL. RICHARDS....................Principal.
MISS R. E. SPARROW......................First Assistant.
MISS A. L. STEADMAN . .........................Teacher.
MISS F. M. CHENEY............................Teacher.
MISS A. M. TOWNSEND.........................Teacher.
MISS S. M. GILL...............................Teacher.
MISS A. D. WARD..............................Teacher.

Miss J. L. RUGGLES...........................

MR. C. M. HUNT.......................Teacher of Sloyd

MR. W. H. GOODALE.....:..........Teacher of Printing

MRS. N. W. GISBURNE.....................Housekeeper

MR. FRED ANDERSON ...........................Janitor

Also, nine other persons—employed as cook, laundress, seam
stress, table and chamber girls, and attendants.

### FINANCIAL REPORT.

The sum of fifteen thousand dollars was appropriated for th
. year of 1896 for maintenance, and the same is accounted for a
follows :

Paid salaries for the months of

| | |
|---|---:|
| January ................................. | $666 0 |
| February................................ | 668 2 |
| March................................... | 681 2 |
| April.................................... | 681 5 |
| May..................................... | 672 0 |
| June .................................... | 661 0 |
| July..................................... | 50 0 |
| August.................................. | 65 0 |
| September............................... | 633 8 |
| October ................................. | 647 0 |
| November ............................... | 676 0 |
| December ............................... | 671 0 |

| | |
|---|---:|
| Total amount of salaries...................... | $6,772 0 |
| Total amount of other expenses................ | 8,215 5 |
| Total amount expended.................... | $14,987 7 |
| Balance covered into treasury.............. | 12 5 |
| Amount of appropriation...................... | $15,000 0 |

Expenses in detail :

| | |
|---|---:|
| Paid Salaries | $6,772 50 |
| Coal | 830 95 |
| Gas | 317 41 |
| Water | 164 12 |
| Ice | 70 67 |
| Meat, milk; etc | 1,920 06 |
| Groceries | 1,561 86 |
| Water pipe | 154 00 |
| Improvements and repairs | 1,293 27 |
| Medicines and medical attendance | 325 03 |
| Telephone | 99 90 |
| Printing | 55 55 |
| School supplies | 260 00 |
| Furnishings | 628 37 |
| Miscellaneous | 534 08 |
| Total | $14,987 77 |

For the purpose of comparison we append the items of expenditure for 1895 :

| | |
|---|---:|
| Paid Salaries | $6,139 17 |
| Coal | 724 44 |
| Gas | 220 74 |
| Water | 162 01 |
| Ice | 88 40 |
| Meats, milk, etc | 1,981 94 |
| Groceries | 1,916 83 |
| Sewer | 364 00 |
| Improvements and repairs | 934 70 |
| Concreting walks | 275 60 |
| Medicines and medical attendance | 293 79 |
| Telephone | 72 00 |
| Advertising | 33 30 |
| Printing | 55 50 |

Expenditure for 1895—continued.

|  |  |  |
|---|---|---|
| School supplies..... . .................... | 251 | 00 |
| Furnishings............................. | 624 | 12 |
| Miscellaneous........................... | 553 | 99 |

Total ..................................... $14,692 96

Average attendance for 1895 ......61 pupils.
Cost per pupil, $240.87.

Average attendance for 1896 ......62 pupils.
Cost per pupil, $241.73.

In January, 1893, the Institute was opened in its present quar—
ters with thirty-eight pupils, six teachers, including the Principal,
and seven attendants and servants—the sum of fifteen thousand
dollars being appropriated for their maintenance. To-day we
have sixty-two pupils enrolled, with faculty, attendants and servants to the number of twenty-one. It is only by the greatest
economy and care, cheerfully seconded in our efforts by our able
and experienced Principal, that we have been enabled to meet
current expenses on the same sum the past year.

As our number will be increased, in order to successfully carry
on our work and aims we respectfully ask for the sum of nineteen
thousand dollars to meet the necessary expenses and to properly
maintain the establishment for the ensuing year.

### IMPROVEMENTS.

The laundry building and the addition to the schoolhouse, containing gymnasium, sloyd, printing and two other rooms, were
finisned, and appropriately opened by the General Assembly in
April last. They are well furnished throughout,—the laundry
with washing machine, mangle, extractor and other conveniences,
operated by an electric motor; the gymnasium with a reasonable
amount of apparatus and furniture. There are, also, increased

facilities in the sloyd and printing departments, and a larger
water-pipe was found necessary to connect the street with the
laundry.  To effect these improvements the sum of ten thousand
dollars was appropriated at the January session of 1895, and the
additional sum of five thousand dollars at the January session of
1896.  The same is accounted for as follows :

CONSTRUCTION ACCOUNT.

Total appropriation ................................. $15,000 00

| | | |
|---|---:|---:|
| 1895.  Paid to Robert Wilson, contractor : | | |
| First payment................... | $3,200 | 00 |
| Second payment .............. | 3,200 | 00 |
| 1896. | | |
| Feb.  Paid to The Samuel Jackson Co. (on account of steam heating contract) in part payment................... | 950 | 00 |
| Mar.  Paid to The Samuel Jackson Co. for gas and water-pipe connections between the school building and the laundry building.................. | 65 | 18 |
| Paid to The Samuel Jackson Co. for changing radiator................ | 7 | 10 |
| Apr.  Paid to Robert Wilson, third payment on account of contract for erection of laundry building and addition to school building, as per agreement.. | 2,500 | 00 |
| Paid to The Samuel Jackson Co. as part payment on account, for steam heating apparatus in the laundry and in the addition to the school building | 400 | 00 |
| Paid to J. H. Tower contract price for putting up fire-escapes on the new addition to school building........ | 100 | 00 |

1896.

May.  Paid for laundry machinery and labor
      .and expense of setting up the same,
      as per bill rendered and in accord-
      ance with written contract.........      913 73
      Paid extras for laundry..............      6 80
      Paid to The Samuel Jackson Co. for
      plumbing........................      14 08
      Paid to Brown Bros. for sundry items
      of belting used in the laundry......      33 71
      Paid Chandler & Barber for sloyd fur-
      nishings.........................  .      55 23
      Paid Phillips & Phillips for plumbers'
      supplies .........................      14 79
      Paid Golding & Co. for furnishings for
      printing-room....................      23 23
      Paid E. T. Turner sundry freight bills
      and charges for carting...........      7 78
      Paid City of Providence for driveway.      15 56
      Paid to The Samuel Jackson Co. bal-
      ance due on written contract.......      247 00
      Paid to The Samuel Jackson Co. sun-
      dry charges for material and labor
      outside of contract ...............      158 37
      Paid for one electric motor, five-horse
      power, as per bill attached—(con-
      tract made through Marsden J.
      Perry, Esq.).....................      175 00
      Paid to J. M. Magoon for installing
      electric motor in the laundry build-
      ing..............................      21 65
      Paid to Anthony, Cowell & Co. (fur-
      nishings)........................      63 00
      Paid to Robert Wilson, balance of
      original building contract..........      1,135 93

'aid to Woonsocket Machine & Press
Co . . . . . . . . . . . . . . . . . . . . . . . . . . . . . .    40 10

'aid to Charles Taft, for use of barges
for General Assembly . . . . . . . . . . . . .    20 25

'aid to Narragansett Machine Co. for
gymnastic apparatus. . . . . . . . . . . . . .    122 23

'aid to P. O'Connor for material and
labor in extending gas pipes to
laundry building from the Pabodie
mansion, for material and labor in
laundry building, extending sewer
pipes, removing set tubs, piping for
laundry machinery, water-closets,
etc., outside of plumbing contract. .    254 17

'aid to P. O'Connor amount of contract for plumbing the new addi-
tion . . . . . . . . . . . . . . . . . . . . . . . . . . . .    300 00

'aid Golding & Co. (printers' sup-
plies) . . . . . . . . . . . . . . . . . . . . . . . . . . .    17 36

'aid Ames Plow Co. . . . . . . . . . . . . . . .    13 00

'aid J. M. Magoon, electrical en-
gineer. . . . . . . . . . . . . . . . . . . . . . . . . . .    18 99

'aid Robert Wilson for material and
labor . . . . . . . . . . . . . . . . . . . . . . . . . . .    437 51

'aid J. M. Magoon, electrical en-
gineer. . . . . . . . . . . . . . . . . . . . . . . . . .    15 40

'aid Union Steam and Gas Pipe Co. .    2 39

'aid Stone, Carpenter & Willson. . . . .    400 00

'aid to The Samuel Jackson Co. for
removing radiators and for putting
in gas pipe. . . . . . . . . . . . . . . . . . . . . .    49 60

      Total. . . . . . . . . . . . . . . . . . . . . . $14,998 64

Balance in treasury. . . . . . . . . . . . . . . . .  . . . . . . . . .

For further and more particular information as to the condition and needs of the School we submit, appended hereto, the Report of the Principal covering the year 1896.

This is the first report submitted which was not drawn by the late Hon. Daniel B. Pond. We cannot close it without referring to the great loss the Board of Trustees sustained in the sudden death at the Institute, in September last, of their honored President and associate. We constantly miss his intelligent care and oversight, his patient attention to detail, and his never-failing interest and sympathy in all pertaining to the well-being of our institute.

Respectfully submitted.

CHARLES WARREN LIPPITT, *Governor*,
EDWIN R. ALLEN, *Lieutenant-Governor*,

*Members ex-officio.*

LIVINGSTON SCOTT, *President*,
MRS. ELLEN T. McGUINNESS, *Secretary*,
MRS. JEANIE L. WEEDEN,
DR. ROWLAND R. ROBINSON,
WILLIAM K. POTTER,
HOWARD SMITH,
MRS. LILLIE B. CHACE WYMAN,
JOHN C. B. WOODS,
MARSDEN J. PERRY,

*Board of Trustees.*

PROVIDENCE, R. I.,
*January, 1897.*

# MEDICAL REPORT

*To the Board of Trustees of the Rhode Island Deaf:*

I have the honor to report that the year past h... severe illness at the Institute. During February ... were five cases of diphtheria, mild in type, which ... isolated as to prevent a general spread of the dis... school. At the same time there were several case... of which made good recoveries. During the F... were three cases of tonsillitis—in marked contras... general prevalence of this condition in every p... largely, it seems probable, to the careful watching ... tion of the cases. There have been a few minor ... nesses incident to an institution for children. T... as in previous years, most faithfully carried out ... made for the care of the children.

Yours faithfully,

FRANK ...

PROVIDENCE,
December 31, 1896.

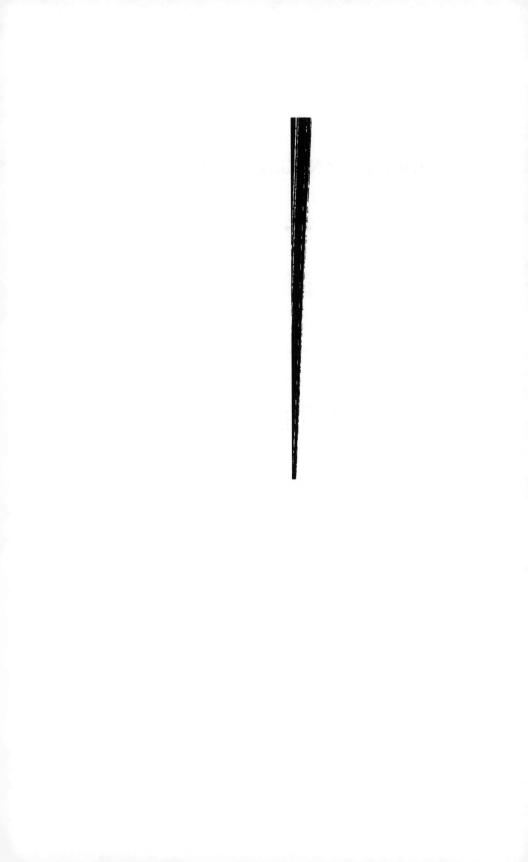

# FOURTH ANNUAL REPORT

OF THE

# PRINCIPAL

OF THE

# RHODE ISLAND INSTITUTE FOR THE DEAF,

PROVIDENCE, R. I.,

FOR THE

YEAR ENDING DECEMBER 31,

# 1896.

# REPORT OF THE PRINCIPAL.

*To the Honorable the Board of Trustees of the Rhode Island Institute for the Deaf:*

I have the honor to submit, for your consideration, the following report for the year ending Dec. 31, 1896.

The week before the opening of school in September the Institute met with a very great loss in the death of the Hon. D. B. Pond, who had been President of the Board of Trustees for the school since the first appointment of that Board by Gov. Davis. Mayor Pond was thoroughly interested in the Institute, and it is owing to his kind care and untiring interest that so much has been accomplished for our comfort and advancement.

## ATTENDANCE.

You will see that our number remains about the same as last year. Sixty-one pupils were enrolled during the year, twenty-five girls and thirty-six boys, five pupils have left school and three have been admitted, which makes our number fifty-nine. There are still children whose parents do not avail themselves of the privileges offered here; cases are frequently coming to our notice of deaf children who ought to be at school. At present there is one fifteen years of age who has *never* attended *any* school, and the parents do not see the great importance of it. As seen on page 32 an act in amendment of and in addition to Chapter 86 of the General Laws, of the R. I. School for the Deaf, requires that every deaf child between the age of seven and eighteen years *must* attend school somewhere.

3

## HEALTH.

Like similar institutions we were visited, during the spring, b
some of the diseases at that time epidemic throughout the countr
diphtheria and measles, which caused the children afflicted t
lose several weeks of school.  We were very fortunate that th
cases were of a mild type, which yielded readily to the wise an
skilful care of our attending physician, Dr. F. L. Day, who wa
untiring in his watchfulness over the school during the epidemi
Under his direction care was taken to thoroughly disinfect th
buildings and try to guard against a recurrence of the disease
Since the opening of school in September the health throughou
the school has been unusually good, and we hope it will continu

## CLASS WORK.

The course of instruction employed is practically the same as i
previous years.  The pupils take greater interest and show com
mendable progress in their studies.  Our aim is to fit them f
their duties in active life; and when we consider that the thre
and in most cases four, first years in school are spent in gaining
vocabulary, that is in learning to talk, because they do not kno
the names of the most common objects before coming to schoc
and this vocabulary must be given them before we can begin wil
the educational work, they cannot, therefore, be expected to com
plete the course and be fully equipped to go out into the worl
in the same length of time as their more fortunate brothers an
sisters who upon, entering school have, at least, a knowledge
how to ask and answer common questions, and who usually cor
tinue their course for about ten years.

Every deaf child should remain in school twelve years, at tl
least, to be able to enter active life successfully.  "Language
the greatest difficulty the deaf have to overcome in acquiring
education," and they should be given ample time in which

master it, and the very best teachers to be found should be provided to impart it.

One of our most successful instructors of the deaf says: "A teacher who is successful in imparting idiomatic English may rest assured that she is a good teacher." She will be able to contrive means that will make the children think of the right things to do or say.

One who has not taught the deaf cannot fully realize to what extent our vernacular is filled with figures of speech. That the pupils may be given all possible assistance in acquiring a ready command of the English language, new books are frequently purchased and added to their library, chosen from the catalogue of the "Model Library," which has been selected especially for the deaf, and I take pleasure in saying they are well appreciated by the pupils.

### CHANGES.

Miss Gill, who was with us last year in training, was appointed in place of Miss March, who did not return. Miss Flint, for several years a successful teacher of hearing children, is taking a course of training with us.

### INDUSTRIAL CLASSES.

Since the completion of the new buildings, last April, the accommodations for our industrial classes have been much improved, and more pupils have been added to each class.

We note with regret the resignation of Mr. Almgren, who was very successful in teaching Sloyd to a class of ten boys. He left to accept a similar position in an institution where his full time would be employed. We were fortunate in securing Mr. C. H. Hunt, a graduate of the Boston Sloyd School, to fill the vacancy. Mr. Hunt is an enthusiastic teacher, greatly interested in the class, which increased after moving into more commodious quarters. We hope soon to have a class of younger pupils taught.

The class in printing, under the direction of Mr. Goodale, is making good progress. Two girls have been added to the class, and their work is very satisfactory.

## IMPROVEMENTS.

The addition to the school building and the new laundry building were completed and ready to be occupied the latter part of April. The assembly hall, in the addition to the school building, was furnished with gymnastic appliances, which the pupils use daily and enjoy much. The hall serves a double purpose, that of a hall for public gatherings and a gymnasium.

The laundry is a great comfort and convenience. The pupils take turns in assisting the laundress, and by so doing become familiar with the use of laundry machinery.

One of the rooms formerly used for laundry purposes has been converted into a sewing room, well fitted with cases and shelves, which fills a need long felt.

The pupils appreciate the improvements made and take pride in the Institution as their home. Heavy wire guards have been put over all the basement windows in the main building and in the addition, which serve as a protection and will also prevent the breaking of windows.

As usual, the children were made happy by a visit from Santa Claus. A tree was provided and well filled with presents, the gift of Mrs. Weeden and Mrs. McGuinness.

## ACKNOWLEDGMENTS.

We acknowledge with thanks a portfolio of copies of fine paintings, from Mrs. W. B. Weeden; Giants of the Republic, from Mayor E. D. McGuinness; Picturesque Europe, from Mrs. E. Chase; three pictures of Mt. Desert, Me., from Miss Adeline Brown; and an architectural portfolio, from Mr. R. Wilson. We also received a copy of Saratoga Battle Grounds, from the late Hon. D. B. Pond.

Thanks are also due Mrs. S. S. Durfee, Mrs. W. B. Weeden and the Misses Weeden for clothing.

Respectfully submitted,

LAURA DE L. RICHARDS,

*Principal.*

TABULAR REPORT OF THE PUPILS OF THE SCHOOL

| NAME OF PUPIL. | RESIDENCE. | AGE. (Approx.) | DATE OF ADMISSION. |
|---|---|---|---|
| Lynch, James E.......... | Wanskuck, Providence... | 18 | Sept.  6, 1880.. |
| Beauchesne, Alphonse..... | Central Falls............ | 16 | Oct.  25, 1896 |
| Sullivan, Nellie.......... | Newport.......... ...... | 13 | Nov.  12, 1886.. |
| Grant, Edith.- .......... | Providence ............. | 10 | Dec.  13, 1886.. |
| Cole, Luella .. .. ..... | South Scituate........... | 12 | March 28, 1887.. |
| Chevers, C. Herbert...... | Providence .......... . | 14 | April  26. 1887.. |
| Jacques, George A........ | Pawtucket........ ...... | 14 | May  11, 1887.. |
| Cove, Margaret.......... | Providence ............. | 13 | Sept.  5, 1887.. |
| Francis, Manuel.......... | Bristol.................. | 14 | Sept.  26, 1887.. |
| Canning, Thomas F...... | Woonsocket............ | 12 | Sept.  3. 1888.. |
| Hackett, Clara L......... | Providence ............. | 10 | Sept.  20, 1888.. |
| Trudell, Albertina..... .. | Warren............ .... | 14 | Nov.  14, 1888.. |
| Gill, Eva G.............. | Providence ...... .. .... | 10 | Dec.  10, 1888.. |
| Goldenofsky, Moses. ..... | Woonsocket............. | 10 | April  29. 1889.. |
| Hackett, Laura..........: | Providence ............. | 8 | Nov.  11, 1889. |
| Dumais, Leander......... | Central Falls. ........... | 13 | May  7, 1890.. |
| Maker, Dora C .......... | Providence ............. | 10 | May  19, 1890.. |
| Egan, Frederick ...... | Providence ............. | 11 | Sept.  1, 1890.. |
| Fletcher, Henrietta M. .. | Johnston ................ | 10 | Sept.  1, 1890 . |
| Trudeau, Leonel ........ | Woonsocket ............ | 12 | Nov.  19, 1890.. |
| O'Brien, William T...... | Providence .......... ... | 12 | Dec.  1, 1890.. |
| Lese, Edwin G ...:..... | Providence ............. | 11 | Feb.  2, 1891.. |
| Beatty, John.... ...... | Johnston.... ......... | 12 | April  27, 1891.. |
| Courtemanche, Henry..... | Woonsocket.......... .. | 12 | June  10, 1891.. |
| Staunton, Annie L .. ... | Providence ... .. ...... | 12 | Sept.  8, 1891.. |
| Staunton, Bertha........ | Providence  ......... .. | 8 | Oct.  5, 1891.. |
| Gay, Frederick........... | Providence ............. | 8 | Nov.  9, 1891.. |
| Jermyn, William......... | Newport................. | 10 | May  5, 1892.. |
| Mills, Annetta........... | Providence ...... .... | 6 | April  3, 1893.. |
| Carr, David. ...... ..... | Pawtucket............ | 6 | Jan.  27, 1893.. |
| Collins, Chester A........ | Providence ............. | 4 | Jan.  30, 1893.. |
| Kleber, Fannie........... | Lymansville............ | 6 | Feb.  7, 1893.. |
| Mercier, Addie C.... .... | Shannock.. ... ....... | 10 | Feb.  7, 1893.. |
| Goldstein, Clara J........ | Providence ............. | 9 | March  1, 1893.. |
| Desonie, Maggie.......... | Lippitt .............. | 8 | March 28, 1893.. |
| Smith, Bernard F........ | Providence ............. | 8 | April  10, 1893.. |
| O'Conner, Mary..... .... | Woonsocket.... .... .. | 6 | May  27, 1893.. |
| Hoen, Alfred. .......... | Kenyon... .......... | .... | Sept.  11, 1893.. |
| Knowles, Grace E. ...... | South Kingstown..... . | 4. | Sept  11, 1893.. |
| Thompson, George........ | Providence ............. | 4 | Sept.  11, 1893.. |
| Pulsifer, M. Hellen.. ..... | River Point ........... | 8 | Sept.  11, 1893.. |
| Savard, Mary C. S. S...... | Woonsocket.. .... ...... | 12 | Sept.  11, 1893.. |
| Flynn, James........ .... | Providence ............. | 6 | Feb.  3, 1894.. |
| Pease, Walter M.......... | Woonsocket............ . | 5 | Sept.  10, 1894.. |
| Comfort, Mae E........... | Newport............ .. .. | 8 | Sept.  10, 1894.. |
| Bradley, William H...... | Woonsocket............. | 11 | Oct.  1, 1894.. |
| Mudrak, Willie . ......... | Geneva...... .......... | 4 | Oct.  18, 1894.. |

| CAUSE OF DEAFNESS, AS FAR AS KNOWN. | AGE WHEN MADE DEAF. (Approx.) | REMARKS. |
|---|---|---|
| Brain fever | 2 years, 2 months. | |
| Scarlet fever | 4 years | |
| Scarlet fever | 2 years | |
| Tumor in ear | 6 months | |
| Congenital | | |
| Brain fever | 6 months | Slight degree of hearing. |
| Meningitis | 2 years, 6 months. | |
| Fever | 2 years | |
| Typhoid fever | 3 years, 6 months. | |
| Congenital | | |
| Congenital | | Hard of hearing. |
| Paralysis | 3 years | |
| Scarlet fever | 5 years | |
| Scarlet fever | 3 years | |
| Congenital | | |
| Typhoid fever | 4 years | |
| Scarlet fever | 3 years | Hard of hearing. |
| Meningitis | 7 years | |
| Congenital | | |
| Congenital | | Slight degree of hearing. |
| Run over | | Hard of hearing. |
| Unknown | 4 years | Hard of hearing. |
| Congenital | | |
| Congenital | | |
| Brain fever | 1 year | Hard of hearing. |
| Brain fever | 3 years | |
| Scarlet fever | 3 years | |
| Congenital | | |
| Measles | 3 years | |
| A fall | 2 years | |
| Measles | 2 years | |
| Congenital | | Deafness partial. |
| Scarlet fever | 5 years | |
| Typhoid fever | 4 years | |
| Congenital | | |
| | | Not deaf. |
| Scarlet fever | 1 year | |
| A fall | 2 years | Deafness partial. |
| Grippe | 2 years | |
| Convulsions | 3 years | |
| Measles | 6 years | |
| Congenital | | |
| Congenital | | |
| Grippe | 2 years | |
| Catarrhal fever | 1 year, 6 months | |
| Diphtheria | 6 years | |
| Congenital | | |

## TABULAR REPORT OF THE PUPILS OF THE SCHOOL

| NAME OF PUPIL. | RESIDENCE. | AGE. (Approx.) | DATE ADMISSI |
|---|---|---|---|
| Canney, John P | Providence | 9 | Dec. 3, |
| Grimes, Mary | Newport | 9 | Feb. 5, |
| O'Riley, Willie F | East Providence | 7 | Feb. 11, |
| Grace, Theresa | Providence | 12 | April 10, |
| Welsh, John | Providence | 7 | May 20, |
| Roe, Albert C. | Hope | 5 | Sept. 21, |
| Stetson, Leroy W | Warren | 10 | Sept. 30, |
| Grebert, Herman | Bristol | 9 | Oct. 14, |
| Boivert, Mary | Providence | 18 | Oct. 27, |
| Smith, Idella | Johnston | 9 | Oct. 28, |
| Lefebre, Isaac | Natick | 18 | May 6, |
| Williams, Charles A. | Pawtucket | 4 | Sept. 14, |
| Cook, Reuben | Peace Dale, | 7 | Oct. 6, |
| Perron, Lena | Warren. | 7 | Oct. 26, |
| Anderson, Edward V | Providence | | |

FOR THE YEAR ENDING DECEMBER 31, 1896.

| CAUSE OF DEAFNESS, AS FAR AS KNOWN. | AGE WHEN MADE DEAF. (Approx.) | REMARKS. |
|---|---|---|
| Taking quinine............ .... .... | 1 year............. .... | ........................... .... |
| Measles.......... ............ | 5 years .......... | Slight degree of hearing. |
| Congenital......................... | ............. ... .. | .............. ............ |
| Congenital......................... | ............. ...... | ....... . ................... |
| Brain fever........ ........... | 8 years ........ | ............................ |
| Inflammation in head.......... | 4 months ........ | ............................ |
| Fall and fever.... ............ | 4 years .......... | Slight degree of hearing. |
| Congenital....... ............... | ...... ...... .. | ......... ...... ...... .... |
| Fever......................... | 8 years .......... | ............................ |
| Congenital. ... ....... ..... | .....,........ | Slight degree of hearing. |
| Scarlet fever................... | 8 years .......... | .......... .... ........ |
| Congenital..................... | ............. ...... | .......................... |
| Congenital.. . .................. | ............. ...... | .......................... |
| Scarlet fever.................. | 1 year. ...... .. | .......................... |
| Scarlet fever......... . ...... | 5 years ......... | Hard of hearing. |

## SUMMARY.

s from date of opening the State school for the deaf, April
ecember 31, 1895...... .. ...............................185
ls who have entered the Institute since Dec. 31, 1895...... 4

nber of pupils who have attended the school............ 139
ho have left the school................................. 80

s Dec. 31, 1896..................... ...................... 59
who have attended school during the year................ 26
who have attended school during the year ................ 84

nber of pupils during the year........... .... ........... 60
ce. .......................................... ........... 59

ally deaf, or made deaf before the age of two ........... 32
hearing between the ages of two and four................ 27
hearing after the age of four, and doubtful cases........ 1

59

e any degree of hearing. .............. ..... .......... 13

ces of all who have attended during the year 1894.

....................................................... 1
ding Wanskuck........................ .............. 25
................................................... ... 1
................................. .................... 8
................................. .................... 9
.................................................... 4
...................................................... 8
.................................................... 4
....................................................... 1
....................................................... 1
....................................................... 1
....................................................... 1

### PERIODICALS.

The receipt of the following periodicals is thankfully acknowledged, and their continuance respectfully requested.

Mute's Companion, Fairibault, Minn.; Daily Paper for Our Little People, Rochester, N. Y.; Our Children's School Journal, The Deaf Mute Journal, New York; Maryland Bulletin, Frederick, Md.; The Deaf Mute Voice, Jackson, Miss.; Kentucky Deaf Mute, Danville, Ky.; The Goodson Gazette, Staunton, Va.; Kansas Star, Olathe, Kansas; Deaf Mute Optic, Little Rock, Ark.; Deaf Mute Index, Colorado Springs, Col.; Juvenile Ranger, Austin, Texas; The Register, Rome, N. Y.; Nebraska Mute Journal, Omaha, Neb.; New Method for the Deaf, Englewood, Ill.; Weekly News, Berkeley, Cal.

### LIPPITT PRIZE FUND AWARDED FOR

*Speech.*

Willie O'Brien,               Mary Boisvert.

*Speech Reading.*

Moses Goldenofsky,            Jennie Goldstein.

*Language.*

Eva Gill,                     Alphonse Beauchesne.

Albertina Trudel,             Herbert Chever,
John Beatty,                  Willie Jermyn,

Bernie Smith.

*Deportment.*

Luella Cole,                  Frank Canning.

*Neatness.*

Maggie Cove,                  Henry Coutermanche.

# COURSE OF STUDY.

## KINDERGARTEN.

### FIRST YEAR.

*a.* KINDERGARTEN EXERCISES.

*b.* ARTICULATION.

*c.* LANGUAGE.

*d.* ARITHMETIC.

*e.* PENMANSHIP.

*a.* Paper cutting and folding; drawing and modeling in clay; designing in shoe pegs; stick laying; embroidery designs sewed on pricked sewing cards; lessons in form and color in all exercises.

*b.* Elements, combinations, simple words and sentences; with reading them from the lips.

*c.* Nouns; objects in class-room, articles of dress, articles of food, different parts of the body, with a limited number of verbs. Adjectives; good, bad, large, small, &c.

*d.* Counting and writing numbers, with addition and subtraction to 10.

*e.* Writing on slate and with lead pencil.

## PRIMARY COURSE.

### SECOND, THIRD, AND FOURTH YEARS.

*a.* ARTICULATION.

*b.* LANGUAGE.

*c.* ARITHMETIC.

*d.* GEOGRAPHY.

*e.* PENMANSHIP.

*f.* DRAWING.

*a.* Drill in elements, combinations and words, and reading them from the lips.

*b.* Thorough review of first year work. Nouns and verbs continued. Adjectives continued; their comparison. Pronouns as in first year, adding myself, herself, himself, with the plurals, and the relatives who and which. Adverbs; not, often, never, &c. Elliptical sentences; action and picture writing; journal and letter writing, and simple stories.

*c.* Practical exercises in addition, subtraction, multiplication and division; United States currency; simple fractions.

*d.* School-room, building and yard, city, and a limited knowledge of the State.

*e.* Copy-book writing.

## INTERMEDIATE COURSE.

### FIFTH, SIXTH AND SEVENTH YEARS.

*a.* ARTICULATION.

*b.* LANGUAGE.

*c.* ARITHMETIC.

*d.* GEOGRAPHY.

*e.* HISTORY.

*f.* PENMANSHIP.

*g.* DRAWING.

*h.* CALISTHENICS.

*a.* Drill in elements, combinations, syllables; words and sentences continued as in Primary Course.

*b.* Nouns, pronouns, adjectives, adverbs, prepositions and conjunctions continued as in Primary Course. Drill in active and passive voices; action and picture writing; stories from Natural History; journal and letter writing.

*c.* Mental and written addition, subtraction, multiplication and division, with practical examples; United States currency and simple fractions continued.

*d.* City, State and New England States.

*e.* Simple historical stories in connection with geography.

*f.* Copy-book writing twice a week.

*g.* Object drawing.

## HIGHER COURSE.

### EIGHTH, NINTH, AND TENTH YEARS.

a. ARTICULATION.

b. LANGUAGE.

c. ARITHMETIC.

d. GEOGRAPHY.

e. HISTORY.

f. PHYSIOLOGY.

g. PENMANSHIP.

h. DRAWING.

i. CALISTHENICS.

a. Drill in difficult combinations and words.

b. Composition; journal and letter writing; miscellaneous reading; newspapers and magazines; lessons on general subjects.

c. Mental, written and practical.

d. Geographical Reader; Manual of Commerce.

e. History of the United States; Outline of General History.

g. Copy-book.

h. Free-hand and object drawing and designing.

# CHAPTER 332.

### AN ACT IN AMENDMENT OF AND IN ADDITION TO CHAPTER 86 OF THE GENERAL LAWS, ENTITLED "OF THE R. I. SCHOOL FOR THE DEAF."

**(Passed May 13, 1896.)**

*It is enacted by the General Assembly as follows:*

SECTION 1. All children of parents, or under the control of guardians or other persons, legal residents of this state, between the ages of three and twenty years, whose hearing or speech, or both, are so defective as to make it inexpedient or impracticable to attend the public schools to advantage, not being mentally or otherwise incapable, may attend the Rhode Island Institute for the Deaf, without charge, under such rules and regulations as the board of trustees of said institute may establish.

SEC. 2. Every person having under his control any such child between the ages of seven and eighteen years, shall cause such child to attend school at said institute for such period of time or such prescribed course, in each individual case, as may be deemed expedient by the board of trustees, and for any neglect of such duty the person so offending shall be fined not exceeding twenty dollars: *Provided*, that if the person so charged, shall prove to the satisfaction of said board that the child has received or is receiving, under private or other instruction, an education suitable to his condition, in the judgment of said board, then such penalty shall not be incurred: *provided further*, that no child shall be removed to said institution or taken from the custody of its parent or guardian except as a day scholar unless such parent or guardian is an improper person to have such custody, and the supreme court in its appellate division shall have jurisdiction in habeas corpus to examine into and revise all findings of said board of trustees under this act.

SEC. 3. Any child having attended said institute a time or course prescribed by said board, upon leaving the institute shall be entitled to receive a certificate of his proficiency from said board.

SEC. 4. This act shall take effect from and after its passage.

# TO PARENTS OF DEAF CHILDREN.

This school is for the benefit of children incapacitated through deafness, total or partial, for receiving proper instruction in common schools, and is free to all pupils who belong in this State.

The aim of the school is to teach deaf children to use the English language with the spontaneity, correctness, and enjoyment of *hearing* children as far as this is practicable.

"Without language there can be no thought, no reason;" and as the highest aim of all instruction is the culture of the mental and moral nature in man, our first effort should be to furnish the deaf with a medium through which knowledge can be imparted and obtained. This can be done by signs, by the finger alphabet, and by speech. Our method is the latter, or oral method, by which the deaf can be educated, and at the same time furnished with the usual and most convenient way of communication in society and the world at large.

It is very desirable that deaf children be sent to school at as early an age as possible. A parent will be amply repaid for sending a child as young as five or six years, even at some inconvenience. The Board of Trustees are authorized to receive pupils between the ages of three and twenty years.

If a child who has learned to talk is made deaf by disease he should immediately, upon his recovery, be sent to a school where his speech will be retained, and where he will be taught to understand from the lips. In such cases it is common to delay so long that serious loss of speech results.

Speech reading is an invaluable acquisition for those who are

5

semi-deaf or even hard of hearing, as well as for those congenitally or totally deaf.

Every effort should be made to encourage the child retain the use of his voice. He should be taught to pronounce common words by watching the lip motion and facial expression, or by feeling the muscular action of the breath; but no attempt should be made to teach him *the names* of the letters of the alphabet.

The English branches are taught here, and every pupil taught some branch of industry.

The school session begins the second Monday in Se mber, and closes the third Friday in June, with a week's at Christmas.

Application for admission should be made to the P at the Institute, corner of East Avenue and Cypress Street, Providence.

State of Rhode Island and Providence Plantations.

# REPORT OF THE BOARD OF TRUSTEES

OF THE

## RHODE ISLAND

# INSTITUTE FOR THE DEAF,

PRESENTED TO THE

## GENERAL ASSEMBLY

AT ITS

## JANUARY SESSION, 1898.

PROVIDENCE:
E. L. FREEMAN & SONS, STATE PRINTERS.
1898.

State of Rhode Island and Providence

# REPORT OF THE BOARD OF TRUS

OF THE

# RHODE ISLAND

# INSTITUTE FOR THE

PRESENTED TO THE

## GENERAL ASSEMBLY

AT ITS

## JANUARY SESSION, 1

PROVIDENCE:

E. L. FREEMAN & SONS, STATE PR

1898.

The present force of employees—housekeeper, janitor, cook laundress, seamstress, table and chamber girls, and attendants consists of thirteen persons.

Salaries and wages paid during the year are as follows :

| | |
|---|---|
| For January...................................... | $676 0 |
| " February................................... | 692 0 |
| " March....................................... | 710 5 |
| " April......................................... | 713 0 |
| " May.......................................... | 665 9 |
| " June.......................................... | 714 0 |
| " July.......................................... | 83 0 |
| " August....................................... | 83 0 |
| " September................................... | 656 5 |
| " October...................................... | 672 0 |
| " November................................... | 695 0 |
| " December................................... | 682 1 |
| Total amount of salaries .................... | $6,876 5 |

Current expenses for maintenance other than salaries and wage were as follows :

| | |
|---|---|
| Coal............................................. | $850 5 |
| Gas.............................................. | 346 8 |
| Water........................................... | 130 9 |
| Ice ............................................. | 64 7 |
| Provisions, etc ................................ | 2,203 6 |
| Improvements and repairs........................ | 3,521 9 |
| Medicines and medical attendance................. | 191 9 |
| Telephone....................................... | 100 0 |
| Printing . ..................................... | 55 0 |
| School and miscellaneous supplies and furnishings.... | 1,643 2 |
| Miscellaneous................................... | 1,943 4 |
| Total current expenses other than salaries and wages, | $11,052 3 |

The whole number of pupils registered during the year was 63. The number now present 58 ;—34 boys and 24 girls.

We feel it our duty at this time to report that the dormitory accommodations are entirely inadequate, even for the present number of pupils: indeed, they are so crowded that during the year it became necessary to assign the rooms originally designed for a hospital to the use of the smaller children and teachers. In this cramped condition it is apparent that the Institute cannot accomplish the best possible results, nor can it extend its advantages and usefulness to meet the full requirements of the public need without an addition in some way to its present dormitory accommodations.

There are now in the State about twenty deaf children of suitable age to become inmates of the Institute, and who ought to have the advantages of the school, and who might enjoy them if we had the necessary room, but who now are necessarily deprived of them.

The board of trustees, therefore, fully realizing the situation and the public need, with a view and in the hope of an extension of the school facilities, are causing plans and estimates to be made of the probable cost of suitable building extensions for submission to your Honorable Body.

These plans and estimates will be communicated to your Honorable Body at an early date, with recommendation of a suitable appropriation for making such extensions of buildings as will both adequately relieve the present crowded condition and accommodate additional pupils.

We believe that the proposed extension is absolutely needed in order to enable the Institute to fully accomplish the humane objects of its creation, and that when finished they will furnish ample accommodation for the pupils we now have, and will also provide for all the natural increase of pupils which may reasonably be anticipated for many years to come.

The health of the pupils has been very good during the year.

The work of the Institute and the results accomplished during the year have been in every way satisfactory, the pupils all exhibiting commendable progress and an increased contentment.

For maintenance during the ensuing year we recommend an appropriation of $19,000.

We submit appended hereto the report of the principal, made to the board of trustees, giving more full and detailed information as to the present condition and needs of the school.

Respectfully submitted,

ELISHA DYER, JR. *Governor*,
ARAM J. POTHIER, *Lieutenant-Governor*,

*Members Ex-officio.*

LIVINGSTON SCOTT, *President*,
MRS. ELLEN T. McGUINNESS, *Secretary*,
MRS. JEANIE L. WEEDEN,
MRS. LILLIE B. CHACE WYMAN,
WILLIAM K. POTTER,
DR. ROWLAND B. ROBINSON,
JOHN C. B. WOODS,
MARSDEN J. PERRY,
JOHN HARE POWEL.

# MEDICAL REPORT.

To the Board of Trustees of the Rhode Island Institute for the
Deaf:

I have the honor to report that during the year just past there
has been but little illness for so numerous a family. During the
earlier part there were a few cases of influenza of a mild type. In
the spring one of the girls had a sharp attack of appendicitis, was
removed to her home, and made a good recovery. This year, as
last, the few cases of tonsillitis stand out in marked contrast with
the great prevalence of that disease in years past. There has
been one case of mumps, and a few minor accidents. During the
latter part of the year there was a single case of diphtheria,
which was sent home, and later removed to the R. I. Hospital,
where the girl recovered; fortunately no other cases followed.
The need of restoring the old hospital rooms to their original purpose, or of providing new ones, cannot be emphasized too strongly.
The larger ward has been used for a dormitory for three years.
This year the smaller ward and the nurses' room have had to be
given up for teachers' sleeping rooms. So we are without any
suitable place for cases of general illness, or for isolating suspected or doubtful cases of contagious diseases, which, from time
to time, are certain to arise among so large a number of children.

Yours faithfully,

FRANK L. DAY, M. D.

PROVIDENCE,
December 31, 1897.

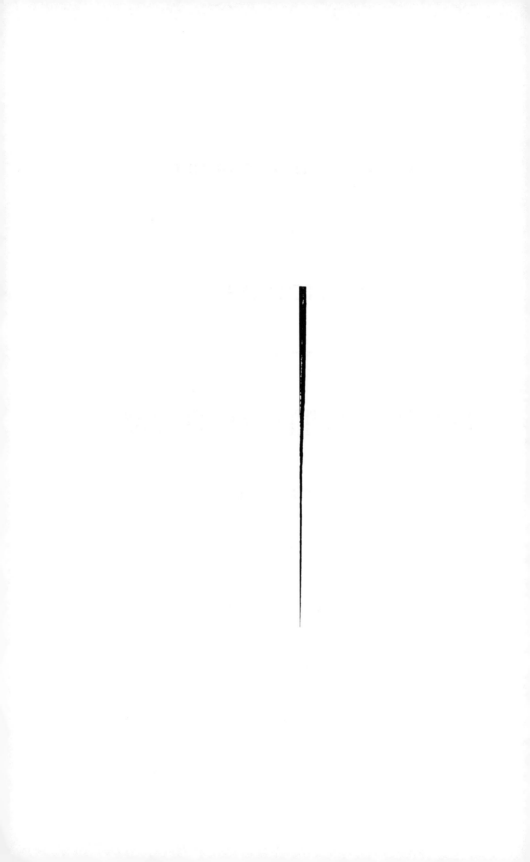

# FIFTH ANNUAL REPORT

OF THE

# PRINCIPAL

OF THE

# RHODE ISLAND INSTITUTE FOR THE DEAF,

PROVIDENCE, R. I.,

FOR THE

YEAR ENDING DECEMBER 31,

# 1897.

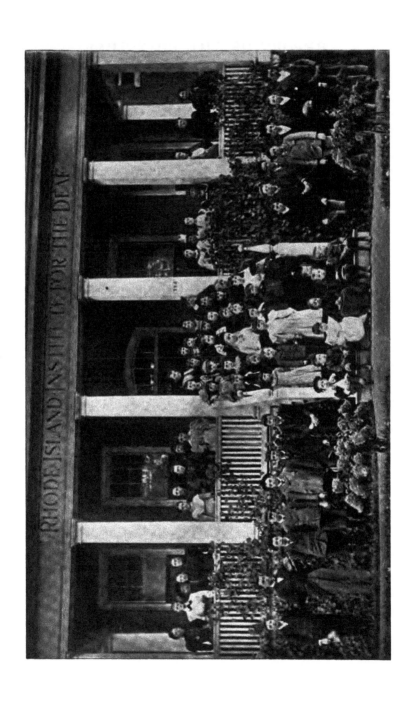

# REPORT OF THE PRINCIPAL.

---

*To the Honorable the Board of Trustees of the Rhode Island Institute for the Deaf:*

During the past year very little has occurred to change the record of previous years.

At the beginning of the year, January 1st, 1897, there were fifty-nine pupils, thirty-three boys and twenty-six girls. Four new pupils were admitted during the year, making our number sixty-three enrolled. Five pupils did not return at the reopening of school in September. Two of the five ought to remain with us for several years yet, and I hope they will return. There are three new pupils waiting to enter when we find accommodations for them, which we shall try to do after the holidays, and there are six others who have never attended school that ought to be here.

## HEALTH.

We are pleased to state that the school has been free from epidemics during the past year, which is due to the skill and care of the attending physician. There have been occasionally minor illnesses, all of which yielded readily to treatment.

After the pupils returned, at the close of the Thanksgiving recess, one of the girls was taken ill with sore throat. She was isolated at once, to the best of our ability under the circumstances, and as soon as it was pronounced diphtheria she was taken to the R. I. Hospital. The case was mild, and the girl was at the hospital but three weeks. We are pleased to say there have been no other cases. We greatly miss our hospital, which has been so invaluable in former years when we were visited by contagious diseases. It has been converted into a nursery for the little boys, owing to the crowded condition of our dormitories, so that now we are totally unable to properly isolate any suspected cases. The hospital has always been found perfectly adequate to our requirements, and will be again if we are only given more dormitory space.

CLASS WORK.

But little that is new can be said with regard to the class work. It has been carried forward with great care and patience. Too great care can not be exercised, the first years of a child's training, in the development of voice and speech.

Our aim is to make the elementary work as interesting and natural, and yet as thorough, as possible. With the young children games form a part of the class work, and each child is encouraged to express its little wants in spoken language as soon as it has a sufficient vocabulary. A very few words will enable it to make a beginning. When a child has something to tell all work is stopped, and the teacher aids the little one to use the few words it has learned to express its desire in words, and then she writes it upon the blackboard so that each member of the class may see it and in seeing learn.

Most of the time in the primary classes is devoted to language work. In teaching elementary arithmetic our aim, especially, is to teach arithmetical language, for without it the pupils are at sea while studying that branch.

To increase the interest in language a new and very interesting set of readers has been provided throughout the school.

In the grammar department much the same course of study is pursued as that in the city schools. The pupils read a great deal and show a lively interest in the general news of the day. They have access to the daily papers, Harper's Weekly and several of the leading magazines, and their library contains several hundred books, to which additions are frequently made.

## CHANGES.

Miss Cheney, after three years of very successful work, decided to rest for a year, Miss Sparrow accepted a position in the Colorado institution, and Miss Gill remained at home. To fill the vacancies Miss Forsythe, for several years a teacher in the Pennsylvania Oral School, Miss Flint, who was with us in training last year, and Miss Currier were appointed. They are doing very commendable work. As there were several pupils too old to enter the kindergarten class, with the youngest pupils, it was decided to form another class, and Miss Wells was appointed to take charge of it November first.

The entire school have lessons in physical culture, under the direction of Prof. Doldt, of the Athletic Association, in which they show great interest and aptitude, and we look for great improvement in health, figure and carriage.

## INDUSTRIAL CLASSES.

The work in the industrial department has been very successfully carried forward. The pupils in the printing-room, under the direction of Mr. Goodale, are doing more satisfactory work than during any previous year. In the spring a large set of type was purchased, and lessons and stories have been printed for use in school. In the sloyd-room, under the supervision of Mr. Hunt, the boys are greatly interested, and are doing excellent work. They are at present working on book cases for the main building. We hope, before long, to have the house filled with their work.

We are arranging for the girls to be taught a system of sewing similar to that taught in the Pratt Institute, in Brooklyn, and we shall be glad when we see them cooking also.

Since the boiler was moved from the basement of the main building to the new laundry building, last summer, it has been found much easier and less expensive to heat the building.

We respectfully call your attention to the crowded condition of the dormitories. From a sanitary point there are far too many children sleeping in each dormitory. There is very little space between the beds. There should be but two beds in the space now occupied by three. There are certainly ten more children, of school age, known in the State, who ought to be here, and probably more whose cases I have so far been unable to investigate, but with our crowded condition, even our hospital being used as it is for a dormitory, it is impossible to admit any more.

Allow me also to call your attention to our school rooms. They are very unattractive, and four of them are much too small and very poorly lighted. And it is quite impossible to ventilate any of the rooms. It is very necessary that our pupils have good light and pure air.

The Christmas festivities were held in the assembly hall, where the children found a beautiful tree laden with all manner of useful gifts, toys, candy and fruit, provided by kinds friends of the school.

### ACKNOWLEDGMENTS.

We acknowledge, with thanks, money for the Christmas gifts from Mrs. W. B. Weeden and Col. J. H. Powel; a large box of clothing, toys, and some nice books for the pupils' library, from the Sunshine Club, of Westminster Church; Christmas candy from Messrs. Arnold & Maine, and Messrs. J. H. Preston & Co.; and a fine box of oranges from the Hon. G. L. Littlefield, formerly one of the trustees; and to Mrs. D. B. Pond, for the St. Nicholas and the Youths' Companion for one year.

Our thanks are also due Mrs. S. S. Durfee and Mrs. W. B. Weeden, for clothing.

Respectfully submitted,

LAURA DE L. RICHARDS.

# APPENDIX.

## TABULAR REPORT OF THE PUPILS OF THE SCHOOL

| Name of Pupil. | Residence. | Age. (Approx.) | Date of Admission. |
|---|---|---|---|
| Lynch, James E. . ...... | Wanskuck, Providence... | 18 | Sept. 6, 1880.. |
| Beauchesne, Alphonse.... | .. .. ............. | 16 | Oct. 25, 1886.. |
| Sullivan, Nellie.......... | Newport................. | 13 | Nov. 12, 1886. |
| Grant, Edith .*............ | Providence... .. ...... | 10 | Dec. 13, 1886.. |
| Cole, Luella ............ | South Scituate........... | 12 | March 28, 1887.. |
| Chevers, C. Herbert...... | Providence............. | 14 | April 26, 1887.. |
| Jacques, George A....... | Pawtucket............ .... | 14 | May 11, 1887.. |
| Francis, Manuel......... | Bristol..... ......... | 14 | Sept. 26, 1887.. |
| Canning, Thomas F...... | Woonsocket............. | 12 | Sept. 3, 1888.. |
| Hackett, Clara L........ | Providence... .. .... ... | 10 | Sept. 20, 1888.. |
| Gill, Eva G.............. | Providence... .. .... ... | 10 | Dec. 10, 1888 . |
| Goldenofsky, Moses....... | Woonsocket............. | 10 | April 29, 1889.. |
| Hackett, Laura........... | Providence............. | 8 | Nov. 11, 1889.. |
| Maker, Dora C .......... | Providence............. | 10 | May 19, 1890.. |
| Egan, Frederick ........ | Providence............. | 11 | Sept. 1, 1890.. |
| Fletcher, Henrietta M .... | Johnston... ............ | 10 | Sept. 1, 1890.. |
| Trudeau, Leonel ........ | Woonsocket.. ... .... ... | 12 | Nov. 19, 1890.. |
| O'Brien, William T........ | Providence ............. | 12 | Dec. 1, 1890.. |
| Lease, Edwin G....... .. | Providence............. | 11 | Feb. 2, 1891.. |
| Beatty, John... . ...... | Johnston............. | 12 | April 27, 1891.. |
| Courtemauche, Henry.... | Woonsocket........ ... | 12 | June 10, 1891.. |
| Staunton, Annie L....... | Providence............. | 12 | Sept. 8, 1891.. |
| Staunton, Bertha......... | Providence............. | 8 | Oct. 5, 1891.. |
| Gay, Frederick. ........ | Providence... ........ | 8 | Nov. 9, 1891.. |
| Jermyn, William.. .. .... | Newport............. | 10 | May 5, 1892.. |
| Mills, Annetta ........... | Providence... .. .... .. | 6 | April 3, 1893.. |
| Carr, David .... ...... | Pawtucket.... . .... | 6 | Jan. 27, 1893.. |
| Collins, Chester A. ...... | Providence............. | 4 | Jan. 30, 1893.. |
| Kleber, Fannie ......... | Lymansville............. | 6 | Feb. 7, 1893.. |
| Mercier, Addie C.. ... . | Shannock............. | 10 | Feb. 7, 1893.. |
| Goldstein, Clara J........ | Providence............. | 9 | March 1, 1893.. |
| Desonie, Maggie ..... .. | Lippitt ............. | 8 | March 23, 1893.. |
| Smith, Bernard F........ | Providence............. | 8 | April 10, 1893.. |
| O'Connor, Mary.......... | Woonsocket ........ .... | 6 | May 27, 1893.. |
| Hoen, Alfred. .......... | Carolina............. | ... | Sept. 11, 1893.. |
| Knowles, Grace E........ | South Kingstown ....... | 4 | Sept. 11, 1893.. |
| Thompson, George. ...... | Providence........ ...... | 4 | Sept. 11, 1893.. |
| Pulsifer, M. Hellen . ..... | River Point.......... ... | 8 | Sept. 11, 1893.. |
| Savard, Mary C. S. S...... | Woonsocket.. ........... | 12 | Sept. 11, 1893.. |
| Flynn, James......... | Providence............. | 6 | Feb. 3, 1894.. |
| Pease, Walter M.......... | Woonsocket.. .. ........ | 5 | Sept. 10, 1894.. |
| Comfort, Mae E. .. .... | Newport...... ...... | 8 | Sept. 10, 1894.. |
| Bradley, William H ...... | Woonsocket............. | 11 | Oct. 1, 1894.. |
| Mudrak, Willie,......... | Geneva .... ......... | 4 | Oct. 13, 1894.. |
| Canney, John P.......... | Providence.. ....... | 9 | Dec. 3, 1894.. |
| Grimes, Mary ........ .... | Newport. ... . .... | 9 | Feb. 5, 1895.. |
| O'Riley, Willie F.. .. .... | East Providence.. ... ... | 7 | Feb. 11, 1895 . |

## FOR THE YEAR ENDING DECEMBER 31, 1897.

| Cause of Deafness, as far as known. | Age when made deaf. (Approx.) | Remarks. |
|---|---|---|
| Brain fever........ ........... | 2 years, 2 months. | ...................... |
| Scarlet fever....... ... ......... | 4 years.......... | ............... ......... |
| Scarlet fever ... ............... | 2 years.......... | .............. ......... |
| Tumor in ear ................. | 6 months........ | ..... .............. ....... |
| Congenital.................... | | |
| Brain fever.. ............... | 6 months........ | Slight degree of hearing. |
| Meningitis................... | 2 years, 6 months. | .................... .... |
| Typhoid fever............ .... | 3 years, 6 months. | ....................... |
| Congenital.. ............... | | |
| Congenital.................... | ....................... | Hard of hearing. |
| Scarlet fever............. .... | 5 years.......... | ........ .......... ..... |
| Scarlet fever................. | 8 years..... .... | ........ ............ .... |
| Congenital.................... | | .................... .... |
| Scarlet fever........ ......... | 8 years.......... | Hard of hearing . |
| Meningitis................... | 7 years.......... | ...................... |
| Congenital... ............... | | ...................... |
| Congenital.... ............... | ....................... | Slight degree of hearing. |
| Run over..................... | .... .......... | Hard of hearing. |
| Unknown..................... | 4 years. ......... | Hard of hearing. |
| Congenital.................... | | ............. .. ..... .... |
| Congenital..................... | | |
| Brain fever.. ............... | 1 year........... | Hard of hearing. |
| Brain fever....... ........... | 3 years............ | ................... |
| Scarlet fever........ ......... | 3 years........... | ..................... .. |
| Congenital..... ... ......... | .. .............. | ............ ........... .. |
| Measles.............. ......... | 3 years. ........ | .... .............. .. ...... |
| A fall..................... | 2 years...... ... | ........ ............. ...... |
| Measles........ ............. | 2 years........ .. | .......... ......... ...... |
| Congenital.... ............... | ................. | Deafness partial. |
| Scarlet fever....... ... ...... | 5 years........ | ......... ............... |
| Typhoid fever................. | 4 years.......... | ....... ................ |
| Congenital.................... | ....... .... .. | ...... ..... ........ |
| ......... ............... ...... | 1 year.. .... ...... | Not deaf. |
| Scarlet fever................. | 1 year........ | ...................... |
| A fall........................ | 2 years.... ...... | Deafness partial . |
| Grippe ................... | 2 years........... | ............. ........... ... |
| Convulsions.................. | 3 years.......... | .................. ........... |
| Measles..... ............. | 6 years........... | ..................... .. |
| Congenital.................. | ......... ..... ... | |
| Congenital.... ............... | | |
| Grippe........ ............. | 2 years........... | ............ ................ |
| Catarrhal fever .............. | 1 year, 6 months.. | ..................... |
| Diphtheria .. ..... ... ..... | 6 years............ | ..................... ... |
| Congenital.................... | ..... ......... | ...... ...... ........ |
| Taking quinine..... .......... | 1 year............ | ...................... |
| Measles.. ..... ............. | 5 years........... | Slight degree of hearing. |
| Congenital..... ............. | ................ | .......... .. ... .... |

TABULAR REPORT OF THE PUPILS OF THE SCHOOL

| NAME OF PUPIL. | RESIDENCE. | AGE. (Approx.) | DATE OF ADMISSION. |
|---|---|---|---|
| Grace, Theresa............ | Providence.............. | 12 | April 10, 1895.. |
| Welsh, John..... ... ... | Providence.............. | 7 | May 20, 1895.. |
| Roe, Albert C........... ..... | Hope............ ...... | 5 | Sept. 21, 1895.. |
| Stetson, Leroy W. ...... | Warren................. | 10 | Sept. 30, 1895.. |
| Grebert, Herman.......... | Bristol. ................. | 9 | Oct. 14, 1895.. |
| Boivert, Mary........... ...... | Providence.............. | 18 | Oct. 27, 1895.. |
| Smith, Idella.. .. ........ | Johnston......... ........ | 9 | Oct. 28, 1895.. |
| Lefebre, Isaac............. | Natick................. | 18 | May 6, 1895.. |
| Williams, Charles A....... | Pawtucket.............. | 4 | Sept. 14, 1896.. |
| Cook, Reuben,............ | Peace Dale............. | 7 | Oct. 6, 1896.. |
| Perron, Lena.. ... .. ... | Woonsocket..... ..... .. | 7 | Oct. 26, 1896.. |
| Anderson, Edward V...... | Providence.............. | 9 | ............ ...... |
| Vigeant, Edward.. ....... | Pawtucket,.............. | 7 | May 3, 1897.. |
| Gardner, May. ........... | Scituate..... ......... ... | 10 | April 29, 1897.. |
| Davis, Elsie....... ........ | Shawomet ... .......... | 9 | Sept. 13, 1897.. |
| Essex, Fred E. L...... ... | ............. ....... | 11 | Sept. 13, 1897.. |

## FOR THE YEAR ENDING DECEMBER 31, 1897.

| CAUSE OF DEAFNESS, AS FAR AS KNOWN. | AGE WHEN MADE DEAF. (Approx.) | REMARKS. |
|---|---|---|
| Congenital .................... | .................... | .................... |
| Brain fever.................... | 3 years........... | .................... |
| Inflammation in head.......... | 4 months. ........ | .................... |
| Fall and fever.... .... ....... | 4 years........... | Slight degree of hearing. |
| Congenital......... .. ........ | .................... | .................... |
| Fever.......................... | 3 years........... | .................... |
| Congenital...... .... ... .. | .................... | Slight degree of hearing. |
| Scarlet fever.................. | 3 years........... | .................... |
| Congenital.................. ... | .................... | .... .. ...... ........... |
| Congenital.... ............. ... | .................... | .................... |
| Scarlet fever................. ... | 1 year.... ... ... | .................... |
| Scarlet fever............. ...... | 5 years.... ...... | Hard of hearing. |
| Scarlet fever............. ...... | 4 years........... | .................... |
| Scarlet fever.................. | 5 years... ........ | ... ......... ........... |
| ... .. ... ........... ........ | .................... | .................... |
| Scrofula...................... | 3 years.... .. .. | ....... ................. |

## SUMMARY.

Number of pupils from date of opening the State school for the deaf, April
2, 1877, to December 31, 1897.................................... ..... 139

Number of pupils who have entered the institute since Dec. 31, 1896. ..... 4

Whole number of pupils who have attended the school..... ........ 139

Number who have left the school... ........ ............ ........ 83

Number of pupils Dec. 31, 1897......................................... 58

Number of girls who have attended school during the year............... 26

Number of boys who have attended school during the year.... .. ........ 37

Whole number of pupils during the year ... .... ................. 63

Average attendance............. .............. ... ..................... 52

Number congenitally deaf, or made deaf before the age of two...... ..... 23

Number who lost hearing between the ages of two and four............... 24

Number who lost hearing after the age of four, and doubtful cases......... 11

58

Number who have any degree of hearing.... ....... ... . .... ..... 16

*Residences of all who have attended during the year 1897.*

Geneva.......... ........... ................................ .. ........ 1

Providence, including Wanskuck ........... ............. ............. 25

East Providence ...... ....... .. ............................ .. ......... 1

Pawtucket.. ............ ...... .......... .............................. 4

South Scituate...... ........................... ............ ........ ... 2

Johnston......... .......... ............................. ................ 3

Newport...... ...... ...................................... ............ 4

Lymansville.... .. ...................................................... 1

Shannock... ........... .............................. ................. 1

Lippitt. ... ... ........................................ ... ........... 1

Peace Dale.. ..................................... ...... .. ... ..... ..... 1

Natick............................................................. 1
South Kingstown.................................................. 1
River Point....................................................... 1
Woonsocket....................................................... 9
Carolina.......................................................... 1
Hope............................................................. 1
Bristol........................................................... 2
Warren........................................................... 1
Shawomat......................................................... 1

Nineteen localities........................................... 63

### PERIODICALS.

The receipt of the following periodicals is thankfully acknowledged, and their continuance respectfully requested.

Mute's Companion, Fairibault, Minn.; Daily Paper for Our Little People, Rochester, N. Y.; Our Children's School Journal, The Deaf Mute Journal, New York; Maryland Bulletin, Frederick, Md.; The Deaf Mute Voice, Jackson, Miss.; Kentucky Deaf Mute, Danville, Ky.; The Goodson Gazette, Staunton, Va.; Kansas Star, Olathe, Kansas; Deaf Mute Optic, Little Rock, Ark.; Deaf Mute Index, Colorado Springs, Col.; Juvenile Ranger, Austin, Texas; The Register, Rome, N. Y.; Nebraska Mute Journal, Omaha, Neb; New Method for the Deaf, Englewood, Ill.; Weekly News, Berkeley, Cal.

### LIPPITT PRIZE FUND AWARDED FOR

*Speech.*

Eva Gill.

*Speech Reading.*

Stephanie Savard.

*Greatest Improvement in Speech.*

Willie O'Brien.          Addie Mercier.

*Greatest Improvement in Speech Reading.*

Luella Cole.                    John Beatty.

*Best in Language.*

Fred Egan.

*Greatest General Improvement.*

Edith Grant.

*Greatest Improvement in Deportment.*

Manuel Francis                  Fred Gay.

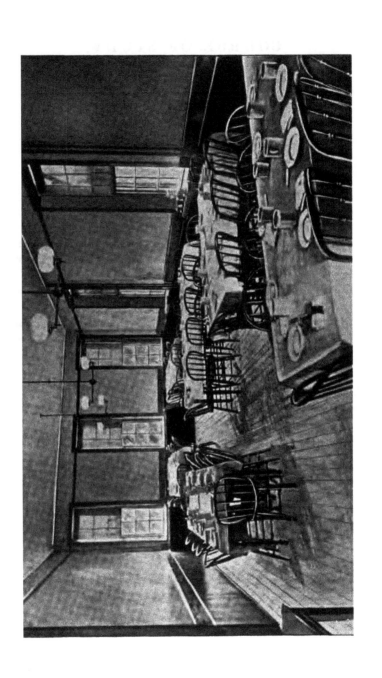

# COURSE OF STUDY.

## KINDERGARTEN.

### FIRST YEAR.

- a. KINDERGARTEN EXERCISES.
- b. ARTICULATION.
- c. LANGUAGE.
- d. ARITHMETIC.
- e. PENMANSHIP.

a. Paper cutting and folding; drawing and modeling in clay; designing in shoe pegs; stick laying; embroidery designs sewed on pricked sewing cards; lessons in form and color in all exercises.

b. Elements, combinations, simple words and sentences; with reading them from the lips.

c. Nouns; objects in class-room, articles of dress, articles of food, different parts of the body, with a limited number of verbs. Adjectives; good, bad, large, small, &c.

d. Counting and writing numbers, with addition and subtraction to 10.

e. Writing on slate and with lead pencil.

## PRIMARY COURSE.

### SECOND, THIRD, AND FOURTH YEARS.

- a. ARTICULATION.
- b. LANGUAGE.
- c. ARITHMETIC.
- d. GEOGRAPHY.
- e. PENMANSHIP.
- f. DRAWING.

*a.* Drill in elements, combinations and words, and reading them from the lips.

*b.* Thorough review of first year work. Nouns and verbs continued. Adjectives continued ; their comparison. Pronouns as in first year, adding myself, herself, himself, with the plurals, and the relatives who and which. Adverbs ; not, often, never, &c. Elliptical sentences ; action and picture writing ; journal and letter writing, and simple stories.

*c.* Practical exercises in addition, subtraction, multiplication, and division ; United States currency ; simple fractions.

*d.* School-room, building and yard, city, and a limited knowledge of the State.

*e.* Copy-book writing.

## INTERMEDIATE COURSE.

### FIFTH, SIXTH AND SEVENTH YEARS.

*a.* ARTICULATION.

*b.* LANGUAGE.

*c.* ARITHMETIC.

*d.* GEOGRAPHY.

*e.* HISTORY.

*f.* PENMANSHIP.

*g.* DRAWING.

*h.* CALISTHENICS.

*a.* Drill in elements, combinations, syllables; words and sentences continued as in primary course.

*b.* Nouns, pronouns, adjectives, adverbs, prepositions and conjunctions continued as in primary course. Drill in active and passive voices; action and picture writing; stories from natural history; journal and letter writing.

*c.* Mental and written addition, subtraction, multiplication and division, with practical examples; United States currency and simple fractions continued.

*d.* City, State and New England States.

*e.* Simple historical stories in connection with geography.

*f.* Copy-book writing twice a week.

*g.* Object drawing.

## HIGHER COURSE.

EIGHTH, NINTH, AND TENTH YEARS.

*a.* ARTICULATION.

*b.* LANGUAGE.

*c.* ARITHMETIC.

*d.* GEOGRAPHY.

*e.* HISTORY.

*f.* PHYSIOLOGY.

*g.* PENMANSHIP.

*h.* DRAWING.

*i.* CALISTHENICS.

*a.* Drill in difficult combinations and words.

*b.* Composition; journal and letter writing; miscellaneous reading; newspapers and magazines; lessons on general subjects.

*c.* Mental, written and practical.

*d.* Geographical reader; Manual of Commerce.

*e.* History of the United States; Outline of General History.

*g.* Copy-book.

*h.* Free-hand and object drawing and designing.

ients, combinations and words, and reading them from th

view of first year work. Nouns and verbs continued. .

inued ; their comparison. Pronouns as in first year, addin

lf, himself, with the plurals, and the relatives who and 1

not, often, never, &c. Elliptical sentences ; action and p

journal and letter writing, and simple stories.

ercises in addition, subtraction, multiplication, and div

ates currency ; simple fractions.

, building and yard, city, and a limited knowledge of the

'riting.

## INTERMEDIATE COURSE.

### FIFTH, SIXTH AND SEVENTH YEARS.

a. ARTICULATION.

b. LANGUAGE.

c. ARITHMETIC.

d. GEOGRAPHY.

e. HISTORY.

f. PENMANSHIP.

g. DRAWING.

h. CALISTHENICS.

ents, combinations, syllables ; words and sentences continu

course.

uns, adjectives, adverbs, prepositions and conjunctions c

primary course. Drill in active and passive voices ; actio

riting, stories from natural history ; journal and letter wri

ritten addition, subtraction, multiplication and division,

examples. United States currency and simple fractions

of New England States.

cal stories in connection with geography.

riting twice a week.

# TO PARENTS OF DEAF CHILDREN.

This school is for the benefit of children incapacitated through deafness, total or partial, for receiving proper instruction in common schools, and is free to all pupils who belong in this State.

The aim of the school is to teach deaf children to use the English language with the spontaneity, correctness, and enjoyment of hearing children as far as this is practicable.

"Without language there can be no thought, no reason;" and as the highest aim of all instruction is the culture of the mental and moral nature in man, our first effort should be to furnish the deaf with a medium through which knowledge can be imparted and obtained. This can be done by signs, by the finger alphabet, and by speech. Our method is the latter, or oral method, by which the deaf can be educated, and at the same time furnished with the usual and most convenient way of communication in society and the world at large.

It is very desirable that deaf children be sent to school at as early an age as possible. A parent will be amply repaid for sending a child as young as five or six years, even at some inconvenience. The board of trustees are authorized to receive pupils between the ages of three and twenty years.

If a child who has learned to talk is made deaf by disease he should immediately, upon his recovery, be sent to a school where his speech will be retained, and where he will be taught to understand from the lips. In such cases it is common to delay so long that serious loss of speech results.

Speech reading is an invaluable acquisition for those who are semi-deaf, or even hard of hearing, as well as for those congenitally or totally deaf.

Every effort should be made to encourage the child to retain the use of his voice.  He should be taught to pronounce common words by watching the lip motion and facial expression, or by feeling the muscular action of the breath; but no attempt should be made to teach him *the names* of the letters of the alphabet.

The English branches are taught here, and every pupil is taught some branch of industry.

The school session begins the second Monday in September, and closes the third Friday in June, with a week's holiday at Christmas.

Application for admission should be made to the principal, at the Institute, corner of East avenue and Cypress street, Providence.

Compliments of

Laura E. L. Richards,

Principal.

State of Rhode Island and Providence Plantations.

# REPORT OF THE BOARD OF TRUSTEES

OF THE

## RHODE ISLAND

# INSTITUTE FOR THE DEAF,

PRESENTED TO THE

## GENERAL ASSEMBLY

AT ITS

## JANUARY SESSION, 1899.

PROVIDENCE:
E. L. FREEMAN & SONS, PRINTERS TO THE STATE.
1899.

# REPORT OF BOARD OF TRUSTEES.

*To the Honorable the General Assembly at its January Session A. D. 1899.*

The Board of Trustees of the Rhode Island Institute for the Deaf respectfully present the following report for the year 1898:

We are happy to be able to say that the past year has been one of even prosperity for the Institute. The children generally have manifested a constantly growing interest and appreciation of the value to them of the instruction and care so freely and generously furnished to them by the State, and exhibit a corresponding improvement in results accomplished.

We are also glad to report that the health of the school during the year has been uniformly good; that while the school has not been exempt from the usual amount of sickness incident to children collected together in large numbers, we have nevertheless thus far fortunately escaped all serious cases of illness.

We are also rejoiced to be able to say that we have every reason to believe that the institution is rapidly gaining in popular favor and appreciation as its scope, objects, and beneficent results become more widely known among the people of the State.

The teaching force of the Institute as it has been maintained throughout the year, consists of the Principal and a corps of nine female and three male teachers.

The corps of teachers as now organized are for the most part experienced in the system of teaching, having had from one to sixteen years' experience therein respectively, and are accomplishing satisfactory results.

A number of changes in the personnel of the teaching force was made during the year, but the *morale* and efficiency of the corps as a whole have been fully maintained and strengthened by the changes made.

During the year an additional class in sloyd has been organized, composed of a younger class of boys, who are manifesting a commendable degree of interest and improvement in the work.

The results of the training in physical culture during the preceding year appeared so satisfactory to the Board that it was deemed highly desirable that the instruction should be continued. They accordingly re-engaged the services of Prof. Doldt, who during the year gave weekly instruction to the whole school.

The pupils entered into these exercises with great interest and zeal, and we believe the course has been of inestimable advantage to them, both physically and mentally.

The value of this instruction is so apparent that it is the intention of the Board to continue the course for the present as a permanent part of the curriculum.

The attendance during the year was as follows:

Whole number of pupils.......................................... 68
"        "       of boys ....................................... 34
"        "       of girls....................................... 29
"        "       at present in attendance ...................... 62
"        "       of boys at present in attendance.............. 34
"        "       of girls at present in attendance............. 28

The corps of attendants and servants at present employed at the Institute is thirteen.

We respectfully submit the following financial report as to maintenance:

Annual appropriation............................ . $19,000 00

## EXPENDITURES.

| | | | | | |
|---|---|---|---|---|---|
| Salaries for January, | 1898.............. | $677 00 | | |
| " | " February, | " ............. ... | 677 50 | | |
| " | " March, | " .............. | 675 00 | | |
| " | " April, | ......... .... | 673 00 | | |
| " | " May, | .............. | 685 00 | | |
| " | " June, | .............. | 690 00 | | |
| " | " July, | .............. | 71 35 | | |
| " | " August, | " .............. | 71 00 | | |
| " | " September, | " .............. | 645 87 | | |
| " | " October, | " .............. | 719 80 | | |
| " | " November, | " ........ ...... | 729 50 | | |
| " | " December, | " .............. | 737 00 | | |

Total amount of salaries................. $7,052 02

Other expenses ......... ................ 11,233 81

Total amount of expenditures............   18,285 83

Balance covered into the treasury........   $714 17

## EXPENDITURES GROUPED IN DETAIL.

| | |
|---|---|
| Salaries and wages............................... | $7,052 02 |
| Coal................... ........ ................. | 1,042 70 |
| Gas....................... .................... | 316 19 |
| Water........... ................ ......... | 135 81 |
| Ice.....: .............. .................... | 107 29 |
| Meat, milk, &c...................................... | 1,289 84 |
| Groceries, &c...................................... | 1,893 19 |
| Improvements and repairs........................ | 1,718 57 |
| Concreting walks and spaces..................... | 242 41 |
| Grading........................................... | 135 35 |

| | | |
|---|---:|---:|
| Storm windows | $135 | 00 |
| Wire guards for windows | 87 | 00 |
| Printing and stationery | 60 | 31 |
| Medicine and medical attendance | 303 | 81 |
| Telephone | 100 | 00 |
| Advertising | 12 | 34 |
| School supplies | 286 | 88 |
| Furnishings | 1,247 | 72 |
| Electric motor | 61 | 00 |
| Physical culture lessons | 100 | 00 |
| Sewing lessons | 57 | 50 |
| Removing and repairing fire escapes | 150 | 00 |
| Covering steam pipes | 86 | 19 |
| Architects' fees | 1,071 | 67 |
| Miscellaneous | 593 | 04 |
| Total | $18,285 | 83 |

## IMPROVEMENTS.

For several years prior to last year the Board had been constantly made to realize that the growth of the school and the extension of its usefulness had reached its possible limits, by reason of insufficient accommodations for pupils and teachers, and that, unless further and additional facilities were supplied by the State, the Institute could not in the future be expected to fully meet the needs of the community in furnishing an education in oral language to that class of unfortunates whose needs and claims the Institute was established to supply and answer.

To the end and in the hope of being able to induce the General Assembly at its January session, 1898, to make a suitable appropriation for the extension of the dormitory and hospital accommodations, so that the advantages of the school should be denied to none entitled to its benefits, the Board of Trustees laid before it the facts of the situation, with plans and estimates of the needed improvements, and requested an appropriation for that purpose.

The General Assembly thereupon, with its accustomed liberality, romptly appropriated $25,000 to purchase the necessary adjoining land, and to erect the necessary additions and alterations of he buildings, under the direction of the Board of Trustees.

We are happy to report that the work has been accomplished. Ve purchased a strip of land adjoining the land already occupied y the Institute on the south, and bounding on East avenue and —— street, platted but not yet laid out.

The title to the land was examined and approved by the attorey-general and the deed prepared and execution approved by im, and the same has been duly recorded and filed with the eneral treasurer of the State.

Both wings and the central division of the old building have een so extended as to furnish ample accommodation for fifty oys and thirty-five girls, with a corresponding increase of class ooms and rooms for teachers and for use as hospitals.

The former crowded condition of the dormitories has been happily relieved, and ample air space, so necessary for the health of he pupils, has been now secured.

We believe that these accommodations will be ample for all the growth and increase that may be reasonably expected for many ears to come.

In making these additions the same general unpretentious style f structure and finish of the old building was employed in the ew, but the work, as we believe, has been done in a better and aore substantial manner.

Following is a statement of the expenditures incurred and paid n making the improvements.

## CONSTRUCTION ACCOUNT.

Appropriation ............................................ ...$25,000 00

1898.

May 20.   Paid Barstow heirs for land....... $5,500 00
June 17.   Paid for recording deed.........    1 80

1898.

| June 17. | Paid for advertising for bids in the Providence Journal............ | $10 58 | |
| July 13. | Paid Maguire & Penniman, on account of building contract...... | 4,905 00 | |
| Aug. 16. | Paid Maguire & Penniman, on account of contract............. | 4,275 00 | |
| Sept. 9. | Paid Maguire & Penniman, on account of contract............. | 2,061 00 | |
| Sept. 19. | Paid Samuel Jackson Co., steam heating, etc ................. | 1,000 00 | |
| Oct. 6. | Paid Maguire & Penniman, on account of contract............. | 1,854 00 | |
| Oct. 6. | Paid Samuel Jackson Co., steam heating, etc.................. | 750 00 | |
| Nov. 19. | Paid Maguire & Penniman, on account of contract............. | 1,520 40 | |
| Nov. 21. | Paid Samuel Jackson Co., steam heating, etc ................. | 500 00 | |
| Dec. | Paid Maguire & Penniman, final payment on building contract... | 1,628 83 | |
| Dec. | Paid Tierney & Co., plumbling.... | 781 50 | |
| Dec. | Paid Samuel Jackson, final payment on account steam heating contract........................ | 207 00 | |
| Total.................................. | | | 24,995 11 |
| Balance in treasury.............. ......... | | | $4 89 |

The above work practically completed the improvements with the exception of some alterations and repairs both upon the old and new building, made necessary by the addition, and which have been paid out of the general appropriation for maintenance.

The above work was commenced early in the season, as soon as possible after the close of the school for the summer vacation.

DINING ROOM.

The contracts for building were made with the lowest bidder, upon bids advertised for in the public newspapers, and the work was forwarded during the summer vacation with all possible speed consistent with good work, in the hope of completing the improvements in season for the opening of the fall term at the usual time in September. In this, however, we were disappointed, on account of unavoidable delays in some parts of the work, and consequently we were not able to open the school until October 18, 1898.

For maintenance during the ensuing year we recommend the usual appropriation, $19,000.

We annex hereto the annual report of the Principal, made to the Board of Trustees, which contains more full and detailed information as to the condition, needs, and work of the school, and also the medical report for the year.

Respectfully submitted,

ELISHA DYER, *Governor,*

WILLIAM GREGORY, *Lieutenant-Governor,*

*Ex-officio.*

LIVINGSTON SCOTT, *President,*

MRS. ELLEN T. McGUINNESS, *Secretary,*

MRS. JEANIE LIPPITT WEEDEN,

MRS. LILLIE B. CHACE WYMAN,

WILLIAM K. POTTER,

DR. ROWLAND R. ROBINSON,

JOHN C. B. WOODS,

MARSDEN J. PERRY,

JEREMIAH HORTON.

*Board of Trustees.*

PROVIDENCE, R. I., January, 1899.

# MEDICAL REPORT.

*To the Trustees of the Rhode Island Institute for the Deaf:*

I have the honor to report concerning the health of the pupils during the year past:

In the early part of the year there were four mild cases of diphtheria, all of them sent to the Rhode Island Hospital, where they made good recoveries. There have been frequent cases of tonsillitis, and a few minor accidents. In November one of the servants developed diphtheria, followed in about two weeks by one case among the boys. At about the same time another of the smaller boys showed signs of scarlet fever and was promptly removed to the Rhode Island Hospital, as were the others. These cases, with a recent case of pleurisy with effusion, made all the sickness for the year. The superior facilities for isolation offered by the new hospital rooms were effective in preventing general spread of contagion. Much credit is due the principal and her assistants for carefully noting, and as promptly reporting all cases of illness, and I have invariably found suspicious cases already isolated on my arrival. The health departments, both of the city and State, should have your especial thanks for the ready and careful way in which they have examined the large number of cultures made from the throats of the children, and for their prompt response to the requests for removal to hospital and thorough disinfection measures adopted in every case.

Respectfully submitted,

FRANK L. DAY, M. D.

PROVIDENCE,
December 31, 1898.

# REPORT OF THE PRINCIPAL.

*To the Board of Trustees of the Rhode Island Institute for the Deaf:*

Allow me to submit for your consideration the following report for the year ending December 31, 1898, being the seventh annual report of this Institute.

January 1, 1898, there were 60 pupils in attendance, 34 boys and 26 girls; eight pupils were admitted during the year, making our enrollment 68. At the opening of school in September four pupils remained at home, and at the beginning of November a boy about fifteen was taken home and placed under a private tutor, and the families of two other boys moved out of the State—which took them from the school—leaving us 61 pupils in attendance.

Owing to the unfinished condition of the additions to the main building, school did not reopen until the 18th of October, when we opened with 57 pupils; four others were admitted the first week of school, and another came the first week in November.

The first few weeks after our return were quite confused, as we were in crowded quarters and greatly inconvenienced by the army of workmen about the place; but now that they have disappeared, leaving us with fine spacious halls and dormitories, we smile at past annoyances and are happy in our delightful building.

The girls and boys each have a pleasant library, leading from their respective sitting-rooms, fitted up with well filled book-cases, writing-tables, &c., which they appreciate and are very proud of.

The dining-rooms for both teachers and children were enlarged, as well as the play-rooms, which were made much lighter and brighter. A part of the large room—on the first floor of the north addition—is used by the kindergarten class, and is a most delightful, bright room for the little ones; the remainder can be used by another class if necessary. The dormitories are much lighter, brighter, and far more airy and healthful than formerly. The nursery for the small boys, which for three years was in a room built for hospital use, has been brought down stairs, and they now are in a cozy little dormitory on the second floor, and the girls have a similar one in the south wing.

### HEALTH.

As in the past two or three years, there was but little illness among the children during the year past. There were at different times a few cases of diphtheria, which, as soon as they came to our knowledge, were isolated to the best of our ability, and as soon as they were pronounced cases were sent to the Rhode Island Hospital—and here I wish to express my sincere thanks to the Superintendent of Health for his great kindness to us whenever we have asked his assistance. New rooms were added to our hospital, and we have, at this early date, found them of great service, as we are now able to isolate all cases of illness at once.

### CLASS WORK.

Work in the class-rooms was carried on as usual, with more attention, if possible, given to articulation and enunciation.

Every day's work represents a development which is very important when acquiring speech, and when a child is out of school for a few days the time cannot be made up, and each teacher should try to inspire her pupils with such desire to work that they will push forward with earnest cheerfulness. Care has been taken to inspire the children with patriotism, temperance, love of animals and nature. Flags have been provided for each class, and flag days have been observed, which both interested and in-

structed the school. The older children have taken great interest in "current events," and have read the newspapers daily to gather what information they could of what has been agitating the public mind for the past year, and they have shown much interest in gaining information about the army and navy. Even the "little people" have learned considerable about the soldiers, war, and the battle-ships. The very young children are taught weaving, stick laying, and other work adapted from the kindergarten, and they are also given, in speech, the elements and such simple words as they can speak from imitation, and those children that have been in school a year are given language work, while the elementary drill and vocal gymnastics are continued. As they progress in the use of the English language they are given primary school work, the same as is taught in the public schools, and the older pupils are given the grammar course.

There is a great deal of enthusiasm in the physical culture class. The instruction is given under the direction of Prof. Doldt. Before the close of the school last June Prof. Doldt gave the class a test drill and awarded prizes to the three who went through the most creditably Mr. Walter Peck, one of the judges, added three other prizes, as there were several pupils between whom it was very difficult to determine which excelled.

## MANUAL TRAINING.

Very little change has been made in this department; two more boys have entered the printing class. In the sloyd-room Mr. Hunt has been given a class of ten small boys in addition to the other two lessons which he has given each week.

He has suggested some form of manual training, either bent iron or card board work, be given the still younger pupils. This has been found very serviceable in hand and eye training among normal children, and we feel that it will be much more so among our children, who depend almost entirely upon the eyes.

Miss Gardiner gives two lessons every Saturday morning in sewing, using the system taught in Pratt Institute, Brooklyn.

As usual the children were provided a beautiful Christmas tree through the kindness of friends. Owing to the appearance of a case of scarlet fever—which was taken to the Rhode Island Hospital at once—the children had the Christmas tree and school was closed two days earlier than usual.

### ACKNOWLEDGMENTS.

Thanks are due our friends Mrs. W. B. Weeden, Mrs. E. D. McGuinness, Mr. Marsden J. Perry, Miss M. H. Flint, and Miss Richards for giving money to provide Christmas presents for the school, and to Messrs. Arnold & Maine and Messrs. J. H. Preston & Co. for Christmas candies. We are very grateful to the Hon. G. L. Littlefield for a fine box of oranges, which was a great delight to a few of the little ones who were not able to go home, and to Mrs. D. B. Pond, for subscribing for the St. Nicholas and the Youth's Companion, which were sent us for a year. We also thank Mrs. W. B. Weeden and Mrs. S. S. Durfee for sending clothing.

Respectfully submitted,

LAURA DE L. RICHARDS.

# APPENDIX.

## TABULAR REPORT OF THE PUPILS OF THE SCHOOL

| Name of Pupil. | Residence. | Age. (Approx.) | Date of Admission. |
|---|---|---|---|
| Sullivan, Nellie........... | Newport .... . ... | 13 | Nov. 12, 1886.. |
| Grant, Edith.............. | Providence... . ....... | 10 | Dec. 13, 1886.. |
| Cole, Luella  .... .... | South Scituate......... | 12 | March 28, 1887.. |
| Chevers, C. Herbert. .... | Providence ............. | 14 | April 26, 1887... |
| Jacques, George A . | Pawtucket... ... .... | 14 | May 11, 1887.. |
| Francis, Manuel........... | Bristol ............ .. ... | 14 | Sept. 26, 1887.. |
| Canning, Thomas F. ..... | Woonsocket. .... | 12 | Sept. 3, 1888.. |
| Gill, Eva G........... | Providence .......... | 10 | Dec. 10, 1888.. |
| Goldenofsky, Moses. .... | Woonsocket .......... | 10 | April 29, 1889.. |
| Hackett, Laura........ .. | Providence .......... | 8 | Nov. 11, 1889.. |
| Maker, Dora C ..... .... | Providence ... .. ... | 10 | May 19, 1890. |
| Egan, Frederick .......... | Providence .......... | 11 | Sept. 1, 1890.. |
| Fletcher, Henrietta M. .. | Johnston .... ........ | 10 | Sept. 1, 1890.. |
| Trudeau, Leonel   .. . | Woonsocket .......... | 12 | Nov. 19, 1890.. |
| O'Brien, William T.. .... | Providence .......... | 12 | Dec. 1, 1890.. |
| Lease, Edwin G........ . | Providence .......... | 11 | Feb. 2, 1891.. |
| Beatty, John.......... | Johnston .......... | 12 | April 27, 1891.. |
| Courtemanche, Henry ... | Woonsocket.. ........ | 12 | June 10, 1891.. |
| Staunton, Annie L ....... | Providence .......... | 12 | Sept. 8, 1891.. |
| Staunton, Bertha......... | Providence .......... | 8 | Oct. 5, 1891.. |
| Gay, Frederick.. .. .... | Providence .......... | 8 | Nov. 9, 1891.. |
| Jermyn, William.. ........ | Newport .............. | 10 | May 5, 1892. |
| Mills, Annetta .... | Providence .......... | 6 | April 3, 1893.. |
| Carr, David............. | Pawtucket............ ... | 6 | Jan. 27, 1893.. |
| Collins, Chester A. ...... | Providence   .. .... | 4 | Jan. 30, 1893.. |
| Kleber, Fannie........ .. | Lymansville......... | 6 | Feb. 7, 1893.. |
| Mercier, Addie C......... | Shannock .... .... | 10 | Feb. 7, 1893.. |
| Goldstein, Clara J........ | Providence .......... | 9 | March 1, 1893.. |
| Desonie, Maggie .... .... | Lippitt ............. | 8 | March 23, 1893.. |
| Smith, Bernard F.... ... | Providence   ........ | 8 | April 10, 1893.. |
| O'Connor, Mary....... ... | Woonsocket .......... | 6 | May 27, 1893.. |
| Hoen, Alfred.. ......... | Carolina............. | .... | Sept. 11, 1893.. |
| Knowles, Grace E........ | South Kingstown .. .... | 4 | Sept. 11, 1893.. |
| Thompson, George... .... | Providence .. .... .... | 4 | Sept. 11, 1893.. |
| Pulsifer. M. Helen........ | River Point....... . | 8 | Sept. 11, 1893.. |
| Savard, Mary C. S. S. ... | Woonsocket .......... | 12 | Sept. 11, 1893.. |
| Flynn, James............. | Providence .......... | 6 | Feb. 3, 1894.. |
| Pease, Walter M.......... | Woonsocket . .. | 5 | Sept. 10, 1894.. |
| Comfort, Mae E. ....... | Newport .... .. .. .. | 8 | Sept. 10, 1894.. |
| Bradley, William H ....... | Woonsocket .......... | 11 | Oct. 1, 1894.. |
| Mudrak, Willie......... | Geneva.............. | 4 | Oct. 18, 1894.. |
| Canney, John P. ......... | Providence ... .. .... | 9 | Dec. 3, 1894.. |
| Grimes, Mary............ | Newport ............ | 9 | Feb. 5, 1895.. |
| O'Riley, Willie F.. ...... | East Providence......... | 7 | Feb. 11, 1895.. |
| Grace, Theresa.. . ....... | Providence .......... | 12 | April 10, 1895.. |
| Welsh, John............. | Providence .... ...... | 7 | May 20, 1895.. |
| Roe, Albert C........... | Hope.................. | 5 | Sept. 21, 1895.. |

FOR THE YEAR ENDING DECEMBER 31, 1898

| Cause of Deafness, as far as known. | Age when made deaf. (Approx.) | Remarks. |
|---|---|---|
| Scarlet fever | 2 years | |
| Tumor in ear | 6 months | |
| Congenital | | |
| Brain fever | 6 months | Slight degree of hearing. |
| Meningitis | 2 years, 6 months. | |
| Typhoid fever | 3 years, 6 months. | |
| Congenital | | |
| Scarlet fever | 5 years | |
| Scarlet fever | 8 years. | |
| Congenital | | |
| Scarlet fever | 3 years. | Hard of hearing. |
| Meningitis | 7 years. | |
| Congenital | | |
| Congenital | | Slight degree of hearing. |
| Run over | | Hard of hearing. |
| Unknown | 4 years. | Hard of hearing. |
| Congenital | | |
| Congenital | | |
| Brain fever | 1 year | Hard of hearing. |
| Brain fever | 8 years | |
| Scarlet fever | 8 years. | |
| Congenital | | |
| Measles | 8 years. | |
| A fall | 2 years. | |
| Measles | 2 years. | |
| Congenital | | Deafness partial. |
| Scarlet fever | 5 years. | |
| Typhoid fever | 4 years. | |
| Congenital | | |
| | | Not deaf. |
| Scarlet fever | 1 year | |
| A fall | 2 years | Deafness partial. |
| Grippe | 2 years. | |
| Convulsions | 8 years | |
| Measles | 6 years | |
| Congenital | | |
| Congenital | | |
| Grippe | 2 years. | |
| Catarrhal fever | 1 year, 6 months. | |
| Diphtheria | 6 years | |
| Congenital | | |
| Taking quinine | 1 year | |
| Measles | 5 years. | Slight degree of hearing. |
| Congenital | | |
| Congenital | | |
| Brain fever | 8 years. | |
| Inflammation in head | 4 months. | |

## TABULAR REPORT OF THE PUPILS OF THE SCHOOL

| Name of Pupil. | Residence. | Age. (Approx.) | Date of Admission. |
|---|---|---|---|
| Stetson, Leroy W......... | Warren..... .... .... | 10 | Sept. 30, 1895.. |
| Boivert, Mary. ......... . | Providence .... ........ | 13 | Oct. 27, 1895.. |
| Smith, Idella.............. | Johnston .... ... ... ... | 9 | Oct. 28, 1895.. |
| Lefebre, Isaac .... .. ... | Natick ............. .. | 18 | May 6, 1895.. |
| Williams, Charles A...... | Pawtucket. ............ | 4 | Sept. 14, 1896.. |
| Cook, Reuben. .... .... | Peace Dale ... ........ | 7 | Oct. 6, 1896.. |
| Perron, Lena...... .... | Woonsocket ............ | 7 | Oct. 26, 1896.. |
| Anderson, Edward V...... | Providence ............. | 9 | ... ............. |
| Vigeant, Edward.......... | Pawtucket............... | 7 | May 3, 1897., |
| Gardner, May............. | Scituate........... ... .. | 10 | April 29, 1897.. |
| Davis, Elsie. ............. | Rumford ... . .... ... | 9 | Sept. 13, 1897.. |
| Essex, Fred E. L.......... | Providence ............ | 11 | Sept. 13, 1897.. |
| Perry, Joseph C........... | Providence ........... .. | 7 | Jan. 7, 1898.. |
| Yuppa, Concetta.... ..... | Providence ........ .. | 4 | Feb. 10, 1898.. |
| Kirk, John.... ...... | Providence ............. | 6 | May 9, 1898.. |
| Forthier, Angelino.... .. | Pawtucket,.... . ...... | 6 | Oct. 24, 1898.. |
| Holborgen, Srina.... .... | Pawtucket..... .... .. | 6 | Oct. 18, 1898.. |
| Bowen, John.. ..... .... | Providence ........ ... | 18 | Oct. 18, 1898.. |
| Bassett, Genevie W ..... | Moosup Valley. ... .... | 4 | Oct. 18, 1898.. |
| Vogel, Alfred............. | Providence .... .. | 11 | Oct. 18, 1898.. |
| Goldman, Samuel..... | Providence ............. | 9 | Nov. 7, 1898.. |

## FOR THE YEAR ENDING DECEMBER 31, 1898.

| CAUSE OF DEAFNESS, AS FAR AS KNOWN. | AGE WHEN MADE DEAF. (Approx.) | REMARKS. |
|---|---|---|
| Fall and fever. | 4 years. | Slight degree of hearing. |
| Fever. | 3 years. | |
| Congenital | | Slight degree of hearing. |
| Scarlet fever | 3 years. | |
| Congenital | | |
| Congenital | | |
| Scarlet fever | 1 year | |
| Scarlet fever | 5 years. | Hard of hearing. |
| Scarlet fever | 4 years. | |
| Scarlet fever | 5 years. | |
| | | |
| Scrofula | 8 years. | |
| Spinal sickness | 2 months. | |
| Congenital | | |
| Scarlet fever | 2 years. 6 months. | Hard of hearing. |
| Congenital | | |
| Measles | 1 year | |
| Convulsions. | 1 year | Hard of hearing. |
| Congenital | | |
| | | Not deaf |
| A fall. | 3 years. | |

## SUMMARY.

Number of pupils from date of opening the State school for the deaf, April
2, 1877, to December 31, 1898...................... ................... 148
Number of pupils who have entered the Institute since Dec. 31, 1896....... 18
                                                                          ——
Whole number of pupils who have attended the school............ .... 148
Number who have left the school  .. ............................. 84
                                                                          ——
Number of pupils Dec. 31, 1898........................... . ... ........ 62
Number of girls who have attended school during the year ............. 29
Number of boys who have attended school during the year..... .......... 89
                                                                          ——
Whole number of pupils during the year..... .................... 68
Average attendance. .. .. ...................... . ...... .............. 52
Number congenitally deaf, or made deaf before the age of two ........ ... 82
Number who lost hearing between the ages of two and four....... ..... 24
Number who lost hearing after the age of four, and doubtful cases. ....... 12
                                                                          ——
                                                                          68
Number who have any degree of hearing. ... .. ........ .. ......... ... 16

———

*Residences of all who have attended during the year 1898.*

Geneva..... .. .......................................... ......................... 1
Providence, including Wanskuck .. .....  .. ..................... ... .... 29
East Providence ... .   ....  .... .. ... .............................. 1
Pawtucket.. ..  ....... .  ... .............. ... ............. . ....... 6
South Scituate.... ... ..  ............... .......... . ............ .... . 2
Johnston.. .. ................... .  ...... ............ .... .. 8
Newport.. ..   ............... ............ ... .. ...... ......... 4
Lymansville............... .... ... .  ........... . .......... ...... 1
Shannock.   .................. ......... ..  ......... ...  . .... 1
Lippitt............................... ........ .. ........ . ..... .... 1
Peace Dale.. ....  .................... ........ ....... ............ 1
Natick ......... ..... ............. ................. ...... ....... ... 1
South Kingstown....................... .  ...................  .....  . ...... 1

### PERIODICALS.

The receipt of the following periodicals is thankfully acknowledged, and their continuance respectfully requested :

Mute's Companion, Fairibault, Minn.; Daily Paper for Our Little People, Rochester, N. Y.; Our Children's School Journal, The Deaf Mute Journal, New York; Maryland Bulletin, Frederick, Md.; The Deaf Mute Voice, Jackson, Miss.; Kentucky Deaf Mute, Danville, Ky.; The Goodson Gazette, Staunton, Va.; Kansas Star, Olathe, Kansas; Deaf Mute Optic, Little Rock, Ark.; Deaf Mute Index, Colorado Springs Col.; Juvenile Ranger, Austin, Texas; The Register, Rome, N. Y.; Nebraska Mute Journal, Omaha, Neb.; New Method for the Deaf, Englewood, Ill.; Weekly News, Berkeley, Cal.

LIPPITT PRIZE FUND AWARDED FOR

*Speech.*

Eva Gill.

*Speech Reading.*

Jennie Goldstein.

# COURSE OF STUDY.

## KINDERGARTEN.

### FIRST YEAR.

    *a.* KINDERGARTEN EXERCISES.

    *b.* ARTICULATION.

    *c.* LANGUAGE.

    *d.* ARITHMETIC.

    *e.* PENMANSHIP.

*a.* Paper cutting and folding ; drawing and modeling in clay ; designing pegs ; stick laying ; embroidery designs sewed on pricked sewing lessons in form and color in all exercises.

*b.* Elements, combinations, simple words and sentences ; with reading from the lips.

*c.* Nouns ; objects in class-room, articles of dress, articles of food, parts of the body, with a limited number of verbs. Adjectives bad, large, small, &c.

*d.* Counting and writing numbers, with addition and subtraction to 10.

*e.* Writing on slate and with lead pencil.

## PRIMARY COURSE.

### SECOND, THIRD, AND FOURTH YEARS.

    *a.* ARTICULATION.

    *b.* LANGUAGE.

    *c.* ARITHMETIC.

    *d.* GEOGRAPHY.

    *e.* PENMANSHIP.

    *f.* DRAWING.

*a.* Drill in elements, combinations and words, and reading them from the lips.

*b.* Thorough review of first year work. Nouns and verbs continued. Adjectives continued; their comparison. Pronouns as in first year, adding myself, herself, himself, with the plurals, and the relatives who and which. Adverbs; not, often, never, &c. Elliptical sentences; action and picture writing; journal and letter writing, and simple stories.

*c.* Practical exercises in addition, subtraction, multiplication, and division; United States currency; simple fractions.

*d.* School-room, building and yard, city, and a limited knowledge of the State.

*e* Copy-book writing.

## INTERMEDIATE COURSE.

### FIFTH, SIXTH, AND SEVENTH YEARS.

*a* ARTICULATION.

*b.* LANGUAGE.

*c.* ARITHMETIC.

*d.* GEOGRAPHY.

*e.* HISTORY.

*f.* PENMANSHIP.

*g.* DRAWING.

*h.* CALISTHENICS.

*a.* Drill in elements, combinations, syllables; words and sentences continued as in primary course.

*b.* Nouns, pronouns, adjectives, adverbs, prepositions, and conjunctions continued as in primary course. Drill in active and passive voices; action and picture writing; stories from natural history; journal and letter writing.

*c.* Mental and written addition, subtraction, multiplication, and division, with practical examples; United States currency and simple fractions continued.

*d.* City, State, and New England States.

*e.* Simple historical stories in connection with geography.

*f.* Copy-book writing twice a week.

*g.* Object drawing.

## HIGHER COURSE.

EIGHTH, NINTH, AND TENTH YEARS.

    *a.* ARTICULATION.

    *b.* LANGUAGE.

    *c.* ARITHMETIC.

    *d.* GEOGRAPHY. ·

    *e.* HISTORY.

    *f.* PHYSIOLOGY.

    *g.* PENMANSHIP.

    *h.* DRAWING.

    *i.* CALISTHENICS.

*a.* Drill in difficult combinations and words.

*b.* Composition; journal and letter writing; miscellaneous reading; news papers and magazines; lessons on general subjects.

*c.* Mental, written and practical.

*d.* Geographical reader; Manual of Commerce.

*e.* History of the United States; Outline of General History.

*g.* Copy-book.

*h.* Free-hand and object drawing, and designing.

# CHAPTER 332.

## AN ACT IN AMENDMENT OF AND IN ADDITION TO CHAPTER 86 OF THE GENERAL LAWS, ENTITLED "OF THE R. I. SCHOOL FOR THE DEAF."

(Passed May 13, 1896.)

*It is enacted by the General Assembly as follows :*

SECTION 1. All children of parents, or under the control of guardians or other persons, legal residents of this state, between the ages of three and twenty years, whose hearing or speech, or both, are so defective as to make it inexpedient or impracticable to attend the public schools to advantage, not being mentally or otherwise incapable, may attend the Rhode Island Institute for the Deaf, without charge, under such rules and regulations as the board of trustees of said institute may establish.

SEC. 2. Every person having under his control any such child between the ages of seven and eighteen years shall cause such child to attend school at said institute for such period of time or such prescribed course, in each individual case, as may be deemed expedient by the board of trustees, and for any neglect of such duty the person so offending shall be fined not exceeding twenty dollars : *Provided,* that if the person so charged shall prove to the satisfaction of said board that the child has received or is receiving, under private or other instruction, an education suitable to his condition, in the judgment of said board, then such penalty shall not be incurred : *provided further,* that no child shall be removed to said institution or taken from the custody of its parent or guardian except as a day scholar unless such parent or guardian is an improper person to have such custody, and the supreme court in its appellate division shall have jurisdiction in habeas corpus to examine into and revise all findings of said board of trustees under this act.

SEC. 3. Any child having attended said institute a time or course prescribed by said board upon leaving the institute shall be entitled to receive a certificate of his proficiency from said board.

SEC. 4. This act shall take effect from and after its passage.

# TO PARENTS OF DEAF CHILDREN.

This school is for the benefit of childen incapacitated through deafness, total or partial, for receiving proper instruction in common schools, and is free to all pupils who belong in this State.

The aim of the school is to teach deaf children to use the English language with the spontaneity, correctness, and enjoyment of *hearing* children as far as this is practicable.

"Without language there can be no thought, no reason;" and as the highest aim of all instruction is the culture of the mental and moral nature in man, our first effort should be to furnish the deaf with a medium through which knowledge can be imparted and obtained. This can be done by signs, by the finger alphabet, and by speech. Our method is the latter, or oral method, by which the deaf can be educated and at the same time furnished with the usual and most convenient way of communication in society and the world at large.

It is very desirable that deaf children be sent to school at as early an age as possible. A parent will be amply repaid for sending a child as young as five or six years, even at some inconvenience. The Board of Trustees are authorized to receive pupils between the ages of three and twenty years.

If a child who has learned to talk is made deaf by disease, he should immediately, upon his recovery, be sent to a school where his speech will be retained, and where he will be taught to understand from the lips. In such cases it is common to delay so long that serious loss of speech results.

Speech reading is an invaluable acquisition for those who are semi-deaf, or even hard of hearing, as well as for those congenitally or totally deaf.

Every effort should be made to encourage the child to retain the use of his voice. He should be taught to pronounce common words by watching the lip motion and facial expression, or by feeling the muscular action of the breath; but no attempt should be made to teach him *the names* of the letters of the alphabet.

The English branches are taught here, and every pupil is taught some branch of industry.

The school session begins the second Monday in September, and closes the third Friday in June, with a week's holiday at Christmas.

Application for admission should be made to the principal, at the Institute, corner of East avenue and Cypress street, Providence.

Compliments of

Laura D. L. Richards,

Principal

State of Rhode Island and Providence Plantations.

# REPORT OF THE BOARD OF TRUSTEES

OF THE

## RHODE ISLAND

# INSTITUTE FOR THE DEAF,

PRESENTED TO THE

## GENERAL ASSEMBLY

AT ITS

## JANUARY SESSION, 1900.

PROVIDENCE:

E. L. FREEMAN & SONS, STATE PRINTERS.

1900.

---

*To the Honorable the General Assembly at its January Session
    A. D. 1900.*

The closing of the year finds the Institute in a prosperous condition. The scholars appear to have a just appreciation of the many benefits which the State has made it possible for them to obtain and enjoy. When we consider the irresponsibility and dependence of the uneducated deaf, surely no more deplorable condition can be imagined ; and to no class of education can the State give its aid and maintenance with better results than to these unfortunates. Each officer and assistant seems to take an intelligent interest in the welfare of the pupils, and the children themselves look upon the school as a well-ordered home, where the little children and those of larger growth are taught to observe the laws of health, to restrain their passions, and are educated from kindergarten to high school studies, and where the rich and the poor are equally well cared for and protected.

The teaching force of the Institute numbers the same as in the previous year, and the results obtained have been satisfactory. The number of attendants has been slightly increased, as in the judgment of the Board it was found necessary for the welfare of the school.

During the summer vacation many needed repairs were made, and others will have to be done during the coming year.

The attendance during the year was as follows :

Whole number of pupils.................................... 75

  "  "  of boys.................................... 44

 "  "  of girls.................................... 31

Present attendance........................................ 61

We respectfully submit the financial report as follows:

| | | |
|---|---:|---:|
| Annual appropriation.......................... | | $19,000 00 |
| Paid salaries............................ | $7,780 60 | |
| All other expenses...................... | 10,419 40 | |
| | | 18,200 00 |
| Balance covered into treasury ........... | | $800 00 |

For maintenance during the ensuing year we recommend the sum of $20,000.00.

Annexed hereto will be found the annual report of the principal, which contains more full and detailed information as to the condition and work of the school.

We are pleased to be able to say there have been no serious cases of illness during the year, although we have had ample opportunity to test the benefits of our hospital. For more detailed statement concerning the health of the pupils see report of Frank L. Day, M. D.

Respectfully submitted,

ELISHA DYER, *Governor,*
WILLIAM GREGORY, *Lieutanant-Governor,*
*Ex-Officio.*
WILLIAM K. POTTER, *President,*
MRS. ELLEN T. McGUINNESS, *Secretary,*
MRS. JEANIE LIPPITT WEEDEN,
MRS. LILLIE B. CHACE WYMAN,
EDWIN FARNELL,
DR. ROWLAND R. ROBINSON,
JOHN C. B. WOODS,
J. EDWARD STUDLEY,
JEREMIAH HORTON.
*Board of Trustees.*

PROVIDENCE, R. I., January, 1900.

# MEDICAL REPORT.

*To the Trustees of the R. I. Institute for the Deaf:*

I have the honor to report that while there have been several severe cases of sickness during the past year, the general health of the school has been excellent. During the winter there were four cases of pneumonia, two of them being severe, but fortunately ending in recovery. There has been much less tonsillitis than formerly, not more than a half dozen cases during the year. There were three minor accidents among the children, and a former pupil who was employed about the school fell from a second-story window, sustaining a dislocation of one foot and a severe sprain of the other, which kept him confined for about a month. These, with a few colds and trifling febrile disturbances, were all the illnesses until, November 11, a case of diphtheria developed. This child was sent to the Rhode Island Hospital at once, and cultures taken from the entire school resulting in the discovery of the bacillus of diphtheria in two other throats. These two children were also immediately sent to the same hospital. A subsequent general culture-taking showed the germs in ten other children, one teacher, and an attendant—all of whom were promptly isolated in our own hospital ward and received treatment aiming at prevention of the development of the disease. Through the ready and prompt co-operation of the health department in furnishing materials and examining repeated cultures, and in rigorously disinfecting all contaminated rooms, an entire absence of germs was secured on November 29th, and at the Thanksgiving recess the school was pronounced free from danger—and in none of the cases where the bacilli were found in throat or nose did the disease develop. This result could not have been attained but for the wise action of the Board in providing a suitable place for isolating and treating contagious diseases in response to recommendations previously made, as well as the ready co-operation of the principal and her assistants in cheerfully and unquestioningly carrying out every suggestion made to them.

Respectfully submitted,

FRANK L. DAY, M. D.

PROVIDENCE, December 31, 1900.

# REPORT OF THE PRINCIPAL.

*To the Trustees of the R. I. Institute for the Deaf:*

GENTLEMEN :—I have the honor to submit for your consideration the following report for the school year closing December 31, 1899.

January 1, 1899, there were 63 pupils in attendance, 34 boys and 29 girls ; 12 were admitted during the year, making 75 that were enrolled. Fourteen did not return at the opening of school in September. Some of the older pupils remained at home to engage in work, and others had moved out of the State, which brings our number down to 61. We hope two of the large girls, who remained at home on account of illness, will return after the holidays.

The additions of a year ago have added greatly to our comfort, and were a great benefit from a sanitary point. The health has been good throughout the school, but for a few cases of pneumonia, which were treated here, and all recovered without any serious effects.

We were unusually free from colds during the spring ; on the whole the health throughout the school has been better than during any previous year. After re-opening in September there was very little illness until a case of diphtheria developed November 11th, which was immediately taken to the Rhode Island Hospital ; and we might have had an epidemic but for the constant watchfulness and care of our attending physician and the Superintendant of Health and his assistants. After the first case developed cultures were taken from each member of the family, and diphtheria germs were found in the throats of two of the small boys. They were also taken to the Rhode Island Hospital and cultures

were taken from each one again, which resulted in finding germs
in the throats or noses of ten boys, one teacher, and one of the
women employed in the house. They were immediately sent up
to *our* hospital and shut off from the main part of the house.
Although none were sick, all were treated to prevent diphtheria
developing. Cultures were again taken all around, and this was
repeated until every one showed a throat perfectly free from diphtheria germs. During all this time there was no illness among
those in whose throat or nose germs had been found, yet but for
the untiring care of the health department and our physician
diphtheria might have been epidemic.

CLASS WORK.

The class work has varied but little from former years. The 61
pupils are divided into kindergarten, primary, and grammar departments, the classes numbering from five to eleven pupils each.

There are in the kindergarten eleven pupils whose ages range
from three to eight years. The admission of so many very young
children necessarily entails great care and responsibility on the
part of both teachers and attendants; but it is very important to
begin the education of these children at an early age.

One must understand the work done here in order to appreciate
it. Deaf children usually come to us without any knowledge of
language, not even knowing their own names or the names of the
most common objects with which they are surrounded. They
have no understanding of this life and its responsibilities, and it
is our work to awaken their understanding and help them to lead
useful and happy lives. Were it not for this school a large majority of them would grow up in utter ignorance; and even now,
when the school is so well known, a boy or girl is occasionally
brought, sixteen or eighteen years old, who has never attended
school and who cannot write, nor does he know the names of anything he sees. There should be a law *compelling every* deaf child
in the State to attend school from five years of age until nineteen.

The principle pursued in this school is that the pupils be re-

quired to use colloquial English, and this year they are showing a deeper interest and a stronger desire to improve in it.

The libraries have been a source of great assistance and pride to the older pupils, as they are well supplied with numerous books of reference and other books well adapted to their use.

The teachers are earnest, sympathetic workers, and I wish here to thank them for their hearty co-operation in all of our undertakings.

The class in physical culture is doing excellent work; the teacher comes twice each week, and the teachers supplement her work by repeating the lesson each day.

The girls are very enthusiastic over the Saturday morning sewing class. Their work is very commendable.

### MANUAL TRAINING.

The work in the sloyd-room remains about the same as the last year. Three classes are taught each week in sloyd. One class under the direction of Mr. Hunt, taught by Miss MacCrosson, has been formed in cardboard sloyd as an elementary course to the regular sloyd work.

The course in cardboard is based upon sloyd principles, and is designed to give the pupil training by which he can pursue the regular sloyd work with better results.

Very good work has been done in all the classes, the children are interested in their work, and when interest is gained good results are to sure follow.

A class of boys and girls is still taught printing by Mr. Goodale, and much of the printing for the school is done by the pupils.

Christmas was observed as usual by a visit from Santa Claus, which was anxiously watched for by our little ones.

### ACKNOWLEDGMENTS.

Thanks are due Messrs. J. H. Preston and Messrs. Arnold & Maine for Christmas candies, also to the Hon. G. L. Littlefield

2

for a nice box of oranges.  We are also very grateful to Mrs. W. B. Weeden, Mrs. E. D. McGuinness, Mr. Marsden J. Perry, and Mr. Samuel Jackson for giving money to provide presents for the Christmas tree; to Mrs. D. B. Pond for a very interesting book— "Story of the World and its People," and for subscribing for the *St. Nicholas*; to Miss A. Brown for Bible pictures, and to Dr. F. L. Day for pictures for hall and libraries; and we thank Mrs. Weeden and Mrs. S. S. Durfee for clothing.

Prizes were awarded, for the best talking, to Annie Mercier ; the best in speech-reading, Stephanie Sevard ; greatest improvement in speech, Nellie Pulsifer and Jimmie Flynn ; greatest improvement in speech-reading, Laura Hackett and Henry Courtemanche.

Respectfully submitted,

LAURA DE L. RICHARDS.

# APPENDIX.

# TABULAR REPORT.

TABULAR REPORT OF THE PUPILS OF THE SCHOOL.

| NAME OF PUPIL. | RESIDENCE. | AGE. (Approx.) | DATE OF ADMISSION. |
|---|---|---|---|
| Sullivan, Nellie | Newport | 13 | Nov. 12, 1886. |
| Grant, Edith | Providence | 10 | Dec. 13, 1886. |
| Cole, Luella | South Scituate | 12 | March 28, 1887. |
| Chevers, C. Herbert | Providence | 14 | April 26, 1887. |
| Francis, Manuel | Bristol | 14 | Sept. 26, 1887. |
| Canning, Thomas F. | Woonsocket | 12 | Sept. 3, 1888. |
| Goldenofsky, Moses | Woonsocket | 10 | April 29, 1889. |
| Hackett, Laura | Providence | 8 | Nov. 11, 1889. |
| Maker, Dora C | Providence | 10 | May 19, 1890. |
| Fletcher, Henrietta M | Johnston | 10 | Sept. 1, 1890. |
| O'Brien, William T | Providence | 12 | Dec. 1, 1890. |
| Lease, Edwin G | Providence | 11 | Feb. 2, 1891. |
| Beatty, John | Johnston. | 12 | April 27, 1891. |
| Courtemanche, Henry | Woonsocket | 12 | June 10, 1891. |
| Staunton, Annie L | Providence | 12 | Sept. 8, 1891. |
| Staunton, Bertha | Providence | 8 | Oct. 5, 1891. |
| Jermyn, William | Newport | 10 | May 5, 1892. |
| Mills, Annetta | Providence | 6 | April 3, 1893. |
| Carr, David | Pawtucket | 6 | Jan. 27, 1893. |
| Collins, Chester A | Providence | 4 | Jan. 30, 1893. |
| Kleber, Fannie | Lymansville | 6 | Feb. 7, 1893. |
| Mercier, Addie C | Shannock | 10 | Feb. 7, 1893. |
| Goldstein, Clara J | Providence | 9 | March 1, 1893. |
| Desonie, Maggie | Lippitt. | 8 | March 23, 1893. |
| Smith, Bernard F. | Providence | 8 | April 10, 1893. |
| O'Connor, Mary | Woonsocket | 6 | May 27, 1893. |
| Hoen, Alfred | Carolina | | Sept. 11, 1893. |
| Knowles, Grace E | South Kingstown | 4 | Sept. 11, 1893. |
| Thompson, George | Providence | 4 | Sept. 11, 1893. |
| Pulsifer, M. Helen | River Point | 8 | Sept. 11, 1893. |
| Savard, Mary C. S. S. | Woonsocket | 12 | Sept. 11, 1893. |
| Flynn, James | Providence | 6 | Feb. 3, 1894. |
| Pease, Walter M. | Woonsocket | 5 | Sept. 10, 1894. |
| Comfort, Mae E. | Newport | 8 | Sept. 10, 1894. |
| Bradley, William H. | Woonsocket | 11 | Oct. 1, 1894. |
| Mudrak, Willie | Geneva | 4 | Oct. 13, 1894. |
| Canney, John P. | Providence | 9 | Dec. 3, 1894. |
| Grimes, Mary | Newport | 9 | Feb. 5, 1895. |
| O'Riley, Willie F | Providence | 7 | Feb. 11, 1895. |
| Grace, Theresa | Providence | 12 | April 10, 1895. |
| Welsh, John | Providence | 7 | May 20, 1895. |
| Roe, Albert C. | Hope. | 5 | Sept. 21, 1895. |
| Stetson, Leroy W. | Warren | 10 | Sept. 30, 1895. |
| Boivert, Mary | Providence | 13 | Oct. 27, 1895. |
| Smith, Idella | Johnston | 9 | Oct. 28, 1895. |
| Lefebre, Isaac | Natick | 18 | May 6, 1895. |
| Williams, Charles A | Pawtucket | 4 | Sept. 14, 1896. |

FOR THE YEAR ENDING DECEMBER 31, 1899.

| Cause of Deafness, as far as Known. | Age when made Deaf. (Approx.) | Remarks. |
|---|---|---|
| Scarlet fever................. | 2 years......... | ................... |
| Tumor in ear................. | 6 months........ | ................... |
| Congenital.................... | | ................... |
| Brain fever.................. | 6 months....... | Slight degree of hearing. |
| Typhoid fever............... | 3 years, 6 mo's .. | ................... |
| Congenital................... | | ................... |
| Scarlet fever................ | 3 years........ | ................... |
| Congenital................... | | ................... |
| Scarlet fever................ | 3 years......... | Hard of hearing. |
| Congenital................... | | ................... |
| Run over..................... | | Hard of hearing. |
| Unknown..................... | 4 years........ | Hard of hearing. |
| Congenital................... | | ................... |
| Congenital................... | | ................... |
| Brain fever................. | 1 year......... | Hard of hearing. |
| Brain fever ................ | 3 years........ | ................... |
| Congenital................... | | ................... |
| Measles..................... | 3 years........ | ................... |
| A fall....................... | 2 years........ | ................... |
| Measles..................... | 2 years........ | ................... |
| Congenital................... | | Deafness partial. |
| Scarlet fever................ | 5 years........ | ................... |
| Typhoid fever............... | 4 years........ | ................... |
| Congenital................... | | ................... |
| ............................. | | Not deaf. |
| Scarlet fever................ | 1 year......... | ................... |
| A fall....................... | 2 years........ | Deafness partial. |
| Grippe....................... | 2 years........ | ................... |
| Convulsions.................. | 3 years........ | ................... |
| Measles..................... | 6 years........ | ................... |
| Congenital................... | | ................... |
| Congenital................... | | ................... |
| Grippe....................... | 2 years........ | ................... |
| Catarrhal fever.... .......... | 1 year, 6 months. | ................... |
| Diphtheria................... | 6 years........ | ................... |
| Congenital................... | | ................... |
| Taking quinine............... | 1 year......... | ................... |
| Measles..................... | 5 years........ | Slight degree of hearing. |
| Congenital................... | | ................... |
| Congenital................... | | ................... |
| Brain fever ................ | 3 years........ | ................... |
| Inflammation in head........ | 4 months....... | ................... |
| Fall and fever............... | 4 years........ | Slight degree of hearing. |
| Fever....................... | 3 years........ | ................... |
| Congenital................... | | Slight degree of hearing. |
| Scarlet fever................ | 3 years........ | ................... |
| Congenital................... | | ................... |

## TABULAR REPORT OF THE PUPILS OF THE SCHOOL

| Name of Pupil. | Residence. | Age. (Approx.) | Date of Admission. |
|---|---|---|---|
| Cook, Reuben........... | Peace Dale............ | 7 | Oct.     6, 1896.. |
| Perron, Lena........... | Woonsocket........... | 7 | Oct.    26, 1896.. |
| Anderson, Edward V.... | Providence............ | 9 | ................. |
| Vigeant, Edward........ | Pawtucket............ | 7 | May     3, 1897.. |
| Gardner, May........... | Scituate.............. | 10 | April   29, 1897.. |
| Davis, Elsie........... | Rumford.............. | 9 | Sept.   13, 1897.. |
| Essex, Fred E. L........ | Providence............ | 11 | Sept.   13, 1897.. |
| Perry, Joseph C........ | Providence........... | 7 | Jan.     7, 1898.. |
| Yuppa, Concetta........ | Providence............ | 4 | Feb.    10, 1898.. |
| Kirk, John............ | Providence............ | 6 | May     9, 1898.. |
| Forthier, Angelina...... | Pawtucket............ | 6 | Oct.    24, 1898.. |
| Horlbogen, Trina........ | Pawtucket ........... | 6 | Oct.    18, 1898.. |
| Bowen, John........... | Providence............ | 13 | Oct.    18, 1898.. |
| Bassett, Genevive W.... | Moosup Valley......... | 4 | Oct.    18, 1898.. |
| Vogel, Alfred........... | Providence. ........... | 11 | Oct.    18, 1898.. |
| Goldman, Samuel....... | Providence............ | 9 | Nov.     7, 1898.. |
| Myers, Arthur.......... | Providence............ | 7 | Jan.     3, 1899.. |
| McLean, Ernest C...... | Manville ............. | 6 | March  14, 1899.. |
| Wilcox, Olive I......... | East Providence....... | 8 | April    3, 1899.. |
| Smith, Everett A........ | Slocumville............ | 3 | May    19, 1899.. |
| Williams, Harold K..... | Pawtucket............ | 4 | Sept.   13, 1899.. |
| Sweet, Fannie M....... | Centredale............ | 8 | Sept.   13, 1899.. |
| Newberg, Charles A..... | Pawtucket............ | 7 | Sept.   25, 1899.. |
| Johnson, Benj. F........ | Kingston............. | 8 | Sept.   26, 1899.. |
| Paquin, Adolard........ | Providence............ | 5 | Oct.     2, 1899.. |
| Cleary, John........... | Newport............. | 5 | Oct.     2, 1899.. |
| Rose, William........... | Providence............ | 10 | Oct.     4, 1899.. |
| Holmes, Thomas........ | Providence............ | 7 | Oct.    17, 1899.. |

FOR THE YEAR ENDING DECEMBER 31, 1899.

| Cause of Deafness, as far as Known. | Age when made Deaf. (Approx.) | Remarks. |
|---|---|---|
| Congenital.................. | .................. | .................. |
| Scarlet fever.............. | 1 year........... | |
| Scarlet fever.............. | 5 years.......... | Hard of hearing. |
| Scarlet fever.............. | 4 years.......... | .................. |
| Scarlet fever.............. | 5 years.......... | |
| .................. | .................. | |
| Scrofula.................. | 8 years.......... | .................. |
| Spinal sickness............ | 2 months......... | |
| Congenital.................. | .................. | |
| Scarlet fever.............. | 2 years, 6 mo's.. | Hard of hearing. |
| Congenital.................. | .................. | .................. |
| Measles.................... | 1 year........... | |
| Convulsions................ | 1 year........... | Hard of hearing. |
| Congenital.................. | .................. | |
| .................. | .................. | Not deaf. |
| A fall..................... | 3 years.......... | |
| Grippe..................... | 6 years.......... | .................. |
| Meningitis................. | 3 years.......... | .................. |
| Congenital.................. | .................. | |
| Congenital.................. | .................. | |
| Congenital.................. | .................. | |
| Spinal meningitis.......... | 7 years.......... | .................. |
| A fall..................... | 5 years.......... | .................. |
| Illness.................... | 4 years.......... | .................. |
| Congenital.................. | .................. | |
| Congenital.................. | .................. | |
| Congenital.................. | .................. | .................. |
| .................. | .................. | Not deaf. |

## SUMMARY.

| | |
|---|---|
| Number of pupils from date of opening the State school for the deaf, April 2, 1877, to December 31, 1899 | 160 |
| Number of pupils who have entered the Institute since Dec. 31, 1898 | 13 |
| Whole number of pupils who have attended the school | 160 |
| Number who have left the school | 96 |
| Number of pupils Dec. 31, 1899 | 61 |
| Number of girls who have attended school during the year | 31 |
| Number of boys who have attended school during the year | 44 |
| Whole number of pupils during the year | 75 |
| Average attendance | 53 |
| Number congenitally deaf, or made deaf before the age of two | 42 |
| Number who lost hearing between the ages of two and four | 16 |
| Number who lost hearing after the age of four, and doubtful cases | 17 |
| | 75 |
| Number who have any degree of hearing | 17 |

*Residences of all who have attended during the year 1899.*

| | |
|---|---|
| Geneva | 1 |
| Providence, including Wanskuck | 31 |
| East Providence | 1 |
| Pawtucket | 1 |
| South Scituate | 2 |
| Johnston | 3 |
| Newport | 2 |
| Lymansville | 1 |
| Shannock | 1 |
| Lippitt | 1 |
| Peace Dale | 1 |
| Natick | 1 |
| Kingstown | 2 |
| Slocumville | 1 |

Centredale............................................................. 1
Manville.............................................................. 1
River Point........................................................... 1
Woonsocket........................................................... 8
Carolina.............................................................. 1
Hope................................................................. 1
Bristol............................................................... 1
Warren............................................................... 1
Rumford.............................................................. 1
Moosup Valley........................................................ 1

Twenty-four localities ........................................ 75

## PERIODICALS.

The receipt of the following periodicals is thankfully acknowledged, and their continuance respectfully requested :

Mute's Campanion, Faribault, Minn.; Daily Paper for Our Little People, Rochester, N. Y.; Our Children's School Journal, The Deaf Mute Journal, New York; Maryland Bulletin, Frederick, Md.; The Deaf Mute Voice, Jackson, Miss.; Kentucky Deaf Mute, Danville, Ky.; The Goodson Gazette, Staunton, Va.; Kansas Star, Olathe, Kansas; Deaf Mute Optic, Little Rock, Ark.; Deaf Mute Index, Colorado Springs, Col.; Juvenile Ranger, Austin, Texas; The Register, Rome, New York; Nebraska Mute Journal, Omaha, Neb.; New Method for the Deaf, Englewood, Ill.; Weekly News, Berkeley, Cal.

# COURSE OF STUDY.

## KINDERGARTEN.

### FIRST YEAR.

  *a.*  KINDERGARTEN EXERCISES.

  *b.*  ARTICULATION.

  *c.*  LANGUAGE.

  *d.*  ARITHMETIC.

  *e.*  PENMANSHIP.

*a.* Paper cutting and folding; drawing and modeling in clay; designing in shoe pegs; stick laying; embroidery designs sewed on pricked sewing-cards; lessons in form and color in all exercises.

*b.* Elements, combinations, simple words and sentences; with reading them from the lips.

*c.* Nouns; objects in class-room, articles of dress, articles of food, different parts of the body, with a limited number of verbs. Adjectives, good, bad, large, small, &c.

*d.* Counting and writing numbers, with addition and subtraction to 10.

*e.* Writing on slate and with lead pencil.

## PRIMARY COURSE.

### SECOND, THIRD, AND FOURTH YEARS.

  *a.*  ARTICULATION.

  *b.*  LANGUAGE.

  *c.*  ARITHMETIC.

  *d.*  GEOGRAPHY.

  *e.*  PENMANSHIP.

  *f.*  DRAWING.

*a.* Drill in elements, combinations, and words, and reading them from the lips.

*b.* Thorough review of first year work. Nouns and verbs continued. Adjectives continued; their comparison. Pronouns as in first year, adding myself, herself, himself, with the plurals, and the relatives who and which. Adverbs; not, often, never, etc. Elliptical sentences; action and picture writing; journal and letter writing, and simple stories.

*c.* Practical exercises in addition, subtraction, multiplication, and division; United States currency; simple fractions.

*d.* School-room, building, and yard, city, and a limited knowledge of the State.

*e.* Copy-book writing.

### INTERMEDIATE COURSE.

FIFTH, SIXTH, AND SEVENTH YEARS.

    *a.* ARTICULATION.

    *b.* LANGUAGE.

    *c.* ARITHMETIC.

    *d.* GEOGRAPHY.

    *e.* HISTORY.

    *f.* PENMANSHIP.

    *g.* DRAWING.

    *h.* CALISTHENICS.

*a.* Drill in elements, combinations, syllables; words and sentences continued as in primary course.

*b.* Nouns, pronouns, adjectives, adverbs, prepositions, and conjunctions continued as in primary course. Drill in active and passive voices; action and picture writing; stories from natural history; journal and letter writing.

*c.* Mental and written addition, subtraction, multiplication, and division, with practical examples; United States currency and simple fractions continued.

*d.* City, State, and New England States.

*e.* Simple historical stories in connection with geography.

*f.* Copy-book writing twice a week.

*g.* Object drawing.

## HIGHER COURSE.

EIGHTH, NINTH, AND TENTH YEARS.

     *a.* ARTICULATION.

     *b.* LANGUAGE.

     *c.* ARITHMETIC.

     *d.* GEOGRAPHY.

     *e.* HISTORY.

     *f.* PHYSIOLOGY.

     *g.* PENMANSHIP.

     *h.* DRAWING.

     *i.* CALISTHENICS.

*a.*  Drill in difficult combinations and words.

*b.*  Composition ; journal and letter writing ; miscellaneous reading, newspapers and magazines ; lessons on general subjects.

*c.*  Mental, written and practical.

*d.*  Geographical reader ; Manual of Commerce.

*e.*  History of the United States ; Outline of General History.

*g.*  Copy-book.

*h.*  Free-hand and object drawing, and designing.

# CHAPTER 332.

AN ACT IN AMENDMENT OF AND IN ADDITION TO CHAPTER 86 OF THE GENERAL LAWS, ENTITLED "OF THE R. I. SCHOOL FOR THE DEAF."

(Passed May 13, 1896.)

*It is enacted by the General Assembly as follows :*

SECTION 1.   All children of parents, or under the control of guardians or other persons, legal residents of this state, between the ages of three and twenty years, whose hearing or speech, or both, are so defective as to make it inexpedient or impracticable to attend the public schools to advantage, not being mentally or otherwise incapable, may attend the Rhode Island Institute for the Deaf, without charge, under such rules and regulations as the board of trustees of said institute may establish.

SEC. 2.   Every person having under his control any such child between the ages of seven and eighteen years shall cause such child to attend school at said institute for such period of time or such prescribed course, in each individual case, as may be deemed expedient by the board of trustees, and for any neglect of such duty the person so offending shall be fined not exceeding twenty dollars : *Provided*, that if the person so charged shall prove to the satisfaction of said board that the child has received or is receiving, under private or other instruction, an education suitable to his condition, in the judgment of said board, then such penalty shall not be incurred : *provided, further*, that no child shall be removed to said institution or taken from the custody of its parent or guardian except as a day scholar unless such parent or guardian is an improper person to have such custody, and the supreme court in its appellate division shall have jurisdiction in habeas corpus to examine into and revise all findings of said board of trustees under this act.

SEC. 3.   Any child having attended said institute a time or course prescribed by said board, upon leaving the institute shall be entitled to receive a certificate of his proficiency from said board.

SEC. 4.   This act shall take effect from and after its passage.

effort should be made to encourage the child to retain
of his voice.  He should be taught to pronounce common
y watching the lip motion and facial expression, or by
he muscular action of the breath ; but no attempt should
to teach him *the names* of the letters of the alphabet.

nglish branches are taught here, and every pupil is taught
anch of industry.

chool session begins the second Monday in September,
es the third Friday in June, with a week's holiday at
as.

ation for admission should be made to the principal, at
itute, corner of East avenue and Cypress street, Provi-

**State of Rhode Island and Providence Plantations.**

# REPORT OF THE BOARD OF TRUSTEES

OF THE

# RHODE ISLAND

# NSTITUTE FOR THE DEAF,

PRESENTED TO THE

## GENERAL ASSEMBLY

AT ITS

## JANUARY SESSION. 1901.

ᴀtion............................. $19,000 00

......................... $8,349 87

ᴇs..................... 10,635 57

18,985 44

into treasury............ $14 56

ce during the ensuing year we recommend the

e found the annual **report** of the principal, which
ᴇtailed information as to the condition and work

ᴊectfully submitted,

WILLIAM GREGORY, *Governor*,
CHARLES D. KIMBALL, *Lieutenant-Governor*,
*Ex-Officio.*
WILLIAM K. POTTER, *President*,
MRS. ELLEN T. McGUINNESS, *Secretary*,
MRS. JEANIE LIPPITT WEEDEN,
MRS. LILLIE B. CHACE WYMAN,
EDWIN FARNELL,
DR. ROWLAND R. ROBINSON,
JOHN C. B. WOODS,
WILLIAM H. BALLOU,
JEREMIAH W. HORTON,

*Board of Trustees.*

I., January, 1901.

State of Rhode Island and Providence Plantations.

# REPORT OF THE BOARD OF TRUSTEES

OF THE

## RHODE ISLAND

# INSTITUTE FOR THE DEAF,

PRESENTED TO THE

## GENERAL ASSEMBLY

AT ITS

## JANUARY SESSION, 1901.

PROVIDENCE:

E. L. FREEMAN & SONS, STATE PRINTERS.

1901.

# REPORT OF THE BOARD OF TRUSTEES.

*To the Honorable the General Assembly at its January Session
  A. D. 1901:*

The Institute has had a year of even prosperity. Many new
pupils have been admitted, and some of the older ones have left
the school and found employment. The number of teachers and
assistants remain about the same as at the last report of the
trustees. The number of pupils has increased during the last
year, there being sixty-six at the present time, five in excess of the
last report. The health of the scholars is good, and no serious
cases of illness have occurred during the year. We would refer
to the report of Dr. Day for detailed report on the health of the
school. The teachers are all well qualified for their various positions, and are to be congratulated on the progress the children
have made, and for the interest and ability they have shown.
During the summer the sanitary condition of the building was
thoroughly looked into, and many changes and improvements were
made; conveniences for the children's bathing were added, and
are well appreciated. The attendance during the year was as
follows:

Whole number of pupils............................... ..... 68
  "      "      " boys..................................... 39
  "      "      " girls.................................... 29
Present attendance........................................ 66

We respectfully submit the financial report, as follows:

| | | |
|---|---|---|
| Annual appropriation........................ | | $19,000 00 |
| Paid salaries............................ | $8,349 87 | |
| All other expenses...................... | 10,635 57 | |
| | | 18,985 44 |
| Balance covered into treasury............ | | $14 56 |

For maintenance during the ensuing year we recommend the sum of $20,000.00.

Annexed will be found the annual report of the principal, which contains more detailed information as to the condition and work of the school.

Respectfully submitted,

WILLIAM GREGORY, *Governor*,
CHARLES D. KIMBALL, *Lieutenant-Governor*,
*Ex-Officio.*
WILLIAM K. POTTER, *President*,
MRS. ELLEN T. McGUINNESS, *Secretary*,
MRS. JEANIE LIPPITT WEEDEN,
MRS. LILLIE B. CHACE WYMAN,
EDWIN FARNELL,
DR. ROWLAND R. ROBINSON,
JOHN C. B. WOODS,
WILLIAM H. BALLOU,
JEREMIAH W. HORTON,
*Board of Trustees.*
PROVIDENCE, R. I., January, 1901.

# MEDICAL REPORT.

*To the Trustees of the R. I. Institute for the Deaf:*

I have the honor to submit this report of the health of the pupils during the past year:

Directly after the re-opening of school in January, two children, one from Pawtucket and one living on the border of Pawtucket and Providence, developed diphtheria and were promptly sent to the Rhode Island Hospital, where they made good recoveries, though somewhat tardily. Cultures were then taken from the whole school, and the germs of diphtheria were found in many throats, among pupils, teachers, officers, and servants, although only occasionally were there other symptoms of the illness. Such cases were isolated until three negative cultures had been secured, both from throat and nose. With the active coöperation of the health department of the city of Providence and the State Board of Health, during the next three months extraordinary efforts were made, by rigid isolation and repeated culture-takings and faithful treatment of the noses and throats of all the inmates, to render the school free from germs. This was finally given up as practically impossible; for, although bacilli were still present in the throats and noses of several otherwise healthy persons, it was evident that they were of a mild strain and were not making their possessors, clinically speaking, sick. So, with your approval and the sanction of the health department, these infected persons were allowed to resume their respective positions, and very fortunately no active case of diphtheria followed; thus seeming to suggest that the Klebs-Loeffler bacillus may be present at times in people's throats and noses without appreciably harming its possessor or others. It is probable that no such prolonged and determined effort to dislodge the diphtheria germ has been made in any institution for the deaf, and it certainly taxed to the extreme the patience of all concerned; yet even at the end it was with reluctance that it was given up and had to be admitted to be a failure.

There was one case of measles in one of the teachers, promptly isolated and not followed by others. After the Easter recess the school was remarkably free from illness.

In the early fall one of the younger boys, in playing, fell, breaking an arm, but recovered promptly without deformity. Since then a few minor illnesses and accidents have constituted all the departures from perfect health among the children and staff.

The experience of this year goes to emphasize the wisdom of amply providing isolated hospital accommodations in such an institution as this.

Respectfully submitted,

FRANK L. DAY, M. D.

PROVIDENCE, Dec. 31, 1900.

"DINING ROOM."

# REPORT OF THE PRINCIPAL.

*To the Trustees of the R. I. Institute for the Deaf.*

GENTLEMEN:—I have the honor to submit for your consideration the following report for the school year ending December
31st, 1900.

We are closing our eighth year as a boarding-school, and in
reviewing the work accomplished we find we have not stood still.

We opened school in the new buildings January 1st, 1893, with
38 pupils. January 1st, 1900, there were 62 pupils in attendance—
an increase of 24 pupils. Six have been admitted during the past
year, which makes our number enrolled 68. Three did not return
at the re-opening of school in September; one had moved out of
the State, one remained at home on account of ill health, and the
other to help in the support of the family.

It is to be regretted that parents of deaf children do not realize
how much their future happiness and usefulness is enhanced by
an education and do not hasten to take advantage of the privileges so freely offered in this school by the State.

We earnestly entreat all who know of one or more deaf children not in school, or those whose hearing is so defective as to
make it impracticable to attend the public schools, to urge upon
the parents the necessity of bringing them to us.

### HEALTH.

During the first three months of the past year there was a continuation of the epidemic of diphtheria germs which commenced the
previous autumn, and in that time five children taken with diphtheria
were removed to the Rhode Island Hospital, where they were

treated. They were not severe cases. Owing to the untiring watchfulness of the attending physician and the superintendent of health and his assistants, there was no serious sickness. The superintendent of health made a thorough inspection and examination of the buildings, but failed to find any local cause for the epidemic. It proved very expensive and tedious to rid the place of it, although every disinfectant we could get was used and every effort put forth.

We record with sorrow the death of one of our number—Ernest McLean, a bright little fellow. He was taken home for a short visit, where he took cold and died April 3rd, after an illness of only a few days.

After the spring vacation the health of the pupils was excellent, and since school re-opened, September 11th, there has been no real sickness, only slight colds and an occasional accident.

In the spring Miss Katharine MacCrosson resigned her position as teacher, to be married, and Mrs. Smith, *née* Miss Fannie Cheney, who had been a former teacher, came and filled the vacancy for the remainder of the term, but was unable to return to us in the fall, to our regret, on account of home duties. Miss Edith Hillman, who had been with us as student a year, was appointed to fill the vacancy. Miss Lizzie Green, from the Home for the Training in Speech of Little Deaf Children, Philadelphia, near Bala, was appointed to take the place of Miss Peet, and Miss Mabel I. Clark was appointed to take the place of Miss Guinness.

### CLASS WORK.

There has been no change in our methods of instruction since our last report. The work in the kindergarten is very satisfactory. There have been promotions from it to the next higher class, which are very gratifying. Through the kindness of those in authority at the Normal School, and of the School of Practice, on Benefit street, our kindergartner and the teacher of the next class are permitted to observe in those schools, and by so doing

keep in touch with that work in the public schools, and they gain many new ideas, which they adopt.

The little children are acquiring the habit of watching people during conversation and of imitating them, so that their speech will be smoother and more agreeable than if they remained at home until they were older. The beginning primary class is taught almost entirely by speech; they write very little. They are taught simple colloquial language, so that they may be able to communicate their wants and answer simple questions readily. As they advance, they are taught writing, but it must always be secondary to speech.

In the intermediate department there is a continuation of the primary work, as they are taught language, *language* continually, but with it they are given beginning work in geography, history, and physiology. Numbers are taught from the first. In the grammar department text-books, such as are in use in the city schools, are given the pupils. Our first class is working with the hope of graduating in '92·

The pupils' reading-rooms are provided with suitable books and magazines, which are a great source of enjoyment as well as benefit to all. The older pupils have the privilege of reading the magazines and papers to be found on the table in the teachers' library. The daily papers are highly prized by all the children— some of the smaller ones, even, telling the morning news to the class after school begins.

A class in drawing was formed the first of April, and lessons have been given, twice a week, to the pupils in the grammar department. They are much interested, and, under the guidance of Miss Ethel A. Dunn, are doing good work.

### MANUAL TRAINING.

The sewing class is making good progress, and we hope soon to add dressmaking to the course. The girls are already learning to cut, and they take great interest in it.

There has been no change in the number of the classes in the sloyd department. The class of beginners started last year by Miss MacCrosson has been continued by Miss Florence Russell. They have finished the work in sloyd cardboard and have started upon a course in whittling. The use of the drawing-board and the instruments used in drawing have been explained and a few simple drawings made. The class will will take up the regular sloyd work next year, and we feel sure that the time given to elementary work has been well spent. The work among the older boys is in about the same lines as last year. Some small pieces in cabinet work have been made, but the benches are not large enough to admit of very large work. The interest in the work remains unabated, and it is hoped that good sloyd principles have been formed.

The work is carried on in the printing-room on the same lines as formerly. The children are interested in their own contributions, and thus it is a means of teaching language.

### ACKNOWLEDGMENTS.

We thank Messrs. J. H. Preston & Co. and Messrs. Arnold & Maine for Christmas candies, and the Hon. G. L. Littlefield for a box of oranges which the children thoroughly enjoyed. We also thank Mrs. W. B. Weeden, Mrs. E. D. McGuinness, and Miss Richards for giving money to provide a Christmas tree and presents; Mrs. D. B. Pond for subscription for the St. Nicholas, and Mrs. W. B. Weeden and Mrs. S. S. Durfee for clothing.

### PRIZES.

At the close of school in June prizes were awarded Fannie Kleber and George Thompson for the best speech, Laura Hackett and Moses Goldenofsky for the best speech-reading, Luella Cole and Mary Grimes for the best in language in the two departments in which they were, Edith Grant and Mamie O'Conner for the best penmanship, and Nellie Sullivan for the greatest improvement in deportment.

Respectfully submitted,

LAURA DE L. RICHARDS.

# TABULAR REPORT.

## TABULAR REPORT OF THE PUPILS OF THE SCHOOL

| NAME OF PUPIL. | RESIDENCE. | AGE. (Approx.) | DATE OF ADMISSION. |
|---|---|---|---|
| Sullivan, Nellie.......... | Newport...... ........ | 13 | Nov. 12, 1886.. |
| Grant, Edith.............. | Providence............. | 10 | Dec. 13, 1886.. |
| Cole, Luella.............. | South Scituate.......... | 12 | March 28, 1887.. |
| Goldenofsky, Moses...... | Woonsocket............. | 10 | April 29, 1889.. |
| Hackett, Laura.......... | Providence............. | 8 | Nov. 11, 1889.. |
| Fletcher, Henrietta M... | Johnston............... | 10 | Sept. 1, 1890.. |
| Lease, Edwin G.......... | Providence............. | 11 | Feb. 2, 1891.. |
| Courtemanche, Henry.... | Woonsocket............. | 12 | June 10, 1891.. |
| Staunton, Bertha........ | Providence............. | 8 | Oct. 5, 1891.. |
| Jermyn, William........ | Newport. ............... | 10 | May 5, 1892.. |
| Mills, Anneta............ | Providence............. | 6 | April 3, 1893.. |
| Carr, David............. | Pawtucket............. | 6 | Jan. 27, 1893.. |
| Collins, Chester A....... | Providence...... .... | 4 | Jan. 30, 1893.. |
| Kleber, Fannie.......... | Lymansville..... ...... | 6 | Feb. 7, 1893.. |
| Goldstein, Clara J....... | Providence............. | 9 | March 1, 1893.. |
| Desouie, Maggie........ | Lippitt................ | 8 | March 23, 1893.. |
| Smith, Bernard F....... | Providence............. | '8 | April 10, 1893.. |
| O'Connor, Mary.......... | Woonsocket............. | 6 | May 27, 1893.. |
| Hoen, Alfred............. | Carolina............... | ... | Sept. 11, 1893.. |
| Thompson, George...... | Providence............. | 4 | Sept. 11, 1893.. |
| Pulsifer, M. Helen...... | River Point............ | 8 | Sept. 11, 1893.. |
| Flynn, James............ | Providence............. | 6 | Feb. 3, 1894.. |
| Comfort, Mae E......... | Newport............... | 8 | Sept. 10, 1894.. |
| Bradley, William H..... | Woonsocket............. | 11 | Oct. 1, 1894.. |
| Mudrak, Willie.......... | Geneva..... ...... | 4 | Oct. 13, 1894.. |
| Canney, John P......... | Providence............. | 9 | Dec. 3, 1894.. |
| Grimes, Mary............ | Newport............... | 9 | Feb. 5, 1895.. |
| O'Riley, Willie F........ | Providence............. | 7 | Feb. 11, 1895.. |
| Grace, Theresa........... | Providence............. | 12 | April 10, 1895.. |
| Welsh, John............. | Providence......... | 7 | May 20, 1895.. |
| Roe, Albert C........... | Hope.................. | 5 | Sept. 21, 1895.. |
| Stetson, Leroy W........ | Warren............... | 10 | Sept. 30, 1895.. |
| Smith, Idella............. | Johnston............... | 9 | Oct. 28, 1895.. |
| Williams, Charles A .... | Pawtucket............. | 4 | Sept. 14, 1896.. |
| Cook, Reuben........... | Peace Dale............. | 7 | Oct. 6, 1896.. |
| Perron, Lena............. | Woonsocket............. | 7 | Oct. 26, 1896.. |
| Anderson, Edward V .... | Providence............. | 9 | .... ........... |
| Vigeant, Edward........ | Pawtucket............. | 7 | May 3, 1897.. |
| Gardner, May............ | Scituate............... | 10 | April 29, 1897.. |
| Davis, Elsie............. | Rumford............... | 9 | Sept. 13, 1897.. |
| Essex, Fred E. L......... | Providence............. | 11 | Sept. 13, 1897.. |
| Perry, Joseph C......... | Providence............. | 7 | Jan. 7, 1898.. |
| Yuppa, Concetta........ | Providence............. | 4 | Feb. 10, 1898.. |
| Kirk, John.............. | Providence............. | 6 | May 9, 1898.. |
| Forthier, Angelina....... | Pawtucket............. | 6 | Oct. 24, 1898.. |
| Holborgen, Trina........ | Pawtucket............. | 6 | Oct. 18, 1898.. |

## FOR THE YEAR ENDING DECEMBER 31, 1900.

| CAUSE OF DEAFNESS, AS FAR AS KNOWN. | AGE WHEN MADE DEAF (Approx.). | REMARKS. |
|---|---|---|
| Scarlet fever. | 2 years. | |
| Tumor in ear. | 6 months. | |
| Congenital. | | |
| Scarlet fever. | 3 years. | |
| Congenital. | | |
| Congenital. | | |
| Unknown. | 4 years | Hard of hearing. |
| Congenital. | | |
| Brain fever. | 3 years. | |
| Congenital. | | |
| Measles. | 3 years. | |
| A fall. | 2 years. | |
| Measles. | 2 years. | |
| Congenital. | | Deafness partial. |
| Typhoid fever. | 4 years. | |
| Congenital. | | |
| | | Not deaf. |
| Scarlet fever. | 1 year. | |
| A fall. | 2 years. | Deafness partial. |
| Convulsions. | 3 years. | |
| Measles. | 6 years. | |
| Congenital. | | |
| Catarrhal fever. | 1 year, 6 months. | |
| Diphtheria. | 6 years. | |
| Congenital. | | |
| Taking quinine. | 1 year. | |
| Measles. | 5 years. | Slight degree of hearing. |
| Congenital. | | |
| Congenital. | | |
| Brain fever. | 3 years. | |
| Inflammation in head. | 4 months. | |
| Fall and fever. | 4 years. | Slight degree of hearing. |
| Congenital. | | Slight degree of hearing. |
| Congenital. | | |
| Congenital. | | |
| Scarlet fever. | 1 year. | |
| Scarlet fever. | 5 years. | Hard of hearing. |
| Scarlet fever. | 4 years. | |
| Scarlet fever. | 5 years. | |
| | | |
| Scrofula. | 8 years. | |
| Spinal sickness. | 2 months. | |
| Congenital. | | |
| Scarlet fever. | 2 years, 6 mo's. | Hard of hearing. |
| Congenital | | |
| Measles | 1 year. | |
| Convulsions. | 1 year. | Hard of hearing. |

## TABULAR REPORT OF THE PUPILS OF THE SCHOOL

| NAME OF PUPIL. | RESIDENCE. | AGE (Approx.). | DATE OF ADMISSION. |
|---|---|---|---|
| Bowen, John | Providence | 13 | Oct. 18, 1898 |
| Bassett, Genevive W | Moosup Valley | 4 | Oct. 18, 1898 |
| Vogel, Alfred | Providence | 11 | Oct. 18, 1898 |
| Goldman, Samuel | Providence | 9 | Nov. 7, 1898 |
| Myers, Arthur | Providence | 7 | Jan. 3, 1899 |
| McLean, Ernest C. | Manville | 6 | March 14, 1899 |
| Wilcox, Olive I | East Providence | 3 | April 3, 1899 |
| Smith, Everett A | Slocumville | 3 | May 19, 1899 |
| Williams, Harold K | Pawtucket | 4 | Sept. 13, 1899 |
| Sweet, Fannie M | Centredale | 8 | Sept. 13, 1899 |
| Newberg, Charles A | Pawtucket | 7 | Sept. 25, 1899 |
| Paquin, Adolard | Providence | 5 | Oct. 2, 1899 |
| Cleary, John | Newport | 5 | Oct. 2, 1899 |
| Ross, William | Providence | 16 | Oct. 4, 1899 |
| Holmes, Thomas | Providence | 7 | Oct. 17, 1899 |
| Grabert, Herman | Bristol | 12 | March 1, 1900 |
| McGowan, Terry | Newport | 17 | May 2, 1900 |
| Brennan, Sarah A | Pawtucket | 7 | May 6, 1900 |
| Terrill, Louise E | White River Jc., Vt. | 14 | May 7, 1900 |
| Olin, Millie I | East Providence | 13 | Sept. 11, 1900 |
| Arel, Joseph I | Woonsocket | 10 | Sept. 19, 1900 |
| Brown, Lola B | Davisville | 12 | Nov. 19, 1900 |

## FOR THE YEAR ENDING DECEMBER 31, 1900.

| CAUSE OF DEAFNESS, AS FAR AS KNOWN. | AGE WHEN MADE DEAF (Approx.). | REMARKS. |
|---|---|---|
| Congenital............ | | |
| ..................... | ................ | Not deaf. |
| A fall................ | 3 years........ | |
| Grippe............... | 6 years........ | |
| Meningitis............ | 3 years........ | |
| Congenital............ | | |
| Congenital............ | | |
| Congenital............ | | |
| Spinal meningitis...... | 7 years........ | |
| A fall................ | 5 years........ | |
| Congenital............ | | |
| Congenital............ | | |
| Congenital............ | | |
| ..................... | | Not deaf. |
| Measles............... | | Deafness partial. |
| A fall................ | 2 years........ | Hard of hearing. |
| Congenital............ | | |
| La Grippe............. | 5 years........ | Hard of hearing. |
| Scarlet fever.......... | 10 years....... | |
| Congenital............ | | |
| Adenoid growth........ | 3 years........ | Hard of hearing. |

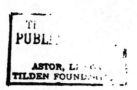

Davisville................................................................. 1
Centredale............................................................... 1
Manville.................................................................. 1
River Point............................................................... 1
Woonsocket............................................................... 6
Carolina.................................................................. 1
Hope..................................................................... 1
Bristol................................................................... 1
Warren................................................................... 1
Rumford.................................................................. 1
Moosup Valley............................................................ 1
White River Junction, Vermont............................................ 1
_____

Twenty-three localities.................................... 58

## PERIODICALS.

The receipt of the following periodicals is thankfully acknowledged, and their continuance respectfully requested :

Mute's Companion, Faribault, Minn.; Daily Paper for Our Little People, Rochester, N. Y.; Our Children's School Journal, The Deaf Mute Journal, New York; Maryland Bulletin, Frederick, Md.; The Deaf Mute Voice, Jackson, Miss.; Kentucky Deaf Mute, Danville, Ky.; The Goodson Gazette, Staunton, Va.; Kansas Star, Olathe, Kansas; Deaf Mute Optic, Little Rock, Ark.; Deaf Mute Index, Colorado Springs, Col.; Juvenile Ranger, Austin, Texas; The Register, Rome, New York; Nebraska Mute Journal, Omaha, Neb.; New Method for the Deaf, Englewood, Ill.; Weekly News, Berkeley, Cal.; The Mount Airy World, Philadelphia; The Canadian Deaf Mute, Bellville, Ontario; The New Era, Jacksonville, Ill.

## RHODE ISLAND INSTITUTE FOR THE DEAF.

## HIGHER COURSE.

### EIGHTH, NINTH, AND TENTH YEARS.

- *a.* ARTICULATION.
- *b.* LANGUAGE.
- *c.* ARITHMETIC.
- *d.* GEOGRAPHY.
- *e.* HISTORY.
- *f.* PHYSIOLOGY.
- *g.* PENMANSHIP.
- *h.* DRAWING.
- *i.* CALISTHENICS.

ı difficult combinations and **words.**

sition; journal and letter writing; miscellaneous readi

papers and magazines; lessons on general subjects.

. written, and practical.

phical reader; Manual of Commerce.

of the United States; **Outline of General History.**

ook.

and object drawing and designing.

. Drill in elements, combinations, and words, and reading them from the lips.

. Thorough review of first year work. Nouns and verbs continued. Adjectives continued ; their comparison. Pronouns as in first year, adding myself, herself, himself, with the plurals, and the relatives who and which. Adverbs ; not, often, never, etc. Elliptical sentences ; action and picture writing ; journal and letter writing, and simple stories.

. Practical exercises in addition, subtraction, multiplication, and division ; United States currency ; simple fractions.

. School-room, building, and yard, city, and a limited knowledge of the State.

. Copy-book writing.

## INTERMEDIATE COURSE.

### FIFTH, SIXTH, AND SEVENTH YEARS.

> *a.* ARTICULATION.
> *b.* LANGUAGE.
> *c.* ARITHMETIC.
> *d.* GEOGRAPHY.
> *e.* HISTORY.
> *f.* PENMANSHIP.
> *g.* DRAWING.
> *h.* CALISTHENICS.

. Drill in elements, combinations, syllables ; words and sentences continued as in primary course.

. Nouns, pronouns, adjectives, adverbs, prepositions, and conjunctions continued as in primary course. Drill in active and passive voices ; action and picture writing ; stories from natural history ; journal and letter writing.

. Mental and written addition, subtraction, multiplication, and division, with practical examples ; United States currency and simple fractions continued.

. City, State, and New England States.

. Simple historical stories in connection with geography.

. Copy-book writing twice a week.

. Object drawing.

## HIGHER COURSE.

### EIGHTH, NINTH, AND TENTH YEARS.

    *a.*   ARTICULATION.

    *b.*   LANGUAGE.

    *c.*   ARITHMETIC.

    *d.*   GEOGRAPHY.

    *e.*   HISTORY.

    *f.*   PHYSIOLOGY.

    *g.*   PENMANSHIP.

    *h.*   DRAWING.

    *i.*   CALISTHENICS.

*a.*   Drill in difficult combinations and words.

*b.*   Composition; journal and letter writing; miscellaneous reading; newspapers and magazines; lessons on general subjects.

*c.*   Mental, written, and practical.

*d.*   Geographical reader; Manual of Commerce.

*e.*   History of the United States; Outline of General History.

*g.*   Copy-book.

*h.*   Free-hand object drawing and designing.

# CHAPTER 332.

AN ACT IN AMENDMENT OF AND IN ADDITION TO CHAPTER 86 OF THE GENERAL LAWS, ENTITLED "OF THE R. I. SCHOOL FOR THE DEAF."

(Passed May 13, 1896.)

*It is enacted by the General Assembly as follows :*

SECTION 1. All children of parents, or under the control of guardians or other persons, legal residents of this state, between the ages of three and twenty years, whose hearing or speech, or both, are so defective as to make it inexpedient or impracticable to attend the public schools to advantage, not being mentally or otherwise incapable, may attend the Rhode Island Institute for the Deaf, without charge, under such rules and regulations as the board of trustees of said institute may establish.

SEC. 2. Every person having under his control any such child between the ages of seven and eighteen years shall cause such child to attend school at said institute for such period of time or such prescribed course, in each individual case, as may be deemed expedient by the board of trustees, and for any neglect of such duty the person so offending shall be fined not exceeding twenty dollars : *Provided*, that if the person so charged shall prove to the satisfaction of said board that the child has received or is receiving, under private or other instruction, an education suitable to his condition, in the judgment of said board, then such penalty shall not be incurred : *provided, further*, that no child shall be removed to said institution or taken from the custody of its parent or guardian except as a day scholar unless such parent or guardian is an improper person to have such custody, and the supreme court in its appellate division shall have jurisdiction in habeas corpus to examine into and revise all findings of said board of trustees under this act.

SEC. 3. Any child having attended said institute a time or course prescribed by said board, upon leaving the institute shall be entitled to receive a certificate of his proficiency from said board.

SEC. 4. This act shall take effect from and after its passage.

# TO PARENTS OF DEAF CHILDREN.

This school is for the benefit of children incapacitated through deafness, total or partial, for receiving proper instruction in common schools, and is free to all pupils who belong in this State.

The aim of the school is to teach deaf children to use the English language with the spontaneity, correctness, and enjoyment of *hearing* children as far as this is practicable.

"Without language there can be no thought, no reason;" and as the highest aim of all instruction is the culture of the mental and moral nature in man, our first effort should be to furnish the deaf with a medium through which knowledge can be imparted and obtained. This can be done by signs, by the finger alphabet, and by speech. Our method is the latter, or oral, method, by which the deaf can be educated and at the same time furnished with the usual and most convenient way of communication in society and the world at large.

It is very desirable that deaf children be sent to school at as early an age as possible. A parent will be amply repaid for sending a child as young as five or six years, even at some inconvenience. The Board of Trustees are authorized to receive pupils between the ages of three and twenty years.

If a child who has learned to talk is made deaf by disease, he should immediately, upon his recovery, be sent to a school where his speech will be retained, and where he will be taught to understand from the lips. In such cases it is common to delay so long that serious loss of speech results.

Speech reading is an invaluable acquisition for those who are semi-deaf, or even hard of hearing, as well as for those congenitally or totally deaf.

State of Rhode Island and Providence

# REPORT OF THE BOARD OF TRU

OF THE

## RHODE ISLAND

# NSTITUTE FOR THE

PRESENTED TO THE

## GENERAL ASSEMBL

AT ITS

## JANUARY SESSION,

PROVIDENCE:
E. L. FREEMAN & SONS, STATE PRIN
1902.

State of Rhode Island and Providence Plantations.

# REPORT OF THE BOARD OF TRUSTEES

OF THE

## RHODE ISLAND

# INSTITUTE FOR THE DEAF,

PRESENTED TO THE

## GENERAL ASSEMBLY

AT ITS

## JANUARY SESSION, 1902.

PROVIDENCE:

E. L. FREEMAN & SONS, STATE PRINTERS.

1902.

State of Rhode Island and Providence Plantations.

# REPORT OF THE BOARD OF TRUSTEES

OF THE

## RHODE ISLAND

# INSTITUTE FOR THE DEAF,

PRESENTED TO THE

## GENERAL ASSEMBLY

AT ITS

## JANUARY SESSION, 1902.

PROVIDENCE, R. I.
E. L. FREEMAN & SONS, STATE PRINTERS.
1902.

# REPORT OF THE BOARD OF TRUSTEES.

*To the Honorable the General Assembly at its January Session, A. D. 1902 :*

With a constantly increasing number of pupils our school has made substantial progress during the year. Improved methods of instruction are being constantly adopted, and the teachers and pupils seem to be working with the harmony and good feeling that is productive of excellent results. There has been no change made of assistant teachers during the year, with the single exception of the teacher of sloyd, Mr. C. M. Hunt, whose business took him out of the State; he was well liked, and a great favorite with the children. Mr. H. G. Hatch was engaged to fill the vacancy, and is giving good satisfaction. Marked improvement in speech is manifest in the pupils, especially among those who entered the institute when very young. The health of the scholars has been uniformly good. There was one death during the year (the first since the institute was opened). One of the boys had double pneumonia, and, notwithstanding he had the best of medical attendance and care, his illness terminated fatally.

The buildings and grounds are in fairly good condition, but it will be necessary to paint all outside work on the school building and on the main building during the coming spring.

| | |
|---|---:|
| Whole number of pupils. | 72 |
| " " " boys | 39 |
| " " " girls | 33 |
| Present attendance | 64 |

We respectfully submit the financial report, as follows:

| | | |
|---|---:|---:|
| Special appropriation............................. | | $1,000 00 |
| Annual        "        ...................... ......... | | 20,000 00 |
| Paid salaries .......................... ............ | $8,765 85 | |
| All other expenses....................... | 12,221 30 | |
| | ——————— | 20,987 15 |

**$12 85**

For maintenance during the ensuing year we recommend the sum of ($20,000.00) twenty thousand dollars.

Annexed will be found the annual report of the principal, also the reports of F. L. Day, M. D., and F. P. Capron, M. D., which contain more detailed information as to the condition and work of the school.

Respectfully submitted,

CHARLES D. KIMBALL,
*Lieutenant-Governor, Acting Governor, Ex-officio.*
WILLIAM K. POTTER, *President,*
MRS. ELLEN T. McGUINNESS, *Secretary,*
MRS. JEANIE LIPPITT WEEDEN,
MRS. LILLIE B. CHACE WYMAN,
EDWIN FARNELL,
DR. ROWLAND R. ROBINSON,
JOHN C. B. WOODS, .
WILLIAM H. BALLOU,
JEREMIAH W. HORTON,

*Board of Trustees.*

PROVIDENCE, R. I., January, 1902.

# MEDICAL REPORT.

---

*To the Trustees of the R. I. Institute for the Deaf:*

I have the honor to make the following report of the children's health during the year just past :

No epidemic has prevailed this year among the children. In January there was a fatal case of double pneumonia in a defective boy, being the first death that has occurred in the institute since its opening. Later in the winter a single case of diphtheria was sent to the R. I. Hospital, and was not followed by other cases. In the fall, aside from a few minor accidents and cases of indigestion, there was singular freedom from illness.

Respectfully submitted,

FRANK L. DAY, M. D.

PROVIDENCE, January 1, 1902.

PROVIDENCE, R. I., December 23, 1901.

*To the Trustees of R. I. Institute for the Deaf.*

GENTLEMEN:—The following patients have been under my care during the past year: Chester Collins, Edward Anderson, Terence McGovern, Louise Terrell, May Gardiner, and Millie Olin. The first three named are still under treatment, and very much improved as to the condition of their ears, but their trouble is of long standing, resulting in a state of chronic purulent inflammation, which is accompanied with polyps or proud flesh, necessitating a persistent and long course of treatment. Any interruption in treatment, such as might result from a long vacation, will give the proud flesh an opportunity to again spring up, and thus undo all that was before accomplished. Such cases require attention not alone on account of the ears, but because of the resultant effect upon their general health, together with the danger of a serious result from extension of the inflammation to the brain.

Louise Terrell was seen but a few times, and was treated for a chronic dry catarrh of ears, as well as for catarrh of the nose. The result was beneficial to a certain extent.

May Gardiner had a discharge from her ears, and had she been left in the institute awhile longer would have been cured of the discharge.

Millie Olin had purulent middle ear catarrh of left side with granulation tissue, which was cured. She was also fitted to glasses for astigmatism.

Respectfully submitted,

F. P. CAPRON, M. D.

# REPORT OF THE PRINCIPAL.

*To the Trustees of the R. I. Institute for the Deaf.*

GENTLEMEN :—In accordance with our custom I present to you a report of the school year just past, ending December 31, 1901. The number enrolled is 39 boys and 33 girls. Seven have been admitted during the year. Three have remained at home. One, a girl with some hearing, who is attending a hearing school; another, a boy of seventeen, has been put to work, so that he may assist in the support of the family; and the other is permitted to remain at home and no doubt will soon be put to work. It is to be regretted that so many of the parents of deaf children seem to think that as soon as the child acquires a small amount of speech there is no longer need for it to attend school. They disregard the fact that most deaf children have no language when first brought to school and that they learn very little *away* from *school*, while their hearing brothers and sisters have much more, when they enter the kindergarten even, than most deaf children have after four or five years of patient work in school. It *is real* work for the deaf to acquire language, while a hearing child gains language sufficient for his use without labor. *Its* education was begun in infancy, its mother being the teacher, and it has continued from day to day, through years, by intercourse with those with whom it has come in contact. It ought to learn language much more readily than the deaf child, because it hears it spoken continually. Most hearing children attend school ten years at least, but often twelve or fifteen, while deaf children are usually taken from school after six or, at the most, eight years instruction. We are constantly searching for deaf children of school age who ought to be in school. Many of the parents are very reluctant to part with them, disregarding entirely the benefit they will *all* derive from the separation. A mother said, only a few days ago: "Daughter is such a nice girl. She helps me so much now." She was speaking of a young girl who has been with us eight years, and we hope to keep her several years more. .

HEALTH.

Owing to the continued care of our attending physician, Dr. F. L. Day, we are able to report that the past year was unusually free from sickness. With the exception of one fatal case, we were visited by only the minor diseases incident to childhood. It is with regret that we record the death of John Canney, of pneumonia, January 25, after an illness of only three days. He had never been strong, either physically or mentally, and therefore not able to throw off disease. This is the first death *here* among the children since we removed from Fountain street nine years ago. Since re-opening school, last September, the pupils have had universally good health, and they have also been free from serious accidents.

CLASS WORK.

The work in the school during the year past has been very gratifying. As we review the past few years we are encouraged to see our older pupils more and more interested in their work, and desirous to continue their studies.

The girls are more womanly and the boys more manly. There has been no change in our regular corps of teachers during the year. In this department eight teachers are employed, with four teachers in training to assist.

In teaching language we follow the object method. When a new word is taught, the object, or picture of the object, is shown the class, and the children are made familiar with the object, or its picture, by seeing and handling it. The verbs, or action words, are taught by performing, before the class, the action expressed by the verb.

method, and speech-rea
ns of instruction. Grea
ind mental development
tice for one to learn to
movements of the face
the greatest importance
l that a child is deaf, its
ns which will teach it
ye, and articulate spe
ly the necessity of a de
ns whatever should be
speech-reader.

## DUSTRIAL DEPARTMENT.

ight departure in the s
s begun to draft and cu
a small scale, of the ga
ilarges it, cuts her patt
s it entirely herself by ha
ake up the same work,
rk in their class. Ther

school year Mr. Hunt, w
his connection to accep
atly regret his resigna
securing the services
veral years experience in
utting, card-board const
nce M. Russell, has beei
l a class of younger pup
he older boys are making
iome at Christmas. The
les, bureaus, and chair
r room, which was much

We employ the oral method, and speech-reading and articulation are the chief means of instruction. Great facility in speech-reading, articulation, and mental development are aimed at. It requires years of practice for one to learn to understand what is said by watching the movements of the face, lips, and tongue. Speech-reading is of the greatest importance in our work. As soon as it is discovered that a child is deaf, its parents should surround it with conditions which will teach it *speech-reading*, language, through the eye, and articulate speech. We cannot emphasize too strongly the necessity of a deaf child acquiring *speech-reading*. No signs whatever should be used if the child is to become a successful speech-reader.

## INDUSTRIAL DEPARTMENT.

There has been a slight departure in the sewing department. The advanced class has begun to draft and cut garments. Each girl draws a design, on a small scale, of the garment which she is to cut, and then she enlarges it, cuts her pattern, and then cuts the garment and makes it entirely herself by hand. The younger girls are ambitious to take up the same work, and the little girls are doing excellent work in their class. There is also a class in embroidery.

At the end of the school year Mr. Hunt, who had been with us four years, severed his connection to accept a more responsible position. We greatly regret his resignation, but consider ourselves fortunate in securing the services of Mr. Harvey G. Hatch, who has had several years experience in sloyd work.

The class in paper-cutting, card-board construction, and whittling, under Miss Florence M. Russell, has been advanced to the regular sloyd work, and a class of younger pupils formed in cardboard construction. The older boys are making desks, book-cases, and hat-racks to take home at Christmas. They have done most of the repairing of tables, bureaus, and chairs, and have partitioned off a refrigerator room, which was much needed.

At the close of school, last June, Mr. Goodale severed his connection with the school. Work in the printing-room was, therefore, discontinued. We hope to resume the work at the beginning of the coming year, with Mr. Hatch as director.

The morning of December 24th, before going home, the children were provided with a bountifully laden Christmas tree, which was appreciated by all; and Santa Claus, who was thoroughly enjoyed, took a lively interest in the children as they went forward to receive presents from their genial friend. The tree was made unusually attractive by the great number of stockings hung upon it, filled with candy, pop-corn, and toys, presented by St. Hope Society, of the Church of The Saviour, to whom we extend thanks.

### ACKNOWLEDGMENTS.

Thanks are due Mrs. W. B. Weeden, for money for the Christmas tree; Messrs. Arnold & Maine, and Messrs. J. H. Preston & Co., for Christmas candies; Mrs. D. B. Pond, for subscription for the Youths' Companion; and Mrs. W. B. Weeden, Mrs. S. S. Durfee, Mrs. H. A. Waldron, and Mrs. J. R. Gladding, for clothing.

### PRIZES.

At the close of the school in June, prizes were awarded Jennie Goldstein for the best speech in the grammar grade, and John Welch for the best speech in the intermediate grade; Moses Goldenofsky and Laura Hackett for the best speech-reading; Terry McGowan for the greatest general improvement; Luella Cole and Willie Jermyn for best deportment; Teresa Grace for the best conduct in study hour; Herman Grebert and Jimmie Flynn for neatness; and Henry Courtemanche and Lena Perron for the best penmanship.

Respectfully submitted,

LAURA DeL. RICHARDS.

MAIN VIEW

# TABULATED STATEMENT.

## TABULAR REPORT OF THE PUPILS OF THE SCHOOL

| Name of Pupil. | Residence. | Age. (Approx.). | Date of Admission. |
|---|---|---|---|
| Sullivan, Nellie.......... | Newport............... | 13 | **Nov.** 12, 1886. |
| Grant, Edith............. | Providence............ | 10 | **Dec.** 13, 1886. |
| Cole, Luella............. | South Scituate........ | 12 | March 28, 1887. |
| Goldenofsky, Moses....... | Woonsocket........... | 10 | April 29, 1889. |
| Hackett, Laura.......... | Providence............ | 8 | Nov. 11, 1889. |
| Fletcher, Henrietta M.... | Johnston.......... | 10 | Sept. 1, 1890. |
| Lease, Edwin G.......... | Providence............ | 11 | Feb. 2, 1891. |
| Courtemanche, Henry..... | Woonsocket........... | 12 | June 10, 1891. |
| Staunton, Bertha......... | Providence............ | 8 | Oct. 5, 1891. |
| Jermyn, William......... | Newport............... | 10 | May 5, 1892. |
| Mills, Anneta............ | Providence............ | 6 | April 3, 1893. |
| Carr, David............. | Pawtucket............ | 6 | Jan. 27, 1893. |
| Collins, Chester A........ | Providence............ | 4 | Jan. 30, 1893. |
| Kleber, Fannie........... | Lymansville........... | 6 | Feb. 7, 1893. |
| Goldstein, Clara J........ | Providence............ | 9 | March 1, 1893. |
| Desonie, Maggie ........ .. | Lippitt................ | 8 | March 23, 1893. |
| Smith, Bernard F........ | Providence............ | 8 | April 10, 1893. |
| O'Connor, Mary.......... | Woonsocket........... | 6 | May 27, 1893. |
| Hoen, Alfred............. | Carolina................ | .. .. | Sept. 11, 1893. |
| Thompson, George....... | Providence............ | 4 | Sept. 11, 1893. |
| Flynn, James............. | Providence............ | 6 | Feb. 3, 1894. |
| Comfort, Mae E.......... | Newport............... | 8 | Sept. 10, 1894. |
| Bradley, William H...... | Woonsocket........... | 11 | Oct. 1, 1894. |
| Mudrak, Willie.......... | Geneva............... | 4 | Oct. 13, 1894. |
| Canney, John P.......... | Providence............ | 9 | Dec. 3, 1894. |
| Grimes, Mary............ | Newport............... | 9 | Feb. 5, 1895. |
| O'Riley, Willie F......... | Providence............ | 7 | Feb. 11, 1895. |
| Grace, Theresa........... | Providence............. | 12 | April 10, 1895. |
| Welsh, John ............. | Providence............. | 7 | May 20, 1895. |
| Roe, Albert C........... | Hope................. | 5 | Sept. 21, 1895. |
| Stetson, Leroy W......... | Warren................ | 10 | Sept. 30, 1895. |
| Smith, Idella............. | Johnston ............. | 9 | Oct. 28. 1895. |
| Williams, Charles A ..... | Pawtucket............ | 4 | Sept. 14, 1896. |
| Cook, Reuben............ | Peace Dale............. | 7 | Oct. 6, 1896. |
| Perron, Lena............. | Woonsocket............ | 7 | Oct. 26, 1896. |
| Anderson, Edward V..... | Providence ............ | 9 | ............ |
| Vigeant, Edward......... | Pawtucket............. | 7 | May 3, 1897. |
| Gardner, May............ | Scituate ............... | 9 | April 29, 1897. |
| Davis, Elsie............. | Rumford............... | 9 | Sept. 13, 1897. |
| Essex, Fred E. L......... | Providence............ | 1 | Sept. 13, 1897. |
| Perry, Joseph C.......... | Providence............ | 7 | Jan. 7, 1898. |
| Yuppa, Concetta......... | Providence............ | 4 | Feb. 10, 1898. |
| Forthier, Angelina........ | Pawtucket............. | 6 | Oct. 24, 1898. |
| Holborgen, Trina......... | Pawtucket............. | 6 | Oct. 18, 1898. |
| Bowen, John............. | Providence............ | 3 | Oct. 18, 1898. |
| Bassett, Genevive W...... | Moosup Valley......... | 4 | Oct. 18, 1898. |

FOR THE YEAR ENDING DECEMBER 31, 1901.

| CAUSE OF DEAFNESS, AS FAR AS KNOWN. | AGE WHEN MADE DEAF (Approx.). | REMARKS. |
|---|---|---|
| Scarlet fever | 2 years | |
| Tumor in ear | 6 months | |
| Congenital | | |
| Scarlet fever | 8 years | |
| Congenital | | |
| Congenital | | |
| Unknown | 4 years | Hard of hearing. |
| Congenital | | |
| Brain fever | 3 years | |
| Congenital | | |
| Measles | 3 years | |
| A fall | 2 years | |
| Measles | 2 years | |
| Congenital | | Deafness partial. |
| Typhoid fever | 4 years | |
| Congenital | | |
| | | Not deaf. |
| Scarlet fever | 1 year | |
| A fall | 2 years | Deafness partial. |
| Convulsions | 3 years | |
| Congenital | | |
| Catarrhal fever | 1 year, 6 months | |
| Diphtheria | 6 years | |
| Congenital | | |
| Taking quinine | 1 year | |
| Measles | 5 years | Slight degree of hearing. |
| Congenital | | |
| Congenital | | |
| Brain fever | 3 years | |
| Inflammation in head | 4 months | |
| Fall and fever | 4 years | Slight degree of hearing. |
| Congenital | | Slight degree of hearing. |
| Congenital | | |
| Congenital | | |
| Scarlet fever | 1 year | |
| Scarlet fever | 5 years | Hard of hearing |
| Scarlet fever | 4 years | |
| Scarlet fever | 5 years | |
| Scrofula | 8 years | |
| Spinal sickness | 2 months | |
| Congenital | | |
| Congenital | | |
| Measles | 1 year | |
| Convulsions | 1 year | Hard of hearing |
| Congenital | | |

TABULAR REPORT OF THE PUPILS OF THE SCHOOL

| Name of Pupil. | Residence. | Age (Approx.). | Date of Admission. |
|---|---|---|---|
| Vogel, Alfred............... | Providence............. | 11 | Oct. 18, 1898. |
| Goldman, Samuel......... | Providence............. | 9 | Nov. 7, 1898. |
| Myers, Arthur............. | Providence............. | 7 | Jan. 3, 1899. |
| Wilcox, Olive I........... | East Providence........ | 3 | April 3, 1899. |
| Smith, Everett A......... | Slocumville............. | 3 | May 19, 1899. |
| Williams, Harold K....... | Pawtucket.............. | 4 | Sept. 13, 1899. |
| Sweet, Fannie M.......... | Centredale............. | 8 | Sept. 13, 1899. |
| Newberg, Charles A....... | Pawtucket.............. | 7 | Sept. 25, 1899. |
| Paquin, Adolard.......... | Providence............. | 5 | Oct. 2, 1899. |
| Cleary, John............. | Newport............... | 5 | Oct. 2, 1899. |
| Ross, William............ | Providence............. | 16 | Oct. 4, 1899. |
| Holmes, Thomas......... | Providence............. | 7 | Oct. 17, 1899. |
| Grabert, Herman......... | Bristol................. | 12 | March 1, 1900. |
| McGowan, Terry......... | Newport............... | 17 | May 2, 1900. |
| Brennan, Sarah A........ | Pawtucket............. | 7 | May 6, 1900. |
| Terrill, Louise E......... | White River Jc., Vt.... | 14 | May 7, 1900. |
| Olin, Millie I............. | East Providence........ | 13 | Sept. 11, 1900. |
| Arel, Joseph I............ | Woonsocket............ | 10 | Sept. 19, 1900. |
| Brown, Lola B........... | Davisville............. | 12 | Nov. 19, 1900. |
| Gardiner, Earl F......... | Providence............. | 7 | April 16, 1901. |
| Notorantonio, Maggie..... | Providence............. | 8 | April 22, 1901. |
| Mitchell, Fred G......... | Providence............. | 8 | Sept. 10, 1901. |
| Blanchard, S. Gertrude.... | Providence............. | 14 | Sept. 10, 1901. |
| Cohen, Esther........... | Providence............. | 14 | Sept. 12, 1901. |
| Lindsay, Mary E......... | Providence............. | 5 | Oct. 5, 1901. |
| Burke, Bessie............ | Providence............. | | |

## FOR THE YEAR ENDING DECEMBER 31, 1901.

| CAUSE OF DEAFNESS, AS FAR AS KNOWN. | AGE WHEN MADE DEAF (Approx.). | REMARKS. |
|---|---|---|
| ............................ | ............ | Not deaf. |
| A fall...................... | 3 years........... | ........................ |
| Grippe..................... | 6 years........... | ........................ |
| Congenital................. | ................ | ........................ |
| Congenital................. | ................ | ........................ |
| Congenital................. | ................ | ........................ |
| Spinal meningitis.......... | 7 years........... | ........................ |
| A fall...................... | 5 years........... | ........................ |
| Congenital................. | ................ | ........................ |
| Congenital................. | ................ | ........................ |
| Congenital................. | ................ | ........................ |
| ............................ | ................ | Not deaf. |
| Measles.................... | ................ | Deafness partial. |
| A fall...................... | 2 years........... | Hard of hearing. |
| Congenital................. | ................ | ........................ |
| La Grippe.................. | 5 years........... | Hard of hearing. |
| Scarlet fever.............. | 10 years......... | ........................ |
| Congenital................. | ................ | ........................ |
| Adenoid growth............ | 3 years........... | Hard of hearing. |
| Spinal meningitis.......... | 4 years........... | ........................ |
| Fever...................... | 4 years........... | ........................ |
| Congenital................. | ................ | Hard of hearing. |
| Scarlet fever.............. | 5 years........... | Hard of hearing. |
| Congenital................. | ................ | ........................ |
| Congenital................. | ................ | ........................ |

## SUMMARY.

Number of pupils from date of opening the State school for the deaf,
April 2, 1877, to December 31, 1900........... ..................... 17◄

Number of pupils who have entered the Institute since Dec. 31, 1900.. ◄7

Whole number of pupils who have attended the school.......... 1▬◄4

Number who have left the school............................... 1 ▬◄0

Number of pupils Dec. 31, 1901........................................ ◄64

Number of girls who have attended school during the year............ ◄33

Number of boys who have attended school during the year............ ◄39

Whole number of pupils during the year....................... 72

Average attendance...................................................

Number congenitally deaf, or made deaf before the age of two........ 39

Number who lost hearing between the ages of two and four....'........ 13

Number who lost hearing after the age of four, and doubtful cases.... 13

Number who have perfect hearing................................... 3

72

Number who have any degree of hearing............................ 16

*Residences of all who have attended during the year 1901.*

| | |
|---|---|
| Genevå................................................. | 1 |
| Providence............................................. | 32 |
| East Providence....................................... | 2 |
| Pawtucket............................................. | 8 |
| South Scituate........................................ | 2 |
| Johnston.............................................. | 2 |
| Newport............................................... | 6 |
| Lymansville........................................... | 1 |
| Lippitt............................................... | |
| Peace Dale............................................ | |
| Slocumville........................................... | |

BOYS' LIBRARY.

a. Drill in elements, combinations, and words, :
   lips.
b. Thorough review of first year work. No'
   Adjectives continued; their comparison,
   adding myself, herself, himself, with the
   who and which. Adverbs; not, often, i
   tences; action and picture writing: jourı
   simple stories.
c. Practical exercises in addition, subtraction,
   ion; United States currency; simple frac
d. School-room, building, and yard, city, and a
   State.
e. Copy-book writing.

### INTERMEDIATE COUі

#### FIFTH, SIXTH, AND SEVENTH

a. ARTICULATION.
b. LANGUAGE.
c. ARITHMETIC.
d. GEOGRAPHY.
e. HISTORY.
f. PENMANSHIP.
g. DRAWING.
h. CALISTHENICS.

a. Drill in elements, combinations, syllables;
   tinued as in primary course.
b. Nouns, pronouns, adjectives, adverbs, preı
   continued as in primary course. Drill in
   action and picture writing; stories from
   and letter writing.
c. Mental and written addition, subtraction, ı
   with practical examples; United States
   tions continued.
d. City, State, and New England States.
e. Simple historical stories in connection with
f. Copy-book writing twice a week.
   Object drawing.

# COURSE OF STUDY.

## KINDERGARTEN.

### FIRST YEAR.

    *a.* KINDERGARTEN EXERCISES.

    *b.* ARTICULATION.

    *c.* LANGUAGE.

    *d.* ARITHMETIC.

    *e.* PENMANSHIP.

*a.* Paper cutting and folding; drawing and modeling in clay; design in shoe pegs; stick laying; embroidery designs sewed on pric sewing-cards; lessons in form and color in all exercises.

*b.* Elements, combinations, simple words, and sentences; with rea them from the lips.

*c.* Nouns; objects in class-room, articles of dress, articles of food, ent parts of the body, with a limited number of verbs. Adjec good, bad, large, small, &c.

*d.* Counting and writing numbers, with addition and subtraction t

*e.* Writing on slate and with lead pencil.

## PRIMARY COURSE.

### SECOND, THIRD, AND FOURTH YEARS.

    *a.* ARTICULATION.

    *b.* LANGUAGE.

    *c.* ARITHMETIC.

    *d.* GEOGRAPHY.

    *e.* PENMANSHIP.

    *f.* DRAWING.

. Drill in elements, combinations, and words, and reading them from the lips.

. Thorough review of first year work. Nouns and verbs continued. Adjectives continued; their comparison. Pronouns as in first year, adding myself, herself, himself, with the plurals, and the relatives who and which. Adverbs; not, often, never, etc. Elliptical sentences; action and picture writing; journal and letter writing, and simple stories.

. Practical exercises in addition, subtraction, multiplication, and division; United States currency; simple fractions.

l. School-room, building, and yard, city, and a limited knowledge of the State.

. Copy-book writing.

## INTERMEDIATE COURSE.

### FIFTH, SIXTH, AND SEVENTH YEARS.

        *a.* ARTICULATION.

        *b.* LANGUAGE.

        *c.* ARITHMETIC.

        *d.* GEOGRAPHY.

        *e.* HISTORY.

        *f.* PENMANSHIP.

        *g.* DRAWING.

        *h.* CALISTHENICS.

. Drill in elements, combinations, syllables; words and sentences continued as in primary course.

. Nouns, pronouns, adjectives, adverbs, prepositions, and conjunctions continued as in primary course. Drill in active and passive voices; action and picture writing; stories from natural history; journal and letter writing,

. Mental and written addition, subtraction, multiplication, and division, with practical examples; United States currency and simple fractions continued.

l. City, State, and New England States.

. Simple historical stories in connection with geography.

f. Copy-book writing twice a week.

g. Object drawing.

## HIGHER COURSE.

### EIGHTH, NINTH, AND TENTH YEARS.

- *a.* ARTICULATION.
- *b.* LANGUAGE.
- *c.* ARITHMETIC.
- *d.* GEOGRAPHY.
- *e.* HISTORY.
- *f.* PHYSIOLOGY.
- *g.* PENMANSHIP.
- *h.* DRAWING.
- *i.* CALISTHENICS.

*a.* Drill in difficult combinations and words.

*b.* Composition; journal and letter writing; miscellaneous reading newspapers and magazines; lessons on general subjects.

*c.* Mental, written, and practical.

*d.* Geographical reader; Manual of Commerce.

*e.* History of the United States; Outline of General History.

*g.* Copy-book.

*h.* Free-hand object drawing and designing.

# CHAPTER 332.

AN ACT IN AMENDMENT OF AND IN ADDITION TO CHAPTER
86 OF THE GENERAL LAWS, ENTITLED "OF THE R. I. SCHOOL
FOR THE DEAF."

[Passed May 18, 1896.]

*It is enacted by the General Assembly as follows:*

SECTION 1. All children of parents, or under the control of guardians
or other persons, legal residents of this state, between the ages of three
and twenty years, whose hearing or speech, or both, are so defective as to
make it inexpedient or impracticable to attend the public schools to advantage, not being mentally or otherwise incapable, may attend the Rhode
Island Institute for the Deaf, without charge, under such rules and regulations as the board of trustees of said institute may establish.

SEC. 2. Every person having under his control any such child between
the ages of seven and eighteen years shall cause such child to attend school
at said institute for such period of time or such prescribed course, in each
individual case, as may be deemed expedient by the board of trustees, and
for any neglect of such duty the person so offending shall be fined not
exceeding twenty dollars: *Provided,* that if the person so charged shall
prove to the satisfaction of said board that the child has received or is
receiving, under private or other instruction, an education suitable to his
condition, in the judgment of said board, then such penalty shall not be
incurred: *provided, further,* that no child shall be removed to said institution or taken from the custody of its parent or guardian except as a day
scholar unless such parent or guardian is an improper person to have such
custody, and the supreme court in its appellate division shall have jurisdiction in habeas corpus to examine into and revise all findings of said
board of trustees under this act.

SEC. 3. Any child having attended said institute a time or course prescribed by said board, upon leaving the institute shall be entitled to receive
a certificate of his proficiency from said board.

SEC. 4. This act shall take effect from and after its passage.

# TO PARENTS OF DEAF CHILDREN.

This school is for the benefit of children incapacitated through deafness, total or partial, for receiving proper instruction in common schools, and is free to all pupils who belong in this State.

The aim of the school is to teach deaf children to use the English language with the spontaneity, correctness, and enjoyment of *hearing* children as far as this is practicable.

"Without language there can be no thought, no reason;" and as the highest aim of all instruction is the culture of the mental and moral nature in man, our first effort should be to furnish the deaf with a medium through which knowledge can be imparted and obtained. This can be done by signs, by the finger alphabet, and by speech. Our method is the latter, or oral, method, by which the deaf can be educated and at the same time furnished with the usual and most convenient way of communication in society and the world at large.

It is very desirable that deaf children be sent to school at as early an age as possible. A parent will be amply repaid for sending a child as young as five or six years, even at some inconvenience. The Board of Trustees are authorized to receive pupils between the ages of three and twenty years.

If a child who has learned to talk is made deaf by disease, he should immediately, upon his recovery, be sent to a school where his speech will be retained, and where he will be taught to understand from the lips. In such cases it is common to delay so long that serious loss of speech results.

Speech reading is an invaluable acquisition for those who are semi-deaf, or even hard of hearing, as well as for those congenitally or totally deaf.

PRESENTED TO THE

# GENERAL ASSEMBL

AT ITS

# ANUARY SESSION.

———— — -

PROVIDENCE, R. I.
E. L. FREEMAN & SONS, STATE PRINTERS.
1903.

State of Rhode Island and Providence Plantations.

# Report of the Board of Trustees

OF THE

# RHODE ISLAND

# INSTITUTE FOR THE DEAF.

PRESENTED TO THE

# GENERAL ASSEMBLY

AT ITS

# JANUARY SESSION, 1903.

PROVIDENCE, R. I.

E. L. FREEMAN & SONS, STATE PRINTERS

1903

FRONT VIEW

State of Rhode Island and Providence Plantations.

# Report of the Board of Trustees

OF THE

## RHODE ISLAND

# INSTITUTE FOR THE DEAF,

PRESENTED TO THE

## GENERAL ASSEMBLY

AT ITS

## JANUARY SESSION, 1903.

—— ·· ——· ·

PROVIDENCE, R. I.
E. L. FREEMAN & SONS, STATE PRINTERS.
1903.

# REPORT OF THE BOARD OF TRUSTEES.

*To the Honorable the General Assembly at its January Session*
  *A. D. 1903:*

The Board of Trustees of the Rhode Island Institute for the Deaf respectfully present the following report for the year 1903.

We greatly regret the enforced resignation, on account of ill-health, of our co-trustee, Mrs. John C. Wyman. Appointed by Gov. John W. Davis in 1891, one of the original members of the board of trustees, Mrs. Wyman has worked with us continuously all these years. Her constant sympathy, wise advice, and broad-mindedness have been invaluable in our often difficult decisions for the best interests and welfare of the school and its inmates. We are fortunate in the appointment, by Governor Kimball, of Mrs. Louise Prosser Bates to take Mrs. Wyman's place. Upon the resignation of another member, Mr. Edwin Farnell, Rabbi Gustav N. Hausmann was appointed.

For the first time since the opening of our institute in its present quarters in 1893, we are pleased and gratified to report that the practical results now show the faithful and conscientious work done by both teachers and pupils, in the graduation in June, with credit and honor, of six of our older pupils. They received their diplomas in public, with the class at the Doyle avenue grammar school, after having successfully taken the same course of study.

We are glad to be able to say that the year just past finds the institute in a prosperous and healthy condition. With 74 pupils on the rolls, 65 now in attendance, no serious epidemic has marred our work, with the exception of a few cases of whooping cough in the early spring. Among such a large number of children colds

and minor ills are to be expected—emphasizing the great impor-
ance of our convenient and comfortable hospital, and the watchful
care of our efficient nurse.

For several years the pupils have had instruction in printing,
but this year the board decided to replace it with a course in practical cooking for the girls,  The class in sewing, under the tuition
of an experienced teacher, remains the same as last year, while
the boys have increased facilities in sloyd and drawing.  A young
man, also, is employed to coach them in football.

Our corps of efficient teachers remains the same as the previous
year, also the same number of attendants.

We respectfully submit the financial report, as follows:

Annual appropriation.......................................... $20,000 00
Paid salaries......................................... $8,905 10
All other expenses................................... 10,945 90
                                                    ————— 19,851 00
                                                          ————————
                                                          $149 00

For maintenance during the ensuing year the board respectfully ask for the same appropriation, viz., the sum of ($20,000.00)
twenty thousand dollars.

### IMPROVEMENTS.

Our increased expenses during the year, caused by the higher
price of provisions, fuel, etc., rendered it necessary to forego some
needed improvements and repairs inside the buildings.  We have,
however, painted all the outside woodwork on the school building and the main building, which could not be left any longer
without great injury to the woodwork.  We sadly need better
facilities for our work inside the present schoolhouse, which is
the old Pabodie mansion, and to which only the most necessary
changes have been made, from time to time, in order to adapt it to
school purposes.  The rooms are now too small and inconvenient,
and absolutely without adequate ventilation.  By tearing out

some partitions, changing somewhat the old chimneys, and putting on some kind of an addition, we think the substantial old homestead could be turned into an ideal school, suitable for our needs and work—for which we hope your honorable body will be able to grant us the means in the near future.

Respectfully submitted,

CHARLES D. KIMBALL, *Governor,*
GEORGE L. SHEPLEY, *Lieutenant-Governor,*
*Members ex-officio.*

WILLIAM K. POTTER, *President,*
ELLEN T. McGUINNESS, *Secretary,*
JEANIE LIPPITT WEEDEN,
LOUISE PROSSER BATES,
GUSTAV N. HAUSMANN,
DR. ROWLAND R. ROBINSON,
JOHN C. B. WOODS,
WILLIAM H. BALLOU,
JEREMIAH W. HORTON,
*Board of Trustees.*

PROVIDENCE, R. I., January, 1903.

# MEDICAL REPORT.

*To the Board of Trustees of the R. I. Institute for the Deaf:*

I have the honor to report concerning the health of the children during the past year.

Until the development of whooping cough in one of the boys, in March, there was little illness in the school. This case was soon followed by five others, of which all except one recovered without complications. This one showed signs pointing to trouble in the lung, but after some weeks of out-door life, he was quite well again.

In the fall, one boy sustained a fracture of the collar bone, and there were several cases of digestive trouble; but the year ends with everybody well.

A feature worthy of note during the past three years is the almost entire freedom from tonsilitis, which prevailed in the school so generally and was of such severe type during the first few years in the new building.

Respectfully submitted,

FRANK L. DAY, M. D.

PROVIDENCE, Dec. 31, 1902.

DINING ROOM.

PROVIDENCE, R. I., Dec. 31, 1902.

*To the Trustees of the R. I. Institute for the Deaf :*

GENTLEMEN:—In rendering to you my brief report of the result of treatment of such of the students as I have had the privilege of attending, will say that one of the worst cases is now nearly ready for discharge, one ear being well healed, the other rapidly gaining. There have been no new patients worthy of record during the past year.

Respectfully submitted,

F. P. CAPRON, M. D.

# REPORT OF THE PRINCIPAL.

*To the Trustees of the R. I. Institute for the Deaf.*

GENTLEMEN:—I have the honor to submit the following statement of our work, during the past year, for your consideration. School re-opened September 9th. Nearly all of the pupils were very prompt returning. Five did not return. Nine pupils have entered this fall. One, a boy of three, that can hear perfectly, but does not talk. We think it is because he will not make the attempt, as he seems bright in every way. There are two four and two five-year-old-children; and one came from another institution, and one from the public school. She is too deaf to gain much in a hearing school. A boy of nine, who has never been in school; and a girl of fifteen, who entered four years ago and remained only a week—because her mother could not be separated from her—and now she is brought back, a large girl, unable to speak or write. What mistaken kindness! If the girl had remained here the past four years, she would have been able, by this time, to talk and read and write; and her voice, which is now unpleasant and sharp, might have been made more agreeable. To acquire a pleasant voice, a child should begin to talk as early as possible.

During the year there were seventy-four pupils enrolled, thirty-four girls and forty boys. There are at present sixty-five pupils in attendance.

It is our aim to provide the best of care for the children committed to our care. One not acquainted with the work cannot realize the immense amount of care, watchfulness, and labor necessary to the domestic control of an institution peopled with these girls and boys.

## HEALTH.

The general health of the pupils was excellent until March, when an epidemic of whooping-cough appeared. There were six cases, all of which yielded readily to treatment with the exception of one, a boy of sixteen. As he was not very strong or active, it took hold of him with a firmer grasp, and serious trouble seemed imminent. He was sent home at once, where he could have the benefit of sunshine and fresh air; therefore he returned to us in the autumn strong and well, with a determination to ward off all such attacks.

Since the re-opening of school there have been several cases of indigestion and one of tonsilitis, and one boy had his collar bone broken.

## CLASS WORK.

Considerable advancement has been made in the schoolrooms. The kindergarten, under the care of Miss Edith Hillman, is doing good work. It was thought best to move this department from the main building into the school building. It now occupies the large, sunny, and airy room formerly used as a printing-room, which seems to have an excellent influence upon the children.

During the beginning of the term several of the children were promoted to the primary grade, to make room for the little new ones who entered. Promotions and changes were made throughout the school, and we now have each class as well graded as is possible in a small school. The beginning primary class is doing language and number work, and making good progress, as are all of the more advanced classes.

We are gratified to report that we graduated a class of six pupils last June: Jennie Goldstein, Gertrude Blanchard, Moses Goldenofsky, William Jermyn, Luella Cole, and Henry Courtermanche. This class took the same course of study as was given in the Doyle avenue grammar school, of this city, and passed the examinations with credit. One of the city school examiners sent, with some of our pupils' papers that she had looked over, a slip of paper on which she had written "I consider these papers excellent."

Mr. Kingsley, principal of the Doyle avenue school, kindly requested us to permit our pupils to go to that school to receive their diplomas with his class, which they did; and it is needless to say that they were very proud indeed when they stepped upon the platform to receive the precious documents.

All but one member of the class returned at the opening of school to take a post-graduate course.

We shall not graduate a class next June, but nearly all of the pupils have a strong desire to become graduates of this school.

### INDUSTRIAL DEPARTMENT.

We are still fortunate in having Mrs. Gibson as teacher of sewing. She is teaching the girls to cut garments, do new stitches in embroidery and hemstitching. Mr. Hatch still has charge of the sloyd. The boys have made some nice frames and book-cases, and have done some of the mending of furniture. Miss Florence M. Russell is teaching the class in cardboard and paper cutting.

An invitation is extended to all to visit the school and see what is accomplished here. Visitors are received with courtesy and shown about, and full explanation of the method of teaching given, and their interest as far as possible enlisted for the school.

### BUILDINGS.

Very little has been done in improvements for the past few years. It was, however, thought necessary to repaint the woodwork on the outside of the buildings, and it was accordingly done, and a flight of stairs, leading into the basement, on the girls' side, put in.

As our numbers increase, we feel the need of larger and more commodious schoolrooms, which would enable us to have proper ventilation. Some of our rooms are very poorly lighted, and there is not sufficient space to pass comfortably from pupil to pupil.

In the assembly hall, on Tuesday, the 23d, the usual Christmas exercises took place.

## ACKNOWLEDGMENTS.

Our thanks are due the United States Bureau of Education, and the Volta Bureau, for books and pamphlets sent us; Keith's Opera Co., for admission to the theatre; Mr. William B. Weeden for a case of beautiful stuffed birds; Mrs. William B. Weeden, for money for the Christmas tree; Messrs. J. H. Preston & Co., and Messrs. Arnold & Maine, for Christmas candies; J. H. Althans, for ice cream; Mrs. D. B. Pond, for subscription for the *Youth's Companion;* and Mrs. William B. Weeden, Mrs. H. A. Waldron, and Mrs. S. S. Durfee, for clothing.

## PRIZES.

At the close of the school in June, prizes were awarded Fannie Sweet, Arthur Myers, Maggie Notorantonio, and Olive Wilcox for the best speech; Mary Grimes, Bertha Stanton, Angelina Forthier, and Adolard Paquin for the best speech-reading; Willie O'Riley for good deportment; Herman Grabert for greatest improvement in speech; and Alfred Vogel for greatest improvement in writing.

## GRADUATES.

| | |
|---|---|
| Jennie Goldstein, | William Jermyn, |
| Gertrude Blanchard, | Luella Cole, |
| Moses Goldonofsky, | Henry Courtemanche. |

We sincerely thank you, the members of the board, on behalf of the deaf children of the State, for your watchful care of their interests, and we respectfully submit to you this report.

LAURA DeL. RICHARDS.

SOUTH VIEW MAIN BUILDING

# TABULAR STATEMENT.

## TABULAR REPORT OF THE PUPILS OF THE SCHOOL

| NAME OF PUPIL. | RESIDENCE. | AGE (Approx.). | DATE OF ADMISSION. |
|---|---|---|---|
| Grant, Edith. | Providence | 10 | Dec. 13, 1886. |
| Cole, Luella | South Scituate | 12 | March 28, 1887. |
| Goldenofsky, Moses. | Woonsocket | 10 | April 29, 1889. |
| Hackett, Laura | Providence | 8 | Nov. 11, 1889. |
| Courtemauche, Henry | Providence | 12 | June 10, 1891. |
| Staunton, Bertha | Providence | 8 | Oct. 5, 1891. |
| Jermyn, William | Newport | 10 | May 5, 1892. |
| Mills, Anneta | Providence | 6 | April 3, 1893. |
| Carr, David. | Pawtucket | 6 | Jan. 27, 1893. |
| Collins, Chester A | Providence | 4 | Jan. 30, 1893. |
| Kleber, Fannie | Lymansville | 6 | Feb. 7, 1893. |
| Goldstein, Clara J | Providence | 9 | March 1, 1893. |
| Desonie, Maggie | Lippitt. | 8 | March 23, 1893. |
| O'Connor, Mary | Woonsocket | 6 | May 27, 1893. |
| Thompson, George | Providence | 4 | Sept. 11, 1893. |
| Flynn, James | Providence | 6 | Feb. 3, 1894. |
| Comfort, Mae E | Newport | 8 | Sept. 10, 1894. |
| Mudrak, Willie | Geneva. | 4 | Oct. 13, 1894. |
| Grimes, Mary | Newport | 9 | Feb. 5, 1895. |
| O'Riley, Willie F | Providence | 7 | Feb. 11, 1895. |
| Grace, Theresa | Providence | 12 | April 10, 1895. |
| Welsh, John | Providence | 7 | May 20, 1895. |
| Roe, Albert C. | Hope | 5 | Sept. 21, 1895. |
| Stetson, Leroy W | Warren | 10 | Sept. 30, 1895. |
| Smith, Idella | Providence | 9 | Oct. 28, 1895. |
| Williams, Charles A | Pawtucket | 4 | Sept. 14, 1896. |
| Cook, Reuben | Peace Dale | 7 | Oct. 6, 1896. |
| Perron, Lena. | Woonsocket | 7 | Oct. 26, 1896. |
| Anderson, Edward V. | Providence | 9 | .......... |
| Vigeant, Edward | Pawtucket | 7 | May 3, 1897. |
| Davis, Elsie | East Providence | 9 | Sept. 13, 1897. |
| Perry, Joseph C. | Providence | 7 | Jan. 7, 1898. |
| Yuppa, Concetta. | Providence | 4 | Feb. 10, 1898. |
| Forthier, Angelina. | Pawtucket | 6 | Oct. 24, 1898. |
| Holborgen, Trina. | Pawtucket. | 6 | Oct. 18, 1898. |
| Bowen, John | Providence | 13 | Oct. 18, 1898. |
| Bassett, Genevive W | Moosup Valley | 4 | Oct. 18, 1898 |
| Vogel, Alfred. | Providence | 11 | Oct. 18, 1898. |
| Goldman, Samuel | Providence | 9 | Nov. 7, 1898. |
| Myers, Arthur | Providence | 7 | Jan. 3, 1899. |
| Wilcox, Olive I | East Providence | 3 | April 3, 1899. |
| Smith, Everett A | Slocumville | 3 | May 19, 1899. |
| Willams, Harold K | Pawtucket | 4 | Sept. 13, 1899. |
| Sweet, Fannie M | Centredale | 8 | Sept. 13, 1899. |
| Newberg, Charles A | Pawtucket | 7 | Sept. 25, 1899. |
| Paquin, Adolard | Providence | 5 | Oct. 2, 1899. |

| OF DEAFNESS, AS FAR AS KNOWN. | AGE WHEN MADE DEAF (Approx.). | REMA |
|---|---|---|
| in ear.................. | 6 months........ | ............. |
| iital.......... ......... | ...................... | ........ ..... |
| ; fever....... .......... | 3 years.......... | .............. |
| iital..... ......... .... | ...................... | ............. |
| iital.............. | ...................... | ............. |
| fever...................... | 3 years. | .............. |
| iital...... .............. | ...................... | ............. |
| s...... ............... | 3 years.......... | .............. |
| ,.. ....... ......... | 2 years.......... | .............. |
| s......... . ........... | 2 years.......... | .............. |
| iital.............. | ................... | Deafness par |
| ld fever................. | 4 years.......... | .............. |
| iital............. ...... | ...................... | ... ......... |
| t fever................. | 1 year.... ..... | ............; |
| lsions................. | 3 years.......... | .............. |
| iital............. | ...................... | .............. |
| hal fever.... .......... | 1 year, 6 months. | ............} |
| iital................... | ...................... | .............. |
| s............. | 5 years.......... | Slight degree |
| iital............... | ...................... | .............. |
| iital.............. | ...................... | .............. |
| fever...... ......... | 3 years.......... | .............. |
| mation in head........ | 4 months........ | ............/ |
| nd fever............. | 4 years.......... | Slight degree |
| iital...... | ................... | Slight degree |
| iital.............. | ...................... | .............. |
| iital.............. | ...................... | .............. |
| t fever................. | 1 year.......... | ............. |
| t fever................. | 5 years.......... | Hard of hear |
| t fever................. | 4 years.......... | .............. |
| sickness............... | 2 months........ | ............} |
| iital............... | ...................... | .............. |
| iital............... | ...................... | .............. |
| s ................. | 1 year.......... | ............. |
| lsions...... ........... | 1 year.......... | Hard of hea |
| iital ..... ............ | ................... | .............. |
| ................... .... | ................... | Not deaf. |
| .................... .... | 3 years.......... | ............. |
| ?...... .............. | 6 years.......... | ............. |
| iital................. | ...................... | ............. |
| iital................. | ...................... | ............. |
| iital................. | ...................... | ............. |
| meningitis............ | 7 years.......... | ............. |
| ...... ............. | 5 years.......... | ............. |
| iital.............. | ...................... | ............. |

## TABULAR REPORT OF THE PUPILS OF THE SCHOOL

| Name of Pupil. | Residence. | Age (Approx.). | Date of Admission. |
|---|---|---|---|
| Cleary, John | Newport | 5 | Oct. 2, 1899. |
| Holmes, Thomas | Providence | 7 | Oct. 17, 1899. |
| Grabert, Herman | Bristol | 12 | March 1, 1900. |
| McGowan, Terry | Newport | 17 | May 2, 1900. |
| Brennan, Sarah A | Pawtucket | 7 | May 6, 1900. |
| Olin, Millie I | Providence | 13 | Sept. 11, 1900. |
| Arel, Joseph I | Woonsocket | 10 | Sept. 19, 1900. |
| Brown, Lola B | Davisville | 12 | Nov. 19, 1900. |
| Gardiner, Earl F | Providence | 7 | April 16, 1901. |
| Notorantonio, Maggie | Providence | 8 | April 22, 1901. |
| Mitchell, Fred G | Providence | 8 | Sept. 10, 1901. |
| Blanchard, S. Gertrude | Providence | 14 | Sept. 10, 1901. |
| Cohen, Esther | Providence | 14 | Sept. 12, 1901 |
| Lindsay, Mary E | Providence | 5 | Oct. 5, 1901. |
| Burke, Bessie | Providence | 11 | Sept. 15, 1901. |
| Johnson, Benjamin F | Kingston | 8 | Sept. 26, 1899. |
| Bruncell, Berger B | Woonsocket | 7 | Dec. 10, 1900. |
| Marden, James B | East Providence | 12 | Jan. 20, 1902. |
| Kinney, Charles H | Newport | 13 | March 17, 1902. |
| Shine, Philip | Providence | 6 | Sept. 9, 1902. |
| Bowser, Gertrude | Providence | 4 | Sept. 15, 1902. |
| Daudelin, E. Albert | Albion | 10 | Sept. 22, 1902. |
| Burke, Sarah C | Pawtucket | 5 | Sept. 23, 1902. |
| VanValkinburg, Fred. E. | East Providence | 3 | Sept. 25, 1902. |
| Finnegan, Francis H | Pawtucket | 8 | Oct. 21, 1902. |
| Martinelli, Emira | Thornton | 15 | Nov. 18, 1902. |
| Ashton, Agnes A | Providence | 11 | Nov. 18, 1902. |
| Williams, ——— | Pawtucket | .... | Dec. 1, 1902. |

BOYS' LIBRARY.

FOR THE YEAR ENDING DECEMBER 31, 1902.

| Cause of Deafness, as far as Known. | Age when made Deaf (Approx.). | Remarks. |
|---|---|---|
| Congenital................................ | ................................ | Not deaf. |
| ................................ | ................................ | Deafness partial. |
| Measles................................ | ................................ | Hard of hearing. |
| A fall................................ | 2 years.......... | |
| Congenital................................ | | |
| Scarlet fever................ | 10 years... ...... | |
| Congenital................................ | | |
| Adenoid growth.............. | 3 years..... .... | Hard of hearing. |
| Spinal meningitis............ | 4 years.......... | |
| Fever................................ | 4 years.......... | |
| Congenital................................ | | Hard of hearing. |
| Scarlet fever............ ...... | 5 years.......... | Hard of hearing. |
| Congenital................................ | | |
| Congenital................................ | | |
| ................................ | ................................ | Not deaf. |
| Congenital................................ | | |
| Brain fever...... ............ | 1 year, 6 months | |
| Scarlet fever............... ..... | 4 years.......... | Hard of hearing. |
| Scarlet fever................ | 4 years.......... | Hard of hearing. |
| Measles................................ | 2 years.......... | |
| Congenital................................ | | |
| Teething................ | 1 year.......... | |
| Measles................ | 1 year.......... | |
| ................................ | ................................ | Not deaf. |
| Fall................ | 4 years.......... | |
| Congenital................................ | | |
| Measles................ | 9 years.......... | Hard of hearing. |
| Congenital................ | ................................ | |

## SUMMARY.

Number of pupils from date of opening the State school for the deaf,
April 2, 1877, to December 31, 1902................................... 185
Number of pupils who have entered the Institute since Dec. 31, 1901.. 11

Whole number of pupils who have attended the school.......... 185
Number who have left the school.............................. 120

Number of pupils Dec. 31, 1902........................................ 65
Number of girls who have attended school during the year............ 34
Number of boys who have attended school during the year............ 40

Whole number of pupils during the year........................ 74

Average attendance..................................................... 5

Number congenitally deaf, or made deaf before the age of two........ 45
Number who lost hearing between the ages of two and four............ 15
Number who lost hearing after the age of four, and doubtful cases.... 10
Number who have perfect hearing...................................... 4

                                                                     74
Number who have any degree of hearing.............................. 18

*Residences of all who have attended during the year 1902.*

Geneva.................................................................. 1
Providence............................................................. 33
East Providence........................................................ 4
Pawtucket.............................................................. 11
South Scituate......................................................... 1
Newport................................................................ v
Lymansville............................................................ 1
Lippitt................................................................ 1
Peace Dale............................................................. 1
Slocumville............................................................ 1
Kingston............................................................... 4

| | |
|---|---|
| Albion | 1 |
| Thornton | 1 |
| Davisville | 1 |
| Centredale | 1 |
| Woonsocket | 5 |
| Hope | 1 |
| Bristol | 1 |
| Warren | 1 |
| Moosup Valley | 1 |
| Twenty localities | 74 |

# COURSE OF STUDY

## KINDERGARTEN.

### FIRST YEAR.

    *a.* KINDERGARTEN EXERCISES.

    *b.* ARTICULATION.

    *c.* LANGUAGE.

    *d.* ARITHMETIC.

    *e.* PENMANSHIP.

*a.* Paper cutting and folding; drawing and modeling in clay; designing in shoe pegs; stick laying; embroidery designs sewed on pricked sewing-cards; lessons in form and color in all exercises.

*b.* Elements, combinations, simple words, and sentences; with reading them from the lips.

*c.* Nouns; objects in class-room, articles of dress, articles of food, different parts of the body, with a limited number of verbs. Adjectives, good, bad, large, small, &c.

*d.* Counting and writing numbers, with addition and subtraction to 10.

*e.* Writing on slate and with lead pencil.

## PRIMARY COURSE.

### SECOND, THIRD, AND FOURTH YEARS.

    *a.* ARTICULATION.

    *b.* LANGUAGE.

    *c.* ARITHMETIC.

    *d.* GEOGRAPHY.

    *e.* PENMANSHIP.

    *f* DRAWING.

*a.* Drill in elements, combinations, and words, and reading them from the lips.

*b.* Thorough review of first year work. Nouns and verbs continued. Adjectives continued ; their comparison. Pronouns as in first year, adding myself, herself, himself, with the plurals, and the relatives who and which. Adverbs ; not, often, never, etc. Elliptical sentences ; action and picture writing ; journal and letter writing, and simple stories.

*c.* Practical exercises in addition, subtraction, multiplication, and division ; United States currency ; simple fractions.

*d.* Schoolroom, building, and yard, city, and a limited knowledge of the State.

*e.* Copy-book writing.

## INTERMEDIATE COURSE.

### FIFTH, SIXTH, AND SEVENTH YEARS.

*a.* ARTICULATION.
*b.* LANGUAGE.
*c* ARITHMETIC.
*d.* GEOGRAPHY.
*e.* HISTORY.
*f.* PENMANSHIP.
*g.* DRAWING,
*h.* CALISTHENICS.

*a.* Drill in elements, combinations, syllables : words and sentences continued as in primary course.

*b.* Nouns, pronouns, adjectives, adverbs, prepositions, and conjunctions continued as in primary course. Drill in active and passive voices ; action and picture writing : stories from natural history ; journal and letter writing.

*c.* Mental and written addition, subtraction, multiplication, and division, with practical examples ; United States currency and simple fractions continued.

*d.* City, State, and New England States.

*e.* Simple historical stories in connection with geography.

*f.* Copy-book writing twice a week.

*g.* Object drawing.

## IIIGHER COURSE.

### EIGHTH, NINTH, AND TENTH YEARS.

    *a.* ARTICULATION.

    *b.* LANGUAGE.

    *c.* ARITHMETIC.

    *d.* GEOGRAPHY.

    *e.* HISTORY.

    *f.* PHYSIOLOGY.

    *g.* PENMANSHIP.

    *h.* DRAWING.

    *i.* CALISTHENICS.

*a.* Drill in difficult combinations and words.

*b.* Composition; journal and letter writing; miscellaneous reading; newspapers and magazines; lessons on general subjects.

*c.* Mental, written, and practical.

*d.* Geographical reader; Manual of Commerce.

*e.* History of the United States; Outline of General History.

*g.* Copy-book.

*h.* Free-hand object drawing and designing.

# CHAPTER 332.

AN ACT IN AMENDMENT OF AND IN ADDITION TO CHAPTER
86 OF THE GENERAL LAWS, ENTITLED "OF THE R. I. SCHOOL
FOR THE DEAF."

[Passed May 13, 1896.]

*It is enacted by the General Assembly as follows:*

SECTION 1.   All children of parents, or under the control of guardians
or other persons, legal residents of this state, between the ages of three
and twenty years, whose hearing or speech, or both, are so defective as to
make it inexpedient or impracticable to attend the public schools to advantage, not being mentally or otherwise incapable, may attend the Rhode
Island Institute for the Deaf, without charge, under such rules and regulations as the board of trustees of said institute may establish.

SEC. 2.   Every person having under his control any such child between
the ages of seven and eighteen years shall cause such child to attend school
at said institute for such period of time or such prescribed course, in each
individual case, as may be deemed expedient by the board of trustees, and
for any neglect of such duty the person so offending shall be fined not
exceeding twenty dollars : *Provided,* that if the person so charged shall
prove to the satisfaction of said board that the child has received or is
receiving, under private or other instruction, an education suitable to his
condition, in the judgment of said board, then such penalty shall not be
incurred : *provided, further,* that no child shall be removed to said institution or taken from the custody of its parent or guardian except as a day
scholar unless such parent or guardian is an improper person to have such
custody, and the supreme court in its appellate division shall have jurisdiction in habeas corpus to examine into and revise all findings of said
board of trustees under this act.

SEC. 3.   Any child having attended said institute a time or course prescribed by said board, upon leaving the institute shall be entitled to receive
a certificate of his proficiency from said board.

SEC. 4.   This act shall take effect from and after its passage.

# TO PARENTS OF DEAF CHILDREN.

This school is for the benefit of children incapacitated through deafness, total or partial, for receiving proper instruction in common schools, and is free to all pupils who belong in this State.

The aim of the school is to teach deaf children to use the English language with the spontaneity, correctness, and enjoyment of *hearing* children as far as this is practicable.

"Without language there can be no thought, no reason;" and as the highest aim of all instruction is the culture of the mental and moral nature in man, our first effort should be to furnish the deaf with a medium through which knowledge can be imparted and obtained. This can be done by signs, by the finger alphabet, and by speech. Our method is the latter, or oral, method, by which the deaf can be educated and at the same time furnished with the usual and most convenient way of communication in society and the world at large.

It is very desirable that deaf children be sent to school at as early an age as possible. A parent will be amply repaid for sending a child as young as five or six years, even at some inconvenience. The Board of Trustees are authorized to receive pupils between the ages of three and twenty years.

If a child who has learned to talk is made deaf by disease, he should immediately, upon his recovery, be sent to a school where his speech will be retained, and where he will be taught to understand from the lips. In such cases it is common to delay so long that serious loss of speech results.

Speech reading is an invaluable acquisition for those who are semi-deaf, or even hard of hearing, as well as for those congenitally or totally deaf.

Every effort should be made to encourage the child to retain the use of his voice. He should be taught to pronounce common words by watching the lip motion and facial expression, or by feeling the muscular action of the breath; but no attempt should be made to teach him *the names* of the letters of the alphabet.

The English branches are taught here, and every pupil is taught some branch of industry.

The school session begins the second Monday in September, and closes the third Friday in June, with a week's holiday at Christmas.

Application for admission should be made to the principal, at the Institute, corner of Hope street and Cypress street, Providence.

Every effort should be made to encourage the child to retain the use of his voice.  He should be taught to pronounce common words by watching the lip motion and facial expression, or by feeling the muscular action of the breath ; but no attempt should be made to teach him *the names* of the letters of the alphabet.

The English branches are taught here, and every pupil is taught some branch of industry.

The school session begins the second Monday in September, and closes the third Friday in June, with a week's holiday at Christmas.

Application for admission should be made to the principal, at the Institute, corner of Hope street and Cypress street, Providence.

State of Rhode Island and Providence Plantations.

# REPORT OF THE BOARD OF TRUSTEES

OF THE

## RHODE ISLAND

# INSTITUTE FOR THE DEAF,

PRESENTED TO THE

## GENERAL ASSEMBLY

AT ITS

## JANUARY SESSION, 1904.

PROVIDENCE, R. I.

E. L. FREEMAN & SONS, STATE PRINTERS.

1904.

**State of Rhode Island and Providence Plantations.**

# REPORT OF THE BOARD OF TRUSTEES

OF THE

## RHODE ISLAND

# INSTITUTE FOR THE DEAF.

PRESENTED TO THE

## GENERAL ASSEMBLY

AT ITS

## JANUARY SESSION, 1904.

---

PROVIDENCE, R. I.

E. L. FREEMAN & SONS, STATE PRINTERS.

1904.

# RHODE ISLAND INSTITUTE FOR THE DEAF.

HOPE STREET, CORNER OF CYPRESS STREET,

## PROVIDENCE, R. I.

---

UNDER THE SUPERVISION OF

## THE BOARD OF TRUSTEES,

CONSISTING OF

**PRINCIPAL.**

LAURA DeL. RICHARDS.

---

**PHYSICIANS.**

FRANK L. DAY, M. D.................. ............*Physician and Surgeon.*
F. P. CAPRON, M. D................................................*Oculist and Aurist.*

---

**TEACHERS.**

| | | |
|---|---|---|
| M. AGNES GRIMM, | GRACE A. BALCH, | FLORENCE M. RUSSELL, |
| CLAUDIA REDD, | GRACE I. RUSSELL, | KITTY YOUNG, |
| | MABEL I. CLARK. | |

---

**SPECIAL TEACHERS.**

ETHEL DUNN DROWNE.............................*Teacher of Drawing.*
SARAH M. ALDRICH.....................................*Teacher of Sloyd.*
FLORENCE M. RUSSELL.......*Teacher of Pasteboard Work and Basketry.*
CLAUDIA REDD.......................................*Teacher of Cooking.*
——————— .......................................*Teacher of Sewing.*

---

**HOUSEHOLD DEPARTMENT**

*Matron,*
HETTIE SCOTT.

ELIZABETH GRAHAM...............................................*Nurse.*
JANE STUART ....................................................*Night Nurse.*
—————— ...........................................*Girls' Attendant.*
KATHARINE BROWN....................................*Girls' Attendant.*
JESSIE MACKIE......................................*Boys' Attendant.*
JENNIE WALLS......................................*Boys' Attendant.*

*Janitor,*
FRED ANDERSON.

# REPORT OF THE BOARD OF TRUSTEES.

*To the Honorable the General Assembly, at its January Session,*
    *A. D. 1904:*

We are gratified that we are able to report a prosperous year
for the institute, and that it continues to hold the high standard
of previous years. The teachers are practically the same as in
the preceding year, and have continued to use their best endeavors
for the interest of the school. The buildings are all in fairly good
condition, and will need but slight repairs. With the increase in
the number of pupils the school building proper has become too
small for the best advantage of the several classes, having been
originally designed for a dwelling house. The rooms are naturally
small for school purposes, as well as being unsuitable in many
other respects. It will be necessary in the near future to make
extensive alterations, or to replace the building by something
more modern and roomy. There have been 72 pupils in attendance during the year, and 65 at the present time. The school has
been remarkably free from contagious diseases and from serious
illness of any kind.

We refer to the report of the principal for a detailed account of
matters appertaining to the work of the school.

The financial report is respectfully submitted, as follows:

Amount of annual appropriation............................ $20,000 00
Paid salaries and wages............................. $9,128 20
All other expenses................................... 10,871 80
                                          ————— 20,000 00

For maintenance during the ensuing year the board respectfully ask the sum of twenty thousand dollars.

Respectfully submitted,

LUCIUS F. C. GARVIN, *Governor,*
ADELARD ARCHAMBAULT, *Lieut.-Governor,*
*Members ex-officio.*
WILLIAM K. POTTER, *President,*
ELLEN T. McGUINNESS, *Secretary,*
JEANIE LIPPITT WEEDEN,
LOUISE PROSSER BATES,
GUSTAV N. HAUSMANN,
DR. ROWLAND R. ROBINSON,
JOHN- C. B. WOODS,
WILLIAM H. BALLOU,
JEREMIAH W. HORTON,
*Board of Trustees.*

PROVIDENCE, R. I., January, 1904.

Dining Room

# MEDICAL REPORT.

*To the Board of Trustees of the R. I. Institute for the Deaf:*

During the winter months one moderately severe case of bronchitis was the only serious illness among the children. In the spring one case of diphtheria appeared, was isolated in the hospital, and made a good recovery.

Soon after the beginning of the fall term one of the larger boys sustained a fracture of the leg in playing foot-ball; another boy dislocated his elbow from a fall, both making uneventful recoveries.

With the exception of some minor illnesses, this constitutes the health report for the year.

Each additional year only serves to emphasize the wisdom of the board in providing a suitable hospital ward for the isolation and proper treatment of the illnesses that are certain to arise among so large a number of children.

Respectfully submitted,

FRANK L. DAY, M. D.

PROVIDENCE, December 31, 1904.

PROVIDENCE, R. I., Jan. 19, 1904.

*To the Honorable Board of Trustees of the R. I. Institute for the Deaf:*

GENTLEMEN :—In submitting my brief report of attendance upon the pupils of the school, have only to say that all of the patients seen during 1903 have been treated for slight disturbances, excepting the two long continued ones, Edward Anderson and Chester Collins. Of these can report that the former is now about ready to be discharged cured, and the latter is in a much better condition than ever before, and I hope he, too, will, not long hence, be able to get on without treatment.

Respectfully submitted,

F. P. CAPRON, M. D.

Giulio' Tishman'

# REPORT OF THE PRINCIPAL.

*To the Trustees of the R. 1. Institute for the Deaf:*

GENTLEMEN:—I have the honor to once more submit, for your consideration, the following report of the school and its work for the year ending December, 31, 1903.

There are sixty-four pupils in attendance. Seven left at the close of the school, last June. Four of them were graduated the previous June, but were anxious to return and continue their studies another year. Nine new pupils have entered since the reopening of school in September. Several of them are quite young children.

We think there is an advantage gained in taking children at as early an age as their parents will let us have them, because they very quickly begin to understand simple commands given them, and they are proud to perform those given them to do. It is in this way that we begin to teach them to understand spoken language, or speech reading. We also give them vocal gymnastics, that is, we teach them to imitate the different positions which we take with our lips and tongue when talking; then, later, they are given words which are easy for them to speak, such as ball, top, arm, etc.

The work of the past year was similar to that of previous years. The usual routine was followed with good results in all of the classes. We endeavored to bestow great care upon the work in the schoolrooms, as well as upon the domestic arrangements of the institution. The general affairs of the household department have been efficiently and carefully managed. One unaccustomed to this work can not appreciate the thought, watchfulness, and labor necessary to insure the well-being of an establishment

2

peopled as this is with deaf children, or with the same number of chidren, even though they could hear; but the deaf require more care, as one must come in contact with them to gain their attention, while with the hearing the attention may be gained by simply raising the voice.

At the close of the school Miss Lizzie T. Green left us, and Miss M. Agnes Grimm was appointed to fill the vacancy. Miss Grimm is a teacher of much experience, and we are fortunate in securing her services. Miss Edith Hillman also left us in June, and Miss Kitty Young, who has been with us for some years, took charge of the kindergarten when school opened in September.

HEALTH.

The health of the children has been carefully guarded. The location of the school, its liberality of space and abundance of fresh air, combined with the attractive surroundings, make this a very healthful location. There were but few serious cases of illness. During the latter part of May a case of diphtheria appeared. The patient was a little fellow of three years. As it was a light case and the child was so very young, he was cared for here. The treatment was so prompt and careful that he recovered in a short time.

There were a series of accidents during the first few weeks after the opening of the school in the fall. The first was a boy, who fractured a leg near the ankle, and a small boy had a dislocated elbow. The others were only slight accidents, such as bruises and scratches.

CLASS WORK.

The schoolroom work has continued about the same as the year previous. In the kindergarten there are twelve bright little ones from three to eight years old. They are given vocal gymnastics, simple words, such as ball, thumb, nose, apple, etc., and later simple commands are given, first of single words, as bow, run, walk, then we add fall down, shut the door, open the door, etc.

The kindergarten work is similar to that given in the kindergartens for hearing children. They have paper cutting and folding, peas work, simple drawing, clay modeling, weaving, and games. Sewing cards are used. The eye is trained in exercises in color, form, and motion. The habit of speech is laid by imitating positions taken by the lips and tongue, also of spoken words that are easy to pronounce; and speech is used during the playing of games, which the children enjoy much.

In the first class in the primary grade the greater part of the time is given to language. The children talk, *talk*, TALK, constantly, with *very* little or almost no writing. They are given numbers up to five, from the start, because they are constantly trying to tell something which requires them.

After the second year, geography of the schoolroom, yard, and the city is taught, then the location of their homes in different parts of the State; and after they are thoroughly familiar with that, they take up geography and history, but then only in its easiest form are the lessons given.

In the grammar department the course prescribed for the city schools is followed as nearly as possible, in which geography and history, physiology, and the natural sciences are taught. The pupils in the first class are making strenuous efforts to become a *graduating* class as soon as possible. It requires a longer time for our pupils to complete the course than for hearing children. The class numbers six, and they are doing very good work.

We consider it of the first importance for deaf children to form the habit of *speech*, of talking so as to make it their vernacular, that they may become as near like hearing people as possible, and it is because of that that our little ones are given very little to do where it is not necessary to use spoken language. Every command and every reply are given by speech, so that they will express themselves spontaneously in spoken language and will also expect it from others. We also give them pictures and picture books during recreation, as the first step toward reading

ard the habit of reading the next in importanc

drawing, under the direction of Mrs. Ethel D
ig excellent work and making good progress.
lying light and shade, which has done mucl
terest in the class work.

### MANUAL TRAINING.

change made in the sloyd room. Mr. Ha
at the close of school, and was succeeded
Aldrich, who has been very successful in awal
y interest in our boys, in sloyd work, which t
oy.

he year they were interested in making diffei
y useful articles. At present the large boys
ielves, boot-blacking stands, and scrap-baskets
d they do considerable repairing about the plac
oyd is not merely to teach boys to plane, saw, t

On the contrary, it is intended to give, prii
nd a moral development, and incidentally it has
. It has been proven that the power to coördin
ements is a mental power. The training of
h sloyd involves this coördination, and increa
he brain.

he educators has said: "There is nothing tha
ning than what we call manual training." Th
really educates the head, heart, and hand m

ak requires planning, and much of it exact test
and rule, in order to produce correct results. T
the pupil the importance of carefulness, accur

successful business or professional men of to-
on training when boys. They were required
he farm or in the home, and use all their muscl

—

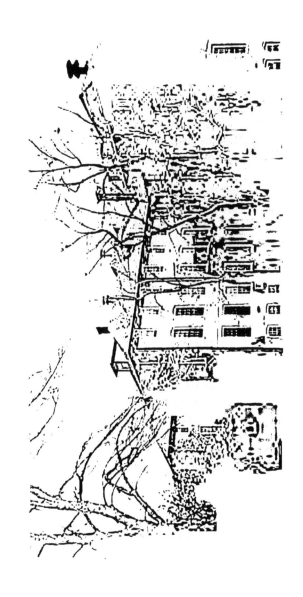

work helped to streng
y to apply themselves
he aim of sloyd to train
and thus help turn out
able to do something,

e that there was a change
three years taught th
pelled to leave us and re
deep interest in her wo
Campau, who has bee
of the sewing. Towai
The girls enjoy the worl
n that direction.

## BUILDINGS.

airing and some paintin
ry to do more next sur
s always more or less br
of the need of improves
ine assembly hall, kind
ry much, better schoolr
il of them poorly light
and until there is an i
iplete. Additions could
r of our buildings whic
eed, and we sincerely h

## ACKNOWLEDGMENTS.

the United States Bureo
books and pamphlets ser
the theatre; Mrs. Will
nas tree; Messrs. J. H.
Christmas candies; M

because we regard the habit of reading the next in importance to speech.

The class in drawing, under the direction of Mrs. Ethel Dunn Drowne, is doing excellent work and making good progress. The pupils are studying light and shade, which has done much to arouse their interest in the class work.

There was a change made in the sloyd room. Mr. Harvey Hatch left us at the close of school, and was succeeded by Miss Sarah M. Aldrich, who has been very successful in awakening a very lively interest in our boys, in sloyd work, which they thoroughly enjoy.

The first of the year they were interested in making different games and many useful articles. At present the large boys are making book-shelves, boot-blacking stands, and scrap-baskets for their rooms, and they do considerable repairing about the place.

The aim of sloyd is not merely to teach boys to plane, saw, and use a few tools. On the contrary, it is intended to give, primarily, a mental and a moral development, and incidentally it has an economic value. It has been proven that the power to coördinate muscular movements is a mental power. The training of the muscles through sloyd involves this coördination, and increases the activity of the brain.

One of our able educators has said: "There is nothing that is more brain training than what we call manual training." There is nothing that really educates the head, heart, and hand more than sloyd.

All of the work requires planning, and much of it exact testing with try square and rule, in order to produce correct results. This impresses upon the pupil the importance of carefulness, accuracy, and patience.

Most of the successful business or professional men of to-day had active motor training when boys. They were required to labor hard on the farm or in the home, and use all their muscular

Rear View Main Building.

energy. This manual work helped to strengthen their character, and gave them ability to apply themselves in whatever pursuit they followed. It is the aim of sloyd to train the executive power, and the ability to do, and thus help turn out more of these self-reliant men, who are able to do something, and not only know how things are done.

We are sorry to note that there was a change in the sewing class. Mrs. Gibson, who for three years taught the sewing class very successfully, was compelled to leave us and return to her home in England. She took a deep interest in her work as well as in each girl personally. Mrs. Campau, who has been with us for some time, now has charge of the sewing. Toward spring a class in cooking was formed. The girls enjoy the work and are very proud of what they can do in that direction.

## BUILDINGS.

There was some repairing and some painting done last summer, and it will be necessary to do more next summer. Where there are many boys there is always more or less breakage.

Last year I spoke of the need of improvements in our school-house. We have a fine assembly hall, kindergarten, and sloyd room, and we need, very much, better schoolrooms. Our present ones are small, several of them poorly lighted, and all of them very badly ventilated, and until there is an improvement our institution will be incomplete. Additions could easily be made and changes in the interior of our buildings which would make it all that we could ask or need, and we sincerely hope that it will soon be given us.

## ACKNOWLEDGMENTS.

Our thanks are due the United States Bureau of Education, and the Volta Bureau, for books and pamphlets sent us; Keith's Opera Co., for admission to the theatre; Mrs. William B. Weeden, for money for the Christmas tree; Messrs. J. H. Preston & Co., and Alexander White, for Christmas candies; Mrs. D. B. Pond, for subscription for the *Youth's Companion;* and Mrs. William B. Weeden, for clothing.

The receipt of the following periodicals is thankfully acknowledged, and their continuance respectfully requested:

Mute's Companion, Faribault, Minn.; Daily Paper for Our Little People, Rochester, N. Y.; Our Children's School Journal, The Deaf Mute Journal, New York; Maryland Bulletin, Frederick, Md.; The Deaf Mute Voice, Jackson, Miss.; Kentucky Deaf Mute, Danville, Ky.; The Goodson Gazette, Staunton, Va.; Kansas Star, Olathe, Kansas; Deaf Mute Optic, Little Rock, Ark.; Deaf Mute Index, Colorado Springs, Col.; Juvenile Ranger, Austin, Tex.; The Register, Rome, New York; Nebraska Mute Journal, Omaha, Neb.; New Method for the Deaf, Englewood, Ill.; Weekly News, Berkeley, Cal.; The Mount Airy World, Philadelphia; The Canadian Deaf Mute, Bellville, Ontario; The New Era, Jacksonvile, Ill., Mentor.

### PRIZES.

At the close of school in June, prizes were awarded Millie Olin, John Welch, Joe Arel, and Sarah Brennan for the best speech; Mamie O'Conner, George Thompson, Bert Williams, and Olive Wilcox for the best speech reading; Mae Comfort and Frank Finnigan for greatest improvement in speech; Henry Courtemanche and Laura Hackett for the best in conversation; for excellence in deportment, Willie O'Riley; for the greatest improvement in deportment, Elsie Davis and Chester Collins.

We sincerely thank you, the members of the board, on behalf of the deaf children of the State, for your watchful care of their interests, and we respectfully submit to you this report.

LAURA DeL RICHARDS.

# TABULAR STATEMENT.

## TABULAR REPORT OF THE PUPILS OF THE SCHOOL.

| NAME OF PUPIL. | RESIDENCE. | AGE (Approx.). | DATE OF ADMISSION. |
|---|---|---|---|
| Goldenofsky, Moses | Woonsocket | 10 | April 29, 1889. |
| Hackett, Laura | Providence | 8 | Nov. 11, 1889. |
| Courtemanche, Henry | Providence | 12 | June 10, 1891. |
| Jermyn, William | Newport | 10 | May 5, 1892. |
| Carr, David | Pawtucket | 6 | Jan. 27, 1893. |
| Collins, Chester A | Providence | 4 | Jan. 30, 1893. |
| Kleber, Fannie | Lymansville | 6 | Feb. 7, 1893. |
| Goldstein, Clara J | Providence | 9 | March 1, 1893. |
| O'Connor, Mary | Woonsocket | 6 | May 27, 1893. |
| Thompson, George | Providence | 4 | Sept. 11, 1893. |
| Flynn, James | Providence | 6 | Feb. 3, 1894. |
| Cofnfort, Mae E | Newport | 8 | Sept. 10, 1894. |
| Mudrak, Willie | Geneva | 4 | Oct. 13, 1894. |
| Grimes, Mary | Newport | 9 | Feb. 5, 1895. |
| O'Riley, Willie F | Providence | 7 | Feb. 11, 1895. |
| Grace, Theresa | Providence | 12 | April 10, 1895. |
| Welsh, John | Providence | 7 | May 20, 1895. |
| Roe, Albert C | Hope | 5 | Sept. 21, 1895. |
| Stetson, Leroy W | Warren | 10 | Sept. 30, 1895. |
| Williams, Charles A | Pawtucket | 4 | Sept. 14, 1896. |
| Perron, Lena | Warren | 7 | Oct. 26, 1896. |
| Anderson, Edward V | Providence | 9 | Oct. 1, 1897. |
| Vigeant, Edward | Pawtucket | 7 | May 3, 1897. |
| Davis, Elsie | East Providence | 9 | Sept. 13, 1897. |
| Perry, Joseph C | Providence | 7 | Jan. 7, 1898. |
| Yuppa, Concetta | Providence | 4 | Feb. 10, 1898. |
| Forthier, Angelina | Pawtucket | 6 | Oct. 24, 1898. |
| Holborgen, Trina | Pawtucket | ·6 | Oct. 18, 1898. |
| Bassett, Genevie W | Moosup Valley | 4 | Oct. 18, 1898. |
| Vogel, Alfred | Providence | 11 | Oct. 18, 1898. |
| Goldman, Samuel | Providence | 9 | Nov. 7, 1898. |
| Myers, Arthur | Providence | 7 | Jan. 3, 1899. |
| Wilcox, Olive I | East Providence | 3 | April 3, 1899. |
| Smith, Everett A | Slocumville | 3 | May 19, 1899. |
| Williams, Harold K | Pawtucket | 4 | Sept. 13, 1899. |
| Sweet, Fannie M | Centredale | 8 | Sept. 13, 1899. |
| Newberg, Charles A | Pawtucket | 7 | Sept. 25, 1899. |
| Paquin, Adolard | Providence | 5 | Oct. 2, 1899. |
| Cleary, John | Newport | 5 | Oct. 2, 1899. |
| Holmes Thomas | Providence | 7 | Oct. 17, 1899. |
| Grabert, Herman | Bristol | 12 | March 1, 1900. |
| Brennan, Sarah A | Pawtucket | 7 | May 6, 1900. |
| Olin, Millie I | Providence | 13 | Sept. 11, 1900. |
| Arel, Joseph I | Woonsocket | 10 | Sept. 19, 1900. |
| Brown, Lola B | Davisville | 12 | Nov. 19, 1900. |
| Gardiner, Earl F | Providence | 7 | April 16, 1901. |

## FOR THE YEAR ENDING DECEMBER 31, 1903.

| CAUSE OF DEAFNESS, AS FAR AS KNOWN. | AGE WHEN MADE DEAF (Approx.). | REMARKS. |
|---|---|---|
| Scarlet fever | 3 years | |
| Congenital | | |
| Congenital | | |
| Congenital | | |
| A fall | 2 years | |
| Measles | 2 years | |
| Congenital | | Deafness partial. |
| Typhoid fever | 4 years | |
| Scarlet fever | 1 year | |
| Convulsions | 3 years | |
| Congenital | | |
| Catarrhal fever | 1 year, 6 months | |
| Congenital | | |
| Measles | 5 years | Slight degree of hearing. |
| Congenital | | |
| Congenital | | |
| Brain fever | 3 years | |
| Inflammation in head | 4 months | |
| Fall and fever | 4 years | Slight degree of hearing. |
| Congenital | | |
| Scarlet fever | 1 year | |
| Scarlet fever | 5 years | Hard of hearing. |
| Scarlet fever | 4 years | |
| Spinal sickness | 2 months | Hard of hearing. |
| Congenital | | |
| Congenital | | |
| Measles | 1 year | |
| Congenital | | |
| | | Not deaf. |
| A fall | 3 years | |
| Grippe | 6 years | |
| Congenital | | |
| Congenital | | |
| Congenital | | |
| Spinal meningitis | 7 years | |
| A fall | 5 years | |
| Congenital | | |
| Congenital | | |
| | | Not deaf. |
| Measles | | Deafness partial. |
| Congenital | | |
| Scarlet fever | 10 years | |
| Congenital | | |
| Adenoid growth | 3 years | Hard of hearing. |
| Spinal meningitis | 4 years | |

3

## TABULAR REPORT OF THE PUPILS OF THE SCHOOL.

| Name of Pupil. | Residence. | Age (Approx.) | Date of Admission. |
|---|---|---|---|
| Notorantonio, Maggie.... | Providence............. | 8 | April 22, 1901. |
| Mitchell, Fred G......... | Providence............. | 8 | Sept. 10, 1901. |
| Cohen, Esther........... | Providence............. | 14 | Sept. 12, 1901. |
| Lindsay, Mary E......... | Providence............. | 5 | Oct. 5, 1901. |
| Burke, Bessie............ | Providence............🔹. | 11 | Sept. 15, 1901. |
| Johnson, Benjamin F.... | Kingston............... | 8 | Sept. 26, 1899. |
| Bruncell, Berger B....... | Woonsocket........... | 7 | Dec. 10, 1900. |
| Marden, James B........ | East Providence....... | 12 | Jan. 20, 1902. |
| Kinney, Charles H....... | Newport............... | 13 | March 17, 1902. |
| Shine, Philip............. | Providence............ | 6 | Sept. 9, 1902. |
| Bowser, Gertrude........ | Providence............. | 4 | Sept. 15, 1902. |
| Daudelin, E. Albert...... | Albion................. | 10 | Sept. 22, 1902. |
| Burke, Sarah C.... ..... | Pawtucket............. | 5 | Sept. 23, 1902. |
| VanValkinburg, Fred E.. | East Providence....... | 3 | Sept. 25, 1902. |
| Finnegan, Francis H..... | Pawtucket............. | 8 | Oct. 21, 1902. |
| Martinelli, Emira........ | Thornton...... ........ | 15 | Nov. 18, 1902. |
| Williams, Margaret...... | Pawtucket............. | 4 | Dec. 1, 1902. |
| Ferris, William A....... | Woonsocket........... | 6 | April 11, 1903. |
| Kingsley, Eleanor M..... | Hope.................. | 3 | Sept. 9, 1903. |
| Brinkman, Weldon...... | Providence............ | 5 | Sept. 10, 1903. |
| Barse, Howard S........ | Providence............. | ..... | Sept. 14, 1903. |
| Colvin, C. Henry.... .... | Providence............ | 7 | Oct. 13, 1903. |
| McCue, John............ | Providence............ | 6 | Oct. 15, 1903. |
| Bryer, Lydia A.... ...... | Newport...... ........ | 6 | Oct. 28, 1903. |
| Legge, Frederick W...... | Bayside............... | 13 | Oct. 26, 1903. |
| Derosier, Rosa........... | Forestdale............. | 9 | Nov. 4, 1903. |

## FOR THE YEAR ENDING DECEMBER 31, 1903.

| Cause of Deafness, as far as Known. | Age when made Deaf (Approx.). | Remarks. |
|---|---|---|
| Fever....... ................ | 4 years.......... | ......................... |
| Congenital.................... | .................. | ......................... |
| Congenital.................... | .................. | Hard of hearing. |
| Congenital.................... | .................. | ......................... |
| ............................. | .................. | Not deaf. |
| Congenital.................... | .................. | ......................... |
| Brain fever..... ............ | 1 year, 6 months. | ......................... |
| Scarlet fever............ ... | 4 years.......... | Hard of hearing. |
| Scarlet fever................. | 4 years.......... | Hard of hearing. |
| Measles...................... | 2 years.......... | ......................... |
| Congenital.................... | ............. ... | ......................... |
| Teething..................... | 1 year........... | ......................... |
| Measles...................... | 1 year·.......... | ......................... |
| ............................. | .................. | Not deaf. |
| Fall......................... | 4 years.......... | ...................... ... |
| Congenital.................... | .................. | ......................... |
| Congenital.................... | .................. | ......................... |
| Diphtheria................... | 1 year. | ......................... |
| Fall......................... | 2 years.......... | ......................... |
| Spinal meningitis..... ...... | .................. | ...................... ... |
| ............................. | .................. | Not deaf. |
| Unknown..................... | 1 year........... | ......................... |
| Brain fever..... .. .......... | 1 year........... | ......................... |
| Congenital.................... | .................. | ......................... |
| Abscess...................... | 4 years.......... | Hard of hearing. |
| Unknown..................... | 3 years.......... | ......................... |

## SUMMARY.

Number of pupils from date of opening the State school for the deaf,
April 2, 1877, to December 31, 1903 .................................... 194
Number of pupils who have entered the Institute since Dec 31, 1902.. 0

    Whole number of pupils who have attended the school. ....... 194
    Number who have left the school........................ ....... 131

Number of pupils Dec. 31, 1903...................................... 63
Number of girls who have attended school during the year........... 29
Number of boys who have attended school during the year.... ...... 43

    Whole number of pupils during the year....................... 72

Average attendance.............. ....................................

Number congenitally deaf, or made deaf before the age of two........ 43
Number who lost hearing between the ages of two and four.......... 15
Number who lost hearing after the age of four, and doubtful cases... 9
Number who have perfect hearing.................................. 5

                                                     72
Number who have any degree of hearing......... .................... 16

*Residences of all who have attended during the year 1903 :*

Geneva........................................................... 1
Providence............... . .................................... 31
East Providence................................................ 4
Pawtucket...................................................... 11
Newport........................................................ 6
Lymansville.................................................... 1
Slocumville.................................................... .
Kingston....................................................... 1
Forestdale .. .................................................. .
Bayside........................................................ 1

Laundry and Boiler House

Albion................................................................ 1

Thornton............................................................. 1

Davisville........................................................... 1

Centredale........................................................... 1

Woonsocket........................................................... 5

Hope................................................................. 2

Bristol.............................................................. 1

Warren............................................................... 2

Moosup Valley........................................................ 1

Twenty localities................................................... 74

# COURSE OF STUDY.

## KINDERGARTEN.

### FIRST YEAR.

    *a.* KINDERGARTEN EXERCISES.
    *b.* ARTICULATION.
    *c.* LANGUAGE.
    *d.* ARITHMETIC.
    *e.* PENMANSHIP.

*a.* Paper cutting and folding; drawing and modeling in clay; designing in shoe pegs; stick laying; embroidery designs sewed on pricked sewing-cards; lessons in form and color in all exercises.

*b.* Elements, combinations, simple words, and sentences; with reading them from the lips.

*c.* Nouns; objects in class-room, articles of dress, articles of food, different parts of the body, with a limited number of verbs. Adjectives, good, bad, large, small, &c.

*d.* Counting and writing numbers, with addition and subtraction to 10.

*e.* Writing on slate and with lead pencil.

## PRIMARY COURSE.

### SECOND, THIRD, AND FOURTH YEARS.

    *a.* ARTICULATION.
    *b.* LANGUAGE.
    *c.* ARITHMETIC.
    *d.* GEOGRAPHY.
    *e.* PENMANSHIP.
    *f.* DRAWING.

a. Drill in elements, combinations, and words, and reading them from the lips.

b. Thorough review of first year work. Nouns and verbs continued. Adjectives continued ; their comparison. Pronouns as in first year, adding myself, herself, himself, with the plurals, and the relatives who and which. Adverbs ; not, often, never, etc. Eliptical sentences ; action and picture writing ; journal and letter writing, and simple stories.

c. Practical exercises in addition, subtraction. multiplication, and division ; United States currency ; simple fractions.

d. Schoolroom, building, and yard, city, and a limited knowledge of the State.

e. Copy-book writing.

## INTERMEDIATE COURSE.

### FIFTH, SIXTH, AND SEVENTH YEARS.

a. ARTICULATION.
b. LANGUAGE.
c. ARITHMETIC.
d. GEOGRAPHY.
e. HISTORY.
f. PENMANSHIP.
g. DRAWING.
h. CALISTHENICS.

a. Drill in elements, combinations, syllables ; words and sentences continued as in primary course.

b. Nouns, pronouns, adjectives, adverbs, prepositions, and conjunctions continued as in primary course. Drill in active and passive voices ; action and picture writing ; stories from natural history ; journal and letter writing.

c. Mental and written addition, subtraction, multiplication, and division, with practical examples ; United States currency and simple fractions continued.

d. City, State, and New England States.

e. Simple historical stories in connection with geography.

f. Copy-book writing twice a week.

g. Object drawing.

## HIGHER COURSE.

### EIGHTH, NINTH, AND TENTH YEARS.

     *a.*   ARTICULATION.

     *b.*   LANGUAGE.

     *c.*   ARITHMETIC.

     *d.*   GEOGRAPHY.

     *e.*   HISTORY.

     *f.*   PHYSIOLOGY.

     *g.*   PENMANSHIP.

     *h.*   DRAWING.

     *i.*   CALISTHENICS.

*a.*   Drill in difficult combinations and words.

*b.*   Composition; journal and letter writing; miscellaneous reading; newspapers and magazines; lessons on general subjects.

*c.*   Mental, written, and practical.

*d.*   Geographical reader; Manual of Commerce.

*e.*   History of the United States; Outline of General History.

*g.*   Copy-book.

*h.*   Free-hand object drawing and designing.

# CHAPTER 332.

AN ACT IN AMENDMENT OF AND IN ADDITION TO CHAPTER 86 OF THE GENERAL LAWS, ENTITLED "OF THE R. I. SCHOOL FOR THE DEAF."

[Passed May 18, 1896.]

*It is enacted by the General Assembly as follows :*

SECTION 1. All children of parents, or under the control of guardians or other persons, legal residents of this state, between the ages of three and twenty years, whose hearing or speech, or both, are so defective as to make it inexpedient or impracticable to attend the public schools to advantage, not being mentally or otherwise incapable, may attend the Rhode Island Institute for the Deaf, without charge, under such rules and regulations as the board of trustees of said institute may establish.

SEC. 2. Every person having under his control any such child between the ages of seven and eighteen years shall cause such child to attend school at said institute for such period of time or such prescribed course, in each individual case, as may be deemed expedient by the board of trustees, and for any neglect of such duty the person so offending shall be fined not exceeding twenty dollars : *Provided*, that if the person so charged shall prove to the satisfaction of said board that the child has received or is receiving, under private or other instruction, an education suitable to his condition, in the judgment of said board, then such penalty shall not be incurred : *provided, further,* that no child shall be removed to said institution or taken from the custody of its parent or guardian except as a day scholar unless such parent or guardian is an improper person to have such custody, and the supreme court in its appellate division shall have jurisdiction in habeas corpus to examine into and revise all findings of said board of trustees under this act.

SEC. 3. Any child having attended said institute a time or course prescribed by said board, upon leaving the institute shall be entitled to receive a certificate of his proficiency from said board.

SEC. 4. This act shall take effect from and after its passage.

# TO PARENTS OF DEAF CHILDREN.

This school is for the benefit of children incapacitated through deafness, total or partial, for receiving proper instruction in common schools, and is free to all pupils who belong in this State.

The aim of the school is to teach deaf children to use the English language with the spontaneity, correctness, and enjoyment of *hearing* children as far as this is practicable.

" Without language there can be no thought, no reason ; " and as the highest aim of all instruction is the culture of the mental and moral nature in man, our first effort should be to furnish the deaf with a medium through which knowledge can be imparted and obtained. This can be done by signs, by the finger alphabet, and by speech. Our method is the latter, or oral, method, by which the deaf can be educated and at the same time furnished with the usual and most convenient way of communication in society and the world at large.

It is very desirable that deaf children be sent to school at as early an age as possible. A parent will be amply repaid for sending a child as young as five or six years, even at some inconvenience. The Board of Trustees are authorized to receive pupils between the ages of three and twenty years.

If a child who has learned to talk is made deaf by disease, he should immediately, upon his recovery, be sent to a school where his speech will be retained, and where he will be taught to understand from the lips. In such cases it is common to delay so long that serious loss of speech results.

Speech reading is an invaluable acquisition for those who are semi-deaf, or even hard of hearing, as well as for those congenitally or totally deaf.

Every effort should be made to encourage the child to retain the use of his voice. He should be taught to pronounce common words by watching the lip motion and facial expression, or by feeling the muscular action of the breath ; but no attempt should be made to teach him *the names* of the letters of the alphabet.

The English branches are taught here, and every pupil is taught some branch of industry.

The school session begins the second Monday in September, and closes the third Friday in June, with a week's holiday at Christmas.

Application for admission should be made to the principal, at the Institute, corner of Hope street and Cypress street, Providence.

State of Rhode Island and Providence Plantations.

# Report of the Board of Trustees

## of the

## RHODE ISLAND

# INSTITUTE FOR THE DEAF.

### PRESENTED TO THE

## GENERAL ASSEMBLY

### AT ITS

## JANUARY SESSION, 1905.

PROVIDENCE.
E. L. FREEMAN & SONS, PRINTERS TO THE STATE.
1905

FROST V.                    No. 4.

State of Rhode Island and Providence Plantations.

# Report of the Board of Trustees

OF THE

## RHODE ISLAND

# INSTITUTE FOR THE DEAF,

PRESENTED TO THE

## GENERAL ASSEMBLY

AT ITS

## JANUARY SESSION, 1905.

PROVIDENCE:
E. L. FREEMAN & SONS, PRINTERS TO THE STATE.
1905.

**PRINCIPAL.**

**PHYSICIANS.**

FRANK L. DAY, M. D.............................*Physician and Surgeon.*

F. P. CAPRON, M. D..................................*Oculist and Aurist.*

———

**TEACHERS.**

| M. AGNES GRIMM, | GRACE A. BALCH. | KITTY YOUNG. |
| CLAUDIA REDD, | GRACE I. RUSSELL, | MABEL I. CLARK |
| FANNIE C. SMITH, | | SYBIL RICHARDS, |

———

**SPECIAL TEACHERS.**

ETHEL DUNN DROWNE.............................*Teacher of Drawing.*

SIGNI WILBAR.........................................*Teacher of Sloyd.*

KITTY YOUNG....................*Teacher of Pasteboard Work and Basketry*

CLAUDIA REDD.......................................*Teacher of Cooking.*

LILLIAN TRIMBLE.....................................*Teacher of Sewing.*

———

**HOUSEHOLD DEPARTMENT.**

*Matron.*

BELLE LITTLEFIELD.

CLARA BUCKLEY.......... ..... ............... .................. ..........*Nurse.*

JANE STUART.... ....................................................*Night Nurse.*

LILLIAN TRIMBLE.... ............. .. ................*Girls' Attendant.*

LIZZIE KELLY.... ................ . .................*Girls' Attendant.*

MAY FOSTER.... ............. .....................*Boys' Attendant.*

WILLIAM JERMYN.........................................*Boys' Attendant.*

*Janitor.*

MATTHEW HILL.

# REPORT OF THE BOARD OF TRUSTEES.

*To the Honorable the General Assembly at its January Session, A. D. 1905, the Board of Trustees of the Rhode Island Institute for the Deaf respectfully presents the following report for the year 1904:*

The progress of previous years has been maintained, and to the faithful work of principal and teachers much credit is due.

With few exceptions, scholars have shown an earnest desire to profit by the instruction so generously furnished by the State, and it is a pleasure to commend the efficient work of instructors and pupils.

The staff of teachers remains the same as last year, with one exception.

In the resignation of Mr. William K. Potter, for many years chairman of the board, the trustees lost the services of a valued member. To fill the vacancy caused by the resignation of Mr. Potter, Governor Garvin appointed Mr. John F. McAlevy.

With the exception of diseases incident to children, the health of the pupils has been excellent.

The high cost of provisions and fuel has increased the difficulty of maintenance, but with careful economy the board of trustees has been able to complete the year within the appropriation.

### NECESSARY ALTERATIONS.

We beg to call the attention of your honorable body to the unsuitable condition of the school building. Although a solid, substantial structure, it was built forty or fifty years ago for a private residence, and since 1892 it has been used for school purposes practically in its original condition.

The rooms are small for the requirements, ill ventilated, and inadequate for such use, and we respectfully urge that provision be made for proper alterations and increase.

A moderate expenditure will remove certain partitions, lay new floors where old floors are unsafe from wear, provide proper ventilation, re-arrange a portion of the steam heating, add a small wing and thus furnish adequate facilities for many years to come.

For maintenance the board of trustees respectfully ask for the same appropriation, viz.:—$20,000.00.

### FINANCIAL STATEMENT.

| | |
|---|---:|
| Appropriation by the State | $20,000 00 |
| Paid for salaries | $9,091 10 |
| Paid for all other expenses | 10,632 32 |
| Unexpended balance | 276 58 |
| | 20,000 00 |

Respectfully submitted,

> LUCIUS F. C. GARVIN, *Governor*,
> GEORGE H. UTTER, *Lieut.-Governor*,
> > *Members ex-officio.*
> WILLIAM H. BALLOU, *President*,
> ELLEN T. McGUINNESS, *Secretary*,
> JEANIE LIPPITT WEEDEN,
> LOUISE PROSSER BATES,
> JEREMIAH W. HORTON,
> DR. ROWLAND R. ROBINSON,
> JOHN C. B. WOODS,
> GUSTAV N. HAUSMANN,
> JOHN F. McALEVY,
> > *Board of Trustees.*

PROVIDENCE, R. I., January, 1905.

 PENCIL DRAWING FROM LIFE
BY JENNIE GOLDSTEIN.

# MEDICAL REPORT.

*To the Trustees for the R. I. Institute for the Deaf:*

I have the honor to report concerning the health of the pupils during the year just closing:

Early in January, within a week of her return from the holidays, one little girl developed scarlet fever and was taken to her home, where she subsequently died. From this case two others developed, were removed to the Rhode Island hospital, returning later to the Institute entirely recovered. In the spring there were several cases of tonsilitis; in two of these the diphtheria bacillus was found, the children promptly isolated and kept quarantined until no germs were present. Nothing further developed. There were several minor accidents and trifling ailments such as are inseparable from so large a number of children.

Just before the holidays there were several cases of tonsilitis, and · three rather severe cases of influenza of such severity as to require the services of a trained nurse. All are now well or convalescent. Every successive year emphasizes the wisdom of your body in providing such excellent facilities for isolating suspects; and the absence of general epidemics bears evidence of the continued faithfulness of the principal and her staff in observing every least suggestion concerning hygienic and preventive measures.

Respectfully submitted,

FRANK L. DAY, M. D.

PROVIDENCE, December 31, 1904.

PROVIDENCE, R. I., Dec. 31, 1904.

*To the Board of Trustees for the R. I. Institute for the Deaf:*

During the year just closed I have treated a number of the pupils, but have had no cases of importance. The two long-continued patients, Edward Anderson and Chester Collins, are now in very good condition, the former with improved hearing and slight trouble with one ear, the latter with one ear healed and the other nearly so.

F. P. CAPRON, M. D.

# REPORT OF THE PRINCIPAL.

GENTLEMEN:—I herewith present, for your consideration, this the twenty-seventh report of our school, its work, and progress for the year ending December 31st, 1904.

The number of pupils enrolled was seventy. Of that number forty-six became deaf before the age of two, twelve lost their hearing between the ages of two and four, nine became deaf after they were four, and five became deaf after six years of age. Ten have partial hearing and three have perfect hearing. It must be borne in mind that even a slight degree of hearing aids greatly in developing a pleasant quality of voice; also, if a child has learned to talk before becoming deaf its voice will be much more agreeable and the language which he had acquired before becoming deaf will return to him and aid him greatly to acquire language.

It is to be regretted that every deaf child is not placed in school as soon as it reaches school age, but many parents say they *can not* part with the *afflicted* child; but this is only selfish affection. I know of one pupil whose mother thought she could not be separated from her, but when the girl grew older she had the desire herself to go to school and learn. She is a very satisfactory pupil, but is now doing beginning language work, which she should have done when she was seven years younger.

If parents of deaf children could only feel that the best way to show their affection for them is to educate them and to make them as near like their hearing brothers and sisters as possible! They should be placed in school at an early age as is possible, and they

2

should be given every advantage which the hearing children of the family are given. Deaf children may be fitted to fill almost any position which hearing children can fill, if they are given the same opportunities: but they are frequently put into a mill, while their brothers and sisters are educated for the more agreeable positions.

## HEALTH.

During the past year general good health prevailed, but soon after re-opening school, at the close of the Christmas vacation, one of the loveliest of our little children was taken sick and scarlet fever developed. The child was taken home, where, I regret to say, she died a few days after. Two other cases developed from that case, which were taken to the R. I. Hospital, where they both made excellent recovery. There were several cases of tonsilitis in the spring, also a few accidents such as are likely to occur where a large number of children are brought together. After the opening of school, in September, the health of the school was unusually good until two or three weeks before the Christmas holiday, when several cases of colds and tonsilitis occurred, and three cases of grippe which were quite severe for a few days.

## CLASS WORK.

There is but little that is new to be reported from the class rooms from year to year. The progress is steady, and in some instances very gratifying. As a whole the children are interested and desire to learn.

The course of study is the same as in the primary and grammar departments of the public schools. It is very gratifying that all of the older pupils returned at the re-opening of school in September, and they are doing very good work. Upon taking up the work again the rotary system was adopted with the three higher classes and the results are satisfactory.

Each teacher has a special branch in which she is to perfect herself as she has three grades in that branch to teach.

There will be no graduating class in June, but the first class is looking forward to graduating in 1906.

At the close of the school in June Miss Florence Russell resigned her position, to be married, and Mrs. Fannie Cheney Smith was appointed to fill the vacancy. We are very glad to welcome Mrs. Smith among us again. She was with us as Miss Fannie Cheney for several years, and we are very fortunate to have her return to us as she is a very enthusiastic teacher.

Miss Young is still in charge of the kindergarten, where the children have made marked progress. Many of the little ones are beginning to use speech, and they understand much that is told them, thus preparing the way for their first language lessons.

It is our aim to give the children under our care spoken language as soon as possible, to continue it and to increase the ability to talk as much as we can. All instruction is given by speech, and it is our only means of communication with the children.

It is with pleasure that I report an addition of about fifty new books to the pupils' libraries, as it increases the children's interest in reading, for they, like others, enjoy *new books* and look forward with pleasure to reading them.

The class in physical culture has been reformed in charge of Miss Sibyl Richards. The pupils enjoy the work much, and the training in this direction is of the greatest benefit to them. We have a fine airy hall in which the exercises are given, and great pride is taken in them.

The drawing classes, under the direction of Mrs. Ethel Dunn Drowne, are doing excellent work. During the past year the pupils have studied pencil drawing, color, composition, designing, and memory drawing. They have also made attempts at life drawing with a few worthy results.

Several of the pupils show marked talent, and the instruction, being mostly individual, allows these to advance rapidly. Among the graduates none will be found who can not handle pencil and brush deftly. Of these Jennie Goldstein and Henry Courtemanche deserve special mention.

The drawing room is equipped with many attractive pictures of still life for the use of the pupils, and additions are frequently made to this collection, and every new piece awakens deep interest.

Professor George H. Small has given several "chalk talks" to the pupils, which have been very helpful. He makes very skillful drawings, basing them all on the type form. He gave us several of the drawings for our drawing room, which are a source of much pleasure.

### MANUAL TRAINING.

The sewing class, under the direction of Miss Lillian Trimble, is making good progress. The sewing for the house is done in the class, also cutting, fitting, and dressmaking, to a limited extent. The girls are very interested in dressmaking.

The cooking, under the direction of Miss C. Redd, has proven very successful, the girls doing practical work. They have done some of the cooking for their own tables and have cooked several suppers. They are very proud of their work and anxious for the lessons.

Miss Young is in charge of the class in basketry, which was formed last spring. She also teaches cardboard work and paper cutting. The little children enjoy the work, and we hope to show what they can do in that line at the pupils' sale in the spring.

After school re-opened last September our sloyd teacher, Miss Sarah M. Aldrich, was appointed to a similar position in one of the Boston public schools, and we were compelled to look for some one to fill the vacancy. We regretted much the resignation of Miss Aldrich, because she had filled the position here *completely*. She took a lively interest in the boys, and she had awakened in them a love for the work, and they turned out many useful and ornamental pieces. We were fortunate to find Mrs. Signi Wilbar, who is a thorough sloyd worker, and she has taken up the work very successfully where Miss Aldrich left it. Mrs. Wilbar has taught her pupils pyrography, and some very creditable pieces have been made and sold. So that after a pupil has learned to draw and make an

icle he can also decorate it.   Without some knowledge of sloyd
: can not realize how great a benefit it is to the pupils.   Sloyd
rkers ought to take up nature study and learn about the dif-
ent woods, their growth and various uses in order to perfectly
derstand their work.   It is well known that sloyd work broadens
:; I therefore quote from our report of 1904:   "The aim of sloyd
1ot merely to teach boys to plane, saw, and use a few tools.   On
: contrary, it is intended to give, primarily, a mental and a moral
relopment, and incidentally it has an economic value.   It has been
ven that the power to coördinate muscular movements is a mental
wer.   The training of the muscles through sloyd involves the
irdination, and increases the activity of the brain.

'One of our able educators has said:   'There is nothing that is
re brain training than what we call manual training.'   There is
thing that really educates the head, heart, and hand more than
yd.

'All of the work requires planning, and much of it exact testing
:h try square and rule, in order to produce correct results.   This
presses upon the pupil the importance of carefulness, accuracy,
d patience.

'Most of the successful business or professional men of to-day
d active motor training when boys.   They were required to labor
:d on a farm or in the home, and use all their muscular energy.
is manual work helped to strengthen their character and gave them
lity to apply themselves in whatever pursuit they followed.   It is
: aim of sloyd to train the executive  power and the ability to do,
d thus help turn out more of these self-reliant men, who are able
do something, and not only know how things are done.''

That sloyd work might appeal more practically to the pupils, on
: twentieth of December the boys were allowed to have a sale of
: work done.   Each boy displayed his own work on his work-
ich, and sold it, taking the proceeds himself.,

There was a number of people present, and the boys were much
ased with their receipts.   We are looking forward to another

sale in the spring, when we expect the girls will bring forward some of their handiwork.

### BUILDINGS.

During the holidays, last summer, the boilers were thoroughly overlooked and repaired and the kitchen portion of the basement thoroughly whitened, and painting and varnishing was also done. It is necessary to do repairing and painting each summer, that the building may be kept in good condition.

In our last report I spoke of our need in the school building. I will here emphasize the fact that we are in great need of having nearly all of the school-rooms in the Pabodie building enlarged. They are not sanitary, they are altogether too small, some of them, to enable a teacher to go about inspecting the work of her pupils comfortably. We need more space, more light, and more fresh air. We look to our friends to make it possible that these conditions be improved.

### ACKNOWLEDGMENTS.

We thank Mrs. William B. Weeden for her kind thoughtfulness in sending us a check from Sicily, to provide a Christmas tree for the children, which she has done each year since this became a boarding school, twelve years ago.

Our thanks are due the United States Bureau of Education, and the Volta Bureau, for books and pamphlets sent us; Keith's Opera Co., for admission to the theatre; Messrs. J. H. Preston & Co., and Alexander White, for Christmas candies; Mrs. D. B. Pond, for subscription for the *Youth's Companion;* and Mrs. William B. Weeden, for clothing.

The receipt of the following periodicals is thankfully acknowledged, and their continuance respectfully requested:

Mute's Companion, Faribault, Minn.; Daily Paper for our Little People, Rochester, N. Y.; Our Children's School Journal, The Deaf Mute Journal, New York; Maryland Bulletin, Frederick, Md.;

The Deaf Mute Voice, Jackson, Miss.; Kentucky Deaf Mute, Danville, Ky.; The Goodson Gazette, Staunton, Va.; Kansas Star, Olathe, Kansas; Deaf Mute Optic, Little Rock, Ark.; Deaf Mute Index, Colorado Springs, Col.; Juvenile Ranger, Austin, Tex.; The Register, Rome, New York; Nebraska Mute Journal, Omaha, Neb.; New Method of the Deaf, Englewood, Ill.; Weekly News, Berkeley, Cal.; The Mount Airy World, Philadelphia; The Canadian Deaf Mute, Bellville, Ontario; The New Era, Jacksonville, Ill., Mentor.

### PRIZES.

At the close of school in June prizes were awarded Fannie Sweet and Joe Arel for the best speech; Millie Olin and Chester Collins for the best speech reading; Fannie Kleber, Mamie O'Connor, and Angelina Forthier for the greatest improvement in speech; Eddie Anderson and Alfred Vogel for the greatest improvement in deportment; Chester Collins for the greatest improvement in sloyd work: Fannie Kleber and Herman Grabert for the greatest improvement in drawing.

We sincerely thank you, the members of the board, on behalf of the deaf children of the State, for your watchful care of their interests, and we respectfully submit to you this report.

LAURA DeL. RICHARDS.

WATER COLOR BY SAMUE[

DRAWING FROM LIFE BY JAMES FLYNN.

WATER COLOR BY SAMUEL GOLDMAN.

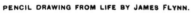

PENCIL DRAWING FROM LIFE BY JAMES FLYNN.

TABULAR STATEMENT.

## TABULAR REPORT OF THE PUPILS OF THE SCHOOL

| NAME OF PUPIL. | RESIDENCE. | AGE (Approx.). | DATE OF ADMISSION. |
|---|---|---|---|
| Carr, David | Pawtucket | 6 | Jan. 27, 1893. |
| Collins, Chester A | Providence | 4 | Jan. 30, 1893. |
| Kleber, Fannie | Lymansville | 6 | Feb. 7, 1893. |
| O'Connor, Mary | Woonsocket | 6 | May 27, 1893. |
| Thompson, George | Providence | 4 | Sept. 11, 1893. |
| Flynn, James | Providence | 6 | Feb. 3, 1894. |
| Comfort, Mae E | Newport | 8 | Sept. 10, 1894. |
| Mudrak, Willie | Geneva | 4 | Oct. 13, 1894. |
| Grimes, Mary | Newport | 9 | Feb. 5, 1895. |
| O'Riley, Willie F | Providence | 7 | Feb. 11, 1895. |
| Grace, Theresa | Providence | 12 | April 10, 1895. |
| Welsh, John | Providence | 7 | May 20, 1895. |
| Roe, Albert C | Hope | 5 | Sept. 21, 1895. |
| Stetson, Leroy W | Warren | 10 | Sept. 30, 1895. |
| Williams, Charles A | Pawtucket | 4 | Sept. 14, 1896. |
| Perron, Lena | Warren | 7 | Oct 26, 1896. |
| Anderson, Edward V | Providence | 9 | Oct. 1, 1896. |
| Vigeant, Edward | Pawtucket | 7 | May 3, 1897. |
| Davis, Elsie | East Providence | 9 | Sept. 13, 1897. |
| Perry, Joseph C | Providence | 7 | Jan. 7, 1898. |
| Yuppa, Concetta | Providence | 4 | Feb. 10, 1898. |
| Forthier, Angelina | Pawtucket | 6 | Oct. 24, 1898. |
| Holborgen, Trina | Pawtucket | 6 | Oct. 18, 1898. |
| Bassett, Genevive W | Moosup Valley | 4 | Oct. 18, 1898. |
| Vogel, Alfred | Providence | 11 | Oct. 18, 1898. |
| Goldman, Samuel | Providence | 9 | Nov. 7, 1898. |
| Myers, Arthur | Providence | 7 | Jan. 3, 1899. |
| Wilcox, Olive I. | East Providence | 3 | April 3, 1899. |
| Smith, Everett A | Slocumville | 3 | May 19, 1899. |
| Williams, Harold K | Pawtucket | 4 | Sept. 13, 1899. |
| Sweet, Fannie M | Centredale | 8 | Sept. 13, 1899. |
| Newberg, Charles A | Pawtucket | 7 | Sept. 25, 1899. |
| Paquin, Adolard | Providence | 5 | Oct. 2, 1899. |
| Cleary, John | Newport | 5 | Oct. 2, 1899. |
| Holmes, Thomas | Providence | 7 | Oct. 17, 1899. |
| Grabert, Herman | Bristol | 12 | Mar. 1, 1900. |
| Brennan, Sarah A | Pawtucket | 7 | May 6, 1900. |
| Olin, Millie I | Providence | 13 | Sept. 11, 1900. |
| Arel, Joseph I | Woonsocket | 10 | Sept. 19, 1900. |
| Brown, Lola B | Davisville | 12 | Nov. 19, 1900 |
| Gardiner, Earl F | Providence | 7 | April 16, 1901. |
| Notorantonio, Maggie | Providence | 8 | April 22, 1901. |
| Mitchell, Fred G | Providence | 8 | Sept. 10, 1901. |
| Lindsay, Mary E | Providence | 5 | Oct. 5, 1901. |
| Burke, Bessie | Providence | 11 | Sept. 15, 1901. |

FOR THE YEAR ENDING DECEMBER 31, 1904.

| Cause of Deafness, as far as Known. | Age when made Deaf (Approx.). | Remarks. |
|---|---|---|
| A fall. | 2 years. | |
| Measles. | 2 years. | |
| Congenital. | | Deafness partial. |
| Scarlet fever. | 1 year. | |
| Convulsions. | 3 years. | |
| Congenital. | | |
| Catarrhal fever. | 1 year, 6 months. | |
| Congenital. | | |
| Measles. | 5 years. | Slight degree of hearing. |
| Congenital. | | |
| Congenital. | | |
| Brain fever. | 3 years. | |
| Inflammation in head. | 4 months. | |
| Fall and fever. | 4 years. | Slight degree of hearing. |
| Congenital. | | |
| Scarlet fever. | 1 year. | |
| Scarlet fever. | 5 years. | Hard of hearing. |
| Scarlet fever. | 4 years. | |
| Spinal sickness. | 2 months. | Hard of hearing. |
| Congenital. | | |
| Congenital. | | |
| Measles. | 1 year. | |
| Congenital. | | |
| | | Not deaf. |
| A fall. | 3 years. | |
| Grippe. | 6 years. | |
| Congenital. | | |
| Conegnital. | | |
| Congenital. | | |
| Spinal meningitis. | 7 years. | |
| A fall. | 5 years. | |
| Congenital. | | |
| Congenital. | | |
| | | Not deaf. |
| Measles. | | Deafness partial. |
| Congenital. | | |
| Scarlet fever. | 10 years. | |
| Congenital. | | |
| Adenoid growth. | 3 years. | Hard of hearing. |
| Spinal meningitis. | 4 years. | |
| Fever. | 4 years. | |
| Congenital. | | Hard of hearing. |
| Congenital. | | |
| | | Not deaf. |

## TABULAR REPORT OF THE PUPILS OF THE SCHOOL

| Name of Pupil. | Residence. | Date of Admission. |
|---|---|---|
| Johnson, Benjamin F...... | Kingston............... | Sept. 26, 1899. |
| Bruncell, Berger B........ | Woonsocket............ | Dec. 10, 1900. |
| Shine. Philip............. | Providence............ | Sept. 9, 1902. |
| Daudelin, E. Albert....... | Albion................. | Sept. 22, 1902. |
| Burke, Sarah C........... | Pawtucket............. | Sept. 23, 1902. |
| Van Valkinburg, Fred E... | East Providence.......... | Sept. 25, 1902. |
| Finnegan, Francis H...... | Pawtucket............. | Oct. 21, 1902. |
| Martinelli, Emira........ | Thornton.............. | Nov. 18, 1902 |
| Williams, Margaret....... | Pawtucket............. | Dec. 1, 1902. |
| Ferris, William A........ | Woonsocket............ | April 11, 1903. |
| Kingsley, Eleanor M...... | Hope.................. | Sept. 9, 1903, |
| Brinkman, Weldon........ | Providence............ | Sept. 10, 1903. |
| Pearse, Howard S........ | Providence............ | Sept. 14, 1903. |
| Colvin, C. Henry......... | Providence............ | Oct. 13, 1903. |
| McCue, John............. | Providence............ | Oct. 15, 1903. |
| Bryer, Lydia A........... | Newport............... | Oct. 28, 1903. |
| Legge, Frederick W...... | Bayside............... | Oct. 26, 1903. |
| Derosier, Rosa........... | Forestdale............. | Nov. 4, 1903. |
| O'Neill, Maurice......... | Pawtucket............. | Feb., 1904. |
| Pelletier, Eva........... | Manville.............. | Mar., 1904. |
| Roberts, Lucia........... | Providence............ | Sept., 1904. |
| Kirk, John.............. | Providence............ | Sept., 1904. |
| Pulsifer, Nellie.......... | Providence............ | Sept., 1904. |
| Aubin, Eva............. | Mapleville............ | Oct., 1904. |
| Barnes, Edith E......... | Westerly.............. | Nov., 1904. |

FOR THE YEAR ENDING DECEMBER 31, 1904.

| USE OF DEAFNESS, AS FAR AS KNOWN. | AGE WHEN MADE DEAF (Approx.). | REMARKS. |
|---|---|---|
| enital.................... | | |
| fever.................... | 1 year, 6 months.. | |
| les...................... | 2 years........... | |
| iing..................... | 1 year........... | |
| les...................... | 1 year........... | |
| ........................ | | Not deaf. |
| ...................... | 4 years........... | |
| enital.................... | | |
| enital.................... | | |
| theria................... | 1 year........... | |
| ......................... | 2 years........... | |
| il meningitis............. | | |
| ........................ | | Not deaf. |
| iown..................... | 1 year........... | |
| fever.................... | 1 year........... | |
| enital.................... | | |
| ess...................... | 4 years........... | Hard of hearing. |
| iown..................... | 3 years........... | |
| oid fever................ | 8 years........... | |
| enital.................... | | |
| iown..................... | | |
| et fever.................. | 2 years, 6 months. | |
| les...................... | 6 years........... | |
| ear...................... | 1 year, 6 months.. | |
| enital.................... | | |

## SUMMARY.

Number of pupils from date of opening the State school for the deaf, April
2, 1877, to December 31, 1904.................................... 201
Number of pupils who have entered the Institute since December 31, 1903.  7

Whole number of pupils who have attended the school............. 201
Number who have left the school................................ 147

———

Number of pupils December 31, 1904.................................. 63
Number of girls who have attended school during the year............... 30
Number of boys who have attended school during the year.............. 40

———

Whole number of pupils during the year......................... 70
Number congenitally deaf, or made deaf before the age of two........... 44
Number who lost hearing between the ages of two and four.............. 12
Number who lost hearing after the age of four, and doubtful cases........ 9
Number who have perfect hearing.................................. 3

———

70
Number who have any degree of hearing........................... 14

———

*Residences of all who have attended during the year 1904.*

Geneva............................................................... 1
Providence.... ...................................................... 28
East Providence....... .............................................. 3
Pawtucket........................................................... 12
Newport............................................................. 4
Lymansville......................................................... ⸱
Slocumville.......... .. ............................................ ⸱
Kingston........... ................................................ ⸱
Forestdale........... ... ........................................... ⸱
Bayside............................................................. ⸱
Albion.............................................................. ⸱
Thornton...... ..................................................... ⸱
Davisville.. .. ..................................................... ⸱
Centredale.......................................................... ⸱

REPORT OF THE PRINCIPAL.

# COURSE OF STUDY.

## KINDERGARTEN.

### FIRST YEAR.

    *a.* KINDERGARTEN EXERCISES.
    *b.* ARTICULATION.
    *c.* LANGUAGE.
    *d.* ARITHMETIC.
    *e.* PENMANSHIP.

*a.* Paper cutting and folding; drawing and modeling in clay; designing in shoe pegs; stick laying; embroidery designs sewed on pricked sewing-cards; lessons in form and color in all exercises.

*b.* Elements, combinations, simple words, and sentences; with reading them from the lips.

*c.* Nouns; objects in class-room, articles of dress, articles of food, different parts of the body, with a limited number of verbs. Adjectives, good, bad, large, small, &c.

*d.* Counting and writing numbers, with addition and subtraction to 10.

*e.* Writing on slate and with lead pencil.

## PRIMARY COURSE.

### SECOND, THIRD, AND FOURTH YEARS.

    *a.* ARTICULATION.
    *b.* LANGUAGE.
    *c.* ARITHMETIC.
    *d.* GEOGRAPHY
    *e.* PENMANSHIP.
    *f.* DRAWING.

Drill in elements, combinations, and words, and reading them from the lips.

Thorough review of first year work. Nouns and verbs continued. Adjectives continued; their comparison. Pronouns as in first year, adding myself, herself, himself, with the plurals, and the relatives who and which. Adverbs; not, aften, never, etc. Eliptical sentences; action and picture writing; journal and letter writing, and simple stories.

Practical exercises in addition, subtraction, multiplication, and division; United States currency; simple fractions.

Schoolroom, building, and yard, city, and a limited knowledge of the State.

Copy-book writing.

## INTERMEDIATE COURSE.

### FIFTH, SIXTH, AND SEVENTH YEARS.

*a.* ARTICULATION.

*b.* LANGUAGE.

*c.* ARITHMETIC.

*d.* GEOGRAPHY.

*e.* HISTORY.

*f.* PENMANSHIP.

*g.* DRAWING.

*h.* CALISTHENICS.

Drill in elements, combinations, syllables; words and sentences continued as in primary course.

Nouns, pronouns, adjectives, adverbs, prepositions, and conjunctions continued as in primary course. Drill in active and passive voices; action and picture writing; stories from natural history; journal and letter writing.

Mental and written addition, subtraction, multiplication, and division, with practical examples; United States currency and simple fractions continued.

City, State, and New England States.

Simple historical stories in connection with geography.

Copy-book writing twice a week.

Object drawing.

## HIGHER COURSE.

EIGHTH, NINTH, AND TENTH YEARS.

- *a.* ARTICULATION.
- *b.* LANGUAGE.
- *c.* ARITHMETIC.
- *d.* GEOGRAPHY.
- *e.* HISTORY.
- *f.* PHYSIOLOGY.
- *g.* PENMANSHIP.
- *h.* DRAWING.
- *i.* CALISTHENICS.

*a.* Drill in difficult combinations and words.
*b.* Composition; journal and letter writing; miscellaneous reading; newspapers and magazines; lessons on general subjects.
*c.* Mental, written, and practical.
*d.* Geographical reader; Manual of Commerce.
*e.* History of the United States; Outline of General History.
*g.* Copy-book.
*h.* Free-hand object drawing and designing.

REAR VIEW MAIN BUILDING.

# CHAPTER 332.

AN ACT IN AMENDMENT OF AND IN ADDITION TO CHAPTER 86 OF THE GENERAL LAWS, ENTITLED "OF THE R. I. SCHOOL FOR THE DEAF."

[Passed May 13, 1896.]

*It is enacted by the General Assembly as follows:*

SECTION 1. All children of parents, or under the control of guardians or other persons, legal residents of this state, between the ages of three and twenty years, whose hearing or speech, or both, are so defective as to make it inexpedient or impracticable to attend the public schools to advantage, not being mentally or otherwise incapable, may attend the Rhode Island Institute for the Deaf, without charge, under such rules and regulations as the board of trustees of said institute may establish.

SEC. 2. Every person having under his control any such child between the ages of seven and eighteen years shall cause such child to attend school at said institute for such period of time or such prescribed course, in each individual case, as may be deemed expedient by the board of trustees, and for any neglect of such duty the person so offending shall be fined not exceeding twenty dollars: *Provided*, that if the person so charged shall prove to the satisfaction of said board that the child has received or is receiving, under private or other instruction, an education suitable to his condition, in the judgment of said board, then such penalty shall not be incurred; *provided, further*, that no child shall be removed to said institution or taken from the custody of its parent or guardian except as a day scholar unless such parent or guardian is an improper person to have such custody, and the supreme court in its appellate division shall have jurisdiction in habeas corpus to examine into and revise all findings of said board of trustees under this act.

SEC. 3. Any child having attended said institute a time or course prescribed by said board, upon leaving the institute shall be entitled to receive a certificate of his proficiency from said board.

SEC. 4. This act shall take effect from and after its passage.

# TO PARENTS OF DEAF CHILDREN.

This school is for the benefit of children incapacitated through deafness, total or partial, for receiving proper instruction in common schools, and is free to all pupils who belong in this State.

The aim of the school is to teach deaf children to use the English language with the spontaneity, correctness, and enjoyment of *hearing* children as far as this is practicable.

"Without language there can be no thought, no reason;" and as the highest aim of all instruction is the culture of the mental and moral nature in man, our first effort should be to furnish the deaf with a medium through which knowledge can be imparted and obtained. This can be done by signs, by the finger alphabet, and by speech. Our method is the latter, or oral, method, by which the deaf can be educated and at the same time furnished with the usual and most convenient way of communication in society and the world at large.

It is very desirable that deaf children be sent to school at as early an age as possible. A parent will be amply repaid for sending a child as young as five or six years, even at some inconvenience. The Board of Trustees are authorized to receive pupils between the ages of three and twenty years.

If a child who has learned to talk is made deaf by disease, he should immediately, upon his recovery, be sent to a school where his speech will be retained, and where he will be taught to understand from the lips. In such cases it is common to delay so long that serious loss of speech results.

Speech reading is an invaluable acquisition for those who are semi-deaf, or even hard of hearing, as well as for those congenitally or totally deaf.

Every effort should be made to encourage the child to retain the use of his voice. He should be taught to pronounce common words by watching the lip motion and facial expression, or by feeling the muscular action of the breath; but no attempt should be made to teach him *the names* of the letters of the alphabet.

The English branches are taught here, and every pupil is taught some branch of industry.

The school session begins the second Tuesday in September, and closes the third Friday in June, with a week's holiday at Christmas.

Application for admission should be made to the principal, at the Institute, corner of Hope street and Cypress street, Providence.

FRONT VIEW OF MAIN BUILDING, WITH NEW WING.

**State of Rhode Island and Providence Plantations.**

# Report of the Board of Trustees

### OF THE

## RHODE ISLAND

# INSTITUTE FOR THE DEAF,

### PRESENTED TO THE

## GENERAL ASSEMBLY

### AT ITS

## JANUARY SESSION, 1906.

PROVIDENCE:

E. L. FREEMAN & SONS, PRINTERS TO THE STATE.

1906.

# RHODE ISLAND INSTITUTE FOR THE DEAF.

## HOPE STREET, CORNER OF CYPRESS STREET,

## PROVIDENCE, R. I.

UNDER THE SUPERVISION OF

## BOARD OF TRUSTEES,

CONSISTING OF

LAURA DEE RICHARDS.

## PHYSICIANS.

FRANK L. DAY, M. D.............................Physician and Surgeon.

F. P. CAPRON, M. D.................................Oculist and Aurist.

## TEACHERS.

M. AGNES GRIMM,          GRACE A. BALCH,          E. ETHEL RICHARDS,

CLAUDIA REDD,            GRACE I. RUSSELL,        OLIVE JACQUES,

FANNIE C. SMITH,                                  SYBIL RICHARDS.

## SPECIAL TEACHERS.

ETHEL DUNN DROWNE............................Teacher of Drawing.

ERNEST B. WALKER.............................Teacher of Sloyd.

M. AGNES GRIMM...................Teacher of Pasteboard Work and Basketry.

CLAUDIA REDD.................................Teacher of Cooking.

FLORENCE B. LYON.............................Teacher of Sewing

## HOUSEHOLD DEPARTMENT.

*Matron.*

LOUISE A. LADD.

*Assistant Matron.*

FLORENCE B. LYON.

FLORENCE B. LYON....................................Girls'

ADA FORREST........................................Girls'

MARY KEOUGH.......................................Boys'

CHESTER A. COLLINS.............................Assistant Boys'

HERMAN GRABERT.................................Assistant Boys'

EVA PUBLICOVER...........................................

JANE STUART......................................Night Nurse.

*Janitor.*

JOHN SIDAWAY.

DINING ROOM

# REPORT OF THE BOARD OF TRUSTEES.

*To the Honorable the General Assembly at its January Session, A. D. 1906:*

*The Board of Trustees of the Rhode Island Institute for the Deaf respectfully presents the following report for the year 1905:*

The number of pupils has varied but little from that of the previous year, but individual cases show gratifying improvement.

The aim and endeavor of the management to take charge of and instruct all deaf children of the State, of suitable age, is frequently defeated by the unwillingness of parents and guardians to be separated from their children, and it is a matter of regret that many are thus deprived of the advantages furnished by the school.

Repairs to buildings and steam apparatus are necessarily paid for from the sum appropriated for maintenance, but these repairs have been made and the property continued in good physical condition.

The general health of pupils has been excellent, the school having been practically exempt from contagious disease during the year.

To fill vacancies caused by expiration of term of office and resignation, Honorable Elisha Dyer and Professor George G. Wilson have been appointed members of the board of trustees.

Each year accentuates the inconvenient and unsanitary features of the school building, and we feel that it is impossible to emphasize too strongly the need of improved conditions and increased space.

The State of Rhode Island in taking these children should furnish them with an ample, well-lighted, properly ventilated and comfortably heated school building, and we respectfully ask your honorable body to furnish the money to provide these necessities.

| | | |
|---|---:|---:|
| Appropriation for year 1905 | | $20,000 00 |
| Paid for salaries | $9,212 96 | |
| Paid for fuel | 1,649 99 | |
| Paid for repairs | 2,119 79 | |
| Paid for all other expenses | 6,981 24 | |
| Unexpended balance | 36 02 | |
| | | $20,000 00 |

For maintenance for the year 1906 the board of trustees respectfully ask for the same amount, viz.—$20,000.00.

Respectfully submitted,

GEORGE H. UTTER, *Governor*,

FREDERICK H. JACKSON, *Lieut.-Governor*,

*Members ex-officio.*

WILLIAM H. BALLOU, *President*,

ELLEN T. McGUINNESS, *Secretary*,

JEANIE LIPPITT WEEDEN,

LOUISE PROSSER BATES,

JEREMIAH W. HORTON,

DR. ROWLAND R. ROBINSON,

ELISHA DYER,

GEORGE G. WILSON,

JOHN F. McALEVY,

*Board of Trustees.*

PROVIDENCE, R. I., January, 1906.

# MEDICAL REPORT.

---

*To the Trustees for the R. I. Institute for the Deaf:*

During the year just closed the children have generally been re-markably well. Early in the year there were a few cases of ton-silitis, and one of the girls had malarial fever. A crushed finger re-quired partial amputation. One boy sprained his ankle by falling from a tree. Roy Stetson developed tuberculosis and was taken home, where he died after an illness of several months.

In the fall months there were only minor ailments, except one case of catarrhal appendicitis which recovered. One of the smaller girls is at present convalescing from a severe lobar pneumonia.

Respectfully submitted,

FRANK L. DAY, M. D.

PROVIDENCE, R. I., December 31, 1905.

GRADUATING CLASS, 1900.

# REPORT OF THE PRINCIPAL.

*To the Trustees for the R. I. Institute for the Deaf:*

GENTLEMEN:—Allow me to present to you a report of the school work for the year just closed.

This school was opened by Mrs. Henry Lippitt, in 1876, and adopted as a State school, by an act of the legislature, in 1877.

It was created a State institution April 21, 1891.

During the past year it has cared for sixty-nine pupils, thirty girls, and thirty-nine boys. There were seven admitted, four boys and three girls. Two of the older boys left before the close of school in June, one on account of poor health and the other found work.

All of the others returned at the opening of school in September, except one of the larger girls, who was so late returning that her room was taken by a new pupil.

The rooms for the *large* girls are all filled, so that no more can be accommodated. As a whole the past year was prosperous and successful. The school work must be similar from year to year, but we adopt new methods as they are brought to our attention, when they are proven to be better than those in use. There are still some children that we have been unable to bring into school, because their parents feel that they can not be separated from them: they fail to realize the fact that an education is much more necessary to a deaf child than it is to one who hears, or that an early start in this very important work should be made. Parents should do all in their power toward the education of the deaf child of the family. They should teach it to write the names of familiar objects, and when the child can speak it should be required to use speech when making its wants known. Because a child is deaf, parents and friends should *not* give up all thought of instruction and discipline: they ought to take more pains to teach the child. We are continually looking for children that we ought to have with us, and we hope that later we shall succeed in bringing them all in. If the truant law was more strictly enforced in some of the rural districts it would aid us greatly.

### HEALTH.

We are thankful to report that the health of the pupils was excellent during the greater part of the year. We must again record the death of one of our number. Leroy Stetson, a youth of eighteen, developed tuberculosis, and died, at his home, after an illness of several months. He was an intelligent, manly boy and is greatly missed by all.

### CHANGES.

In September there were some changes among the teachers. Miss Young and Miss Clark resigned their positions to be married, and Miss Ethel Richards and Miss Olive Jacques were appointed to fill the vacancies. Miss Richards, who takes Miss Young's place in the kindergarten, was with us as a student last year, and Miss Jacques comes from Simmons College. We expect Miss Richards to maintain the high degree of excellence to which Miss Young had brought the kindergarten, where the children are taught weaving, stick-laying, drawing and clay modeling, the same as that given in kindergarten for hearing children. They are provided with building blocks and taught how to use them, sliced animals and games suited to the work laid out.

They are also given exercises in form, color and motion, and in vocal gymnastics and simple phonetics, that the habit of speech may be begun with them as soon as possible. If a child has ever talked it is required to use speech as much as possible when trying to communicate with others. The children that are beginning to form sentences and express themselves in spoken language are expected to talk constantly in the class room, but it is very simple language indeed. At first they are taught the names of familiar objects and a few verbs, then they are given commands, and later they are taught simple sentences, such as, "I love mamma," "I love you," and others similar. In all of the younger classes speech is taught instead of writing, because we wish them to become so familiar with speech that they will prefer to use it rather than signs.

They begin regular study when they enter the primary grade; then they have written work and lessons to commit to memory. They have lessons in numbers, home geography, simple history stories, and lessons on the care of the body. We copy from a former report: "In the grammar department the course prescribed for the city schools is followed, in which arithmetic, grammar, geography, history, physiology, and the natural sciences are taught." We frequently add new books to our library and try to select books that will equip each grade with reading matter suited to its work. The first class, which is in two divisions, is doing excellent work. There are four in the first division, which forms our graduating class and will graduate in June. The second division is also doing good work, but they have not been in school as long as the pupils in the first division, therefore they will *remain* in school and will form the next class to be graduated. They are interested in reading, taking books from our library, and some of the pupils enjoy going to the Public Library to read. Our aim is to cultivate in the pupils a taste for good, healthy reading. We also try to have them acquire the habit of strict attention to duty at the time set for duty, and that they consider school a real business and a business to which they must attend if they wish to become strong men and women, for good in the world.

The drawing classes have been doing well the past year. The time has been devoted, principally, to studying repeating patterns and historical ornament. Considering the limited time for drawing, the pupils have done some exceedingly good work. Many things have been added to the equipment of the room, casts, still-life, screens, etc. Clay modeling has recently been added to the course, for which the pupils show marked appreciation.

Miss Sibyl Richards is still in charge of the classes in physical culture. She is very interested in this branch of study and is doing excellent work with the pupils.

### MANUAL TRAINING.

While the cultivation of the mind should be our first and principal work with the deaf, we should keep before us the thought that we must teach them to be self-supporting. That they may be so, the girls are taught sewing and embroidery and different kinds of fancy work. They are taught dress making, cutting and fitting, by Miss Florence B. Lyon, who takes a great interest in the girls and their work. They have done some very creditable work.

Miss C. Redd has charge of the class in cooking, which the girls enjoy very much. They are also taught basketry by Miss Grimm, one of the teachers, in which they are very much interested, because they see the practical side, as it has brought them in some money. Miss Grimm gives instruction to a class of small boys in card-board work and measurement, preparatory to Sloyd. In June Mrs. Signi Wilbur resigned her position as teacher of Sloyd, and Mr. Ernest B. Walker was appointed to fill the vacancy. He began work at the opening of school in September. Mr. Walker is a teacher of experience, and he has gained the confidence of the boys. They have made several pieces, both small and large, for the main building, which does them credit. We are looking for a man who can teach the boys printing, and when he is found we shall re-open the printing-room, which is very well equipped.

### BUILDINGS.

It was necessary to do something more than the usual repairing last summer, as the boiler, laundry, and the place generally, needed repairing. The whole place was put in good order. Where there are a great many active children it is necessary to make repairs yearly, as there is more or less breakage. In our last report your attention

was called to the fact that we needed a better school building. The need still exists. We have occupied the old Pabodie mansion, as a school building, for years, *without any change.* It was built for a dwelling house, to accommodate a family of six or thereabout, and we have been occupying *this same building* for school purposes, sending from sixty to seventy children and from eight to twelve teachers and officers there to spend five hours and more, daily, where we have very inadequate means of ventilation and no possible means of improving the situation. With such surroundings can we be expected to ward off contagious diseases? We need more space, more light, better heat, and a newer, fresher building, where we can have more fresh air. And we look to our friends in the General Assembly to make it possible for these conditions to be improved.

### ACKNOWLEDGMENTS.

We thank Mrs. William B. Weeden for her kindness in sending us a check to provide a Christmas tree for the children, which she has done each year since this became a boarding school, fourteen years ago.

Our thanks are due the United States Bureau of Education, and the Volta Bureau, for books and pamphlets sent us; Keith's Opera Co., for admission to the theatre; Messrs, J. H. Preston & Co., and R. L. Rose Co., for Christmas candies; Mrs. D. B. Pond, for subscription for the *Youth's Companion;* and Mrs. William B. Weeden, for clothing.

The receipt of the following periodicals is thankfully acknowledged, and their continuance respectfully requested:

Mute's Companion, Faribault, Minn.; Daily Paper for our Little People, Rochester, N. Y.; Our Children's School Journal, The Deaf Mute Journal, New York; Maryland Bulletin, Frederick, Md.; The Deaf Mute Voice, Jackson, Miss.; Kentucky Deaf Mute, Danville, Ky.; The Goodson Gazette, Staunton, Va.; Kansas Star, Olathe, Kansas; Deaf Mute Optic, Little Rock, Ark.; Deaf Mute Index, Colorado Springs, Col.; Juvenile Ranger, Austin, Tex.; The Register, Rome, New York; Nebraska Mute Journal, Omaha, Neb.; New

Method of the Deaf, Englewood, Ill.; Weekly News, Berkeley, Cal.; The Mount Airy World, Philadelphia; The Canadian Deaf Mute, Bellville, Ontario; The New Era, Jacksonville, Ill., Mentor.

## PRIZES.

At the close of school in June prizes were awarded Fannie Kleber and Mary Grimes, for the best speech; Millie Olin and Eddie Vigeant, for the best speech reading; Emira Martinnelli, for greatest improvement in speech; Mae Comfort, for greatest improvement in speech reading; Herman Grebert and Fannie Sweet, for being the best in conversation; David Carr, for best deportment; Elise Davis and Chester Collins, for the greatest improvement in deportment.

LAURA DeL. RICHARDS.

# TABULAR STATEMENT

# TABULAR STATEMENT.

## TABULAR REPORT OF THE PUPILS OF THE SCHOOL

| NAME OF PUPIL. | RESIDENCE. | AGE. (Approx.) | DATE OF ADMISSION. |
|---|---|---|---|
| Carr, David | Pawtucket | 6 | Jan. 27, 1893. |
| Collins, Chester A | Providence | 4 | Jan. 30, 1893. |
| Kleber, Fannie | Lymansville | 6 | Feb. 7, 1893. |
| Thompson, George | Providence | 4 | Sept. 11, 1893. |
| Flynn, James | Providence | 6 | Feb. 3, 1894. |
| Comfort, Mae E | Newport | 8 | Sept. 10, 1894. |
| Mudrak, Willie | Geneva | 4 | Oct. 13, 1894. |
| Grimes, Mary | Newport | 9 | Feb. 5, 1895. |
| Roe, Albert C | Hope | 5 | Sept. 21, 1895. |
| Stetson, Leroy W | Warren | 10 | Sept. 30, 1895. |
| Williams, Charles A | Pawtucket | 4 | Sept. 14, 1896. |
| Perron, Lena | Warren | 7 | Oct. 26, 1896. |
| Anderson, Edward V | Providence | 9 | Oct. 1, 1896. |
| Vigeant, Edward | Pawtucket | 7 | May 3, 1897. |
| Davis, Elsie | East Providence | 9 | Sept. 13, 1897. |
| Perry, Joseph C. | Providence | 7 | Jan. 7, 1898. |
| Yuppa, Concetta | Providence | 4 | Feb. 10, 1898. |
| Forthier, Angelina | Pawtucket | 6 | Oct. 24, 1898. |
| Holborgen, Trina | Pawtucket | 6 | Oct. 18, 1898. |
| Bassett, Genevive W | Moosup Valley | 4 | Oct. 18, 1898. |
| Vogel, Alfred | Providence | 11 | Oct. 18, 1898. |
| Goldman, Samuel | Providence | 9 | Nov. 7, 1898. |
| Myers, Arthur | Providence | 7 | Jan. 3, 1899. |
| Wilcox, Olive I | East Providence | 3 | April 3, 1899. |
| Smith, Everett A | Slocumville | 3 | May 19, 1899. |
| Williams, Harold K | Pawtucket | 4 | Sept. 13, 1899. |
| Sweet, Fannie M | Centredale | 8 | Sept. 13, 1899. |
| Newburg, Charles A | Pawtucket | 7 | Sept. 25, 1899. |
| Paquin, Adolard | Providence | 5 | Oct. 2, 1899. |
| Cleary, John | Newport | 5 | Oct. 2, 1899. |
| Holmes, Thomas | Providence | 7 | Oct. 17, 1899. |
| Grabert, Herman | Bristol | 12 | Mar. 1, 1900. |
| Brennan, Sarah A. | Pawtucket | 7 | May 6, 1900. |
| Olin, Millie I | East Providence | 13 | Sept. 11, 1900. |
| Arel, Joseph I | Woonsocket | 10 | Sept. 19, 1900. |

FOR THE YEAR ENDING DECEMBER 31, 1905.

| Cause of Deafness, as far as Known. | Age when made Deaf (Approx.). | Remarks. |
|---|---|---|
| A fall | 2 years | |
| Measles | 2 years | |
| Congenital | | Deafness partial. |
| Convulsions | 3 years | |
| Congenital | | |
| Catarrhal fever | 1 year, 6 months | |
| Congenital | | |
| Measles | 5 years | Slight degree of hearing. |
| Inflammation in head | 4 months | |
| Fall and fever | 4 years | Slight degree of hearing. |
| Congenital | | |
| Scarlet fever | 1 year | |
| Scarlet fever | 5 years | Hard of hearing. |
| Scarlet fever | 4 years | |
| | | |
| Spinal sickness | 2 months | Hard of hearing. |
| Congenital | | |
| Congenital | | |
| Measles | 1 year | |
| Congenital | | |
| | | Not deaf. |
| A fall | 3 years | |
| Grippe | 6 years | |
| Congenital | | |
| Congenital | | |
| Congenital | | |
| Spinal meningitis | 7 years | |
| A fall | 5 years | |
| Congenital | | |
| Congenital | | |
| | | Not deaf. |
| Measles | | Deafness partial. |
| Congenital | | |
| Scarlet fever | 10 years | |

2

## TABULAR REPORT OF THE PUPILS OF THE SCHOOL

| NAME OF PUPIL. | RESIDENCE. | AGE (Approx.). | DATE OF ADMISSION. |
|---|---|---|---|
| Brown, Lola B | Davisville | 12 | Nov. 19, 1900. |
| Gardiner, Earl F | Providence | 7 | April 16, 1901. |
| Notorantonio, Maggie | Providence | 8 | April 22, 1901. |
| Mitchell, Fred G | Providence | 8 | Sept. 10, 1901. |
| Lindsay, Mary E | Providence | 5 | Oct. 5, 1901. |
| Johnson, Benjamin F | Kingston | 8 | Sept. 26, 1899. |
| Bruncell, Berger B | Woonsocket | 7 | Dec. 10, 1900. |
| Shine, Philip | Providence | 6 | Sept. 9, 1902. |
| Burke, Sarah C | Pawtucket | 5 | Sept. 23, 1902. |
| Finnegan, Francis H | Pawtucket | 8 | Oct. 21, 1902. |
| Martinelli, Emira | Thornton | 15 | Nov. 18, 1902. |
| Williams, Margaret | Pawtucket | 4 | Dec. 1, 1902. |
| Ferris, William A | Woonsocket | 6 | April 11, 1903. |
| Kingsley, Eleanor M | Hope | 3 | Sept. 9, 1903. |
| Brinkman, Weldon | Providence | 5 | Sept. 10, 1903. |
| Pearse, Howard S | Providence | | Sept. 14, 1903. |
| Colvin, C. Henry | Providence | 7 | Oct. 13, 1903. |
| McCue, John | Providence | 6 | Oct. 15, 1903. |
| Bryer, Lydia A | Newport | 6 | Oct. 28, 1903. |
| Derosier, Rosa | Forestdale | 9 | Nov. 4. 1903. |
| O'Neill, Maurice | Pawtucket | 8 | Feb., 1904. |
| Pelletier, Eva | Manville | 6 | Mar., 1904. |
| Roberts, Lucia | Providence | 4 | Sept., 1904. |
| Kirk, John | Providence | 12 | Sept., 1904. |
| Pulsifer, Nellie | Providence | 19 | Sept., 1904. |
| Aubin, Eva | Mapleville | 10 | Oct., 1904. |
| Barnes, Edith E | Westerly | 15 | Nov., 1904. |
| Plante, Juliette M | Providence | 7 | Mar., 1905. |
| Eidelberg, Rose | Providence | 20 | Sept., 1905. |
| Green, Horace W | Westerly | 6 | Sept., 1905. |
| Ruckdeschel, Frederick | Providence | 13 | Sept., 1905. |
| Gobeille, Antonio | Woonsocket | 15 | Sept., 1905. |
| Epstein, Esther | Arctic | 13 | Sept., 1905. |
| Hardy, Raymond W | Providence | 5 | Oct., 1905. |

FOR THE YEAR ENDING DECEMBER 31, 1905.

| Cause of Deafness, as far as Known. | Age when made Deaf (Approx.). | Remarks. |
|---|---|---|
| Congenital | | |
| Adenoid growth | 3 years | Hard of hearing. |
| Spinal meningitis | 4 years | |
| Fever | 4 years | |
| Congenital | | Hard of hearing. |
| Congenital | | |
| Congenital | | |
| Brain fever | 1 year, 6 months | |
| Measles | 2 years | |
| Measles | 1 year | |
| Fall | 4 years | |
| Congenital | | |
| Congenital | | |
| Diphtheria | 1 year | |
| Fall | 2 years | |
| Spinal meningitis | | |
| Unknown | 1 year | Not deaf. |
| Brain fever | 1 year | |
| Congenital | | |
| Unknown | 3 years | |
| Typhoid fever | 8 years | |
| Congenital | | |
| Unknown | | |
| Scarlet fever | 2 years, 6 months | |
| Measles | 6 years | |
| Sore ear | 1 year, 6 months | |
| Congenital | | |
| Brain fever | 2 years | |
| Cold | 10 years | Hard of hearing. |
| Unknown | | |
| Spinal meningitis | 12 years | |
| Fits | 1 year, 6 months | |
| Unknown | 9 years | |
| Unknown | | |

## SUMMARY.

Number of pupils from date of opening the State school for the deaf, April 2.
1877, to December 31, 1905.. ............       208
Number of pupils who have entered the Institute since December 31, 1904..    7

Whole number of pupils who have attended the school... ... ...    208
Number who have left the school..............................   145

Number of pupils December 31, 1905................................    63
Number of girls who have attended school during the year...............    30
Number of boys who have attended school during the year..............    39
Average attendance during the year................................    58

Whole number of pupils during the year......................,..........    69
Number congenitally deaf, or made deaf before the age of two............    35
Number who lost hearing between the ages of two and four..............    13
Number who lost hearing after the age of four, and doubtful cases........    18
Number who have perfect hearing...................................     3

                                                                     69
Number who have any degree of hearing       .....................    12


*Residences of all who have attended during the year* 1905.

Geneva...   .............................................................    1
Providence                       ..   ..  ..  .   .........   27
East Providence.                        ...........................    3
Pawtucket............................................................   12
Newport..............................................................    4
Lymansville..        ......................................    ...    ₁
Slocumville...  ....................................................    ₁
Kingston.  ....   .................................................    ₁
Forestdale..  .....   .....   .......................................    ₁
Thornton............................................................    ₁
Davisville  .  ....................................................    ₁
Centredale. ....   ...............................................    ₁
Arctic....        ...........................................    ₁
Woonsocket........................................................    ₇

Hope............................................................... 2
Bristol............................................................. 1
Warren............................................................. 2
Moosup Valley..................................................... 1
Westerly........................................................... 2
Mapleville......................................................... 1
Manville........................................................... 1
-----
Twenty-one localities.............................................. 69

# COURSE OF STUDY.

## KINDERGARTEN.

### FIRST YEAR.

    *a.* KINDERGARTEN EXERCISES.

    *b.* ARTICULATION.

    *c.* LANGUAGE.

    *d.* ARITHMETIC.

    *e.* PENMANSHIP.

*a.* Paper cutting and folding; drawing and modeling in clay; designing in shoe pegs; stick laying; embroidery designs sewed on pricked sewing-cards; lessons in form and color in all exercises.

*b.* Elements, combinations, simple words, and sentences; with reading them from the lips.

*c.* Nouns; objects in class room, articles of dress, articles of food, different parts of the body, with a limited number of verbs. Adjectives, good, bad, large, small, &c.

*d.* Counting and writing numbers, with addition and subtraction to 10.

*e.* Writing on slate and with lead pencil.

## PRIMARY COURSE.

### SECOND, THIRD, AND FOURTH YEARS.

    *a.* ARTICULATION.

    *b.* LANGUAGE.

    *c.* ARITHMETIC.

    *d.* GEOGRAPHY.

    *e.* PENMANSHIP.

    *f.* DRAWING.

a. Drill in elements, combinations, and words, and reading them from the lips.

b. Thorough review of first year work. Nouns and verbs continued. Adjectives continued; their comparison. Pronouns as in first year, adding myself, herself, himself, with the plurals, and the relatives who and which. Adverbs; not, often, never, etc. Eliptical sentences; action and picture writing; journal and letter writing, and simple stories.

c. Practical exercises in addition, subtraction, multiplication, and division. United States currency; simple fractions.

d. Schoolroom, building, and yard, city, and a limited knowledge of the State.

e. Copy-book writing.

## INTERMEDIATE COURSE.

### FIFTH, SIXTH, AND SEVENTH YEARS.

a. ARTICULATION.

b. LANGUAGE.

c. ARITHMETIC.

d. GEOGRAPHY.

e. HISTORY.

f. PENMANSHIP.

g. DRAWING.

h. CALISTHENICS.

a. Drill in elements, combinations, syllables; words and sentences continued as in primary course.

b. Nouns, pronouns, adjectives, adverbs, prepositions, and conjunctions continued as in primary course. Drill in active and passive voices; action and picture writing; stories from natural history; journal and letter writing.

c. Mental and written addition, subtraction, multiplication, and division, with practical examples; United States currency and simple fractions continued.

d. City, State, and New England States.

e. Simple historical stories in connection with geography.

f. Copy-book writing twice a week.

g. Object drawing.

## HIGHER COURSE.

### EIGHTH, NINTH, AND TENTH YEARS.

- *a.* ARTICULATION.
- *b.* LANGUAGE.
- *c.* ARITHMETIC.
- *d.* GEOGRAPHY.
- *e.* HISTORY.
- *f.* PHYSIOLOGY.
- *g.* PENMANSHIP.
- *h.* DRAWING.
- *i.* CALISTHENICS.

*a.*  Drill in difficult combinations and words.

*b.*  Composition; journal and letter writing; miscellaneous and magasines; lessons on general subjects.

*c.*  Mental, written, and practical.

*d.*  Geographical reader; Manual of Commerce.

*e.*  History of the United States; Outline of General History.

*g.*  Copy-book.

*h.*  Free-hand object drawing and designing.

# CHAPTER 332.

AN ACT IN AMENDMENT OF AND IN ADDITION TO CHAPTER 86 OF THE GÉNERAL LAWS, ENTITLED "OF THE R. I. SCHOOL FOR THE DEAF."

[Passed May 13, 1896.]

*It is enacted by the General Assembly as follows:*

SECTION 1. All children of parents, or under the control of guardians or other persons, legal residents of this state, between the ages of three and twenty years, whose hearing or speech, or both, are so defective as to make it inexpedient or impracticable to attend the public schools to advantage, not being mentally or otherwise incapable, may attend the Rhode Island Institute for the Deaf, without charge, under such rules and regulations as the board of trustees of said institute may establish.

SEC. 2. Every person having under his control any such child between the ages of seven and eighteen years shall cause such child to attend school at said institute for such period of time or such prescribed course, in each individual case, as may be deemed expedient by the board of trustees, and for any neglect of such duty the person so offending shall be fined not exceeding twenty dollars: *Provided,* that if the person so charged shall prove to the satisfaction of said board that the child has received or is receiving, under private or other instruction, an education suitable to his condition, in the judgment of said board, then such penalty shall not be incurred; *provided, further,* that no child shall be removed to said institution or taken from the custody of its parent or guardian except as a day scholar unless such parent or guardian is an improper person to have such custody, and the supreme court in its appellate division shall have jurisdiction in habeas corpus to examine into and revise all findings of said board of trustees under this act.

SEC. 3. Any child having attended said institute a time or course prescribed by said board, upon leaving the institute shall be entitled to receive a certificate of his proficiency from said board.

SEC. 4. This act shall take effect from and after its passage.

# TO PARENTS OF DEAF CHILDREN.

This school is for the benefit of children incapacitated through deafness, total or partial, for receiving proper instruction in common schools, and is free to all pupils who belong in this State.

The aim of the school is to teach deaf children to use the English language with the spontaneity, correctness, and enjoyment of *hearing* children as far as this is practicable.

"Without language there can be no thought, no reason;" and as the highest aim of all instruction is the culture of the mental and moral nature in man, our first effort should be to furnish the deaf with a medium through which knowledge can be imparted and obtained. This can be done by signs, by the finger alphabet, and by speech. Our method is the latter, or oral, method, by which the deaf can be educated and at the same time furnished with the usual and most convenient way of communication in society and the world at large.

It is very desirable that deaf children be sent to school at as early an age as possible. A parent will be amply repaid for sending a child as young as five or six years, even at some inconvenience. The Board of Trustees are authorized to receive pupils between the ages of three and twenty years.

If a child who has learned to talk is made deaf by disease, he should immediately, upon his recovery, be sent to a school where his speech will be retained, and where he will be taught to understand from the lips. In such cases it is common to delay so long that serious loss of speech results.

Speech reading is an invaluable acquisition for those who are semi-deaf, or even hard of hearing, as well as for those congenitally or totally deaf.

Every effort should be made to encourage the child to retain the use of his voice. He should be taught to pronounce common words by watching the lip motion and facial expression, or by feeling the muscular action of the breath; but no attempt should be made to teach him *the names* of the letters of the alphabet.

The English branches are taught here, and every pupil is taught some branch of industry.

The school session begins the second Tuesday in September, and closes the third Friday in June, with a week's holiday at Christmas.

Application for admission should be made to the principal, at the Institute, corner of Hope street and Cypress street, Providence.

MAIN BUILDING

State of Rhode Island and Providence Plantations.

# REPORT OF THE BOARD OF TRUSTEES

### OF THE

## RHODE ISLAND

# INSTITUTE FOR THE DEAF,

### PRESENTED TO THE

## GENERAL ASSEMBLY

### AT ITS

## JANUARY SESSION, 1907.

PROVIDENCE:

E. L. FREEMAN COMPANY, STATE PRINTERS.

1907.

# RHODE ISLAND INSTITUTE FOR THE DEAF.

## HOPE STREET, CORNER OF CYPRESS STREET,

## PROVIDENCE, R. I.

---

UNDER THE SUPERVISION OF

# BOARD OF TRUSTEES,

CONSISTING OF

# OFFICERS OF THE INSTITUTE.

# REPORT OF THE BOARD OF TRUSTEES.

*To the Honorable the General Assembly, at its January Session, A. D. 1907.*

The Board of Trustees of the Rhode Island Institute for the Deaf, respectfully presents the following report for the year 1906:

With the beginning of the present school year a change was made in the principalship of the school, Mr. E. G. Hurd succeeding Miss Laura deL. Richards, who had been the principal since the beginning of the school.

Miss Richards was an expert teacher of the deaf, and a woman of marked executive ability. To her devotion to the school and its interests much credit for the present efficiency of the school is attributable, and her name will always be closely identified with the first years of the institution.

Mr. E. G. Hurd, who is now in charge of the school, came from a successful service of ten years at the North Carolina School for the Deaf, at Morganton, N. C., where he and Mrs. Hurd held high positions in connection with work similar to that now being done. The course of study arranged by the present principal and taught by a force of efficient teachers, coupled with the admirable administration of the domestic department, has given marked and satisfactory results.

There are in the State between twenty and thirty more deaf children who should be taught in this school, and without doubt a large proportion of them will be admitted during the year 1907. The trustees respectfully urge that your honorable body increase the appropriation to a sufficient sum to provide for the increased number, and to defray the expense of additional industrial training necessary to equip them with the means to earn their living. With contagious disease so prevalent it is gratifying to report the general good health of the pupils, and we feel that it reflects credit upon the management of principal and assistants. It is our duty to again call attention to the unsatisfactory condition of the school building, a condition that would not be allowed to exist in any other like institution. We venture the assertion that there is not in this State another building, used for public school purposes, so deficient in proper ventilation, adequate heating, and suitable school equipment.

Ample space, good ventilation, and light are essential to the successful teaching of hearing pupils; but with the deaf, where teaching is practically personal, these are prime requisites. The school building was built for a private residence, fifty years ago, and has been used for school purposes for the past fifteen years as originally built.

The trustees earnestly request that funds be provided to remodel this building.

In the resignation of Mrs. Jeanie Lippitt Weeden the school lost an earnest supporter and the Board of Trustees a valued member. Mrs. Weeden's intimate association with the institution dated from its inception, and it was due largely to her indomitable efforts that the present buildings were secured. The death of Hon. Elisha Dyer was a severe loss to all connected with the school, for he was always the cordial friend and adviser, giving freely of his time, and the members of the Board of Trustees will sadly miss the active co-operation of that courteous gentleman.

To fill these vacancies Governor Utter appointed Mrs. Richard W. Jennings and Mr. Herbert W. Rice, both of Providence.

For maintenance the Board of Trustees respectfully asks for $25,000.00.

### FINANCIAL STATEMENT.

| | | |
|---|---:|---:|
| Appropriation by the General Assembly | | $20,000 00 |
| Bills of 1905 paid in 1906 | $1,060 40 | |
| Salaries and labor | 8,586 72 | |
| Fuel and ashes removed | 1,528 67 | |

| | | |
|---|---:|---:|
| Gas for light, cooking, fixtures.............. | 416 | 82 |
| Water................................. | 148 | 09 |
| Fire protection......................... | 29 | 25 |
| Boiler inspection........................ | 7 | 00 |
| Electric power for laundry................ | 109 | 47 |
| Telephone.............................. | 76 | 35 |
| Provisions............................. | 4,293 | 50 |
| Repairs................................ | 1,306 | 90 |
| Kitchen range.......................... | 83 | 61 |
| Advertising............................ | 30 | 15 |
| Printing............................... | 53 | 57 |
| Cleaning bedding and blankets............. | 40 | 05 |
| Clothing for pupils, shoes repaired......... | 67 | 52 |
| Medical attendance and nurses............ | 315 | 75 |
| Supplies for hospital..................... | 66 | 81 |
| Furniture, carpets, mattings, curtains, shades, etc................................. | 548 | 25 |
| Supplies for sewing room.................. | 78 | 12 |
| Supplies for kitchen...................... | 50 | 61 |
| Supplies for laundry...................... | 50 | 18 |
| Supplies for school, including books........ | 367 | 72 |
| Supplies for dining room.................. | 84 | 32 |
| Supplies for household, linens, towels, mattresses, blankets, supplies for bathroom and for cleaning.................... | 471 | 05 |
| Miscellaneous expenses................... | 129 | 12 |

$20,000 00

Respectfully submitted,

# REPORT OF THE PRINCIPAL.

*To the President and Board of Trustees of the Rhode Island Institute for the Deaf.*

GENTLEMEN:—I hereby submit to you the following annual report of the affairs of the Institute for the year ending December 31, 1906. There have been in attendance, since the opening of school, September 11, 1906, sixty (60) pupils. Of this number six (6) were new pupils, four of whom had never attended school before; one comes from the public schools, having become too deaf to finish her education in hearing schools; and one comes from the Maryland School for the Deaf, Baltimore, Md. Of thirty-five (35) are boys and twenty-five (25) girls-

22 were born deaf.
9 became deaf at 1 year or under.
8 " " under 2 years.
8 " " " 5 years.
8 " " between 5 years and 12 years.
4 unknown.

44 were born in Rhode Island.
2 " " " Canada.
1 was " " Russia.
1 " " " Sweden.
1 " " " Italy.
1 " " " Minnesota.
6 were " " Massachusetts.
1 was " " Austria.
2 were " " Maine.
1 was " " Maryland.

FIRST LESSON IN SPEECH.

Since coming upon the field, August 1st, I have devoted considerable time and effort to ascertain the location of deaf children in the State who hav enever attended school, and as a result I have secured the names of twenty-two (22) deaf children whose attendance I am endeavoring to secure.

### HEALTH.

The health of the pupils has been good. As will be seen by the physician's report, there have been few cases of illness, and these of a trivial nature. Since the opening of school, September 11th, 1906, the physician has made but twenty visits, which is twenty-eight less than for the corresponding period of last year. For further information upon this point I refer you to the physician's report, upon another page. Great care is taken to secure good sanitary conditions in all parts of the buildings, and much attention is paid to the personal cleanliness and neatness of the pupils at all times. They are furnished with an abundance of plain, but nourishing, food and all are compelled to take exercise out of doors each day when the state of the weather does not prohibit. Once or twice a week all of the pupils are allowed to take a walk outside of the Institute grounds, accompanied by an attendant. By careful attention to these matters we have secured a state of good physical well-being in the pupils, and it is gratifying to note the many expressions of appreciation that are constantly coming from them.

### THE BUILDINGS.

During the past summer much work was done to put the buildings in good condition for the opening of school. The interior walls received a new finish, and much of the woodwork was revarnished and painted. The gutters were in a bad condition and were repaired temporarily, but another year new gutters will be needed. It was found necessary to purchase new rugs and carpets to replace those that were long past use, and to repair and purchase some new furniture. In the school building we have fitted up the kindergarten

2

room in such a manner as to make it suitable and possible to carry on kindergarten work. We have done little to the older part of the school building, except to have it thoroughly cleaned and put in a better sanitary condition. The older portion of the school building is so ill adapted to school purposes, in every way, that it will be necessary to rebuild it before we can hope to have a school building in any way suitable for our needs. No school children in the city of Providence, or, I venture to say, in the State, attend school in rooms of this character.

### THE HOUSEHOLD DEPARTMENT.

The affairs of the household are administered with care and economy. They are under the immediate charge of a competent matron, who, with the assistance of attendants, has direction of the pupils at all times when not in school, and an inspection of this part of our work shows a continuous and steady improvement. By baking all of our bread instead of buying it, we have bread of a better quality at a less price. We also buy our meat in larger quantities than heretofore, at a considerable gain both in cost and quality.

### THE INTELLECTUAL DEPARTMENT.

The method of instruction pursued in the Rhode Island Institute is the Oral Method. By this method deaf children are taught speech and speech-reading, and by this means, with writing, their entire education is accomplished.

Early in the fall the school was entirely re-organized. A new class was formed by promoting a portion of the kindergarten pupils who had long outgrown kindergarten work. This class is now doing well and is making considerable progress in speech and language. A regrading of classes throughout the school resulted in the formation of eight classes in all. These classes are arranged for the year as follows:

*Primary Classes.*

Kindergarten, 9 pupils, Miss Hill.
First Grade, 10 pupils, Mrs. Hurd, substitute, Miss Clarke.
Second Grade, 8 pupils, Miss McClelland.
Third Grade, 9 pupils, Miss Richards.

*Intermediate Class.*

Fourth Grade, 7 pupils, Miss Woodcock.

*Grammar Classes.*

D. C. B. A.    14 pupils.    Rotating.

Miss Grimm,
- Language.
- Reading.
- Grammar.

Miss Balch,
- Arithmetic.
- Information Lessons

Miss Russell,
- Speech.
- Geography.
- U. S. History.
- Physical Geography.
- English History.

For an examination of the course of study outlined for the present year I refer you to another part of this report.

Two Sunday-school classes have been formed for the Protestant pupils, which are taught each Sunday by the teachers in turn.

The Catholic pupils are sent each Sunday to their own church, where they attend service and receive instruction in classes formed especially for them.

Each morning before school and on Sunday afternoon, the pupils all assemble in the chapel, where we have responsive readings, and I give them talks upon subjects tending to instruct them in matters connected with good conduct and right living.

Upon assuming the duties of principal there were three vacancies in the regular corps of instructors, which I filled by appointing the following teachers, all of whom have had special training for the teaching of the deaf: Miss Frances McClelland, from the North Carolina School; Miss Ellen Woodcock, from the Myrtle, Oral School; and Miss Marion Hill, who was trained at the Pa., Oral School for the Deaf. Miss Elizabeth Clarke, who a part of her training in the Rhode Island Institute returned to complete her training and to fill the position stitute teacher, and Miss Urania Sturdivant, of Hartford us to take training. I also re-appointed Mrs. Drown of drawing, and Mr. Walker, teacher of sloyd. The matron, also vacant, was filled by the appointment of Gogin, of the Mt. Airy School, Philadelphia, Pa., a perience and success in this line of work. Miss of the Portland School, was appointed girls' supervisor of sewing.

During the past summer I attended the meeting of the Association for the Promotion of the Teaching of Speech to Deaf, held at the Western Penna. Institution for the Deaf, at Edgewood Park, Pittsburg. The meeting was well attended, there being over two hundred present, and the sessions were of unusual interest and profit to all present.

### INDUSTRIAL TEACHING.

The importance and value of teaching useful trades to the deaf is recognized by all educators, and all institutions, with few exceptions, teach their pupils some useful occupation by means of which they are enabled to make their own way and become self-supporting.

The teaching of trades is helpful, not only because of its practical value, but on account of the mental training and discipline it gives. Teaching of this character, in which both the mind and muscles are actively and harmoniously employed, will do much to secure

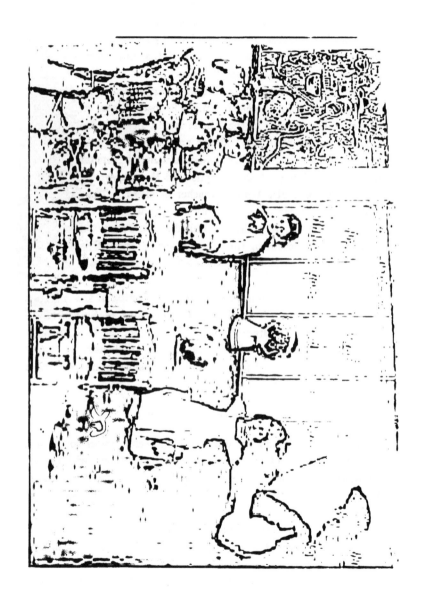

a healthful physical and moral development. I hope in the near future to have in this Institute two useful trades taught to the boys. At present we have no teaching of this kind except sloyd, which, although of some value for our youngest pupils, is of little use to boys of a larger growth. The girls in our Institute are taught sewing for a time each day, and we shall begin the teaching of cooking as soon as we are able to secure the desks and utensils necessary for this purpose. Twice each week a class of girls is taught basketry by Miss Grimm, and both boys and girls receive instruction in drawing from Mrs. Drown. The pupils also have gymnastic exercises in the morning before school, taught by Miss Sybil Richards. We hope in the near future to improve this important branch of instruction by re-arranging one of the large rooms of the main building for a gymnasium and putting the apparatus in better order, so that better work will be possible. We have this year started a small class of boys in baking, who bid fair to become proficient in this line of work.

### FUTURE NEEDS.

I wish to call attention to the need of a larger appropriation for the coming year. Much repair work will be necessary, and varnishing and painting to keep the buildings in good condition. The floors in some parts of the buildings are in bad condition and will need to be replaced in the near future. At present the basement rooms are floored with wood, which, owing to the natural dampness of such a situation, are sure to decay in time and endanger the health of the pupils. The great need of rebuilding a part of the schoolbuilding I have already referred to in another part of this report. The number of pupils in attendance is sure to be increased, and this will necessitate an increased expense for maintenance.

In closing this report I wish to express my gratification at the atmosphere of harmony and good feeling among the teachers

# OUTLINE OF WORK FOR THE CLASSES

## IN THE

# RHODE ISLAND INSTITUTE FOR THE DEAF.

## 1906—1907.

### KINDERGARTEN CLASS.

#### Miss Hill.

Motion Exercises:
> Marching, Running, Walking, Standing, Sitting.
> Motions of Arms, Head, Hands, Mouth.

Touch Exercises.

Tongue Exercises.

Breathing Exercises.

Kindergarten Exercises:
> To develop (a) Observation, (b) Imitation.
> To develop idea of Form and Color.

Speech Reading.

Voice Development.

Speech Development—following "First Lessons in Speech."

Penmanship—Formation of letters.

Short Sentences—read from lips and spoken to cultivate continuity and smoothness of speech.

No written sentence work required.

### FIRST GRADE

#### Mrs. Hurd, Ass't. Miss Clarke.

Review Elements and Combinations and Words—following "First Lessons in Speech."

Writing (a) from copy, (b) from Dictation—using pencil.

3

Busy Work—Practical Exercises.

Breathing and Calisthenic Exercises for Recreation Periods.

Second Half of Year:

Sentence Work begun—following "The Language Outline," by Mrs. Hurd.

Sentence Forms:

(1) Intransitive Verb:

    (a) One subject and one verb.

    (b) Two subjects and one verb.

    (c) One subject and two verbs.

    (d) Compound sentence.

    (e) Compound sentence when one subject or one predicate is compound.

(2) Transitive Verb—Simple sentence.

    (f) One object to verb.

    (g) Two objects to verb.

    (h) Compound transitive sentence.

    (i) One subject for both clauses.

Personal Pronouns.

Possessive Case of Nouns.

Verb—to be—Present, Past, and Future Tense.

The Verbs (in Present Tense):

to have, to want, to love, to like.

Declarative and Negative Forms.

Time Expressions: to-day, yesterday, to-morrow, last...., next.....

Nouns—(about 200) including those previously learned in "First Lessons in Speech." Singular and Plural Number.

Verbs—(about 75) Past Tense.

Declarative and Negative Form (did not....).

Adjectives (about 25).

    (a) Colors.

    (b) Numerals to 10.

    (c) Good, bad, sick, etc.

Questions—using Am? Are? Is? Was? Were? Will....be? Can? Have? Has? Do....? Does....? Did....?

Also the meaning of Interrogative Forms:

Who? What? Whose? Whom? When?

Notes: *All* written sentence work to be written in the columns—according to the "Six Column Diagram."

New words to be given *first* through Speech Reading always.

Oral work and Written work to be in proportion of 4 to 1.

Busy Work:

Useful, Practical exercises arranged.

Neatness and accuracy to be required in all exercises and at all times.

Original Exercises (oral and written):

Statements.

Questions.

News,

Letters.

Nature Lessons.

## SECOND GRADE.

### Miss McClelland.

Review *all* of "First Grade Work" and strengthen the weak places.

Questions—using all interrogative forms in "First Grade Work," and later Where? Why?

The Future Tense.

Prepositions.

The Negative Form of Verbs—"Could not.....," "Would not....."

Infinitives—as "Want to go," "Like to sew," etc.

Because—in declarative sentences and in answer to Why?

Time Expressions: a long time ago, sometimes, bye and bye, one day, in a little while, etc.

New Sentence Forms—Prepositional Sentence.

(a) Transitive verb with prepositional phrase.

(b) Intransitive verb with prepositional phrase.

(c) Sentence containing two prepositional phrases with same verb or different verbs.

Number Work—"Number Primer," Gibbs.

Simple problems involving four principles, addition, subtraction, multiplication, and division, with numbers to 25, using objects.

Notes:

*All* written work to be written in the columns according to the "Six Column Diagram."

New words given *first* through Speech Reading.

Oral work and written to be in proportion of 3 to 2.

Neatness and accuracy to be required in all exercises and at all times.

Original exercises, oral and written:

News.

Questions.

Letters.

Reading Book, Miss Sweet's No. 1 (revised edition).
Penmanship—Copy book, with pen and ink.
Conversation—Daily.
Nature Lessons.

## THIRD GRADE.

### MISS RICHARDS.

Review all of First and Second Grade Work.
The Definite Article.
"Ask and Tell," followed by "Asked and Told."
The Progressive Forms of the Verb.
Notes:

> *All* written work to be written in the columns according to the "Six Column Diagram."

> New work and explanations to be given *orally*.

> Oral Work and Written Work to be in the proportion of 3 to 2.

> Neatness and accuracy to be required in all exercises and at all times.

Original Exercises—Oral and Written.

> News, Questions, Letters, Reproductions of stories read, and stories told.

Reading Books: Miss Sweet's No. 2.

> Miss Hammond's No. 1.

> Supplementary Reading also.

Nature Lessons.
Number Work: Number Primer, "Gibbs."

> Practical Problems—using numbers to 100.

Conversation Daily.

## FOURTH GRDAE.

### MISS WOODCOCK.

Review rapidly all of First, Second, and Third Grade Work.
Here, There.
The Expletives—There is.  There are.

| some. | something. | somebody |
| any, | anything, | anybody, |
| none, | nothing, | nobody. |

Comparison of Adjectives.
Interrogative: Which....?
The use of :

| While......, | When......, |
| Before......, | After......, |

he following expressions:

    to set the table,
    to wash the dishes,
    to make the fire,
    to pump some water,
    to get some water,
    to sweep.....
    to scour the knives,
    to dust,
    to pare potatoes,
    to get into bed,
    to scrub the floor,
    to empty,
    to stitch on the machine,
    to dig a hole.
    to plant....,
    to hoe,
    to harness a horse,
    to milk a cow,
    to saw some wood,
    to split some wood,
    to cut down,
    to mend,
    to build,
    to make a.....
    to feed,
    to water,
    to rake, etc.

Iames of work in sloyd room:

    to hammer,
    to drive a nail,
    to sharpen....,
    to put in a screw,
    to saw,
    to plane,
        etc.

Time Expressions:

| | |
|---|---|
| two years ago, | last year, |
| a week ago last ......, | a week from ......, etc. |
| at once. | before ......, |
| for a long time, | after ......, etc. |

The Conditional *if*.

The Participial Constructions:

    to go skating,

    to go swimming,

    saw ...... flying, etc.

    to stop playing, etc.

    ......fond of playing, etc.

    tired of playing, etc.

    ...... heard ......talking, etc.

The Pronouns:

| mine, | hers, | his, |
|---|---|---|
| yours, | theirs, | ours. |

Compound Personal Pronouns:

| myself, | himself, | herself, etc. |
|---|---|---|

The Expressions :

| a piece of ......, | one of ......, |
|---|---|
| a slice of ......, | some of ......, |
| a pair of ......, | any of ......, |
| a loaf of ......, | more of ......, |
| a glass of ......, | a part of ......, |
| a lump of ......, | the rest of ......, |
| the top of ......, | the bottom of ......, |
| the front of ......, | the back of ......, |
| the side of ......, | each of ....... |

The Habitual Present Tense of Verbs.

*But* (conjunction).

    (a) Comparison ex.  Your dress is brown but mine is blue.

    (b) Contrary to—ex.  You told Henry to open the door but he opened a
        window.

The Expressions :

    to intend to ....,

    to pretend to ......,

    to pretend that ......,

| except, | until, | instead of. |
|---|---|---|

    would rather go,

    would rather have,

    would rather stay, etc.

| out of breath, | in a hurry, |
|---|---|
| made a face at ......, | pointed at ......, |

| | |
|---|---|
| had to ......, | began to ......, |
| tried to ......, | had on ......, |
| tied ...... with a ribbon, | led .... with, |
| held up ...... by ......, | led ...... by. |

Adjectives that resemble verbs in form.

| | | | |
|---|---|---|---|
| sleepy, | dead, | shut, | torn, |
| asleep, | alive, | open, | broken. |

Notes: Special attention to be paid to the Speech at all times.
   Oral and Written work to be in proportion of 3 to 2.

Reading: Miss Hammond's No. 2,
   Nature Stories from "September to June,"
   "Classic Stories for Little Ones,"
   "Robinson Crusoe,"
   The Dog of Flanders,
   Graded Classics No. 2.

Speech Reading—Special exercises to be written up.

Arithmetic—Winslow's Natural Arithmetic, Part 1.

Original Exercises: News, Letters, Reproduction of stories read and stories told.

Questions—to bring out reasoning and judgment in answers.

Exercises to cultivate the imagination: Imaginary conversations, etc.

Nature Lessons.

Geography: Points of compass.

   Direction, etc.

   Stories of people in other countries.

History: Stories of United States History for Youngest Readers to be read.

## D. C. B. A. ROTATING CLASSES.

Language,
Reading,      } Miss Grimm.
Grammar,

Arithmetic,
Speech Reading, } Miss Balch.

Speech,
Geography,
History—U. S.,      } Miss Russell.
Physical Geography,
History—English.

## D GRADE.

Language: Work up any point in previous year's work that pupils are weak
The Perfect Tenses of Verbs—following Mr. Davidson's plan.
Conjugation of verbs in all forms and tenses.
Relative Pronouns.

Common Idioms and Expressions:

| | |
|---|---|
| to cut out, | to hem, |
| to baste, | to try on, |
| to fit, | to press, |
| to buy, | to sell, |
| to own, | to trade, |
| to pay to, | to pay for. |
| too large, | too small, |
| too tight, | worn out, |
| wrong side out, | right side out. |
| to look like, | to look nice, |
| to wipe dry, | to rub bright. |

The Interrogative *How?*

| | |
|---|---|
| to do it again, | to go on an errand, |
| to take a trip to, | to use, |
| to catch fire, | to set fire to, |
| to give it up, | to take cold. |
| to have a picture taken, | to upset, |
| to get a scolding, | to turn over, |
| to get a whipping, | to waste time, |
| to catch up, | to set out, |
| to take aim, | to walk in, |
| to take a seat, | to get out of the way, |
| to call on, | to get home, |
| to take ...... choice ......, etc. | |

Reading: "Robinson Crusoe,"
"Stories for Language Study,"
"Little Lame Prince."
"The Dog of Flanders."
Graded Classics—No. 3.
Supplementary Reading:
Stories of Indian Children.

Nature Study.

Geography: Morton's Elementary.
    "Fairbanks' Home Geography."

History: Hazen's United States History.
    Supplementary Reading.

Arithmetic: Winslow's Natural Arithmetic, Part 1.

Speech Reading: Stories.
    Information Lessons.

Speech:
    Special drill upon defects in articulation and voice.
    Concert recitations.
    Special attention to be given to speech in *all* recitations.

Written tests to be given for study hour work and from time to time in class room.

## C CLASS.

Language: Review any work in Language Outline that may be necessary, especially the perfect tenses and conjugation of verbs in all forms.

Grammar: Longmans' School Grammar—Part 1.

Reading: Robinson Crusoe.
    Little Lame Prince.
    Bob Tail Dixie.
    Child of Urbino.
    The Golden Touch.
    Graded Classics—No. 4.
    King of the Golden River.
    Stories of Indian Children.

Nature Study.

History—Hazen's United States.
    Supplementary Reading.

Geography: Morton's Elementary Geography,
    Fairbanks' Home Geography.

Arithmetic: Winslow's Natural Arithmetic—Part 2.

Speech Reading: Stories and Information Lessons.

Speech: Special drill upon defects in articulation and voice.
    Concert recitations.
    Special attention given to speech in all recitations.

Written tests from time to time.

## B CLASS.

Language: Review Work on Perfect Tenses of Verbs.
Conjugation in all forms.

Grammar: Longmans' School Grammar.

Reading: Robinson Crusoe.
Stories of Indian Chieftains.
Child of Urbino.
Graded Classics—No. 5.
Bob Tail Dixie.
Rip Van Winkle.
The Great Stone Face.

Nature Study.

History: Higginson's United States.
Supplementary Reading.

Geography: Frye's Grammar School Geography.

Arithmetic: Winslow's Natural Arithmetic—Part 2.

Speech Reading: Information Lessons.

Speech: Drill upon defects in articulation and voice.
Special attention to speech in *all* recitations.

Written tests from time to time.

## A CLASS.

Geography: Frye's Grammar School Geography completed.

United States History completed.

Physical Geography: Houston's begun.

English History: Higginson's begun.

Grammar.

Reading: Robinson Crusoe.
Stories of Our English Grandfathers.
The Children's Shakespeare.
The Courtship of Miles Standish.
The Legend of Sleepy Hollow.
Evangeline.

Nature Study.

Arithmetic: Winslow's Natural Arithmetic.

Speech Reading

Speech.

GIRLS' LIBRARY.

## BOYS.

| NAME OF PUPIL. | RESIDENCE. | DATE OF ADMISSION. |
|---|---|---|
| Arel, Joseph I | Woonsocket | 1900. |
| Anderson, Edward V | Providence | 1896. |
| Bruncell, Berger B | Woonsocket | 1900. |
| Brinkman, Weldon | Providence | 1903. |
| Carr, David | Pawtucket | 1893. |
| Collins, Chester A | Providence | 1893. |
| Cleary, John | Newport | 1899. |
| Colvin, Henry C | Providence | 1903. |
| Flynn, James | Providence | 1894. |
| Finnegan, Francis H | Pawtucket | 1902. |
| Ferris, William A | Woonsocket | 1903. |
| Gardiner, Earl F | Providence | 1901. |
| Gobeille, Antonio | Woonsocket | 1905. |
| Goldman, Samuel | Providence | 1898. |
| Grabert, Herman | Bristol | 1900. |
| Green, Horace W | Westerly | 1905. |
| Hardy, Raymond W | Providence | 1905. |
| Holmes, Thomas | Providence | 1905. |
| Jaswell, Joseph | Greenville | 1906. |
| Johnston, Benjamin F | Kingston | 1899. |
| Kalman, Harry | Pawtucket | 1906. |
| La Rochelle, Joseph | Providence | 1906. |
| McGinn, Joe | Providence | 1906. |
| McCue, John | Providence | 1903. |
| Meehan, Bernard | Woonsocket | 1906. |
| Mitchell, Fred G. | Providence | 1901. |
| Mudrak, William | Geneva | 1894. |
| Myers, Arthur | Providence | 1899. |
| Newberg, Charles A. | Pawtucket | 1899. |
| O'Neill, Maurice | Pawtucket | 1904. |
| Paquin, Adolard | Providence | 1899. |
| Perry, Joseph | Providence | 1898. |
| Roe, Albert C | Hope | 1895. |
| Ruckdeshel, Frederick | Providence | 1905. |
| Shine, Philip | Providence | 1902. |
| Smith, Everett A | Slocumville | 1899. |
| Vigeant, Edward | Pawtucket | 1897. |
| Williams, Charles A | Pawtucket | 1896. |
| Williams, Harold K | Pawtucket | 1899. |

## Cause of Deafness of Pupils in R. I. Institute.

| | GIRLS. | BOYS. |
|---|---|---|
| Congenital | 13 | 9 |
| Measles | 4 | 3 |
| Spinal meningitis | 2 | 4 |
| Scarlet Fever | 2 | 3 |
| Brain fever | 2 | 2 |
| Fall | 1 | 4 |
| Disease of ear | 1 | 1 |
| Adenoid growth | 1 | .. |
| Catarrhal fever | 1 | .. |
| Convulsions | .. | 1 |
| Diphtheria | .. | 1 |
| Fever | 1 | .. |
| Fits | .. | 1 |
| Grippe | .. | 1 |
| Inflammation in Head | .. | 1 |
| Swollen glands | 1 | .. |
| Typhoid fever | .. | 1 |
| Whooping cough | 1 | .. |
| Unknown | 4 | 3 |
| Not deaf but speech defective | .. | 3 |
| | 34 | 38 |

Total 72

# TERMS OF ADMISSION.

The Rhode Island Institute for the Deaf is free to a[ll]
the State, between the ages of three and twenty, wh[o are]
so defective that they are unable to be educated i[n]
hearing, provided they are not mentally incapab[le.]
guardians of deaf children who wish to secure ad[mission]
should apply to the principal for an application b[lank]
should be filled out as carefully as possible and re[turned]
cipal. The parent or guardian will then receive [word of the ad-]
mission of the child, and a date set when the child [may enter]
the school.

The State provides board, instruction, and indust[rial training]
but the parents must provide clothing. Parents a[re requested to see]
that their children are supplied with at least two c[hanges]
throughout, and care taken that their clothing is re[newed from]
time to time as needed. Parents are requested not to [take]
their children out of school at any time except for the re[gular]
Pupils can not afford to lose any time from school or indust[rial work,]
and by being kept out of school they are liable to lose their [place in]
their class, and so will not be able to advance with the rest. [Report]
cards are sent out each month to the parents, informing the[m of the]
standing, health, conduct, etc., of their children. In cases [of sickness]
pupils have the best of care in an infirmary especially prep[ared for]
this purpose, under the care of a physician and nurse, and in [cases of]
serious illness parents are kept informed of the condition [of their]
child. All pupils should be on hand promptly on the first da[y of the]
opening of school in the fall, and also on the day set for their [return]
after the holidays. By a careful observance of these points th[e work]
of organizing and beginning school is much simplified.

All parents, guardians, and interested persons are requested [to]
send us the names of any deaf children who are not in attendan[ce]
at this school, and we will take steps to look them up.

## Calendar for the School Year 1906-1907.

School begins September 11th, 1906, and closes June 21st, 1907.

### HOLIDAYS.

Thanksgiving, November 28th to December 3rd.

Christmas holidays, December 24th, 1906, to January 3rd, 1907.

Washington's birthday, February 22nd.

Easter Holiday, March 28th to April 2nd (including Good Friday and Easter Monday).

Decoration Day May, 30th.

Fall term, 1907, begins Tuesday, September 10th.

Thanksgiving Day from the Wednesday preceding the day appointed to the following Monday.

Christmas holiday, December 24th, 1907, to January 3rd, 1908.

Teachers' Meetings each Monday evening at 8 P. M.

### PUPILS' PARTIES.

September 29th, 1906.
November 24th, 1906.
February 25th, 1907.
April 29th, 1907.

# CHAPTER 332.

AN ACT IN AMENDMENT OF AND IN ADDITION TO CHAPTER 86 OF THE GENERAL LAWS, ENTITLED "OF THE R. I. SCHOOL FOR THE DEAF."

[Passed May 13; 1896.]

*It is enacted by the General Assembly as follows:*

SECTION 1. All children of parents, or under the control of guardians or other persons, legal residents of this state, between the ages of three and twenty years, whose hearing or speech, or both, are so defective as to make it inexpedient or impracticable to attend the public schools to advantage, not being mentally or otherwise incapable, may attend the Rhode Island Institute for the Deaf, without charge, under such rules and regulations as the board of trustees of said institute may establish.

SEC. 2. Every person having under his control any such child between the ages of seven and eighteen years shall cause such child to attend school at said institute for such period of time or such prescribed course, in each individual case, as may be deemed expedient by the board of trustees, and for any neglect of such duty the person so offending shall be fined not exceeding twenty dollars: *Provided*, that if the person so charged shall prove to the satisfaction of said board that the child has received or is receiving, under private or other instruction, an education suitable to his condition, in the judgment of said board, then such penalty shall not be incurred; *provided, further*, that no child shall be removed to said institution or taken from the custody of its parent or guardian except as a day scholar unless such parent or guardian is an improper person to have such custody, and the supreme court in its appellate division shall have jurisdiction in habeas corpus to examine into and revise all findings of said board of trustees under this act.

SEC. 3. Any child having attended said institute a time or course prescribed by said board, upon leaving the institute shall be entitled to receive a certificate of his proficiency from said board.

SEC. 4. This act shall take effect from and after its passage.

Main Building

State of Rhode Island and Providence Plantations.

# Report of the Board of Trustees

OF THE

## RHODE ISLAND

# INSTITUTE FOR THE DEAF,

PRESENTED TO THE

## GENERAL ASSEMBLY

AT ITS

## JANUARY SESSION, 1908.

PROVIDENCE:
E. L. FREEMAN COMPANY, STATE PRINTERS,
1908.

# OFFICERS OF THE INSTITUTE.

## PRINCIPAL.
EDWIN GALE HURD, M. A.

## TEACHERS.
MRS. ANNA C. HURD,

| | |
|---|---|
| M. AGNES GRIMM, | SIBYL B. RICHARDS, |
| GRACE I. RUSSELL, | ELLEN N. WOODCOCK, |
| GRACE A. BALCH, | FRANCES MCCLELLAND, |
| MARION C. HILL, | EUGENIA T. WELSH, |

M. GERTRUDE WATSON.

## SPECIAL TEACHERS.
Teacher of Cabinet Making and Carpentry............WILLIAM T. RASMUSSEN.
Teacher of Drawing and Sloyd........................FLORENCE M. CLEGG.
Teacher of Cooking..................................EVANGELINE DAVIS.
Teacher of Sewing...................................FLORENCE M. CLEGG.
Teacher in Physical Culture (boys)..................ROBERT H. WHITMARSH.
Teacher in Physical Culture (girls) ................URANIA H. STURDEVANT.

## HOUSEHOLD DEPARTMENT.
Matron..............................................MRS. MATILDA A. GOGIN.
Supervisor of Large Girls ..........................URANIA H. STURDEVANT.
Supervisor of Small Girls...........................EVANGELINE DAVIS.
Supervisor of Large Boys............................MARY DANA.
Supervisor of Small Boys............................ANNIE M. SOUTHWORTH.
Nurse ..............................................BERTHA LOWDERMILK.
Night Watch.........................................JANE STUART.
Cook................................................LOUIS COTE.
Janitor.............................................ALFRED J. MCCLINTOCK.

## PHYSICIANS.
Attending Physician.... ............................FRANK L. DAY, M. D.
Oculist and Aurist..................................F. P. CAPRON, M. D.

# REPORT OF THE BOARD OF TRUSTEES.

*To the Honorable the General Assembly, at its January Session, A. D.* 1908.

The Board of Trustees of the Rhode Island Institute for the Deaf respectfully presents the following report for the year 1907:

The expectations of the Board, when in 1906 it secured the services of Mr. and Mrs. E. G. Hurd as managers of the Institute, have been fully realized during the past year. Mr. and Mrs. Hurd are aiming to make the institution rank with the best of its kind in the country, and their experience and training amply qualify them to carry out such a purpose. The Board has felt that it was your desire that no effort be spared to improve the standard of the school, both in regard to its educational field and the home life of its pupils, and it feels that during the past year a considerable and satisfactory advance has been made in these directions. Especially is this true in regard to the important work of caring for the children out of school hours, and giving to them the best possible substitute for home care and training.

New and practical industrial work has been added to the regular school work, such as carpentry and cabinet making for the boys, sewing and cooking for the girls.

The attitude of the teachers toward their duties is evinced by the fact that every one, at her own expense, attended the four weeks' normal course at the Northampton school during the summer. The latest improved methods of teaching deaf children, which are exemplified in that school, have proven invaluable applied to our own classrooms.

The Board is looking forward to further improvement in its institute work as the result of the opening of the new school building, for which an appropriation of $21,000 was made at the January session in 1907. This building is to be a three-story brick edifice, containing nine schoolrooms, and an unfinished assembly room in the third floor. Messrs. Fontaine and Kinnicut, of Woonsocket, are the architects, and the various contracts have been awarded as follows:

| | |
|---|---|
| Contractor and Builder, William Williams...................... | $15,900 00 |
| For Heating, The Allen Fire Department Supply Co.............. | 1,008 00 |
| For Plumbing, The Tierney Colgan Co......................... | 626 00 |
| For Electric Wiring......................................... | 275 00 |

The building is to be ready for occupancy at the end of May, 1908.

The Board respectfully asks for an increase in the annual appropriation for maintenance from $25,000 to $30,000, owing to the increased number of pupils, the addition of three new teachers (two being for industrial work), the increased cost of provisions, and all expenses for general maintenance, and a deficit of $3,191.73 on this year's account, arising from those causes, which has been carried over in part from year to year.

The main building, used for the boarding home, is greatly in need of some improvements, such as electric lighting in place of gas, new hardwood floors in the main rooms, and new equipment in the gymnasium.

In view of the very inadequate playgrounds for the children, your Board has secured an option upon certain property adjoining the Institute. This matter is brought to your attention at this time, because, if this offer is not accepted, the land in the near future will either be taken for residential purposes or held at a greatly increased price.

There has been one change in the membership of the Board during the year, the appointment of Dr. George D. Ramsay in place of Dr. Rowland R. Robinson, of Newport.

### FINANCIAL STATEMENT.

| | | |
|---|---|---|
| Appropriation by General Assembly......................... | | $25,000 00 |
| Bills of 1906 paid in 1907......................... | $3,675 61 | |

| | | |
|---|---:|---:|
| .nd labor | 10,709 | 02 |
| ashes removed | 2,127 | 39 |
| ater | 185 | 91 |
| ghting and hand ironing, also fixtures | 398 | 89 |
| ipection | 7 | 00 |
| ection | 29 | 25 |
| ower for laundry | 74 | 70 |
| e service | 80 | 35 |
| s | 3,998 | 73 |
| | 630 | 63 |
| | 55 | 98 |
| cleaned | 36 | 80 |
| for pupils, shoes, rubbers, etc | 205 | 26 |
| ittendance | 174 | 00 |
| for hospital | 108 | 71 |
| for school | 252 | 70 |
| for laundry and laundry work | 156 | 98 |
| for cabinet shop, tools, lumber, etc | 397 | 16 |
| for kitchen, range, refrigerator | 424 | 61 |
| for sewing room | 43 | 80 |
| for dining room | 72 | 06 |
| e, carpets, curtains, etc | 415 | 58 |
| ld supplies | 361 | 97 |
| eous expenses | 376 | 91 |

$25,000 00

Respectfully submitted,

# REPORT OF THE PRINCIPAL.

*To the President and Board of Trustees of the Rhode Island Institute for the Deaf.*

GENTLEMEN:—I hereby submit to you a report of the affairs of the Rhode Island Institute for the Deaf for the year 1907.

During this period I have canvassed the State thoroughly, and have found, exclusive of the pupils who were already enrolled in the school, thirty-one (31) children either totally deaf or too deaf to be instructed to advantage in the public schools. Admission has been granted to sixteen (16) of these children to our school, and several others we hope will enter before the close of the session; while a few are so young that I have advised against entering them until another school year.

I have no doubt but that there are other children in the State, of whose whereabouts I have not yet learned, who should come to us, and will as soon as the school and its purposes become better known.

We have had, all told, during the year 1907, seventy (70) pupils under our instruction. The method of instruction employed is the Oral Method. The pupils are taught to speak and to understand speech, and will have, when they shall have completed the full course of instruction outlined, a fair command of the English language and what is equivalent to a grammar school education. In addition to this, it is our purpose to train every child in some form of industrial work.

### THE INTELLECTUAL DEPARTMENT.

At the opening of the fall session the pupils were formed into nine classes.

SEWING CLASS.

In all schools for the deaf, from the fact that the instruction must be largely individual and given in detail, the classes must be small and well graded if satisfactory results are to be obtained.

Owing to the erection of a new school building on the site of the old house that had been used for this purpose heretofore, we are using improvised classrooms in various parts of the main building this year, and the school work is necessarily handicapped on this account, but all are manifesting the best possible spirit under these adverse conditions.

It is hoped that the new building provided for by the last General Assembly will be ready for occupancy early in May. The classes are pursuing the work in the development and use of speech and language, and in the studies of arithmetic, geography, history, nature study, reading, and general information, practically as outlined last year, persistent effort being made to have the pupils very thorough in what is attempted.

Future progress will be much surer and more rapid if a thorough foundation is laid.

The classes for the year are arranged as follows, and are under the general supervision of Mrs. Hurd:

Class 1. Teacher, Miss Watson.
Class 2. Teacher, Miss Hill.
Class 3. Teacher, Miss Welsh.
Class 4. Teacher, Miss McClelland.
Class 5. Teacher, Miss Richards.
Class 6. Teacher, Miss Woodcock.

Classes 7 and 8, and a special rotating class, taught by Miss Russell and Miss Balch.

Ungraded class, taught by Miss Grimm.

One entire class has been added this year, which necessitates the employment of an additional teacher, and I consider that we are fortunate in having secured the services of Miss Eugenia T. Welsh, from the North Carolina school. Miss Welch is a teacher of more than

2

usual ability and known success in this line of work, and adds material strength to our corps. Miss Elizabeth Clarke having resigned, Miss Gertrude Watson was appointed in her stead. Miss Watson is a graduate of the normal training class of the Northampton School, and is well equipped for the work.

At the close of the school last June our entire corps of teachers attended the Summer School for Teachers of the Deaf held at the Clarke School. Northampton, Mass.

This summer school was established by the American Association for the Promotion of the Teaching of Speech to the Deaf. It affords a month's course of instruction to teachers, consisting of lectures and class room work with practical study and demonstration of methods with pupils. We feel that our teachers derived great benefit from this course, as well as from the month's stay in the Clarke School, which is a model school in its equipment and the results obtained there are second to none.

### INDUSTRIAL CLASSES.

The time devoted to industrial work has been greatly increased this year. Now all pupils, except the very youngest, have from one to two hours each day in industrial work. The boys have seventeen (17) hours a week of class instruction in cabinet work, carpentry, and sloyd, as compared with four and one-half (4½) hours a week in sloyd heretofore, and both boys and girls have twenty-three (23) hours a week of drawing in place of three (3) a week.

The instruction in sewing has been made more systematic, and classes in cooking have been added. By increasing the time devoted to industrial work we have materially strengthened the character and efficiency of the school. What before were hours of idleness to the pupils are now times of busy and useful employment. These changes can but result in better habits of industry, as well as better order and discipline in the school.

Miss Florence Clegg, a graduate of the Philadelphia School of Design, with three years' experience in the Mystic Oral School.

Mystic, Conn., was appointed teacher of drawing and sewing, and also has a class of the younger boys in sloyd twice a week.

### DRAWING.

We have no room this year that could be set aside for a studio, but Miss Clegg goes from class to class during the morning session of school, giving each class two or three periods a week of instruction in freehand drawing, so that every child in the school now receives this training of eye and hand. She also gives the two classes of boys, taking cabinet work, instruction in mechanical drawing.

### SEWING.

Twice a week two classes of girls receive instruction in sewing. Here the girls are taught the different branches of plain sewing, as well as dressmaking, and have made a number of blouses for the small boys that, with other work done, shows a fair degree of progress.

### COOKING.

The classes in cooking, taught by Miss Evangeline Davis, alternate with the classes in sewing twice a week, giving the girls opportunity to take both branches. The classes are having practical work in cooking, and are given demonstrations with explanations by the teacher. The lessons are made interesting to the pupils, and they seem to be making much progress in this important and useful art. The room used for this purpose is entirely too small, and the equipment inadequate, but with the expenditure of a comparatively small sum this can be remedied another year.

### CABINET MAKING.

Mr. William T. Rasmussen, for several years instructor in cabinet making at the Sockanosset Reform School, was appointed to take charge of this feature of industrial work in our school, and a temporary room has been fitted up with a limited number of benches and suitable tools.

We expect another year to use a larger, better lighted room in the basement of the new addition to the school building. Two classes of boys are receiving daily instruction in this industry. While not engaged with these classes the instructor is occupied in making general repairs about the buildings.

## SUNDAY.

On Sunday, as heretofore, the Catholic children attend school at the Holy Name Church, a short distance from the Institute, on Camp street, while the Protestant children all attend service, under the supervision of one of the teachers, at the Congregational church next door. The Protestant pupils also have Sunday-school at the Institute for one hour, forming four classes, and are taught by the teachers of the school. In the evening another hour is devoted to reading under their supervision. We have been obliged to discontinue, for a time, the regular chapel services in the afternoon while the new school building is being erected.

## THE SUPERVISION OF PUPILS.

The supervision of the pupils under our charge is a matter of so much importance that I take occasion to speak of it here.

The duties of the supervisor consist of the care of the pupils at all times when not in school or engaged in industrial work. From the time they arise in the morning until they retire at night this constant supervision is necessary. Good supervision consists not only in seeing that the pupils refrain from doing harmful things, but in training them to do the things that normal children do and to enjoy the sports and physical activities which other children enjoy. Out-of-door games furnish some of the most useful means of securing a healthful moral and physical well-being. In all weather when not actually storming we make it a point that the pupils shall go out for a time for a brisk walk if no more. In the evening, after the study hour, the older pupils, under the care of the supervisor, spend an hour in reading or in some occupation or amusement in which they

DINING ROOM.

are interested. On two evenings in the week, this hour is spent in playing basket-ball, or other forms of exercise in the gymnasium.

## THE BUILDINGS.

During the past summer the walls of the central part of the main building, the infirmary rooms, and the boys' sitting room received a new finish. The floors were also oiled or shellacked, thus making this portion of the main building more healthful and more easily kept in good sanitary condition. The gymnasium apparatus has been removed from the assembly room and placed in a large room in the main building, a room more suited for this purpose. To make this room higher, I would suggest that the floor be removed, thus opening it up to the floor below. This would make the room over twenty (20) feet in height, large enough in every way for this purpose.

Another most desirable change would be the substitution of electric lighting for gas in the main building. There is more or less danger of fire with so many gas jets, and as an additional safeguard to the lives and property of all in the building, the installing of electric lights would be a wise precaution.

Shower baths were added in the fall on the boy's side, and we hope to have similar baths added for the girls. Owing to the increase of new pupils it became necessary to purchase a number of new beds and bedding, and more bedding will be needed. There is, however, enough space in the dormitories to accommodate all the pupils that may attend for years to come.

## HEALTH.

The health of the pupils has been very good, there being no cases of serious illness during the entire year. By providing an abundance of nourishing food, and compelling pupils to take some vigorous outdoor exercise each day, we are enabled to secure and keep a good state of health among them. For further information on this point I refer you to the physician's report on another page. .

## MORE GROUND NEEDED.

The present place for playground is insufficient. There is not space enough for base-ball and foot-ball, and other out-of-door games of this nature can not be indulged in satisfactorily. I would therefore recommend the purchase of the land in the rear of the Institute as a very desirable acquisition to our present grounds.

I consider the following to be the immediate future needs of the Institute:

Additional ground.
. Electric lighting for Main Building.
The enlargement of the Gymnasium.
New equipment for Gymnasium.
Additional equipment for Cabinet Shop and Cooking Class Room.
An additional bath for the use of the Infirmary.
Additional shower baths and dressing rooms.
New gutters and down pipes for the Main Building.
New shades for windows in Main Building.
Painting and re-finishing of walls.
New floors in part of Main Building.
New walk connecting Boiler House with Main Building.

In closing this report, permit me to thank you for the ready assisttance given me at all times, and for the interest you have shown in the progress and welfare of the Institute.

Respectfully submitted,

EDWIN G. HURD,

Providence, January 1st, 1908.

# PHYSICIAN'S REPORT.

*To the Trustees of the Rhode Island Institute for the Deaf:*

I have the honor to report that, during the year past, the health of the children has been unusually good. There have been no epidemics, and but little illness of any kind. An occasional case of tonsillitis and a few cases of disturbance of the gastro intestinal tract, with some minor injuries, were all that required attention during the early part of the year, while there were a few mild cases of Influenza and colds later.

The officers have been most faithful in caring for the sick children, and have my thanks for their zealous co-operation.

Respectfully submitted,

FRANK L. DAY, M. D.

PROVIDENCE, R. I., December 31st, 1907.

## Pupils in Attendance During the Year Ending Dec. 31, 1907.

| NAMES OF PUPILS. | RESIDENCE. | DATE OF ADMISSION. |
|---|---|---|
| Aubin, Eva | Mapleville | 1904 |
| Bagley, John | East Providence | 1907 |
| Bassett, Genevieve | Mossup Valley | 1898 |
| Blake, Helen | Newport | 1907 |
| Blanchard, Joseph | Chepachet | 1907 |
| Brennan, Sarah | Pawtucket | 1900 |
| Brinkman, Weldon | Providence | 1903 |
| Bruncell, Berger | Woonsocket | 1900 |
| Bryer, Lydia | Newport | 1903 |
| Burke, Sarah | Providence | 1902 |
| Cleary, George | Newport | 1907 |
| Cleary, John | Newport | 1899 |
| Collins, Chester | Providence | 1893 |
| Colvin, Henry | Providence | 1904 |
| Davis, Elsie | East Providence | 1897 |
| Derosier, Rosea | Forestdale | 1903 |
| Desantels, Rosie | Centerdale | 1906 |
| Eidelberg, Rosie | Providence | 1905 |
| Epstein, Esther | Arctic | 1905 |
| Ferris, William | Woonsocket | 1903 |
| Finnegan, Frank | Pawtucket | 1902 |
| Flynn, James | Providence | 1894 |
| Forthier, Angelina | Pawtucket | 1898 |
| Gardiner, Earle | Providence | 1901 |
| Gobeille, Antonio | Woonsocket | 1903 |
| Goldman, Samuel | Providence | 1898 |
| Green, Horace | Westerly | 1905 |
| Grimes, Mary | Providence | 1895 |
| Hardy, Raymond | Providence | 1905 |
| Holborgen, Trina | Pawtucket | 1898 |
| Jaswell, Joseph | Greenville | 1906 |
| Johnson, Ben | Kingston | 1899 |

| NAMES OF PUPILS. | RESIDENCE. | DATE OF ADMISSION. |
|---|---|---|
| Kingsley, Eleanor | Hope | 1903 |
| Lindsey, Mary | Providence | 1903 |
| Livingston, Margaret | Pawtucket | 1907 |
| Martin, Sarah | Providence | 1907 |
| McAuliffe, Lorna | Providence | 1906 |
| McCue, Johnnie | Providence | 1903 |
| Meehan, Bernard | Woonsocket | 1906 |
| McGinn, Joseph | Providence | 1906 |
| Mitchell, Frederick | Providence | 1901 |
| Mitchell, Howard | Oakland | 1907 |
| Mudrak, William | Geneva | 1894 |
| Mulcahey, Francis | Providence | 1907 |
| Myers, Arthur | Providence | 1907 |
| Newburg, Charles | Pawtucket | 1899 |
| O'Neill, Maurice | Pawtucket | 1904 |
| Pelletier, Eva | Manville | 1904 |
| Paquin, Adolard | Providence | 1899 |
| Plante, Juliette | Providence | 1905 |
| Quirk, Mabel | Woonsocket | 1904 |
| Roe, Albert | Hope | 1895 |
| Roberts, Lucia | Providence | 1904 |
| Rector, Miriam | Pawtucket | 1907 |
| Rogers, Emma | Auburn | 1907 |
| Romagnano, Frank | Providence | 1907 |
| Ruckdeshell, Fritz | Providence | 1905 |
| Rudolph, Victoria | Pawtucket | 1907 |
| Shine, Philip | Pawtucket | 1902 |
| Smith, Everett | Slocumville | 1899 |
| Sweet, Fannie | Slocumville | 1899 |
| Taylor, Sarah | Harmony | 1907 |
| Tanglais, Eustache | Providence | 1907 |
| Thompson, George | Providence | 1893 |
| Wilcox, Olive | East Providence | 1899 |
| Williams, Margaret | Pawtucket | 1902 |
| Williams, Charles | Pawtucket | 1896 |
| Williams, Harold | Pawtucket | 1899 |
| Wood, John | Pawtucket | 1906 |
| Yuppa, Concetta | Providence | 1898 |

2

## Cause of Deafness of Pupils in R. I. Institute.

| | GIRLS. | BOYS. |
|---|---|---|
| Congenital | 12 | 9 |
| Measles | 5 | 2 |
| Spinal meningitis | 4 | 3 |
| Scarlet fever | 2 | 2 |
| Brain fever | 2 | 2 |
| Accident | 1 | 2 |
| Disease of ear | 1 | 3 |
| Convulsions | | 1 |
| Diphtheria | | 1 |
| Fever | 1 | |
| Fits | | 1 |
| Grippe | | 2 |
| Diseased glands | 1 | |
| Typhoid fever | | 2 |
| Unknown | 5 | 6 |
| Totals | 34 | 36 |

Grand Total ................70.

# TERMS OF ADMISSION.

The Rhode Island Institute for the Deaf is free to all children in the State, between the ages of three and twenty, whose hearing is so defective that they are unable to be educated in schools for the hearing, provided they are not mentally incapable. All parents or guardians of deaf children who wish to secure admission for a child should apply to the principal for an application blank. This blank should be filled out as carefully as possible and returned to the principal. The parent or guardian will then receive notice of the admission of the child, and a date set when the child should be sent to the school.

The State provides board, instruction, and industrial training free, but the parents must provide clothing. Parents are urged to see that their children are supplied with at least two changes of clothing throughout, and care taken that their clothing is replenished from time to time as needed. Parents are requested not to ask to take their children out of school at any time except for the regular holidays. Pupils can not afford to lose any time from school or industrial work, and by being kept out of school they are liable to lose their place in their class, and so will not be able to advance with the rest. Report cards are sent out each month to the parents, informing them of the standing, health, conduct, etc., of their children. In cases of illness, pupils have the best of care in an infirmary especially prepared for this purpose, under the care of a physician and nurse, and in case of serious illness parents are kept informed of the condition of their child. All pupils should be on hand promptly on the first day of the opening of school in the fall, and also on the day set for their return after the holidays. By a careful observance of these points the task of organizing and beginning school is much simplified.

All parents, guardians, and interested persons are requested to send us the names of any deaf children who are not in attendance at this school, and we will take steps to look them up.

# Calendar for the School Year, 1907-1908.

---

School begins Wednesday, September 11th, 1907.
School closes Friday, June 19th, 1908.

## Holidays.

Thanksgiving, 1907, from Wednesday, November 27th, to Monday, December 2d.
Christmas Holidays, from Friday, December 20th, 1907, to Monday, January 6th.
Washington's Birthday, Saturday, February 22nd.
Easter Holidays, from Thursday April 16th, to Tuesday, April 21st.
Decoration Day, Saturday, May 30th.

Fall term, 1908, begins Tuesday, September 8th.

Thanksgiving, 1908, from Wednesday, November 26th, to Monday, November 30th.

Christmas Holidays, 1908, begin Thursday, December 24th, continuing to the following Monday, January 4th, 1909.

# CHAPTER 332.

AN ACT IN AMENDMENT OF AND IN ADDITION TO CHAPTER 86 OF THE GENERAL LAWS, ENTITLED "OF THE R. I. SCHOOL FOR THE DEAF."

[Passed May 13, 1896.]

*It is enacted by the General Assembly as follows:*

SECTION 1. All children of parents, or under the control of guardians or other persons, legal residents of this state, between the ages of three and twenty years, whose hearing or speech, or both, are so defective as to make it inex-pedient or impracticable to attend the public schools to advantage, not being mentally or otherwise incapable, may attend the Rhode Island Institute for the Deaf, without charge, under such rules and regulations as the board of trustees of said institute may establish.

SEC. 2. Every person having under his control any such child between the ages of seven and eighteen years shall cause such child to attend school at said institute for such period of time or such prescribed course, in each individual case, as may be deemed expedient by the board of trustees, and for any neglect of such duty the person so offending shall be fined not exceeding twenty dollars: *Provided*, that if the person so charged shall prove to the satisfaction of said board that the child has received or is receiving, under private or other instruction, an education suitable to his condition, in the judgment of said board, then such penalty shall not be incurred; *provided, further*, that no child shall be removed to said institution or taken from the custody of its parent or guardian except as a day scholar unless such parent or guardian is an improper person to have such custody, and the supreme court in its appellate division shall have jurisdiction in habeas corpus to examine into and revise all findings of said board of trustees under this act.

SEC. 3. Any child having attended said institute a time or course prescribed by said board, upon leaving the institute shall be entitled to receive a certificate of his proficiency from said board.

SEC. 4. This act shall take effect from and after its passage.

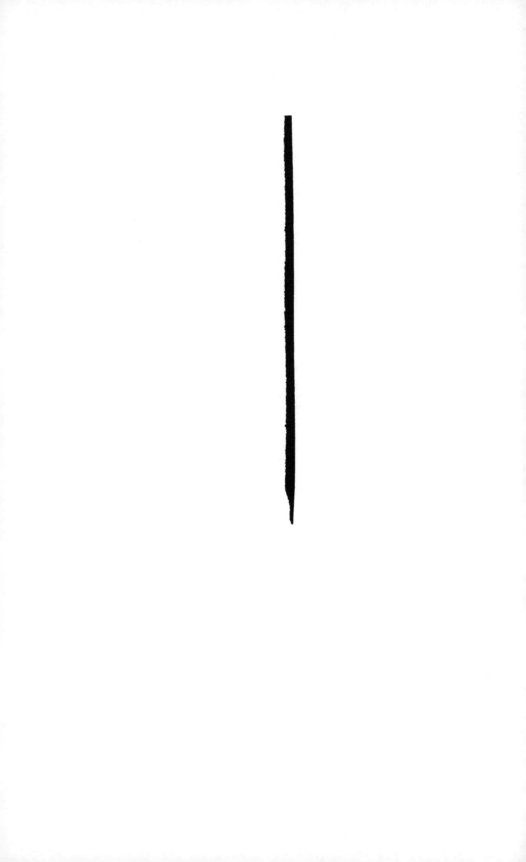

the cause of deaf-mute inst
of an edifice which for all ti
training of the deaf childr
for rejoicing to the frien
more especially to the deaf
the blessed privilege of recei
ngratulate the State, I congrat
ssociates of the Board of Direct
children who shall be here b
ghtenment upon the splendid
ommodious and admirably des
dedicated for all time to the
less cordially and sincerely. I
ving secured as the executive
ll trained and so energetic and
reful. intelligent, and skillful r
tain the highest possible success
Rhode Island has ever stood in
an progress. Here the earl
enjoyment of that liberty of

# ADDRESS

DELIVERED BY DR. A. L. E. CROUTER, SUPERINTENDENT OF THE PENNSYLVANIA
INSTITUTE FOR THE DEAF, MT. AIRY. PHILADELPHIA, PA., AT THE CERE-
MONIES ATTENDING THE LAYING OF THE CORNER-STONE OF THE
NEW SCHOOL BUILDING AT THE RHODE ISLAND INSTI-
TUTE FOR THE DEAF, JANUARY 28TH, 1908.

— ·· — ·· —

*Mr. President, Members of the Board of Directors, and Ladies and ,
Gentlemen:*

We are met to-day on an occasion of great interest and importance,
in the cause of deaf-mute instruction—the laying of the corner-
stone of an edifice which for all time is to be devoted to the education
and training of the deaf children of Rhode Island.  It is an occasion for rejoicing to the friends of human progress everywhere,
but more especially to the deaf of this State who may hereafter enjoy the blessed privilege of receiving instruction within its walls.  I
congratulate the State, I congratulate you,  Mr. President, and your
associates of the Board of Directors, and the parents and friends of
the children who shall be here brought together for instruction and
enlightenment upon the splendid prospects awaiting you when this
commodious and admirably designed building shall be completed
and dedicated for all time to the cause of humanity, and lastly, but
not less cordially and sincerely, I congratulate you, Mr. President, on
having secured as the executive head of your school a gentlemen so
well trained and so energetic and capable as Mr. Hurd, under whose
careful, intelligent, and skillful management your school is sure to
attain the highest possible success in all its departments.

Rhode Island has ever stood in the forefront of human liberty and
human progress.  Here the early settlers of New England, denied
the enjoyment of that liberty of conscience which they had fled the

mother land to secure, sought and obtained, in the primeval forests and among its original inhabitants, entire spiritual and religious freedom; here many of the commercial and civic problems that have vexed our country have been wisely and permanently solved; here educational privileges of the most liberal and unfettered character have ever been enjoyed by all classes of citizens; here, too, in this very city, struggling to secure public recognition, the first inspirations to the friends of oral methods of instructing the deaf in America were received through the achievements of a loving mother in teaching her afflicted child to speak and read the lips; and here to-day we witness a step which has for its aim the uplifting and enlightenment of all of her silent children for all time to come. At such a time and upon such an occasion I count it a high honor and privilege to be permitted briefly to present the cause of deaf-mute instruction to your consideration.

Let us at the very outset understand what is meant by a school for the instruction of deaf children. It is simply a school (boarding or day) or an institution in which are gathered together a class of children too deaf to be educated in the public schools. It is in no sense, as some erroneously think, a *home* for the care of the infirm, nor an *asylum* or *hospital* for the treatment of the suffering, nor a *reformatory* for the reformation of the delinquent and incorrigible, nor yet a school for the care and training of the mentally deficient. It is a school maintained simply and solely for the instruction of deaf children, and for nothing else. The deaf are not defectives in the general acceptation of the term, which, when applied to a class or to an individual, always carries with it the idea of inferiority, especially of mental deficiency. With opportunity for development and culture the mental faculties of the deaf become as keen and as rich as are those of any other class of children. As with all children of good natural capacity, the question of their mental development is simply one of opportunity and environment. It is true deafness is a defect, but so also are lameness, a diseased liver, a weak heart, forgetfulness, and many other imperfections of body and mind. Few, if any, of us are quite free from all physical and mental defect, but, because of such imperfection, we should hardly enjoy being termed defectives or designated as belonging to the defective classes—the delinquent, the incorrigible, or the feeble-minded, for instance.

Understanding, then, the nature of the work of our special schools for deaf children, let us pass to a consideration of their numbers, the causes of their deafness, and the various methods that have been devised for their instruction.

People generally are not aware of the number of those whom the world calls deaf and dumb. Dr. Alexander Graham Bell, in his very able tabulation of the census of 1900, relating to the deaf and blind, states, that, of the total population at that time, about 75,000,000, 89,287 were returned as being deaf and 51,861 as being partially deaf. The total population at this time is probably nearly 90,000,000, of which, if the percentage of deafness remains the same as in 1900, there must be at the present time in this country about 100,000 deaf persons, of whom 42,000 are totally deaf and 58,000 partially deaf.

These figures, however, include any and all persons who were deaf in 1900 and those who may be deaf at the present time—those born deaf, those deaf after birth, those partially deaf, and those who are semi-mute—without reference to age, cause or degree of deafness. The partially deaf and the semi-mute constitute a class differing psychologically very greatly from the born deaf and those who become deaf at an early age, say before they are three years old. In their mental processes and in their care and training they differ so little from children of perfect hearing that they ought never, for purposes of instruction, to be included in any enumeration of the congenital or the early adventitious deaf. If, therefore, we eliminate the partially deaf, the hard-of-hearing deaf, the semi-mute, youths and adults who have received instruction through their hearing, and who therefore ought not to be included in the class we have under consideration, the number of deaf will be found to be very greatly reduced, probably more than one-half. In Pennsylvania, for instance, we shall find a population of about 4,500 afflicted with what the profession regards as deaf-mutism, 1 to 1,600 of the total population of the State, instead of 9,000, 1 to 835, and in Rhode Island the total deaf population, fit subjects for instruction in your special school, will be about 300 instead of 600. Of the total deaf population, of this state, 300, from 80 to 100 are of school age at the present time, and about 70 of them, a very remarkable proportion, are now under instruction in this school. This latter ratio of one deaf person to about every 1,500 or 1,600 of the total population is, I believe, more nearly correct for our purposes, and will be adhered to in what I shall have to say upon the subject to-day.

In foreign countries the proportion of deafness to the general population is much greater than in our own country, the ratio being as high in some places as 1 to 800. Especially is this true of mountainous regions, such as Switzerland and Bohemia, and in certain elevated regions of Asia and South America. The estimated deaf population of China and India is very great. In the former it is 200,000, in the latter from 75,000 to 100,000.

Of the total deaf population in the United States there are, according to the latest statistics upon the subject, under instruction in our special schools to-day about 12,000 children, twenty-five per cent. of the whole number; 1,500 teachers are employed in their instruction, and 137 schools (boarding and day), representing an investment of nearly 15,000,000 dollars, are maintained at an annual outlay of over three and one-quarter millions of dollars on account of tuition and support. The whole number of children who have received instruction in our American schools for the deaf is nearly 56,000.

The average cost of maintaining and educating deaf children in the various schools of the country is about $275 per pupil; more than this in some schools, and less in others. The amount will be found to vary according to the equipment of the school and the provision made for the care and instruction of its pupils. As a rule the per capita cost will be found highest in our best schools. Poor schools come cheap, but they never pay. They are always found to be a bad investment. One of the chief reasons for what may be considered by some a high per capita cost for the maintenance of a school for deaf children is the absolute necessity of maintaining small classes. In some of our schools ten pupils is considered a sufficient load for any teacher to carry; in some even a less number is considered highly advisable.

You will find our best schools conducting the work of instruction in small classes. In fact, other things being equal, it may be laid down as a maxim that the smaller the class the better the work. Then again, teachers of the deaf, good teachers, enthusiastic teachers, come high. It can not be expected that a young man or woman of good education, after spending years in securing her professional training, will labor for little or nothing; they should be well paid, and should hold their positions for merit only. Small classes, well-paid teachers, and careful household provision for the needs and comforts of the pupils make the average cost of maintaining our special schools for the instruction of deaf children come seemingly high. But it is money wisely expended. Far better maintain good schools for their instruction and training in their childhood and youth, making them self-supporting, self-respecting citizens, than maintain almshouses and prisons for their care and correction in adult life when left uneducated.

The causes of deafness are various, and presumably the same to-day as five hundred or a thousand years ago, although, owing to the great advance made in medical science and in the general intelligence of the people, the proportion of the population affected is undoubtedly much less than formerly. Assuming that the causes of deafness among the pupils at the Mt. Airy School are similar to the causes that obtain the country over (there is no good reason why they should greatly differ), we find as follows in every 500 deaf children: born deaf, 206; deaf from scarlet fever, 47; from meningitis, 40; from falls, 25; from disease of the ear and throat, 23; from measles, 18; from brain fever, 16; from convulsions, 13; from abscesses, 12; from la grippe, 7; from accident (nature not stated), 7; from whooping

cough, 7; from typhoid fever, 6; diphtheria, 6; mumps, 5; from paraly-
sis, 4; marasmus, 4; pneumonia, 2; dentition, 2; chicken-pox, 1;
poisoning, 1; intermittent fever, 1; gastric fever, 1; sickness (nature
not stated), 8; unknown causes, 38.

The chief cause of deafness is seen to be a congenital one. From 35
to 40 per cent. of the pupils attending our schools are deaf born. It
is quite probable that one of the chief causes of congenital deafness is
consanguineous marriage. Especially is this the case when the defect is hereditary in one or the other or in both the families of the
contracting parties. Statistics, carefully collected for years, prove
conclusively that the percentage of born deafness is greatest in families and communities where persons nearly related are permitted to
marry. This is notably true of Jews, Quakers, Menonites and Dun-
kards, both in this country and in Europe, where statistics upon the
subject have been carefully verified. A remarkable instance of
deafness resulting from consanguineous marriages was investigated
by Dr. Bell some years ago on Cape Cod. The intermarriage of the
congenital deaf, particularly in families in which the defect is
hereditary, is also a contributing cause. There is more deafness
traceable to these two causes than to all other causes combined, and
it is greatly to be hoped that the time is near at hand when such
unions shall be prohibited by legislative enactment.

The unfortunate effects of deafness when it occurs in early life
are psychological rather than physiological. They are noticeable
in the retarded mental development, rather than in any lack of physical growth, in those who suffer from the defect. Unless there be
other causes present creating an enfeebled physical condition, the
deaf are known to be as strong, as vigorous, as active, and as long-
lived as the hearing. Insurance companies are coming to insure
them quite as readily, and on quite as generous terms as are those
accorded the hearing. Indeed it has been shown by comparative
tests that the deaf under proper training develop physically quite
as well, in some respects even better than the hearing. Dr. James
Kerr Love, of Glasgow, a well-known authority on the subject, in a

recent work on Deaf-mutism publishèd a series of interesting tests
as to the comparative average height, weight, chest measurement,
and head measurement of a number of lads attending two Glasgow,
Scotland, hearing schools, and a like number of deaf boys under instruction in the school for the deaf in that city, in which an excellent
gymnasium is maintained, and clearly showed that the deaf boys,
far from being physically inferior, were actually superior at most
points of the comparison: they were found to be taller, heavier,
bigger-chested, and, in many instances, bigger-headed. It is not,
therefore, in any physical weakness or discomfort, or disadvantage,
that we are to seek for the almost overpowering calamity which deafness in early life entails, but rather in the stunted, retarded, undeveloped activities of the mind that inevitably follow its infliction.

Usually there is little or nothing in the outward appearance of a
deaf child to indicate to the ordinary observer the nature and serious-
ness of the infirmity under which he labors. He goes about his simple
duties much as normal children do. He eats, sleeps, goes and comes,
engages in games and plays with all the joyous zest that is wont to
accompany active child-life. He feels, and, upon occasion, suffers
hunger and pain; he laughs, cries, endures sorrow and distress, and
experiences many of the joys and happinesses common to human existence without attracting any special attention to his unfortunate
condition.

According to the manner and effectiveness of his early training,
the deaf child is found to be cheerful, affectionate, orderly, obedient,
polite and sociable, or unhappy, peevish, irritable, disobedient, suspicious, and morose and melancholy. He sometimes walks with un-
certain, swaggering gait, especially at night, the cause of which wise
men thus far have been unable satisfactorily to account for. In
passing along the street he frequently shuffles his feet rather more
than hearing children do, and, if closely observed, will be seen to
look forward and backward, to the right and to the left, as if fearful
and watchful of approaching danger. He often makes unfamiliar
and disagreeable noises with his voice simply for the pleasure it

pressions
hievous,
liarities,
, or the
k. It is
haracter
, and, if
ts to his
timately
ods pur-
endeavor
l or sign
gers, or,
produce
nted for
educated
y receive
l.

af man is
in it. Be
ables, for
or from al
mains, als
for great's
is not the
e made of
ess, indi-
envelope
they are
ng fingers
ne expres-
his right
and, so

BOOK HAND EIGHTH

may occur at the seemingly
that free the use of the ha
or ridicule. Their feeblen
their mental disposition not to en
may one result being visu
witheld every exhibit consisti
he truly observed.

The uneducated deaf man may truly h
reason. But is always a foreigner, en
His great difficulty is t
He thinks, but can
He uses a language, natural gestures, all
him. His powers of visual ob
developed, but the speech and lang
undeveloped. Verbal memory to
development of his reasoning faculties
has grown with each day's
much. Then, he thinks, not in wor
things that pass his mental visio
his simple ideas he uses s
to enable him to
Without this natural mea
he and completely c

truly stated that
uninformed intellect
ideas of an overruling
strong, and is absolutely
vine. He may be dil
but it will be owing to
good example not to the
children who hear,
and prone to secret
character is generally char

they can only wonder at the seemingly impassable barriers which separate them from the rest of the human family. Without development or cultivation, if their faculties do not ripen into knavery, and their natural dispositions turn to envy and malevolence, their minds must ever remain barren wastes whence every incentive to duty is withheld, every earthly consolation denied, and every hope of a hereafter totally obscured.

The uneducated deaf man may truly be said to be a man without a country. He is always a foreigner, even among his nearest relatives and friends. His great difficulty is to make himself understood by those about him. He thinks, but can not express his thoughts. He has a language, natural gestures, all his own, but few or none understand it. His powers of visual observation and memory are well developed, but the speech and language centers of his brain remain undeveloped. Verbal memory to him is wholly lacking, but the development of his reasoning faculties, while greatly retarded by his condition, has grown with each day's experiences through sight and touch. Thus, he thinks, not in words, but in pictures, images of the things that pass his mental vision, and therefore when he would express his simple ideas he uses a picture language, natural gestures, or pantomime, to enable him to set forth his thoughts in picture form. Without this natural means of expressing his ideas he would be absolutely and completely cut off from all communication with those about him.

It has been well and truly stated that the uneducated deaf child, by his own unaided, uninformed intellect and uninstructed nature, never arrives at the idea of an overruling Providence, or of what is really right or wrong, and is absolutely ignorant of general law, either human or divine. He may be diligent, affectionate, or even habitually honest, but it will be owing to the influence of kind and firm control and good example, not to the higher moral and religious motives, that actuate children who hear. He may often prove self-willed, passionate, and prone to secret vices, but this unfavorable phase of his character is generally chargeable to early injudicious indulgence, to the example of evil companions, and to the lack of those higher motives that are supplied by religious education. If he is suspicious, it is because he has been made the butt of cruel, thoughtless comrades. If he lacks self-control, it is because he can not appreciate the consequences of his unrestrained actions. When he is thwarted in desires, the folly and criminality of which he cannot appreciate, he is apt to think himself the victim of unjust discrimination and oppression, and to wreak vengeance upon those who oppose and refuse his demands.

While the condition of the deaf has at all times excited the notice of writers and thinkers, their systematic instruction is comparatively of modern origin. The sages of antiquity, with all their wisdom and insight into the promptings of the human soul, never conceived of the possibility of the acquisition of language, either spoken or written, by one deprived of his hearing, and did not hesitate to place one thus afflicted on a level with the idiot and the beasts of the fields.

To the Christian era belongs the glory of the intellectual and social advancement of the deaf. Jerome Cardan, a distinguished philosopher of Padua, Italy, in the early part of the sixteenth century, first advanced the principle that there is no absolute connection between thought and articulate speech; that ideas may be presented to the mind through written characters without any intervention of the sounds of those characters; that hearing is not absolutely necessary to the development of the mental faculties, and that, therefore, a deaf person may be taught to comprehend ideas expressed in written language. History does not inform us whether Cardan demonstrated the correctness of his theory by practically instructing a deaf child or not, but that he was right in his ideas has been abundantly proven in thousands of instances. To Spain, however, where the labors of Pedro Ponce de Leon, first teacher of the deaf, and John Paul Bonet, the inventor of the manual alphabet, won for them merited fame, must be given the credit of the first successful efforts to instruct deaf children. These remarkable men taught their pupils to speak and write several languages. They used what would now be called the oral and manual alphabet method.

From Spain the work spread into Italy, Holland, Portugal, and England, exciting the attention of some of the most profound minds of the time, and thence into Germany and France, enkindling the genius and sympathy of Heinicke and De l'Epee, those devoted men who must ever be regarded as the founders of modern methods of instructing the deaf.

As stated, there are two principal methods of teaching the deaf—the oral, or German, method, founded by Samuel Heinicke, and the manual, or sign, method, or, as it is sometimes called, the French method, founded by the Abbe de l'Epee. Under the former, speech, lip-reading, and writing are the means employed to secure mental development and communication between teacher and taught; under the latter, signs, natural and conventional, finger spelling, and writing are the chief means employed. In either case mental development is the chief end to be attained; all else depends upon that. These two methods are employed often side by side in the same class-room, more frequently and more successfully in separate rooms and in separate schools, to secure the mental advancement of deaf children. In former years sign methods were much more generally pursued in this country than oral, but in later years the oral, or speech, method has made rapid gain in popular favor. Fully two-thirds of the pupils under instruction at the present time are taught by speech methods, and more than half the teachers employed in our American schools are oral, or speech, teachers.

But how, you may ask, may the deaf child be taught to comprehend written language? Practically in the same manner that the hearing child learns to comprehend audible or spoken language. To illustrate, let us take some familiar object, for instance a hat, and, as a learner, a little child who has not yet learned its name, or a foreigner beginning to learn English. The sound of the word *hat*, when first pronounced in the hearing of such a learner conveys no idea or meaning. It is a sound which the child may very readily

5

imitate, but as yet it has to him no signification. Now let the object be pointed out, or held up at the same time its name is pronounced. Let this be done several times. Perception of the object, its form, size, shape, etc., in connection with the sound of its name, now arises in the mind of the child. He repeats the sound or name, and hears it repeated, until it becomes so familiar that he has no difficulty in recognizing the idea of the object whenever he hears its name repeated. It is to be noted that the child conceived no idea from the sound until it was closely associated with the object of which it was the name. Now in like manner, the names of objects are presented to the mind of the deaf child *through the eye.* Pursuing the manual, or sign, method, the hat is submitted. The name is written upon the board or slate, or spelled upon the fingers, and by associating it with the object itself the child soon comprehends that the written or spelled word h-a-t stands for the object of which it is the name, and vice versa upon seeing the object will associate the proper name with it. The eye of the deaf child thus becomes the channel, as the ear is to the hearing child, through which ideas may be conveyed to its mind by means of written characters.

In case oral methods are pursued, the visible forms of the sounds constituting the name of the object are taken from the instructor's lips directly instead of from their written forms on the board or slate. For instance, in this case, holding up the object (giving the sounds), h-a-t; h-a-t, hat, hat, till the name is acquired and reproduced by the child, when, if desired, it may be written upon the slate. Now let it be remembered that when words or ideas are presented to the mind of the deaf child, in their written form, or by means of the manual alphabet, or by signs or gestures, the method of instruction is called the manual, or sign, method; and that when they are presented through the sounds composing them, which sounds the child is trained to imitate and read, the method is called the oral method. In the manual method, signs, writing, and finger spelling are used; in the oral method, the voice and writing are used. The former is the French method, the latter is the German method. For purposes of mental development, it is not to be denied that the manual method possesses many excellent features and is accomplishing much good work in many of our combined, or sign, schools. But to me the oral, or speech, method, the method pursued in your own excellent school, is a vastly superior method in that it is an English language (not sign) method, that it brings the deaf child into closer communion and communication with the hearing world about him, and restores him more nearly and more completely to his family and friends and to society than the sign method possibly can restore him. The oral method gives him all that the manual method possibly can give him, and in addition it gives him the great boon of speech, which more nearly than anything else makes him a part of the great hearing and speaking world about him. Indeed, so greatly am I convinced of the superiority of this method of instruction that, were one of my little ones to become deaf, I should spare no expense, nor time nor labor to teach him to speak, to say "father" and "mother," sweetest words in all language, and to repeat his little evening prayer on closing his eyes for the night's rest.

When, therefore, a child is known to be deaf, from whatever cause, the most important question that presents itself to the attention of relatives and friends is *when* and *where* and *how* shall his education be conducted. Answering the first of these inquiries, I would say that long experience has demonstrated the fact that, with a very few exceptions, from five to seven years is usually the best age at which to begin this most serious and most important task. The child's mind is so alert and receptive, his organs of speech so flexible and easily controlled, and his habits of life so susceptible to surrounding influences that surer and better results follow proper care and instruction at this age than when the work is commenced at an earlier or deferred to a still later period. An earlier period takes the child from his mother's care and direction, a very grave mistake in my opinion, and subjects him to restraints and labored tasks as injurious as they are unwise; while on the other hand, if the work be postponed to a much later period, unfortunate consequences may follow: mental development may be less satisfactory, inferior speech and lip-reading may ensue, and the probability of the child becoming an intelligent, independent, and self-supporting member of the family greatly lessened. My reply to the second part of this question, "where shall the education of a deaf child be conducted?" would be "at home if the circumstances of the family are such as to permit of the expense; if not, at some good, well-managed school, within convenient reach of the family home." There is much that may be said favoring the home instruction of a deaf child, and as much that may be said in favor of the school plan. The reasons usually given in support of private or home training are that superior speech and lip-reading are acquired, that mental development along more natural lines is secured, that freedom from institutional or school life and all that it involves is maintained, and that the cultivation of stronger home ties in consequence of uninterrupted family associations is more generally assured. No doubt a young deaf child enjoying at his home the constant association and instruction of a skillful teacher and knowing no method of communication except by and through speech and lip-reading becomes very expert in the art of reading the lips and very fluent and self-reliant in the use of his vocal organs. No doubt, too, institutional life when it extends through several years, from ten to fifteen and sometimes longer, does tend to weaken family ties and to form very strong attachments for school and class associations, sometimes to the extent of rendering after home life burdensome and unhappy. Nor is it to be denied there are certain habits and tendencies, not altogether of a desirable or happy character, engendered by institutional life, which parents and friends find it difficult to eradicate upon the return of their children to the family circle. These disadvantages, to a certain extent, are inherent in any form of institutional or school life, whether for the deaf or for the hearing, and are therefore unavoidable under the most favorable conditions. But, on the other hand, schools and institutions, under proper management, possess certain advantages that private or home instruction can not provide. As a rule they are better equipped, have apparatus unknown to the family circle, have more efficient teachers, are better regulated, more healthful, and, without resorting to harshness or unkindness, enforce better discipline and secure more studious habits. And to these certain and important advantages in the education of children must be added the always important elements of emulation, ambition, and the mental friction that is aroused by the association of children in the performance of school and class work. All these important elements of school and institutional life are largely wanting in private instruction, whatever other advantages it may possess.

The last part of the question as to how the deaf child's education may best be conducted is perhaps sufficiently answered in what has already been said regarding methods of instruction. But at the risk of repeating I would answer, most undoubtedly by oral methods, and by oral methods alone. Neither signs nor the manual alphabet should form any part in the method of instruction pursued. The attempt sometimes made to combine oral and manual methods in the instruction of a deaf child, under what is styled the Combined System, is, for the production of the best results, a demonstrated failure. If it be desired to establish the speech habit in a deaf child, speech communication must always be insisted on, and all sign communication discouraged and as far as possible prohibited. There should be no halfway measures employed, no pleasing compromises allowed, if the child is to become proficient in speech and lip-reading, making those arts potential factors for purposes of communication with the hearing world, of which he must ever form a part.

I have already referred in a general way to the two chief methods of instructing the deaf and to the principles underlying them. There remains one other method, closely allied to the manual method, to which I must very briefly refer. It is the dactylological, or manual alphabet, method. By it the manual alphabet, invented and first used by *Bonet*, is used for all purposes of mental development and classroom instruction. Signs and natural gestures are absolutely discarded. Name words, action words, and the sentence thought are conveyed to the mind of the child in rapid succession by this means, and the individual results attained compare most favorably with those of other methods. As a means of mental development it possesses many advantages, but as a means of placing a child so taught in open and free communication with the hearing world it is objectionable. Few hearing people know how to spell on the fingers, and fewer still are inclined to learn. Therefore, for the most part, the deaf instructed by this method are compelled to resort to the tedious process of writing, a means of communication that soon becomes fatiguing and wearisome to hearing people. Speech and lip-reading, it is true, are included in this method of teaching, but as they are not made the chief means of instruction, they rarely confer sufficient freedom or fluency of speech to enable deaf children thus educated to communicate orally even with their nearest relatives and friends.

I have thus tried to place before you, with more or less distinctness, the three principal methods of teaching deaf children in our American schools, and with your permission will now pass to another important feature of the work, that of trade-teaching. This work is much emphasized in the majority of our schools at the present time; and every boy and girl in good health is given an opportunity, under expert instruction, to acquire a trade by which to support himself after leaving school. No less than sixty-eight different trades, varying with locality and demand, are to-day taught in our special schools for the deaf, with the view to enable their graduates to become immediately self-supporting; and experience and statistics abundantly prove that deaf students thus trained become faithful, skillful, and satisfactory workmen, earning for themselves and those dependent upon them a comfortable livelihood. It is a fact not generally known, but nevertheless true, that the attention given to this subject of trade-teaching in our American schools for the deaf was the origin of the splendid system of manual training now so popular in nearly all our large centers of population. Fully ninety per cent. of the deaf trained in our special schools to some form of wage-earning are by actual investigation found to be self-supporting. They are found in almost every walk of life in which hearing is not an absolute requisite; they become teachers, ministers, lawyers, doctors, dentists, newspaper men, architects, artists, engravers, civil engineers, chemists, railroad men, electricians, mechanics of various kinds, farmers, etc., etc. They are trained to be industrious and home-loving, and unless driven by dire want are seldom or never found begging in the streets or seeking shelter and support in our alms-houses or at the hands of our numerous charitable organizations.

The deaf man exists not through any fault of his own. However pitiable his condition may be, it is the result of inexorable hereditary law, or of disease or accident. He exists, too, as we have seen, in very considerable numbers, so much so that if left to himself unaided and uneducated he becomes a serious burden and menace to society. In self-protection, therefore, as well as from a sense of Christian and humanitarian duty, it becomes the duty of society or of the State to educate him in the best possible manner. This the State and organized societies, with much labor and at great expense, are now doing after the manner all too briefly here described to you.

The deaf man as he is seen and known to-day is, in a peculiar manner, the direct product of opportunity and environment. He was found ignorant, uneducated, unhappy, miserable. He has been given an opportunity to learn, to acquire an education; he has been surrounded by elevating, civilizing, socializing influences, and he is become a capable, intelligent, moral and social being, comprehending and performing his duties as a man and as a citizen with power and credit to himself and to his family. Not knowing law nor the requirements of law, whether human or divine, he has become God-fearing, obedient and law-abiding. Not appreciating or knowing the necessity of labor, he has acquired habits of industry and has learned to be self-supporting. From being a social vagabond, wandering aimlessly and hopelessly about the land, he has become patient, docile, sociable, and home-loving to a very remarkable de-

State of Rhode Island a[nd]

REPORT OF THE B[OARD]

OF

RHODE

[I]NTITUTE F[OR]

PRESENT

GENERAL

AT

JANUARY S[ESSION]

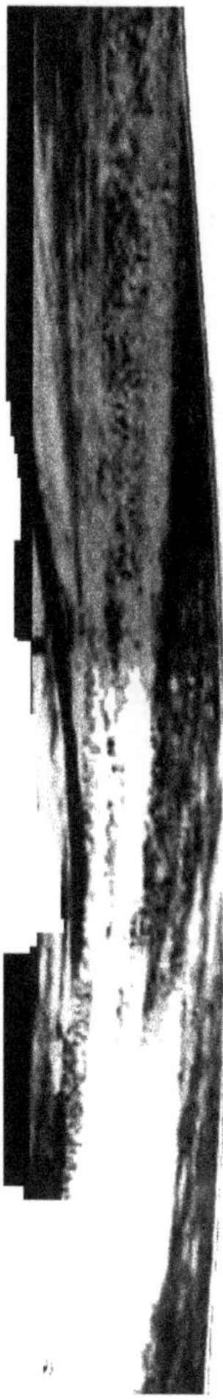

MAIN BUILDING

PROVI[DENCE]

E. L. FREEMAN COM[PANY]

1[9]

State of Rhode Island and Providence Plantations.

# Report of the Board of Trustees

OF THE

## RHODE ISLAND

# INSTITUTE FOR THE DEAF,

PRESENTED TO THE

## GENERAL ASSEMBLY

AT ITS

## JANUARY SESSION, 1909.

PROVIDENCE:

E. L. FREEMAN COMPANY, STATE PRINTERS.

1909.

# RHODE ISLAND

**HOPE STREET,**

UNDER THE SU

# BOARD OF

CONSIST

HIS EXCELLENCY JAMES H. H

HIS HONOR RALPH C. WATRO

WILLIAM H. BAI

MRS. ELLEN T. McC

D. RAMSAY,

LOUISE PROSSER BATES,

GERTRUDE J. JENNINGS,

GEORGE G

GRACE A. BALCH,  
MARION C. HILL,  
SIBYL B. RICHARDS,  

FRANCES I. McCLELAND,  
EUGENIA T. WELSH,  
URANIA H. STURDEVANT.

---

### SPECIAL TEACHERS.

Teacher of Cabinet Making and Carpentry......WILLIAM T. RASMUSSEN.  
Teacher of Drawing and Sloyd.....................FLORENCE M. CLEGG.  
Teacher of Cooking ........................... .....EVANGELINE DAVIS.  
Teacher of Sewing.. ..............................FLORENCE M. CLEGG.  
Teacher in Physical Culture (boys).............ROBERT H.  
Teacher in Physical Culture (girls)............URANIA H. STURDEVANT.

---

### HOUSEHOLD DEPARTMENT

Matron. ...................................................JANE BARCLAY.  
Supervisor of Large Girls............................PAULINE A. CLEGG.  
Supervisor of Small Girls............................EVANGELINE DAVIS.  
Supervisor of Large Boys. ........................ .WINIFRED STOWITTS.  
Supervisor of Small Boys...............................ERVA M. COVEY.  
Nurse......................................................BERTHA LOWDERMILK.  
Night Watch. .................................................JANE STUART.  
Cook...... ...............................................................LOUIS COTE.  
Janitor.........................................ALFRED J. McCLINTOCK.

---

### PHYSICIANS.

Attending Physician.............................FRANK L. DAY, M. D.  
Aurist...............................................EDWARD S. BACON, M. D.

# REPORT OF THE BOARD OF TRUSTEES.

*To the Honorable the General Assembly, at its January Session, A.
D. 1909:*

The Board of Trustees of the Rhode Island Institute for the
Deaf respectfully presents the following report for the year 1908:

The new school building, for which $21,000 was appropriated at
the January session of 1907, was finished in May of the present
year. With abundant light and ventilation, and convenient arrangements for industrial work, the building is well equipped
and admirably adapted for the purposes of a school for the deaf.

The old building was removed and the new one built and furnished within the original appropriation.

The adjoining vacant land acquired during the year will be of
inestimable value as recreation grounds for the pupils, and when
in proper condition will supply a long-felt need.

To teach pupils to express themselves intelligently and with
reasonable clearness; to read the lips and to give them a sound
grammar school education is the aim of the school, and under the
efficient management of Mr. and Mrs. Hurd, assisted by competent
teachers, long strides have been made in this direction.

Industrial training for the boys has been steadily enlarged, and
while it is not expected that every boy will, on leaving the school,
become a carpenter or cabinet-maker, the training of eye and hand
will be of great value.

Sewing, cooking, and household economics as far as possible, are
taught the girls, and commendable progress has been made during
the year by both boys and girls.

It is difficult to adequately express our appreciation of the constant, unselfish attention of Dr. Frank L. Day, who has for many
years devoted so much time to the needs of the Institute.

For maintenance for the year 1909, the Board respectfully asks
for $28,000.

00 00

*io,*

*).*

# REPORT OF THE PRINCIPAL.

*To the President and Board of Trustees of the Rhode Island Institute for the Deaf.*

GENTLEMEN:—I hereby present to you a report of the affairs of the Rhode Island Institute for the Deaf, for the year 1908.

The past year has been marked by continued progress in the intellectual and industrial departments of the Institute. The health of the pupils has been good, and, with the exception of an outbreak of measles, there have been few cases of sickness. For a more detailed report on this point I refer you to the physician's report, on another page.

Owing to the fact that the old school building was torn down to make room for the new building, now erected in its place, we were obliged to use temporary rooms in the main building, where we conducted our school from the opening in the fall of 1907 until its close the following June. Schoolrooms were fitted up in the dormitories, the study rooms, and wherever space could be found. Although these rooms were ill-adapted for this purpose, we were enabled to keep our school together and continue our work. The new building was completed early in the summer, the rooms furnished with new desks and chairs, and was occupied upon the opening of the fall term in 1908. We have had enrolled, all told, during the year, seventy-seven pupils; thirty-six girls and forty-one boys, and I have the names of several other children that will come in soon.

The methods of instruction have been the same as in the past, the oral method being the one employed. An important change was made in the hours of school, upon the opening of school in

oom
1alf.
. M.
ipal
k.
into
er of
This
ivide
cher
on in
1aga.
as to
ches,

and of
pils is
unday-
otestant
ught by
e at one
Chapel
again ou

der Miss
that this
ble condi-
has also
Vednesday
ves, but is

ool course
McArdill,
pupils re-
d work.

At the close of school in June, Miss Grace I. Russell, who had been a teacher in this Institute for eight years, resigned to be married. Miss Gertrude Watson, who had been a teacher here for one year, was obliged to give up work for a time, on account of ill-health, and Miss Agnes Grimm, a teacher for a number of years, did not return.

To fill vacancies thus caused, Miss Mabelle Mallory and Miss Urania H. Sturdevant were appointed, both of whom had received special training for this work.

## INDUSTRIAL CLASSES.

### Sloyd.

We have one class in sloyd, for the younger boys only. In this class they are taught the use of tools, and wood working, as a preliminary step to the more difficult work of the cabinet shop.

### Cabinet Making.

A portion of the large basement in the new school building has been fitted up for a cabinet shop, by building a partition through the centre and laying a floor, all of which was done by the boys, under the direction of the teacher. Not only does the class have systematic instruction in cabinet-work, but in the past year they have made all necessary repairs to furniture, and done much other work of a similar character.

### Sewing.

Two classes in sewing have been continued as heretofore, each class meeting twice a week. The girls in these classes have made good progress, and have shown considerable skill in making various articles of wearing apparel.

### Domestic Science.

There are two classes in cooking. The pupils in these classes have shown much interest in their work, and we are ab'e to report considerable progress here also.

2

s'
ns
ns
re
ng
ed
ion
ave
old
ades
fitted
lls re-
in the
sloyd.
g, and
of the
e main


a week;
tion of
th Miss
uitable

AN ADVANCED CLASS.

ing for the main building; new seats for the chapel; cement floors in the basement, and new bath-tubs for the pupils; grading and fencing of vacant land in the rear; painting the outside woodwork of the main building.

Permit me, in closing this report, to again thank you for the assistance you have given me at all times, and for the interest you have shown in the welfare of the Institute.

Respectfully submitted,

EDWIN G. HURD.

PROVIDENCE, R. I., January 1, 1909.

# PHYSICIAN'S REPORT.

*To the Trustees of the Rhode Island Institute for the Deaf:*

I have the honor to present my report of the health of the school during the year just ended. With the exception of an epidemic of measles, the children have been remarkably well.

Save for three lesser accidents, no medical attendance was required until the end of February, when, a few days after a visit home, one boy developed measles. This case was followed by others, and during March and April there were sixteen cases in the house, all but two being among the pupils. Three of the children had a subsequent broncho pneumonia, one boy being critically ill, with pleurisy superadded. Several of the cases were complicated with middle ear troubles, and were attended by Dr. Capron. There were no deaths from measles nor its complications. There have been two cases of catarrhal jaundice, one being recurrent.

The fall was free from any save trivial illnesses; but one of the larger boys fractured the right arm above the elbow in football; and after the fracture had united and the arm was out of splints, fell, refracturing it. Perfect union again resulted, and there is but slight limitation to free motion, although the fractures involved the elbow joint.

One of the larger girls developed intestinal catarrh before the holidays, was kept in bed and under treatment for a few days, and went home at Christmas. She afterward ran down rapidly, and is now critically ill at her own home. Before the holidays the entire school was vaccinated.

DINING

...terially lightening the burden.

Respectfully subn

FF

PROVIDENCE, R. I., Dec. 31st, 1908.

Thanks are due the entire staff for ready and able assistance freely given at all times, and especially during the measles epidemic.

The teachers have often given willing aid in matters quite outside of their prescribed duties, even cheerfully relinquishing their rooms to accommodate the nurses, and suffering many other inconveniences. Each vied with the other in being helpful, thereby materially lightening the burden.

Respectfully submitted,

FRANK L. DAY, M. D.

PROVIDENCE, R. I., Dec. 31st, 1908.

| NAMES OF PUPILS, | RESIDENCE. | DATE OF ADMISSION. |
|---|---|---|
| Rudolph, Victoria | Providence | 1907 |
| Sweet, Fannie | Providence | 1899 |
| Taylor, Sarah | Greenville | 1907 |
| Wilcox, Olive | East Providence | 1899 |
| Williams, Margaret | Pawtucket | 1902 |
| Yuppa, Concetta | Providence | 1898 |

### BOYS.

| | | |
|---|---|---|
| Arnold, Arthur | Providence | 1908 |
| Bagley, John | East Providence | 1907 |
| Blanchard, Joseph | Pascoag | 1907 |
| Brinkman, Weldon | Providence | 1903 |
| Bruncell, Berger | Providence | 1900 |
| Buckley, Leonard | Central Falls | 1908 |
| Cleary, George | Newport | 1907 |
| Cleary, John | Newport | 1899 |
| Collins, Chester | Providence | 1893 |
| Colvin, Henry | Providence | 1904 |
| Dempster, Thomas | Lonsdale | 1908 |
| Dodge, Samuel | Providence | 1908 |
| Ferris, Willie | Woonsocket | 1903 |
| Finnegan, Frank | Pawtucket | 1902 |
| Flynn, James | Providence | 1894 |
| Gardiner, Earl | Providence | 1901 |
| Gobielle, Antonio | Woonsocket | 1903 |
| Goldman, Sam | Providence | 1898 |
| Green, Horace | Westerly | 1905 |
| Hardy, Raymond | Providence | 1905 |
| Jaswell, Joseph | Greenville | 1906 |
| Johnson, Ben | Kingston | 1899 |
| Lachapelle, Willie | Rockville | 1908 |
| Larochelle, Joseph | Providence | 1908 |
| McCue, Johnnie | Providence | 1903 |
| Meeham, Bernard | Woonsocket | 1906 |
| Mitchell, Fred | Providence | 1901 |
| Mudrake, Willie | Geneva | 1894 |
| Mulcahey, Frances | Providence | 1907 |
| Myers, Arthur | Providence | — |
| Newburg, Charles | Pawtucket | 1899 |

## RHODE ISLAND INSTITUTE FOR THE DEAF.

| NAMES OF PUPILS. | RESIDENCE. | DATE OF Admission. |
|---|---|---|
| O'Niell, Maurice | Pawtucket | 1904 |
| Paquin, Adolard | Providence | 1899 |
| Romagnano, Frank | Providence | 1907 |
| Ruckdeschel, Fritz | Providence | 1905 |
| Shine, Philip | Pawtucket | 1904 |
| Smith, Everett | Slocumville | 1899 |
| Tanglaise, Eustache | Providence | 1907 |
| Williams, Albert | Pawtucket | 1896 |
| Williams, Harold | Pawtucket | 1899 |
| Wood, John | Providence | 1906 |

### *Summary.*

| | |
|---|---|
| Girls | 36 |
| Boys | 41 |
| | — |
| Total | 77 |

GLASS IN CABINET WORK.

Cause of Deafness of Pu|

Congenital..........................|
Scarlet fever.......................
Spinal meningitis..................
Measles.............................
Brain fever.........................
Diseases of ear....................
Accidents...........................
Typhoid fever......................
Fits.................................
Concussion of brain...............
Diphtheria..........................
Fever...............................
Grippe..............................
Catarrh.............................
Pneumonia..........................
Swollen glands.....................
Unknown............................

Totals..............................
Defective speech...................

Total.............

## Cause of Deafness of Pupils in R. I. Institute.

| | Girls. | Boys. |
|---|---|---|
| Congenital | 16 | 12 |
| Scarlet fever | 8 | 2 |
| Spinal meningitis | 2 | 4 |
| Measles | 2 | 2 |
| Brain fever | 1 | 8 |
| Diseases of ear | 1 | 2 |
| Accidents | 1 | 2 |
| Typhoid fever | .. | 8 |
| Fits | .. | 1 |
| Concussion of brain | .. | |
| Diphtheria | .. | |
| Fever | 1 | 1 |
| Grippe | .. | 2 |
| Catarrh | 1 | .. |
| Pneumonia | .. | |
| Swollen glands | 1 | .. |
| Unknown | 0 | 8 |
| | — | — |
| Totals | 35 | 40 |
| Defective speech | 1 | 1 |
| | — | — |
| | 36 | 41 |

Total....................... 77

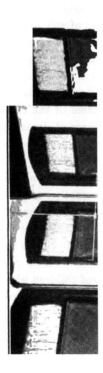

# TERMS OF ADMISSION.

The Rhode Island Institute for the Deaf is free to all children in the State, between the ages of three and twenty, whose hearing is so defective that they are unable to be educated in schools for the hearing, provided they are not mentally incapable. All parents or guardians of deaf children who wish to secure admission for a child should apply to the principal for an application blank. This blank should be filled out as carefully as possible and returned to the principal. The parent or guardian will then receive notice of the admission of the child, and a date set when the child should be sent to the school.

The State provides board, instruction, and industrial training free, but the parents must provide clothing. Parents are urged to see that their children are supplied with at least two changes of clothing throughout, and care taken that their clothing is replenished from time to time as needed. Parents are requested not to ask to take their children out of school at any time except for the regular holidays. Pupils can not afford to lose any time from school or industrial work, and by being kept out of school they are liable to lose their place in their class, and so will not be able to advance with the rest. Report cards are sent out each month to the parents, informing them of the standing, health, conduct, etc., of their children. In cases of illness, pupils have the best of care in an infirmary especially prepared for this purpose, under the care of a physician and nurse, and in case of serious illness parents are kept informed of the condition of their child. All pupils should be on hand promptly on the first day of the opening of school in the fall, and also on the day set for their return after the holidays. By a careful observance of these points the task of organizing and beginning school is much simplified.

All parents, guardians, and interested persons are requested to send us the names of any deaf children who are not in attendance at this school, and we will take steps to look them up.

## Calendar for the Year 1909.

———

Winter Term begins Monday, January 4th.
Term ends Friday, June 18th.
Fall Term begins Tuesday, September 14th.
Fall Term ends Thursday, December 23d.

### HOLIDAYS.

Washington's Birthday, February 22d.
Easter Holidays, Thursday, April 8th, to Monday, April 12th.
Decoration Day, May 30th.
Thanksgiving Holidays, Wednesday, November 24th, to Monday, November 29th.
Christmas Holidays, Thursday, December 23d, 1909, to Monday, January 3d, 1910.

A GYMNASIUM CLASS.

A GYMNASIUM CLASS.

## Rhode Island Institute for the Deaf—Daily Program.

---

Rise (Pupils)............6:15 A. M...................Sunday 6:45 A. M.
Breakfast (Pupils).......7:A. M..................... "    7:30 A. M.
   "    (Teachers) ...7:15 A. M................... "    8:00 A. M.
Chapel .................8:15 A. M...................
School....:...............8:30 A. M...................
Recess...................11:15 to 11:30 A, M ..........
School.......... .........11:30 A. M. to 1:15 P. M .....
Dinner (Pupils)..........1:25 P. M...... .............Sunday 12:30 P. M.
   "    (Teachers)........1:30 P. M................... "    1:00 P. M.
Industrial Work........2:30 to 4:30 P. M..... .. ...
Supper (Pupils)..........6:00 P. M...................Sunday 5:30 P. M.
   "    (Teachers) .......6:30 P. M................... "    6:00 P. M.
Study Hour.............7:00 to 8:00 P. M.............
Bed Time......... ......1st Group, 7:00 P. M.........
   "    ...............2d Group, 8:00 P. M..........
   "    ...............3d Group, 9:00 P. M..........
Sunday Chapel .........8:30 to 9:00 A. M.............
Sunday-School..........9:00 to 10:00 A. M............
Church (Catholics).......9:30 A. M...................
   "    (Protestants)....10:30 A. M...................

and.

M.

TABLEAU.—THANKSGIVING FESTIVAL.

TABLEAU.—THANKSGIVING FESTIVAL.

# CHAPTER 332.

AN ACT IN AMENDMENT OF AND IN ADDITION TO CHAPTER 86
OF THE GENERAL LAWS, ENTITLED "OF THE R. I. SCHOOL
FOR THE DEAF."

[Passed May 13, 1896.]

*It is enacted by the General Assembly as follows:*

SECTION 1. All children of parents, or under the control of guardians or
other persons, legal residents of this state, between the ages of three and twenty
years, whose hearing or speech, or both, are so defective as to make it inexpedient or impracticable to attend the public schools to advantage, not being •
mentally or otherwise incapable, may attend the Rhode Island Institute for the
Deaf, without charge, under such rules and regulations as the board of trustees
of said institute may establish.

SEC. 2. Every person having under his control any such child between the
ages of seven and eighteen years shall cause such child to attend school at said
institute for such period of time or such prescribed course, in each individual
case, as may be deemed expedient by the board of trustees, and for any neglect
of such duty the person so offending shall be fined not exceeding twenty dollars: *Provided,* that if the person so charged shall prove to the satisfaction of
said board that the child has received or is receiving, under private or other
instruction, an education suitable to his condition, in the judgment of said
board, then such penalty shall not be incurred; *provided, further,* that no child
shall be removed to said institution or taken from the custody of its parent or
guardian except as a day scholar unless such parent or guardian is an improper
person to have such custody, and the supreme court in its appellate division
shall have jurisdiction in habeas corpus to examine into and revise all findings
of said board of trustees under this act.

SEC. 3. Any child having attended said institute a time or course prescribed
by said board, upon leaving the institute shall be entitled to receive a certificate
of his proficiency from said board.

SEC. 4. This act shall take effect from and after its passage.

State of Rhode Island and Providence Plantations.

# Report of the Board of Trustees

OF THE

## RHODE ISLAND

# INSTITUTE FOR THE DEAF,

PRESENTED TO THE

## GENERAL ASSEMBLY

AT ITS

## JANUARY SESSION, 1910.

PROVIDENCE:
E. L. FREEMAN COMPANY, STATE PRINTERS.
1910.

# TEACHERS AND OFFICERS.

### PRINCIPAL.
#### EDWIN GALE HURD, M. A.

---

### TEACHERS.
#### MRS. ANNA C. HURD,

LINA HENDERSHOT,  
GRACE A. BALCH,  
OLGA WITTENMEIER,  
M. GERTRUDE WATSON,

EUGENIA T. WELSH,  
FRANCES I. MCCLELLAND,  
E. OGWEN JONES,  
FRANCES F. CARTER.

---

### SPECIAL TEACHERS.
WILLIAM GRAYSON ........... *Teacher of Cabinet Making and Carpentry.*  
FLORENCE M. CLEGG .. *Teacher of Drawing and Primary Manual Training.*  
EVANGELINE DAVIS ........................................ *Teacher of Cooking.*  
MARY MCSWAIN ............ ......................... *Teacher of Sewing.*  
WILLIAM FOGGETT ................... *Teacher of Physical Culture (boys).*  
SARAH L. MURPHY . ................. *Teacher of Physical Culture (girls).*

---

### HOUSEHOLD DEPARTMENT.
CATHERINE J. MYER ............................................. *Matron.*  
ETHEL BRUCE ............................... *Supervisor of Large Girls.*  
EVANGELINE DAVIS ......................... *Supervisor of Small Girls.*  
WILLIAM GRAYSON .......................... *Supervisor of Large Boys.*  
MRS. ABBIE BRADFORD ...................... *Supervisor of Small Boys.*  
MRS. AGNES CHADWICK ....................................... *Nurse.*  
JANE STUART ............................................ *Night Watch.*  
LOUIS COTE ............................................... *Cook.*  
ALFRED J. MCCLINTOCK ................. .................... *Engineer.*

---

### PHYSICIANS.
FRANK L. DAY, M. D ............................ *Attending Physician.*  
EDWARD S. BACON, M. D ....................................... *Aurist.*

MAIN BUILDING.

SCHOOL BUILDING.

# REPORT OF THE BOARD OF TRUSTEES.

*To the Honorable the General Assembly at its January Session, A. D., 1910.*

The Board of Trustees of the Rhode Island Institute for the Deaf respectfully presents the following report for the year :

The record of the year is one of improvement and progress, and under the management of Mr. and Mrs. Hurd the institution has reached a high degree of efficiency, placing it in the front rank of schools for the deaf in this country. Pupils are contented and happy, and their uniformly good physical condition is evidence of the care they have received.

We have to thank Dr. F. L. Day for another year of faithful service, and to express our gratitude to Dr. E. S. Bacon for his courteous attention.

While the new school building is of inestimable value, the increased steam radiation overloads the boilers to such an extent that a change in the heating plant is imperative. The present boilers have been carefully looked after and systematically repaired; but after twenty years' use, we feel that the limit of safety has been reached, and we respectfully ask for an appropriation sufficient to install two boilers of proper capacity and to make the necessary change to the boiler house. Inadequate boiler capacity means constant forcing of fires, and the resultant smoke brings numerous complaints, from the residents of the neighborhood, through the smoke inspector.

The trustees recognize the justice of Mr. Hurd's appeal for electric lighting to replace gas, for, in spite of the greatest care, several serious accidents have been narrowly averted. For the year 1910, the Board respectfully asks $30,000,00.

## FINANCIAL STATEMENT.

| | |
|---|---|
| Appropriation by General Assembly............................, | $28,000 00 |
| By tuition ................................................,...... | 150 00 |
| | $28,150 00 |

| | |
|---|---|
| Salaries............................................... | $12,485 20 |
| Provisions............................................ | 5,744 74 |
| Repairs and labor......... ........................ | 2,215 18 |
| Fuel, and ashes removed............................. | 1,869 88 |
| Household supplies................................ . | 1,843 66 |
| Medical attendance.................................. | 641 23 |
| Gas ................................. ............ .... | 466 14 |
| Water.................................. ...... .......... | 464 72 |
| Clothing..................................... ........ | 416 10 |
| School supplies .................................... | 396 15 |
| Hospital supplies .................................. | 180 74 |
| Electric power and light............................ | 110 62 |
| Hardware........................................... | 109 74 |
| Supplies for the cabinet shop ...................... | 96 40 |
| Telephone service.............................. ............ | 85 54 |
| Kitchen supplies.................................... ..... | 82 77 |
| Supplies for sewing room .......'................... | 76 45 |
| Printing............................................... | 76 16 |
| Fire protection .................................... | 48 75 |
| Gas fixtures........................................ | 30 94 |
| Miscellaneous.................................. ............ | 699 89 |
| Total ...................................... | $28,150 00 |

Respectfully submitted,

His EXCELLENCY ARAM J. POTHIER, *Governor, ex-officio,*
His HONOR ARTHUR W. DENNIS, *Lieut.-Gov., ex-officio,*
WILLIAM H. BALLOU, *President,*
MRS. ELLEN T. McGUINNESS, *Sec.,*
DR. G. D. RAMSAY,
MRS. LOUISE PROSSER BATES,
MRS. GERTRUDE J. JENNINGS,
JEREMIAH W. HORTON,
JOHN F. McALEVY,
HERBERT W. RICE,
GEORGE G. WILSON.

# REPORT OF THE PRINCIPAL.

*To the President and Board of Trustees of the Rhode Island In-
stitute for the Deaf.*

I have the honor to present to you a report of the affairs of the
Rhode Island Institute for the Deaf, for the year nineteen hundred and nine.

There have been under instruction in the institute, during this
period, seventy-eight pupils. Since making my last report, January 1st, 1909, thirteen new pupils have been admitted, and ten
pupils have left the school for the following reasons.

Two pupils were graduated at the close of the school year in
June last, one pupil left after taking an extra year's work following his graduation in June, 1908, one pupil moved to California, three pupils were allowed by their parents to learn a
trade instead of returning for their final year in school, and three
were discharged as not being eligible to this school.

The total number enrolled at the present time is sixty-eight,
thirty-seven girls and thirty-one boys.

Of the thirteen new pupils admitted since January 1st, 1909, ten
are under six years of age, one is eight, one is ten, and one is a
young woman from Bryan, Texas, who has received instruction
from private teachers only heretofore.

Below is given the nationality of the entire number enrolled
during the past year.

|  | Girls. | Boys. |
|---|---|---|
| American | 11 | 18 |
| French | 7 | 4 |
| Irish | 0 | 9 |
| Russian | .) | 1 |
| German | z | 1 |

|            | Girls. | Boys. |
|------------|--------|-------|
| Italian    | 2      | 3     |
| Swedish    |        | 2     |
| Finlander  | 1      | ..    |
| Jewish     | 1      | 2     |
| Portuguese | 1      | ..    |
| Sicilian   | 1      | ..    |
| African    | 2      | 1     |
|            | 37     | 41    |
| Total      | 78     |       |

## THE SCHOOL.

We are occupying the new school building provided by the appropriation of the General Assembly in 1907, and opened in September, 1908. It is well adapted to our needs, the rooms being cheerful, well-lighted, and well-ventilated.

The school is organized into eight classes, averaging a little more than eight pupils each, a very fair number in a school of this size. In schools where from two hundred and fifty to five hundred children are in attendance, the maximum number in a class is ten pupils. In our school of less than one hundred pupils, if we secure fairly well graded classes of eight each, we are doing as well as can be expected. The school work is under the direct supervision of Mrs. Anna C. Hurd, and the classes are organized as follows:

First Class—11 pupils....................Miss Watson.
Second Class—10 pupils..................Miss Jones.
Third Class—9 pupils....................Miss Carter.
Fourth Class—8 pupils...................Miss Hendershot.
Fifth Class—9 pupils....................Miss Welsh.
Sixth Class—8 pupils....................Miss Wittenmeier.
Seventh Class—7 pupils... } rotating.... { Miss McClelland.
Eighth Class—6 pupils.... }            { Miss Balch.

The school hours are from 8:15 to 1:15 each school day and the classes above the fourth have a study-hour from 7:00 to 8:00 P. M., over which a teacher presides.

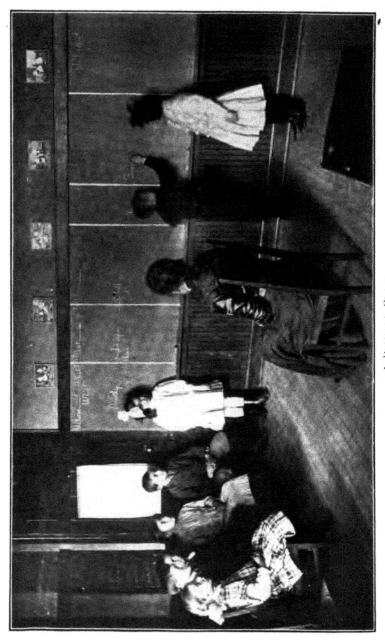

A PRIMARY CLASS.

All of the teachers have had training for the work of teaching the deaf, and all are young women of ability and successful experience, varying from two to fifteen years. We consider our corps of teachers exceptionally strong, and good results cannot help being obtained. The pupils show eagerness to learn, and are interested and happy in their work. The best methods known in the education of the deaf are employed, and we look forward hopefully to seeing the Rhode Island Institute for the Deaf take a place among the best schools of its kind in this country.

At the close of last year, five teachers resigned; one to be married, one to take a needed rest, two to teach in other schools, and one to remain at home. To fill these vacancies, four teachers were added: Miss Jones, from the North Carolina and the Pennsylvania schools; Miss Wittenmeier, from the Ohio school; Miss Watson, who returned to us after a year's absence; and Miss Carter, who had taught a private pupil for several years and was formerly connected with the New Brunswick school. Miss Lina Hendershot, who was added to our corps in February last, is a teacher of marked ability, from the Pennsylvania school, and the Wright school, New York City.

### DRAWING.

In connection with the schoolroom work, each class above the third works in the studio, receiving instruction in freehand drawing for two periods each week, of three-fourths an hour each, under Miss Florence Clegg, who has achieved very satisfactory results in this line. The studio was fitted up and opened in January, 1909.

### INDUSTRIAL WORK.

We have arranged that every child in the school over ten years of age shall have from one and a half to two hours each day in this department. The value and importance of this branch of instruction for all children is now so well recognized that I need not dwell upon it, except to call attention to the effective training and development that it affords our deaf pupils. Skill with the

2

hands, drawing, use of the needle and use of tools furnish our deaf children additional means of expression very helpful to them all through life, handicapped as they must be to a certain extent, and the discipline of wholesome occupation fits them for the struggle of earning a livelihood after their school days.

The very youngest children, ranging in age from five to nine years, spend their afternoons in play. A room in each wing of the living building, one for girls and one for boys, has been fitted up with suitable, substantial toys. Here the little ones spend many happy hours under the direction of their supervisors, when the weather does not permit them to play out of doors.

### PRIMARY MANUAL TRAINING CLASS.

The intermediate boys, ranging in age from ten to thirteen years, have one and a half hours each of four afternoons in the week in this class, when they are taught to use simple tools and the first steps in wood-working, preliminary to the work in the cabinet shop. A room in the basement of the school building has been fitted up for this purpose, and, under the direction of Miss Clegg, the boys are doing very interesting work.

### CLASSES IN SEWING.

The intermediate girls form a class in sewing, under Miss Mc-Swain. The sewing-room, adjoining the girls' sitting-room and play-room, is bright and sunny, and the work shown coming from this class is very creditable.

The older girls form another class where the cutting and making of garments and work of a more advanced nature is undertaken. Both classes meet together in a mending class once a week.

### CLASS IN CABINET WORK.

The oldest boys work in the cabinet shop four afternoons in the week, and on Saturday morning from eight to twelve o'clock, under the instruction of Mr. William Grayson, an expert cabinet maker.

The boys receive instruction in mechanical drawing once a week, under Miss Clegg, and work from their drawings in the cabinet shop. They have thus far nearly completed a set of four heavy oak tables for their study-rooms; several writing-desks, tabourettes, book racks, and other smaller articles, besides doing considerable repairing to furniture and about the buildings.

### CLASS IN COOKING.

The oldest girls receive instruction in the cooking class twice a week, pursuing a systematic course in plain cooking, under Miss Evangeline Davis, and are making good progress in this art. At each regular monthly meeting of the Board of Directors simple refreshments are served by the pupils of this class, entirely their own work.

### OTHER DOMESTIC SCIENCE WORK.

The care of their bedrooms, dining-room, and sitting-room is also taught the girls, and on Saturday morning instruction is given in fine ironing, in a room in the main building fitted up for this purpose.

### GYMNASIUM CLASSES.

Two classes in gymnasium work have been organized: one, of twenty girls, under Miss Sarah Murphy, instructor; and one, of twenty boys, under Mr. William Foggitt, instructor. Each class meets two evenings a week for an hour's work. The members of the classes are furnished appropriate suits, and the room used for a gymnasium is very well adapted as to light and ventilation, but additional equipment is required. It is hoped that sufficient funds will be available to enable us to furnish this in the near future.

### RELIGIOUS INSTRUCTION.

All of the pupils attend church and Sunday School. The Catholic children go to the Cathedral each Sunday morning, where their

instruction is in the hands of Father Hebert, appointed by the Rt.
Rev. Mathew Harkins, Bishop of Rhode Island, to take charge of
the religious instruction of the Catholic deaf in Rhode Island.

The Protestant children attend church services at the Free
Evangelical Church, Hope street, next door to the school. For
Sunday School work they are divided into five classes, taught at
the school by our own teachers.

### THE HOUSEHOLD.

The betterment of the home life in the school for the pupils
under our care has been the subject of most earnest effort on our
part, and under the present organization and arrangement we feel
that we may approach our ideal. We were fortunate at the opening of this session in securing as matron Miss Catherine Myer,
from the Home for Aged Deaf, Doylestown, Pa., and formerly
connected with the Pennsylvania School for the Deaf, Mt. Airy,
Philadelphia.

Her warm sympathy for children, her good judgment and untiring energy have accomplished much in the administration of the
household affairs, while the wise measure of your Honorable
Board, in the naming of a Household Committee, perfects the organization of the household.

The supervisors, who have charge of the children when they are
not with the teachers, work under the direction of the matron, and
are responsible to her in all respects. Each supervisor has from
fifteen to twenty pupils in charge, and the position is one requiring faithfulness, patience, love of children, and energy. These
positions are unusually well filled at the present time.

### THE CARE OF THE SICK.

A dispensary, four rooms, a bath and a nurse's room, at the rear
of the centre wing on the third floor, are set apart for an infirmary. Last summer the walls of all these rooms were painted, and
everything was put in good sanitary condition. A competent
nurse is in charge, and all children who are ill are sent at once

An Intermediate Class.

AN ADVANCED CLASS.

to be cared for by her. If the illness is at all serious, our physician, Dr. Frank L. Day, is at once summoned.

In general, the health of the pupils has been excellent since the opening of school in September. Dr. Day's report for the year is appended, also that of Dr. Edward S. Bacon, Aurist of the school, both of whom have been most faithful in their attention to the children.

### CLOSING EXERCISES.

The closing exercises, marking the completion of the last school year, were held on the morning of June 17th, in the Assembly Hall of the school building, when Miss Fannie Sweet and Mr. Arthur J. Myers were granted diplomas showing their satisfactory completion of the course of study prescribed.

Immediately following the close of school, Mrs. Hurd and myself attended the Eighth Summer Meeting of the American Association for the Promotion of the Teaching of Speech to the Deaf, held in Chicago, Illinois, from June 28th to July 5th, at which over two hundred and fifty principals, teachers, and others interested in the education of the deaf, were present. It was a most profitable meeting.

### IMPROVEMENTS MADE.

The fitting up of two play-rooms in the main building, for the small boys and girls, one in each wing, was completed early in the year. Another room has been fitted up for the use of the large boys as a reading-room, with tables and chairs, and provided with reading matter and games. One hundred and sixty new shades have been put up in the main building.

The infirmary rooms have been thoroughly renovated, the walls painted, etc.

The kitchen in the basement has been painted, both walls and woodwork.

The principal's rooms have been papered and painted; the matron's room, the guest room, and one teacher's room have been papered; the ceilings and walls in several rooms, and the floors in the dining-rooms, halls, and several other rooms, have been re-finished. New furniture has been purchased for several of the teachers' rooms, rugs for the Institute parlor, matron's room, and one teacher's room; also one hundred pairs of blankets, 365 yards of sheeting, and 60 yards of table linen.

The ground purchased in 1908 has been graded and fenced; and the exterior of the main building, and the old wing of the school building, painted.

New chairs for the boys' study-room, and new chairs for the large girls' bedrooms have been purchased; also furnishings for the office in the school building.

IMPROVEMENTS NEEDED.

I wish to call your attention to the following improvements, which are of vital necessity:

1. An enlarged heating plant, necessary because of the added space required to be heated since the construction of the new school building. It is difficult to heat both buildings during moderately cold weather, and in severe weather it is impossible.

2. Electric light in the main building instead of gas. In a place of this kind, where there are so many children, gas is positively dangerous. During the past year there have been two narrow escapes from calamities, even though the closest vigilance is observed.

3. New bathing facilities for both boys and girls. The bathrooms are entirely inadequate. They are located in the basement, far from the dormitories, not well-warmed, and quite out of date.

Permit me, in closing this report, to express my appreciation of the interest you have shown in the welfare of the Institute, and to thank you for the assistance you have given me.

Respectfully submitted,

EDWIN G. HURD.

PROVIDENCE, R. I., Jan. 1st, 1910.

At Work in the Studio.

# PHYSICIAN'S REPORT.

*To the Trustees of the Rhode Island Institute for the Deaf:*

I have the honor to render this report concerning the health of the children during the year past.

During the late winter there were several cases of influenza with accompanying bronchitis, and, in three of the children, pneumonia, with good recoveries in all cases. There were seven cases of chicken-pox; a few of the children have had tonsilitis; and one, catarrhal jaundice. All of the new children, and those of the older ones who did not present good scars of recent origin, have been vaccinated.

Considering the number of children, there has been relatively little illness, a fact that may be credited in large part to the care of their hygiene and diet exercised by the officers of the school.

Respectfully submitted,

FRANK L. DAY, M. D.

Providence, Dec. 31st, 1909.

# AURIST'S REPORT.

*To the Board of Trustees of the R. I. Institute for the Deaf:*

In presenting my first report of the octological condition of the children in the Rhode Island Institute for the Deaf, during the past year, I wish to preface that report with a brief statement concerning the causes of the deafness found in that institution. I wish to do this more as a matter of record and statistics, perhaps, than of especial interest.

In seeking for the causes of the deafness, an examination of the ears, nose, and throat of each child was made, and tests for the possible hearing ability of each case were tried. These reports were supplemented by the reports given by the parents regarding the age at which they first noticed the child's inability to hear, and their knowledge of the possible cause of the deafness.

These reports were in a measure unsatisfactory, and in some degree affect the true percentages of the seventy-one cases examined. Four were found to have hearing, and these were thrown out. Of the sixty-seven deaf-mutes, the causes of the deafness were as follows:

| | | | |
|---|---|---|---|
| Congenital | | | 23 |
| Acquired from intercraneal disease | | | 27 |
| " | " | the exanthemata | 10 |
| " | " | suppurative middle ear from other causes than the exanthemata | 7 |
| | | | 67 |
| In percentages— | | | |
| Congenital | | | 34.3 |
| Acquired | | | 65.7 |

These differ but little from the percentages found in most institutions of like character, and are probably as correct as can be obtained.

There were in the institution, at the beginning of the year, eight cases of chronic suppurative middle ear disease. Five of these were in an active stage, requiring treatment during the entire year. Three were of the intermittent type, requiring treatment only at intervals, when the process was lighted up under the influence of colds or some other exciting cause.

In three of the active cases, the discharge was very profuse and offensive, and an attempt was made to accomplish a cure of them by daily treatment over a period of over six months. In one case a decided improvement was obtained, but in the other two no improvement resulted from the treatment, and these were sent to the Rhode Island Hospital, where an attempt was made to cure the disease by removing the necrosed bone by the canal route. In one of these cases the result was very satisfactory ; in the other no improvement was made, and nothing short of a radical operation will accomplish a cure in this case.

At the institution two cases of acute otitis media were treated, one complicating pneumonia.

Several cases of acute rhinitis, one of chronic purulent rhinitis, and one of atrophic rhinitis received office treatment.

Three cases of adenoids with hypertrophied tonsils were operated upon at the Rhode Island Hospital.

At the present time there are at the institution three cases of suppurative otitis media requiring constant treatment, and two cases requiring occasional treatment.

I wish to thank Mr. Hurd for permitting me to make the attempt to cure the three cases of chronic suppurative otitis media above mentioned, by the prolonged daily treatment, and also the nurses and attendants who brought them to my office, much to their loss of time, and discomfort.

Respectfully submitted,

E. S. BACON, M. D.

JANUARY 1st, 1910.

3

### Rhode Island Institute for the Deaf—Daily Program.

Rise (Pupils).................6:15 A. M..............Sunday 6:30 A. M.

Breakfast (Pupils)............7:00 A. M..............    "    7:00 A. M.

    "    (Teachers).........7:15 A. M...............    "    8:00 A. M.

Chapel.......................8:15 A. M...............

School ......................8:30 A. M...............

Recess.....................11:15 to 11:30 A. M......

School ......................11:30 A. M. to 1:15 P. M.

Dinner (Pupils)....  .........1:25 P. M..............Sunday 12:30 P. M.

    "    (Teachers)............1:30 P. M...............    "    1:00 P. M.

Industrial Work.............2:30 to 4:30 P. M........

Supper (Pupils)..............6:00 P. M..............Sunday 5:30 P. M.

    "    (Teachers)............6:30 P. M..............    "    6:00 P. M.

Study Hour............. ....7:00 to 8:00 P. M........

Bed Time..................1st Group, 7:00 P. M ....

    "        .................2d Group, 8:00 P. M.....

    "        .................3d Group, 9:00 P. M.....

Sunday-School (Protestants)..9:00 to 10:00 A. M.......

Church (Catholics) ..........9:00 to 9:45 A. M .......

Sunday-School (Catholics)....10:00 to 11:00 A. M......

    "        (Protestants)..10:30 A. M..............

SMALL GIRLS AT PLAY.

SMALL BOYS AT PLAY.

## Rhode Island Institute for the Deaf.

### DAILY PROGRAM OF DRAWING, INDUSTRIAL WORK, ETC.

| | Drawing. Miss Clegg. | Elementary Manual Training. Miss Clegg. | Sewing. Miss McSwain. | Cooking. Miss Davis. | Cabinet Work. Mr. Grayson. | Gymnasium. |
|---|---|---|---|---|---|---|
| Monday. School—8:15-1:15. | Class 3, 10:30-11:15. Class 5, 11:30-12:15. Class 6, 12:15-1:00. | 2:30-4:00. | Class 1. 2:30-4:30. | | 2:30-4:30. | Mr. Foggitt. Boys. 8:00-9:00. |
| Tuesday. School—8:15-1:15, | Class 8, 8:15-9:00. Class 7, 9:00-9:45. Class 4, 10:45-11:15. | 2:30-4:00. | Class 2. 2:30-4:30 | 2:30-4:30 | 2:30-4:30. | Miss Murphy. Girls. 8:00-9:00. |
| Wednesday. School—8:15-1:15. | Boys. Mechanical Drawing. 2:30-4:30. | | Class 2. 2:30-4:00. | 2:30-4:30. | | |
| Thursday. School—8:15-1:15, | Class 8, 8:15-9:00. Class 7, 9:00-9:45. Class 4, 10:45-11:15. | 2:30-4:00. | Class 1, 2:30-4:30. | | 2:30-4:30. | Mr. Foggitt. Boys. 8:00-9:00. |
| Friday. School—8:15-1:15. | Class 3, 10:30-11:15. Class 5, 11:30-12:15. Class 6 12:15-1:00. | 2:30-4:00. | Class 1. 2:30-4:30. | | 2:30-4:30. | Miss Murphy. Girls. 8:00-9:00. |
| Saturday. | Boys. Class 2. Mechanical Drawing. 8:00-9:00. | | | | 8:00-12:00. | |

# Rhode Island Institute for the Deaf.

## DAILY PROGRAM OF DRAWING, INDUSTRIAL

| | *Drawing,* Miss Clough. | *Elementary Man- ual Training.* Miss Clough. | *Sewing.* Miss McSwain. | *Cooking.* Miss Davis. |
|---|---|---|---|---|
| | *Class 3.* 10:30–11:15. *Class 5.* 11:30–12:15. *Class 6.* 12:15–1:00. | 2:30–4:00. | *Class 1.* 2:30–4:30. | 2:30–4 |
| **Monday.** School—8:15 1:15. | | | | |
| **Tuesday.** School—8:15 1:15. | *Class 8.* 8:15 9:00. *Class 7.* 9:00–9:45. *Class 4.* 10:45 11:15. | 2:30–4:00 | *Class 6.* 2:30–4:30 | 2:30–4 |
| | | | *Class 5.* | 2:30–4:30 |

A CLASS IN SEWING.

PRIMARY MANUAL. TRAINING CLASS.

## Calendar for the Year 1910.

---

Winter Term begins Tuesday, January 4th.
Term ends Friday, June 17th.
Fall Term begins Tuesday, September 13th.
Fall Term ends Thursday, December 23d.

### HOLIDAYS.

Washington's Birthday, February 22d.
Easter Holidays, Thursday, March 24th, to Tuesday, March 29th.
Decoration Day, May 30th.
Thanksgiving Holidays, Wednesday, November 23d, to Monday, November 28th.
Christmas Holidays, Friday, December 23d, 1910, to Tuesday, January 3d, 1911.

# TERMS OF ADMISSION.

The Rhode Island Institute for the Deaf is free to all children in the State, between the ages of three and twenty, whose hearing is so defective that they are unable to be educated in schools for the hearing, provided they are not mentally incapable. All parents or guardians of deaf children who wish to secure admission for a child should apply to the principal for an application blank. This blank should be filled out as carefully as possible and returned to the principal. The parent or guardian will then receive notice of the admission of the child, and a date set when the child should be sent to the school.

The State provides board, instruction, and industrial training free, but the parents must provide clothing. Parents are urged to see that their children are supplied with at least two changes of clothing throughout, and care taken that their clothing is replenished from time to time as needed. Parents are requested not to ask to take their children out of school at any time except for the regular holidays. Pupils can not afford to lose any time from school or industrial work, and by being kept out of school they are liable to lose their place in their class, and so will not be able to advance with the rest. Report cards are sent out each month to the parents, informing them of the standing, health, conduct, etc., of their children. In cases of illness, pupils have the best of care in an infirmary especially prepared for this purpose, under the care of a physician and nurse, and in case of serious illness parents are kept informed of the condition of their child. All pupils should be on hand promptly on the first day of the opening of school in the fall, and also on the day set for their return after the holidays. By a careful observance of these points the task of organizing and beginning school is much simplified.

All parents, guardians, and interested persons are requested to send us the names of any deaf children who are not in attendance at this school, and we will take steps to look them up.

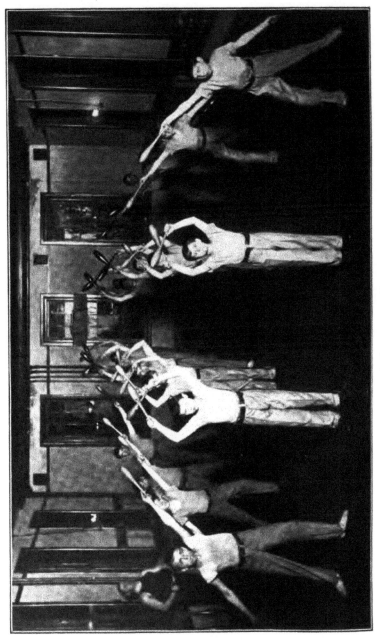

A GYMNASIUM CLASS

A GYMNASIUM CLASS.

CLASS IN COOKING.

CLASS IN CABINET WORK.

# CHAPTER 332.

## AN ACT IN AMENDMENT OF AND IN ADDITION TO CHAPTER 86 OF THE GENERAL LAWS, ENTITLED " OF THE R. I. SCHOOL FOR THE DEAF."

[Passed May 18, 1896 ]

*It is enacted by the General Assembly as follows:*

SECTION 1. All children of parents, or under the control of guardians or other persons, legal residents of this state, between the ages of three and twenty years, whose hearing or speech, or both, are so defective as to make it inexpedient or impracticable to attend the public schools to advantage, not being mentally or otherwise incapable, may attend the Rhode Island Institute for the Deaf, without charge, under such rules and regulations as the board of trustees of said institute may establish.

SEC. 2. Every person having under his control any such child between the ages of seven and eighteen years shall cause such child to attend school at said institute for such period of time or such prescribed course, in each individual case, as may be deemed expedient by the board of trustees, and for any neglect of such duty the person so offending shall be fined not exceeding twenty dollars : *Provided*, that if the person so charged shall prove to the satisfaction of said board that the child has received or is receiving, under private or other instruction, an education suitable to his condition, in the judgment of said board, then such penalty shall not be incurred ; *provided, further,* that no child shall be removed to said institution or taken from the custody of its parent or guardian except as a day scholar unless such parent or guardian is an improper person to have such custody, and the supreme court in its appellate division shall have jurisdiction in habeas corpus to examine into and revise all findings of said board of trustees under this act.

SEC. 3. Any child having attended said institute a time or course prescribed by said board, upon leaving the institute shall be entitled to receive a certificate of his proficiency from said board.

SEC. 4. This act shall take effect from and after its passage.

**AN ACT IN AMENDMENT**
**•• OF THE GENERAL LAW**

*Th*

*enacted by the General Ass*

SECTION 1. All children of
or other persons, legal residents
and twenty years, whose heari
make it inexpedient or imprac
vantage, not being mentally or
Island Institute for the Deaf,
lations as the board of trustees

**SEC. 2. Every person having**
**the ages of seven and eightee**
school at said institute for suc
in each individual case, as may
tees, and for any neglect of s
fined not exceeding twenty d
charged shall prove to the sa
received or is receiving, under
suitable to his condition, in the
ty shall not be incurred: *provi*
to said institution or taken fro
cept as a day scholar unless s
son to have such custody, and
shall have jurisdiction in hal
findings of said board of trust

SEC. 3. Any child having a
scribed by said board, upon le
ceive a certificate of his profic

SEC. 4. This act shall take e